# A
# Consumer's
# Dictionary
# of
# Food
# Additives

# A Consumer's Dictionary of Food Additives

## NEWLY REVISED EDITION

## Ruth Winter

Crown Publishers, Inc.   New York

Published by Crown Publishers, Inc., One Park Avenue, New York, New York
10016, and simultaneously in Canada by General Publishing Company Limited
Manufactured in the United States of America

Library of Congress Cataloging in Publication Data
Winter, Ruth, 1930–
A consumer's dictionary of food additives.
1. Food additives—Dictionaries.   I. Title.
TX553.A3W55   1984        664'.06'0321        83-26135
ISBN 0-517-55287-6

10 9 8 7 6 5 4 3 2 1
First Revised Edition

# INTRODUCTION

Pick up a can, box, or any package of food. Do you understand the label? Do you know what is not on the label but may be added to the food?

When the last revision of this book was published in 1978, the addition of additives to our food was a $1.3-billion-a-year business. By 1990, it is expected to be a $4.5-billion enterprise. In 1978, there were 164.1 million pounds of food additives in processed meat alone. At the current rate of growth, there will be 363 million pounds by 1990.[1]

This book tells you about the additives in your food, where they come from, how they are used, and what is known about how they may affect your health.

A food additive is a substance or mixture of substances, other than basic foodstuffs, present in food as a result of any aspect of production, processing, storage, or packaging. The term does not include chance contaminants.

Food processors have in their armamentaria an estimated 10,000 chemicals they can add to what we eat. Some are deleterious, some are harmless, and some are beneficial.

Every one of these chemicals used in food processing must serve one or more of the following purposes:

- Improve nutritional value
- Enhance quality or consumer acceptability
- Improve the keeping quality
- Make the food more readily available
- Facilitate its preparation[2]

The majority of food additives have nothing to do with *nutritional value,* as anyone can see from the contents of this Dictionary.

Most of the chemicals added to enhance *consumer acceptability* are to feed our illusions. We want enhanced food because all our lives we have been subjected to the beautiful pictures of foods in our magazines and on television. We have come to expect an advertiser's concept of perfection in color and texture, even though Mother Nature may not turn out all her products that way. As a result, the skin of the oranges we eat is dyed bright orange to match our mental image of an ideal orange. Our poultry is fed a chemical to turn the skin yellower and more appetizing, and our

---

[1] *Food Product Development* (December 1980), pp. 36–40.
[2] According to the Food Protection Committee of the National Academy of Sciences, which evaluates the safety of additives.

fruits and vegetables are kept unblemished by fungicides, pesticides, herbicides, and other antispoilants.

To improve the keeping quality of some products, processors embalm them. Bread has sixteen chemicals to keep it feeling "fresh." One type of bread, balloon bread, undergoes rigor mortis thanks to its additive, plaster of Paris. Ironically, when nothing is added to the foods, they cost us considerably more. Unbleached flour is four times as much as bleached; "untreated" tomatoes five times as much as regular canned tomatoes, and unsulfured raisins cost six times as much as the treated ones.

Food purveyors are only responding to the changes in society. We want convenience, which by definition means ease and speed of preparation or use and, of course, higher costs. Women who spend the day on the job outside the home no longer have the time or energy to shop frequently or to spend hours preparing a meal. Households have shrunk in size and the traditional sitdown family dinner has gone the way of the hand-held can opener.

The growth of the microwave oven has also encouraged the use of convenience foods. In 1978, only 11 percent of American homes had the quick-cooking method. It is estimated that by 1990 60 percent will have them.[3]

Those foods that are *easier to prepare* pass through many hands to be mashed, mushed, mangled, and loaded with chemicals so that we can have cake mixes, peeled and sliced potatoes, and instant everything.

Technology has advanced or retreated, depending upon one's view, so far that some foods are almost pure ersatz. One well-known "natural" orange-flavored drink consists of sugar, citric acid, natural flavor, gum arabic, monosodium phosphate, potassium citrate, calcium phosphate, Vitamin C, cellulose gum, hydrogenated coconut oil, artificial flavor, artificial coloring, Vitamin A, and butylated hydroxyanisole. No orange could live in that environment. One whipped topping consists of sodium caseinate, dextrose, corn sugar, polysorbate 60, sorbitan monostearate, carrageenan, and guar gum. All these ingredients are listed on the labels.

By law, the label must identify the product in a language the consumer can understand. It must indicate the manufacturer, the packer, or distributor, and declare the quantity of contents either in net weight or volume, and the ingredients must be declared on the label in order of predominance. The label must be accurate in any statement about the product. Also, if a vignette, or picture, of the product is placed on the label, it must be representative of the container's contents.

[3] *Food Product Development* (December 1980), pp. 36–40.

However, for more than 300 "standard" foods—including ice cream, catsup, and mayonnaise—no ingredients need be listed. For standard foods, processors follow the standard chemical recipes written out by the government. The manufacturer has been given the option to choose among many alternative standard chemicals, and only if he substitutes or adds a nonstandard chemical or uses Yellow No. 5 (*see*), a common allergen, must he indicate the fact on the label. Ice cream, for example, which can have some 30 additives, need indicate no ingredients on the label. In still other products, such as canned fruit and gelatin desserts, instead of indicating the specific artificial coloring or flavoring, the processor need only state "artificial coloring" or "artificial flavoring," again with the exception of Yellow No. 5. The law does not require that chemicals added in small amounts during processing, such as calcium bromate (a maturing agent for dough), be stated on the label.

Sometimes the label can be misleading. For example, when it says "light" or "lite," you assume that the product has fewer calories. However, in a study by Madelyn L. Wheeler, R.D., M.S., coordinator of research dietetics at the Diabetes Research and Training Center, Indiana University Medical Center, Indianapolis, she and her colleagues found that one vegetable oil producer used "light" because their oil was 25 percent paler in color but the calories were the same as any other. A "light" pancake mix had the same calories as any other except that it had no preservatives or artificial flavors and the "light" used on the label of taco shells was found to mean that the tacos were made with wheat flour rather than cornmeal, although the calories were the same.[4]

The only time you can count on "light" foods probably being light—in calories, that is—is when the label has "low calorie" or "reduced calorie" because the FDA requires such products to have at least one-third fewer calories than similar "regular" products.

If you are looking for low-sodium products, you also have to be careful since some processors say "no salt added" although the product itself may be naturally high in sodium.

Food companies test additives ostensibly for acute toxicity. Additives are fed to animals in large amounts at one time. Although most companies do not use control groups—for comparison, animals not fed any additive—or perform autopsies to determine any effects on tissues, they observe the animals for symptoms of ill effects. They also usually determine the lethal dose (if in fact the additive can be determined to be lethal) based on what kills 50 percent of the animals ($L_{50}$). In subacute (*see*) studies, which have also been done for a number of food additives, the

---

[4] Madelyn Wheeler, et al., *Diabetes Forecast* (September–October 1983).

food chemical is fed to groups of animals in varying amounts nearly to the point of death. These tests usually last a minimum of three months and are made on at least two species of animals, most often rats and dogs. The data collected during the study include appetite, thirst, growth rates, weight, blood and urine analyses, and behavior patterns. At the end of the study, all surviving animals are autopsied. These tests are expensive and time-consuming, often costing more than $250,000 for a single chemical.

In the mid-1970s, the FDA discovered that some of the 130 laboratories doing food-additive testing had serious deficiencies, and in the 1980s several laboratory executives were indicted for fraud. The federal agency had relied on the basic accuracy and integrity of the data submitted to make decisions about approving food and color additives for the market. The FDA officials noted: "The submission of faulty, erroneous, or distorted data increases the potential for reaching invalid judgments about the safety of these additives."

In fact, there is a large percentage of food additives that have not been tested long-term, one of the great problems in determining chemical safety. Cancer, for instance, may take 20 years to develop in humans and often more than 2 years in animals. Long-term safety is determined from rats, which live from 18 to 24 months. However, researchers point out that laboratory animals are in a nonnatural, sterile environment and that in two years, 70 to 90 percent of them would be dead anyway and only two or three would be left for evaluation. Therefore, long-term tests may have invalid assurances of safety.

One partial solution, although not accepted by all scientists, is the Ames Test. In the early 1970s, Dr. Bruce Ames, a biochemist at the University of California at Berkeley, developed a simple test using common bacteria that reveals whether a chemical is a mutagen. The test can be done quickly and is relatively inexpensive. Mutagens act by changing the genetic material that is transferred to daughter cells when cell division occurs. Carcinogens also act by fouling up the genetic material within a cell. Almost all of the chemicals known to be carcinogenic have also been shown to be mutagenic in the Ames Test.

Another great problem with testing additives is how they interact with each other and with the 63,000 other chemicals in common use today. In 1976, the *Journal of Food Science* carried a report on a small-scale attempt to determine the extent of the problem. When three additives were tested one at a time on rats, the animals stayed well; two at a time, the rats became ill; and with a three-additive combination, all the animals died within fourteen days.

How valid are animal studies? All but two of the known human carcinogens—benzene and arsenic—are also carcinogenic in rodents. None of the approximately 143 "rodent" carcinogens has been proven to be noncarcinogenic in humans. Animal assays have predicted several human carcinogens, including three that may be contaminants in food: the mold found on nuts, aflatoxin; the plastic used in packaging, vinyl chloride; and the hormone used to increase the weight of meat that the FDA has tried to ban but that is still being used by some meat producers, diethylstilbestrol.

Incidentally, the FDA has set a limit for aflatoxins in nuts of 15 parts per billion. If a batch exceeds that, the producers are able to add noncontaminated nuts to the batch to reduce levels, a system a number of food processors advocate for other undesirable additives such as low-potency carcinogens.[5]

Although the FDA officially claims to know what additives are being used in food, FDA researchers report that it is impossible to check small manufacturers. Efforts have been made through the years to have food manufacturers register and provide the information, but as yet there is no law to require them to do so.

Contrary to public belief, food additives are not a modern innovation. Adding chemicals to food began in the dawn of civilization when man first discovered that by adding salt to meat the meat would last longer.

The father of modern food additives laws was Dr. Harvey W. Wiley, who in the early 1900s led the fight against chemical preservatives such as boric acid, formaldehyde, and salicylic acid. He dramatized the problem by his famous "Poison Squad," comprised of young men willing to be guinea pigs, which meant eating measured amounts of these chemicals to determine toxicity.

As a result of Dr. Wiley's pioneering work, the first Federal Food and Drug Act was passed in 1906. However, as can be determined from the contents of this Dictionary, not all questions concerning food additive safety have been answered.

In the mid-1950s, when Food and Drug Administration scientists pushed for further laws, the FDA could not stop the use of a chemical simply because it was questionable or had not been adequately tested. It was necessary to be able to prove in court that the chemical was poisonous or deleterious. But on September 6, 1958, the Food Additives Amendment was passed. Food and chemical manufacturers, as of that date, were required to run extensive tests on additives before they were

[5] "Public Issues, Private Medicine," symposium sponsored by Smith Kline Corp. and The College of Physicians of Philadelphia, December 6, 1978, in Philadelphia.

marketed. Results of these tests had to be submitted to the FDA.

The famous, or infamous—again depending on one's view—Delaney Amendment was part of the 1958 law. Written by Congressman James Delaney, the law specifically states that no additive may be permitted in any amount if the tests show that it produces cancer when fed to man or animals or by other appropriate tests.

This part of the law has been severely attacked by food and chemical manufacturers, the Nutrition Council of the American Medical Association, and several FDA commissioners. The FDA commissioners claim it is unenforceable and point to the problem with saccharin, a proven carcinogen, although a weak one. The artificial sweetener has been in use since 1879. When it was shown to cause cancer in laboratory animals in 1977, the FDA announced that the use of saccharin in foods and beverages would be banned. There was a public outcry from dieters led by the Calorie Control Council, a trade organization that spent over a million dollars in the first six months to stop the ban. Saccharin is still on the market, the FDA having postponed the ban several times in response to "public" pressure.

The food industry has been pushing for changes in the food laws. Among the new legislation they want:

• Define the term "safe," since a zero-risk standard is neither realistic nor desirable, they claim.
• Allow the comparison of risk and benefits when issuing or revoking approval for an additive, since there is no need to ban a product where risk has been shown to be small or unproven, according to the industry.
• Permit a gradual phaseout of a product, they ask, since immediate bans on food additives disrupt the food supply and can cause severe economic hardship.[6]

The advocates of such changes point out nitrites as an example of risk and benefit. Nitrites combine with natural stomach chemicals to cause nitrosamines, powerful cancer-causing agents, but nitrites also prevent botulism, a potentially fatal illness caused by contaminated food. Since they claim there is no good substitute for nitrites, their benefits outweigh their risks.

Unfortunately, when it comes to potentially harmful food additives, we take the risk while the food processors take the benefits.

[6] "Congress Eyes Major Rewrite of Nation's Food Safety Laws," *American Medical News,* June 24, 1983.

They keep talking about "no effect levels" and pointing out that one part per billion is equal to one inch in 16,000 miles. How much exposure to a carcinogen does it take to damage a gene or to cause cancer in a child or adult? No one knows for certain. The FDA estimates that exposure to DES—diethylstilbestrol—as low as one part per trillion may be associated with the risk of one cancer per million consumer lifetimes. That's pretty low, except, of course, if you are that one consumer.

In 1980 the Surgeon General's Office issued a report setting nutritional objectives for improving the health of Americans by 1990. Some of the specific objectives were weight control; reduction in the population's serum cholesterol levels; reduced daily sodium intake; reduced consumption of potentially carcinogenic foods; and increased promotion and awareness of United States Department of Agriculture Dietary Guidelines.

The National Food Processors Association reaction to the Surgeon General's report was cited in an editorial in the March 1981 issue of *Food Product Development,* a trade journal:

It should not be government's role in a free society to intervene or interfere in the production of manufactured foodstuffs to ensure their nutritional quality and content, a "technologic measure" suggested in the report. Such a policy could lead to government control over the food processing industry, lessening of competition and stagnation in the development of new products with attributes desired by consumers.

Nor is the positioning of products in the supermarkets to make nutrition information readily apparent, also suggested in the report, a province of government. So many factors are involved in shelf positioning of products that it is absurd to suggest that the presentation of nutrition information might become the overriding consideration.

The food processing industry is opposed to promulgation of guidelines to maintain or improve the nutritional quality of the food supply. Again, development of food products should be unfettered by government regulation, even in the guise of guidelines, and left to the play of market forces.[7]

You are part of that market force. By using this book to understand the labels and by selecting wisely, you can affect the sales of more wholesome foods and protect the health of your family.

The FDA personnel, while well intentioned, do not have the resources to prevent all potentially harmful food additives from reaching the market. Your knowledge is your best protection.

[7] Editorial, Fran LaBell, *Food Product Development* (March 1981), p. 70.

## Generally Recognized as Safe (GRAS) List

The GRAS list was established in 1958 by Congress. Those substances that were being added to food over a long time, which, under conditions of their intended use, were generally recognized as safe by qualified scientists, would be exempt from premarket clearance. Congress had acted on a very marginal response—on the basis of returns from those scientists sent questionnaires. Approximately 355 out of 900 responded, and only about 100 of those responses had substantive comments. Three items were removed from the originally published list.

Since then, in recent years, developments in the scientific fields and in consumer awareness brought to light the inadequacies of the testing of food additives and, ironically, the complete lack of testing of the generally recognized as safe list.

Cyclamates, the artificial sweeteners, were shown to be cancer-causing agents in laboratory animals and were removed from the market. They had been on the GRAS list. As a result, in 1969 President Nixon directed the FDA to reevaluate all of the items on the GRAS list.

The study of the GRAS-list substances has been conducted by an expert advisory group—the Select Committee on GRAS Substances of the Federation of American Societies for Experimental Biology.

By 1980, 415 substances that had been in use prior to the 1958 Food Additives Amendment to the Food, Drug and Cosmetic Act were reviewed. The committee's evaluations were based on review of medical and scientific literature and unpublished reports. In some cases the research extended back 60 years. The number of references obtained for a given GRAS substance ranged from 23 reports for carnauba wax to 20,-000 for Vitamin A.

Of the 415 substances reviewed, 305 were given Class 1 status, which means they are considered safe for use at current levels and future anticipated levels under conditions of good manufacturing practices.

Sixty-eight were placed in Class 2. They are considered safe for use at current levels, but the committee advised that more research is needed to determine whether a significant increase in consumption would constitute a dietary hazard. This category includes certain zinc salts, alginates, iron, tannic acid, sucrose, and Vitamins A and D.

Class 3 status was given to 19 substances for which the committee recommended additional studies because of unresolved questions in research data. The FDA issued interim regulations for this class of ingredients requiring that certain safety tests be undertaken within a specific time but meanwhile permitting current use of the substances. Caffeine, BHA, and BHT were listed in this class.

Five substances—salt and four modified starches—were placed in Class 4, which means the committee recommended that FDA establish safer conditions of use or prohibit addition of the ingredients to food.

The committee said there is no evidence that salt hurts most people, but suggested that a reduction of salt in processed foods would benefit the 10 to 30 percent of the United States population genetically predisposed to high blood pressure and might thus reduce the frequency of hypertension.

Restrictions were also recommended on some starches—distarch glycerol and hydroxypropyl, acetylated, and succinyl distarch glycerol—used primarily as thickening agents.

In addition, the use of lactic acid and calcium lactate was placed in this category for exclusion from infant formulas, because of reports of adverse effects. They are no longer used in infant formulas, except when needed in special medical compounds.

Class 5 had 18 substances about which, the committee said, there were insufficient data to make any evaluation. These substances include some glycerides and certain iron salts. The FDA proposes removing these substances from the GRAS list unless sufficient data become available for evaluation.

The expert committee evaluations and the questions raised about food additives continue. In the meantime, the over 31 million Americans who are allergic even to the tiniest amount of some chemicals in foods (with allergic reactions ranging from a mild skin rash to death) can't wait.

The disturbing questions of long-term toxicity and carcinogenicity remain.

Researchers at Albert Einstein College of Medicine in New York have been working with a substance isolated from chickling peas that causes nerve damage similar to amyotrophic lateral sclerosis (ALS), Lou Gehrig's disease. They have been collaborating with Indian and Israeli scientists. The toxic component, BOAA, is chemically related to two approved food additives, glutamate and aspartate.

Many epidemiological studies are being carried out to determine the causes of cancer. Curtis Harris, M.D., chief of the Laboratory of Human Carcinogenesis at the National Institutes of Health, pointed out at a science writers meeting sponsored by the American Cancer Society in San Diego in 1983 that incidence of liver cancers seems to parallel the presence of nitrosamines. Nitrosamines are formed when nitrites combine with natural stomach chemicals. His particular area of interest is finding those who are at risk to cancer because of genetics or environment.

Walter Troll, Ph.D., of New York University, at the same meeting pointed out that seeds seem to contain protease inhibitors, natural cancer-fighting agents.

While such reports are preliminary, there is little doubt that what we eat affects our health. Our bodies are wonderful machines that can detoxify and render harmless many poisons we ingest; however, we don't want to overburden our bodies by taking unnecessary chances. Certainly, not all food additives are harmful. Some, in fact, are greatly beneficial. It's all a matter of judgment. Hopefully, this book will allow you to make wiser choices.

The purpose of this Dictionary is to enable you to look up any additive under its alphabetical listing, to determine the feasibility of continuing with the product because it is beneficial or rejecting it in favor of its betters.

The Dictionary includes most of the food additives in common use. For the sake of clarity and ease of use, their nearly 50 functions are grouped under the following broad categories:

## Preservatives

These "antispoilants" are used to help prevent microbiological spoilage and chemical deterioration. They are of many different types, of which about 100 are in common use.

Preservatives for fatty products are called antioxidants, which prevent the production of off-flavors and off-odors. These include benzoic acid used in margarine, butylated hydroxyanisole (BHA) used in lard, shortenings, crackers, soup bases, and potato chips.

In bread, preservatives are "mold" and "rope" inhibitors. They include sodium and calcium propionate, sodium diacetate, and such acetic substances as acetic acid and lactic acid. Sorbic acid and sodium and potassium salts are preservatives used in cheeses, syrups, and pie fillings. Preservatives used to prevent mold and fungus growth on citrus fruits are called "fungicides." Sequestering agents, still another type of preservative, prevent physical or chemical changes that affect color, flavor, texture, or appearance. Ethylenediaminetetraacetic acid (EDTA) and its salts, for instance, are used to prevent the adverse effects of the presence of metals in such products as soft drinks where metal ions can cause clouding. Sequestrants used in dairy products to keep them "fresh and sweet" include sodium, calcium, and potassium salts of citric, tartaric, and pyrophosphoric acids. Other common multipurpose preservatives are the gas sulfur dioxide, propyl gallate, and, of course, sugar, salt, and vinegar.

## Acids, Alkalies, Buffers, Neutralizers

The degree of acidity or alkalinity is important in many processed foods. An acid such as potassium acid tartrate, sodium aluminum phosphate, or tartaric acid acts on the leavening agent in baked goods and releases the gas which causes the desired "rising." The flavor of many soft drinks, other than cola types, is modified by the use of an acid such as citric acid from citrus fruits, malic acid from apples, or tartaric acid, a component of grapes. Phosphoric acid is used to give colas that "tangy" taste. The same acids that are used in soft drinks are also used in churning cream to help preserve the flavor and keeping quality of butter. Alkalies such as ammonium hydroxide in cocoa products and ammonium carbonate in candy, cookies, and crackers are employed to make the products more alkaline. Buffers and neutralizing agents are chemicals added to foods to control acidity or alkalinity, just as acids and alkalies are added directly. Some common chemicals in this class are ammonium bicarbonate, calcium carbonate, potassium acid tartrate, sodium aluminum phosphate, and tartaric acid.

## Moisture Content Controls

Humectants are necessary in the production of some types of confections and candy to prevent drying out. Without a humectant, shredded coconut, for example, would not remain soft and pliable. Substances used for this purpose include glycerine, which retains the soft, moist texture in marshmallows, propylene glycol, and sorbitol. On the other hand, calcium silicate is used to prevent table salt from caking due to moisture absorption from the air.

## Coloring Agents

Food colors of both natural and synthetic origin are extensively used in processed foods, and they play a major role in increasing the acceptability and attractiveness of these products. However, the indiscriminate use of color can conceal damage or inferiority, or make the product appear better than it actually is. The World Health Organization in delineating some 140 different kinds of colorants found many to be unsafe. Coal-tar colors were subject to a special provision in a 1938 law that required every coal-tar color used in food to be listed with the government as "harmless and suitable for use" and every batch of the color intended for use in food had to be certified by a government agency as safe. Some of the colors originally listed as "harmless" were found to produce injury when fed to animals and were removed from the list. In 1960, the federal government required manufacturers to retest all artificial colors to determine safety. At present, there are six permanently listed as safe. Among them FD and C Blue No. 1 and FD and C Green No. 33 have been shown to cause tumors at the site of injection in animals, but the FDA does not consider this significant because the experiments concerned injection by needle and not ingestion in food or application to the skin. FD and C Red No. 40, one of the most widely used colorings, is also being questioned because it is made from a base known to be carcinogenic and because many scientists feel that it should not have been given permanent listing based solely on the manufacturer's tests.

Among the natural colors used in foods are alkanet, annatto, carotene, chlorophyll, cochineal, saffron, and turmeric. Foods that are frequently colored include candies, baked goods, soft drinks, and such dairy products as butter, cheese, and cream.

## Flavorings

A wide variety of spices, natural extractives, oleoresins, and essential oils are used in processed foods. In addition, the modern flavor chemist has produced many synthetic flavors. Both types of products are used extensively in soft drinks, baked goods, ice cream, and confectionery. Flavoring agents are the most numerous additive, with over 2,000 in use. Of these, some 500 are natural and the balance synthetic. They are usually employed in amounts ranging from a few to 300 parts per million. Amyl acetate, benzaldehyde, carvone, ethyl acetate, ethyl butyrate, and methyl salicylate are typical compounds employed in the preparation of flavoring materials. However, many of the compounds used in synthetic flavorings are also found in natural products or derive from natural acids. Essential oils, such as oil of lemon and oil of orange, are natural flavors made by extraction of the fruit rind. There are also flavor enhancers, the commonest being monosodium glutamate (MSG) and maltol.

## Physiologic Activity Controls

The chemicals in this group are added to fresh foods to serve as ripeners or antimetabolic agents. For instance, ethylene gas is used to hasten the ripening of bananas and maleic hydrazide is used to prevent potatoes from sprouting. Coming into increasing use are enzymes which are of natural origin and generally believed to be nontoxic. Of all the food enzyme additives, amylases which act on starch have the most numerous applications. Various amylases from plant, animal, fungal, and bacterial sources have been used to break down the components of starch to make it more digestible. Enzymes are also used in the fermentation of sugar to make candy, in the brewing industry, and in the manufacture of artificial honey, bread, and frozen milk concentrates.

## Bleaching and Maturing Agents/Bread Improvers

Fresh ground flour is pale yellow. Upon storage, it slowly becomes white and undergoes an aging process that improves its baking qualities. For more than 50 years, processors have added oxidizing agents to the flour to accelerate this process, thus reducing storage costs, spoilage, and the opportunity for insect infestation. Compounds such as benzoyl peroxide bleach the flour without effect on baking qualities. Other compounds, such as oxides of nitrogen, chlorine dioxide, nitrosyl chloride, and chlorine have both a bleaching and maturing, or "improving," ability. Bread improvers used by the baking industry contain oxidizing substances such as potassium bromate, potassium iodate, and calcium peroxide. They also contain inorganic salts such as ammonium or calcium sulfate and ammonium phosphates, which serve as yeast foods and dough conditioners. Quantities used are relatively small since these can easily result in an inferior product. Bleaching agents may also be used in other foods such as cheese to improve the appearance of the finished product.

## Processing Aids

Many chemicals fall into this category. Sanitizing agents, for instance, to clean bacteria and debris from products, are considered such aids. So are clarifying agents which remove extraneous materials. Tannin, for instance, is used for clarifying liquids in the wine and brewing industries. Gelatin and albumen remove small particles and minute traces of copper and iron in the production of vinegar and some beverages. Emulsifiers and emulsion stabilizers help to maintain a mixture and assure a consistency. They affect characteristics such as volume, uniformity, and fineness of grain (bakery products have a softer "crumb" and slower "firming" rate). They influence ease of mixing and smoothness, such as the whipping property of frozen desserts and the smoothness of cake mixes. They help maintain homogeneity and keeping quality in such products as mayonnaise, candy, and salad dressing. Some common emulsifiers are lecithin, the monoglycerides and diglycerides, and propylene glycol alginate. Sorbitan derivatives are used to retard "bloom," the whitish deposits of high-melting components of cocoa butter that occasionally appear on the surface of chocolate candy. Food chemists sometimes call emulsifiers "surfactants" or "surface-active agents."

Texturizers or stabilizers are added to products to give them "body" and maintain a desired texture. For instance, calcium chloride or some other calcium salt is added to canned tomatoes and canned potatoes to keep them from falling apart. Sodium nitrate and sodium nitrite are used in curing meats to develop and stabilize the pink color. Nitrogen, carbon dioxide, and nitrous oxide are employed in pressure-packed containers of certain foods to act as whipping agents or as propellants. The texture of ice cream and other frozen desserts is dependent on the size of the ice crystals in the product. By the addition of agar-agar, gelatin, cellulose gum, or some other gum, the size of the ice crystals is stabilized. Texturizer gums are also used in chocolate milk to increase the viscosity of the product and to prevent the settling of cocoa particles to the bottom of the container. Gelatin, pectin, and starch are used in confectionary products to give a desired texture. Artificially sweetened beverages also need bodying agents because they do not contain the "thickness" normally contributed by sugar. The thickeners employed include such natural gums as sodium alginate and pectins. The foaming properties of brewed beer can also be improved by the addition of texturizers.

## Nutrition Supplements

Enrichment of food means that the natural nutrients have been removed during processing and then replaced. Enrichment of cereal foods, much touted by the big producers, according to them is supposed to provide 12 to 23 percent of the daily supply of thiamine, niacin, and iron, and 10 percent of the riboflavin recommended for human consumption.

Fortification of food means that additional nutrients are added to the product to make it more nutritious than it was before. For instance, Vitamin C is added to orange drinks and Vitamin A to margarine. Vitamin D is used to fortify milk to prevent rickets and potassium iodide is added to iodized salt to prevent goiter, a thyroid tumor caused by iodine deficiency.

Amino acids may become commonly used as additives. The major use of amino acids in the food industry today is monosodium glutamate, which enhances flavor. Actually the human body needs certain amino acids not manufactured in the body in sufficient amounts. Proposals to add these acids as nutrients await FDA testing along with items on the GRAS list at its Pine Bluff, Arkansas, facility.

A number of additional substances are employed for various purposes. Certain sugar substitutes are used in foods for persons who must restrict their intake of ordinary sweets. Saccharin and sorbitol are commonly used for this purpose. Glazes and polishes such as waxes and gum benzoin are used on coated confections to give luster to an otherwise dull surface. Magnesium carbonate and tricalcium phosphate are employed as anticaking agents in table salt, and calcium stearate is used for a similar purpose in garlic salt.

While unique in content, this Dictionary follows the format of most standard dictionaries. The following are sample entries with any explanatory notes that may be necessary:

**MARJORAM, POT. Sweet Marjoram.** The natural extract of the flowers and leaves of two varieties of the fragrant marjoram plant. The *oleoresin* (*see*) is used in sausage and spice flavorings for condiments and meats. The *seed* is used in sausage and spice flavorings for meats (3,500 ppm) and condiments. Sweet marjoram is used in sausage and spice flavorings for beverages, baked goods (2,000 ppm), condiments, meats, and soups. The *sweet oil* is used in vermouth, wine, and spice flavorings for beverages, ice cream, ices, candy, baked goods, and condiments. No known toxicity. GRAS.

We have learned that pot marjoram is a natural flavoring extract, that there are pot and sweet marjoram, that they are utilized as an oleoresin, a seed, and as sweet oil. By looking up "oleoresin" we learn that it means "a thick, sticky product obtained when a substance is extracted from a plant by a solvent and the solvent is then removed." The "ppm" figures stand for "parts per million," that is, 3,500 parts of marjoram is added to a million parts of meat. However, because ppm amounts (they do not appear on labels) represent maximum rather than actual usage, they are not reliable estimates of consumption, and are included here only to show how amounts can be relatively quite large or small. "No known toxicity" is not an assurance that an additive is absolutely harmless but rather that no deleterious effects have been recorded in the literature. GRAS means, of course, that the item is on the government's generally *r*ecognized *a*s *s*afe list, without having undergone thorough laboratory testing. ("GRAS in packaging" means that even though substances from the containers may migrate into the food, they are assumed not harmful.)

**WORMWOOD. Absinthium.** A European woody herb with a bitter taste, used in bitters and liquor flavorings for beverages and liquors. The *extract* is used in bitters, liquor, and vermouth flavorings for beverages, ice cream, candy, and liquors, and in making absinthe. The *oil* is a dark green to brown and a narcotic substance. Used in bitters, apple, vermouth, and wine flavorings for beverages, ice cream, ices, candy, baked goods, and liquors. In large doses or frequently repeated doses, it is a narcotic poison, causing headache, trembling, and convulsions. Ingestion of the volatile oil or of the liqueur (absinthe) may cause gastrointestinal symptoms, nervousness, stupor, coma, and death.

"Absinthium," of course, is another name for wormwood and is cross-referenced in the Dictionary. Source material for the comments on toxicity is indicated in the Notes at the end of the Dictionary. A similar example is the entry for lye.

**SODIUM SESQUICARBONATE. Lye.** Produced on a large scale from sodium carbonate and a slight excess of sodium bicarbonate (*see both*). Used as a neutralizer for butter, cream, fluid milk, ice cream, in the processing of olives before canning, cacao products, and canned peas. Chiefly used in laundering in conjunction with soap. Irritating to skin and mucuous membrane. The final report to the FDA of the Select Committee on GRAS Substances stated in 1980 that it should continue its GRAS status with no limitations other than good manufacturing practices.

Under the entry **Acacia. Gum Arabic. Catechu,** the first two terms are used interchangeably. **Catechu** (from the Latin *Acacia catechu*) is less commonly used. Under the entry **Acetaldehyde. Ethanal,** the term ethanal is used interchangeably with acetaldehyde.

Some chemicals that are derived from a natural source are considered synthetic because they represent only a portion of the original compound or because other chemicals have been added. For instance:

**NONANAL. Pelargonic Aldehyde.** A synthetic flavoring that occurs naturally in lemon oil, rose, sweet orange oil, mandarin, lime, orris, and ginger. Used in lemon and fruit flavorings for beverages, ice cream, ices, candy, baked goods, gelatin desserts, and chewing gum. No known toxicity.

Terminology generally has been kept to a middle road between technician and average-interested-citizen, while at the same time avoiding oversimplification of data. If in doubt, look up any term, listed alphabetically, such as *isolate* (used in its chemical context), or *extract,* or *anhydride,* or *oleoresin,* or *demulcent, emollient, mutogenic, teratogenic, subacute,* and so on.

With *A Consumer's Dictionary of Food Additives* you will be able to work with the current labels to determine the purpose and the desirability or toxicity of the additives listed. You will be able to assert your right to wholesome food along with a wholesome environment. By having options in the marketplace, by rejecting those products that are needlessly costly or unsafe or unpalatable in favor of "clean" food, you strike back at greed and ignorance as practiced by too many in the food industry. And you reward those manufacturers who deserve your purchases.

Presently many legislators are fighting for more pervasive and informed labeling. Consequently, more chemical identities, included in the Dictionary, may be expected to appear on food labels.

Consumer groups are demanding that all foods, including standard foods, carry labeling showing all ingredients. The FDA has published a proposed regulation requiring manufacturers to list sources of fats in processed foods to allow consumers to avoid certain fats, such as polyunsaturated fats, in dietary foods, and requiring labels on baby food to state the protein content. Consumer action groups want more. They want nutritional labeling on all foods, including calories, protein content, mineral elements, vitamins, and fat levels. Hopefully, they will succeed.

In the meantime, this book takes some of the guesswork out of the chemicals you eat.

# A

**ABIES ALBA MILL.** See Pine Needle Oil.

**ABIETIC ACID.** A widely available natural acid prepared from pine rosin, usually yellow, and comprised of either glassy or crystalline particles. Used in the manufacture of soaps, vinyls, lacquers, and plastics. Employed to carry nutrients that are added to enriched rice in amounts up to .0026 percent of the weight of the nutrient mixture. Little is known about abietic acid toxicity; it is harmless when injected into mice but causes paralysis in frogs and is slightly irritating to human skin and mucous membranes.

**ABSINTHIUM. Extract or Oil.** See Wormwood.

**ABSOLUTE.** The term refers to a plant-extracted material that has been concentrated but which remains essentially unchanged in its original taste and odor. For example, see Rose, Absolute.

**ACACIA. Gum Arabic.** Acacia is the odorless, colorless, tasteless dried gummy exudate from the stem of the acacia tree grown in Africa, the Near East, India, and the southern United States. Its most distinguishing quality among the natural gums is its ability to dissolve rapidly in water. The use of acacia dates back 4,000 years when the Egyptians employed it in paints. Its principal use in the confectionery industry is to retard sugar crystallization and as a thickener for candies, jellies, glazes, and chewing gum. As a stabilizer, it prevents chemical breakdown in food mixtures. Gum acacia is a foam stabilizer in soft drink and brewing industries. Other uses are for mucilage, and the gum gives form and shape to tablets. Medically, it is used as a demulcent to soothe irritations, particularly of the mucous membranes. Oral toxicity is low but it can cause allergic reactions such as skin rash and asthmatic attacks. It is one of the additives given priority by the FDA for study of its mutagenic, teratogenic, subacute, and reproductive effects.

In 1976 the FDA placed acacia in the GRAS category as an emulsifier, flavoring agent, processing aid, and stabilizer in beverages at 2.0 percent; as an emulsifier, processing aid, humectant, and surface finishing agent in chewing gum at 5.6 percent; as a formulation aid, stabilizer, and humectant in confections and frostings at 12.4 percent; as a humectant, stabilizer, and formulation aid in hard candy at 46.5 percent; in soft candy at 85 percent; in nut formulations at 1.0 percent; and in all other food categories at 8.3 percent of the product. See Catechu Extract.

**ACER SPICATUM LAM.** See Mountain Maple Extract.

**ACESULFAME POTASSIUM.** In a petition filed in September 1982, the American Hoechst Corporation asked for approval to market this nonnutritive sweetener 200 times sweeter than table sugar. It would be used in chewing gum, dry beverage mixes, confections, canned fruit, gelatins, puddings, custards, and as a tabletop sweetener. The petition said the sweetener is not metabolized and would not add calories to the diet. As of this writing, the FDA was still reviewing the safety data contained in 15 volumes of research studies.

**ACETAL.** A synthetic flavoring agent made from acetaldehyde (*see*) and alcohol. Acetal goes into beverages, ice cream, ices, candy, and baked goods as apple, apricot, peach, banana, and whiskey flavorings. A volatile liquid, it is employed as a solvent in synthetic perfumes such as jasmine. Medically, acetal is administered as a hypnotic—as a central nervous system depressant, similar in action to paraldehyde but more toxic. Paraldehyde is a hypnotic and sedative whose side effects are respiratory depression, cardiovascular collapse, and possibly allergic reactions.

**ACETALDEHYDE. Ethanal.** A flammable, colorless liquid with a pungent odor, made from alcohol and acetylene. It is used in the manufacture of flavorings, perfumes, aniline dyes, synthetic rubber, and to harden gels. It is irritating to mucous membranes, narcotic in large doses, and may cause death by respiratory paralysis. Its ability to depress the central nervous system is greater than that of formaldehyde (*see*), and ingestion produces symptoms of "drunkenness." Acetaldehyde is thought to be a factor in the toxic effect caused by drinking alcohol after taking the antialcohol drug Antabuse.

**ACETALDEHYDE PHENETHYL PROPYL ACETAL PEPITAL.** A synthetic fruit flavoring agent for beverages, ice cream, ices, candy, and baked goods. See Acetaldehyde for toxicity.

**ACETANISOLE.** A synthetic flavoring agent, colorless to pale yellow, solid, with an odor of hawthorne or hay, moderately soluble in alcohol and most fixed oils. Acetanisole is used in butter, caramel, chocolate, fruit, nut, and vanilla flavorings, which go into beverages, ice cream, ices, candy, baked goods, and chewing gum. No known toxicity.

**ACETATE PA.** See Allyl Phenoxyacetate.

**ACETIC ACID.** Utilized as a synthetic flavoring agent, it is one of the earliest known food additives. Occurs naturally in apples, cheese, cocoa, coffee, grapes, grape juice (Concord), milk (skimmed and irradiated), oranges, parsley, peaches, pineapples, raspberries, strawberries, bay, and bay-leaf extract. (Vinegar is about 4 to 6 percent acetic acid; essence of vinegar is about 14 percent.) A colorless liquid, it is used in raspberry, strawberry, butter, butterscotch, chocolate, grape, rum, wine, spice, tobacco, cheese, and vinegar flavorings for beverages, baked goods, confections, pickles, catsup, canned artichokes, cottage cheese, pasteurized processed cheese, and cheese spreads. In its glacial form (less than 1 percent water), it is used as a solvent for oils and resins and is highly corrosive, and the vapors are capable of producing bronchial obstruction. The final report to the FDA of the Select Committee on GRAS Substances stated in 1980 that it should continue its GRAS status for packaging only with no limitations.

**ACETIC ANHYDRIDE.** A dehydrating agent and food starch modifier. A strong acetic odor, it produces irritation and necrosis of tissues in vapor state and carries a warning against contact with skin and eyes. The FDA believes that further study of modified starch (*see*) is necessary.

**ACETIC ETHER.** A synthetic agent, transparent, colorless, liquid, with a fragrant, refreshing odor, used in butter, butterscotch, fruit, nut, and spice flavorings for beverages, ice cream, ices, candy, baked goods (1,000 ppm) and chewing gum (4,000 ppm). Acts as a mild local irritant and a central nervous depressant. It readily vaporizes and is highly flammable.

**(tri-) ACETIN.** A synthetic flavoring agent, colorless, oily liquid, with a fatty odor and bitter taste. Used in butter, butterscotch, fruit, nut, and spice flavorings for beverages, ice cream, ices, candy, baked goods (1,000 ppm), and chewing gum (4,100 ppm). Also a coating for vegetables and fruits and a fixative for perfumes. Laboratory rats have tolerated diets of 50 percent triacetin.

**ACETOACETIC ESTER.** See Ethyl Acetoacetate.

**ACETOIN. Acetyl Methyl Carbinol.** A flavoring agent that occurs naturally in broccoli, grapes, pears, cultured dairy products, cooked beef, and cooked chicken. As a product of fermentation and of cream ripened for churning, it is a colorless or pale yellow liquid or a white powder, it has a characteristic buttery odor and must be stored in a light-resistant container. It is used in raspberry, strawberry, butter, butterscotch, caramel, coconut, coffee, fruit, liquor, rum, nut, walnut, vanilla, cream soda, and cheese flavorings for beverages, ice cream, ices, candy, baked goods, margarine, gelatin desserts, cottage cheese, and shortenings. No known toxicity. GRAS.

**2′ ACETONAPHTHONE.** See Methyl $\beta$-Naphthyl Ketone.

**ACETONE.** A solvent, obtained by fermentation, for fats, oils, and waxes. A tolerance of 30 ppm is allowed for a residue of acetone in spice extracts. It is also used in manufacture of airplane dopes, nail-polish remover, rayon, and photographic films. Continued use may irritate the skin. Inhalation may irritate the lungs, and in large amounts has a narcotic effect, causing symptoms such as "drunkenness."

**ACETONE PEROXIDE.** Acetone (*see*) to which an oxygen-containing compound has been added. A maturing agent for bleaching flour and dough. It has a sharp, acrid odor similar to hydrogen peroxide. A strong oxidizing agent, it can be damaging to the skin and eyes. The FDA is pursuing testing for short- and long-term effects of mutagenic, teratogenic, subacute, and reproductive effects of this widely used additive.

**ACETOOLEIN.** Obtained from fats and oils, it is a glyceride (*see*) that the Select Committee on GRAS Substances stated in 1980 should be GRAS with no limitations. See also Oleic Acid.

**ACETOPHENONE.** A synthetic agent derived from coal tar, with an odor of bitter almonds, used in strawberry, floral, fruit, cherry, almond, walnut, tobacco, vanilla, and tonka bean flavorings for beverages, ice cream, ices, candy, baked goods, gelatin desserts, and chewing gum. It occurs naturally in strawberries and tea and may cause allergic reactions. It has been used as a hypnotic.

**ACETOSTEARIN.** Obtained from fats and oils, it is a glyceride (*see*) that the Select Committee on GRAS Substances stated in 1980 should be GRAS with no limitations. See also Stearic Acid.

*p*-**ACETYL-ANISOLE.** See Acetanisole.

**ACETYL BENZENE.** See Acetophenone.

**ACETYL BUTYRYL.** See 2, 3-Hexandione.

**ACETYL-*o*-CRESOL.** See *o*-Tolyl Acetate.

**ACETYL-*p*-CRESOL.** See *p*-Tolyl Acetate.

**ACETYL EUGENOL.** See Eugenyl Acetate.

**ACETYL FORMALDEHYDE.** See Pyruvaldehyde.

**ACETYL FORMIC ACID.** See Pyruvic Acid.

**ACETYL METHYL CARBINOL.** See Acetoin.

**ACETYL NONYRYL.** See, 2, 3-Undecadione.

**ACETYL PELARGONYL.** See 2, 3-Undecadione.

**ACETYL PENTANOYL.** See 2, 3-Heptanedione.

**ACETYL PROPIONYL.** See 2, 3-Pentanedione.

*p*-**ACETYL TOLUENE.** See 4'-Methyl Acetophenone.

**ACETYL TRIOCETYL CITRATE PECTIN. Citrus Pectin.** A jelly-forming powder obtained from citrus peel and used as a texturizer and thickening agent to form gels with sugars and acids. Light colored. No known toxicity.

**ACETYL VALERYL.** See 2, 4-Heptanedione.

**ACETYL VANILLIN.** See Vanillin Acetate.

**ACETYLATED.** Refers to any organic compound heated with acetic anhydride of acetyl chloride (*see* Acetic Acid), usually in the presence of an inert solvent such as benzene or acetic acid. Acetylation is used to coat candy and other foods to hold in moisture.

**ACETYLATED DISTARCH ADIPATE AND PHOSPHATE.** Starches (*see*) that have been modified to change their solubility and digestibility. The Select Committee on GRAS Substances stated in 1980 that there is no available evidence that demonstrates or suggests a hazard to the public when they are used at levels now current and in the manner now practiced. However, it is not possible to determine, without additional data, whether a significant increase in consumption would constitute a dietary hazard. They can continue GRAS with limitations on amounts that can be added to food.

**ACETYLATED DISTARCH PROPANOL.** A starch (*see*) that has been modified to change its solubility and digestibility. The final report to the FDA of the Select Committee on GRAS Substances stated in 1980 that although no evidence in the available information on it demonstrates a hazard to the public at current use levels, uncertainties exist requiring that additional studies be conducted. GRAS status continues while tests are being completed and evaluated.

**ACHILLEIC ACID.** See Aconitic Acid.

**ACID HYDROLYZED PROTEIN.** Protein that is mixed with water and broken down into smaller molecules by acids. The final report to the FDA by the Select Committee on GRAS Substances stated in 1980 that acid hydrolyzed protein was GRAS with no limitations other than good manufacturing practices.

**ACID-MODIFIED STARCHES.** Usually made by mixing an acid— such as hydrochloric or sulfuric—water, and starch at temperatures too low for gelatinization. When the starch has been reduced in viscosity to the degree desired, the acid is neutralized and the starch is filtered, washed, and dried. It is done so that starches can be cooked and used at higher concentrations than unmodified starches. Acid-modified starches are often used for salad dressings and puddings and as inexpensive thickening agents. The final report to the FDA of the Select Committee on GRAS Substances stated in 1980 that acid-modified starches are GRAS with no limitations.

**ACID POTASSIUM SULFITE.** See Sulfites, Potassium.

**ACIDOPHILUS.** A type of bacteria that ferments milk and has been used medically to treat intestinal disorders.

**ACIDS.** See Acidulants.

**ACIDULANTS. Acids.** An acid is a substance capable of turning blue litmus paper red and of forming hydrogen ions when dissolved in water. An acid aqueous solution is one with a pH less than 7 (*see* pH). Acidulants are acids that make a substance more acid and function as flavoring agents to intensify taste, to blend unrelated flavoring characteristics, and to mask any undesirable aftertaste. Acidulants are used also as preservatives to prevent germ and spore growths that spoil foods. Acidulants control the acid-alkali (pH) balance and are used in meat curings to enhance color and flavor and as a preservative. Among the most common acids added to foods are acetic, propionic, and sorbic (see all).

**ACONITIC ACID. Citridic Acid.** A flavoring agent found in beetroot and cane sugar. Most of the commercial aconitic acids, however, are manufactured by sulfuric acid dehydration of citric acid. It is used in fruit, brandy, and rum flavorings for beverages, ice cream, ices, candy, baked goods, liquors, and chewing gum. Also used in the manufacture of plastics and buna rubber. No known toxicity.

**ACRYLAMIDE RESIN. Acrylic Acid.** A clarifying agent in beet sugar and cane sugar juice. The acid is used in the synthesis of this acrylic resin. No known toxicity.

**ACTADECYLSILOXYDIMETHYLSIOLOXYPOLYSILOXANE.** A component of defoamers (see) used in processing beets and yeast. No known toxicity.

**ACTIVATED CHARCOAL (CARBON).** Used to remove impurities that cause undesirable color, taste, or odor in liquid. The major sources are lignite, coal, and coke. The Select Committee of the Federation of American Societies for Experimental Biology (FASEB) under contract to the FDA concluded that it is not a hazard to human health at current or possible future use levels. However, the Committee said because the substance is extensively used in the food industry, it would be prudent to have purity specifications for food-grade activated carbon to assure the absence of any cancer-causing hydrocarbons in food.

**ACTIVATED 7-DEHYDROCHOLESTEROL.** See Vitamin $D_3$.

**ADIPIC ACID.** Occurs naturally in beets. Used in flavorings for beverages and gelatin desserts (5,000 ppm) to impart a smooth-tart taste. Also used as a buffer and neutralizing agent in confections, but limited to 3 percent of contents, and in the manufacture of plastics and nylons, and as a substitute for tartaric acid (see) in baking powders because it is impervious to humidity. Nontoxic. The final report to the FDA of the Select Committee on GRAS Substances stated in 1980 that it should continue its GRAS status with no limitations other than good manufacturing practices.

**ADIPIC ANHYDRIDE.** A starch-modifying agent, not to exceed .12 percent of the starch compound. No known toxicity. See Modified Starch.

**AGAR-AGAR. Japanese Isinglass.** A stabilizer and thickener, it is transparent, odorless, and tasteless, and obtained from various seaweeds found in the Pacific and Indian oceans and the Sea of Japan. Agar was the first seaweed to be extracted, purified, and dried. Discovered by a Japanese innkeeper around 1658 and introduced in Europe and the

United States by visitors from China in the 1800s as a substitute for gelatin, it goes into beverages, ice cream, ices, frozen custard, sherbet, meringue, baked goods, jelly, frozen candied sweet potatoes, icings, confections, artificially sweetened jellies and preserves. Agar serves as a substitute for gelatin and is used for thickening milk and cream. It is also a bulk laxative, and, aside from causing an occasional allergic reaction, is nontoxic. The final report to the FDA of the Select Committee on GRAS Substances stated in 1980 that there is no evidence in the available information that it is a hazard to the public when used as it is now and it should continue its GRAS status with limitations on amounts that can be added to food.

**ALANINE. L and DL forms.**   Colorless crystals derived from protein. Believed to be a nonessential amino acid (*see*), it is used in microbiological research and as a dietary supplement in the L and DL forms. The FDA has asked for supplementary information. It is now GRAS for addition to food. It caused cancer of the skin in mice and tumors when injected into their abdomens.

**ALBUMIN.**   A group of simple proteins composed of nitrogen, carbon, hydrogen, oxygen, and sulfur that are soluble in water. Albumin is usually derived from egg white and employed as an emulsifier in foods and cosmetics. May cause a reaction to those allergic to eggs, and in large quantities can produce symptoms of lack of biotin, a growth factor in the lining of the cells.

**ALCOHOL C-7.**   See Heptyl Alcohol.

**ALCOHOL C-9.**   See Nonyl Alcohol.

**ALDEHYDE C-7.**   See Heptanal.

**ADELHYDE C-9.**   See Nonanal.

**ALDEHYDE C-10.** See Decanal.

**ALDEHYDE C-11 UNDECYLENIC.** See 9-Undecenal.

**ALDEHYDE C-12 MNA.**   See 2-Methylundecanal.

**ALFALFA. Herb and Seed.**   A natural cola, liquor, and maple flavoring agent for beverages and cordials. Alfalfa is widely cultivated for forage and is a commercial source of chlorophyll. Also called lucerne. No known toxicity.

**ALGAE, BROWN. Kelp.**   Ground, dried seaweed used to carry natural spices, seasonings, and flavorings. A source of alginic acid (*see*). Also used in chewing-gum base. All derivatives of alginic acid are designated "algin." The food industry is one of the major users of alginates (*see*) along with pharmaceutical, cosmetic, rubber, and paper industries. The United States is the largest producer of alginates. Nontoxic. The final report to the FDA of the Select Committee on GRAS Substances stated in

1980 that it should continue its GRAS status with no limitations other than good manufacturing practices.

**ALGAE, RED.** A natural extract of seaweed used to carry natural spices, seasonings, and flavorings. See Alginates. Nontoxic. GRAS.

**ALGINATES. Ammonium, Calcium, Potassium, and Sodium.** A gelatinous substance obtained from certain seaweeds used as stabilizers and water retainers in beverages, ice cream, ices, frozen custard, emulsions, desserts, baked goods, and confectionery ingredients. A clarifying agent for wine, chocolate milk, meat, toppings, cheeses, cheese spreads, cheese snacks, salad dressings, and artificially sweetened jelly and jam ingredients. Alginates are used also as stabilizers in gassed cream (pressure-dispensed whipped cream). The alginates assure a creamy texture and prevent formation of ice crystals in ice creams. Alginates have been used in the making of ice pops to impart smoothness of texture by ensuring that the fruit flavors are uniformly distributed throughout the ice crystals during freezing, helping the pops to retain flavor and color, and to stop dripping. The final report to the FDA of the Select Committee on GRAS Substances stated in 1980 that there is no evidence in the available information that it is a hazard to the public when used as it is now and it should continue its GRAS status with limitations on amounts that can be added to food.

**ALGINIC ACID.** Obtained from seaweeds. It is odorless and tasteless and is used as a stabilizer in ice cream, frozen custard, ice milk, fruit sherbet, water ices, beverages, icings, cheeses, cheese spreads, cheese snacks, French dressing, and salad dressing. It is also used as a defoaming agent in processed foods. Capable of absorbing 200 to 300 times its weight of water and salts. Also used in sizing paper and textiles; as binder for briquettes; in manufacture of artificial horn, ivory, celluloid; and for emulsifying mineral oils and in mucilage. No known toxicity. GRAS.

**ALKALI.** The term originally covered the caustic and mild forms of potash and soda. A substance such as potash, soda, or "animosia" that neutralizes acids. An alkaline aqueous solution is one with a pH (*see*) greater than 7. Sodium bicarbonate is an example of an alkali that is used to neutralize excess acidity in foods.

**ALKANET ROOT.** The extraction of the tree root grown in Asia Minor and the Mediterranean. Used as a colorant in wines, cosmetics, confections, sausage casings, oleomargarine, shortening, and inks. Used in berry, fruit, and meat flavorings for beverages, ice cream, ices, candy, baked goods, icings, and meats. Formerly used as an astringent. Alkanet may be mixed with approved synthetic dyes or harmless inert material such as common salt and sugar. Nontoxic.

**ALKYL.** Meaning from alcohol, usually derived from alkane—any one of a series of saturated hydrocarbons, such as methane. The introduction of one or more alkyls into a compound is for the purpose of making the product more soluble. The compound is usually used with surfactants (*see*), which have a tendency to float if not alkylated.

**ALKYL BETAINES.** See Alkyl Sulfates.

**ALKYL ETHER SULFATES.** See Alkyl Sulfates.

**ALKYL SULFATES.** Surfactants (*see*) used in foods, drugs, and cosmetics. These compounds were developed by the Germans during World War II when vegetable fats and oils were scarce. A large number of alkyl sulfates have been prepared from primary alcohols by treatment with sulfuric acid; the alcohols are usually prepared from fatty acids (*see*). Alkyl sulfates are low in acute and chronic toxicity but may cause skin irritation.

**ALLOMALEIC ACID.** See Fumaric Acid.

**ALLSPICE.** A natural flavoring from the dried berries of the allspice tree. Allspice is used in liquor, meat, and spice flavorings for beverages, ice cream, ices, candy, baked goods (1,400 ppm), chewing gum, condiments (1,000 ppm), and meats. Allspice *oleoresin* (a natural mixture of oil and resin) is used in sausage flavoring for baked goods, meat, and condiments. Allspice *oil* is used in sausage, berry, cola, peach, rum, nut, allspice, cinnamon, ginger, nutmeg, and eggnog flavorings for beverages, ice cream, ices, candy, baked goods, chewing gum (1,700 ppm), condiments, pickles, meats, liquors, and soups. Nontoxic. GRAS.

**ALLYL ANTHRANILATE.** A synthetic citrus fruit and grape flavoring agent for beverages, ice cream, ices, candy, baked goods, and gelatin desserts. No known toxicity.

**ALLYL BUTYRATE.** A synthetic butter, fruit, and pineapple flavoring agent for beverages, ice cream, ices, candy, baked goods, and gelatin desserts. No known toxicity.

**ALLYL CINNAMATE.** A synthetic fruit flavoring agent for beverages, ice cream, ices, candy, and baked goods. No known toxicity.

**ALLYL CYCLOHEXANE ACETATE.** A synthetic pineapple flavoring agent for beverages, ice cream, ices, candy, and baked goods. No known toxicity.

**ALLYL CYCLOHEXANE BUTYRATE.** A synthetic pineapple flavoring agent for beverages, ice cream, ices, candy, and baked goods. No known toxicity.

**ALLYL CYCLOHEXANE HEXANOATE.** A synthetic fruit flavoring agent for beverages, ice cream, ices, candy, and baked goods. No known toxicity.

**ALLYL CYCLOHEXANE PROPIONATE.** A synthetic agent, liquid

and colorless, with a pineapplelike odor, used in pineapple flavorings for beverages, ice cream, ices, candy, baked goods, gelatin desserts, puddings, chewing gum, and icings. No known toxicity.

**ALLYL CYCLOHEXANE VALERATE.** A synthetic pineapple flavoring agent for beverages, ice cream, ices, candy, and baked goods. No known toxicity.

**ALLYL DISULFIDE.** Found naturally in garlic and leeks, but considered a synthetic flavoring. It is used in garlic, onion, and spice flavorings for meats and condiments. No known toxicity.

**ALLYL ENANTHATE.** See Allyl Heptanoate.

**ALLYL 2-ETHYLBUTYRATE.** A synthetic fruit flavoring agent for butter, candy, gelatin desserts, and pudding. No known toxicity. GRAS.

**ALLYL 2-FUROATE.** A synthetic coffee and pineapple flavoring agent for beverages, ice cream, ices, candy, baked goods, and gelatin desserts. No known toxicity. GRAS.

**ALLYL HEPTANOATE.** A synthetic berry, fruit, and brandy flavoring agent for beverages, ice cream, ices, candy, baked goods, gelatin desserts, and chewing gum. No known toxicity. GRAS.

**ALLYL HEXANOATE.** A synthetic orange, strawberry, apple, apricot, peach, pineapple, and tutti-frutti flavoring agent for beverages, ice cream, ices, candy, baked goods, gelatin desserts, and chewing gum. No known toxicity.

**ALLYL α-IONONE. Cetone V.** A synthetic agent, yellow, with a strong, fruity, pineapplelike odor, used in fruit flavoring for beverages, ice cream, ices, candy, baked goods, gelatin desserts, and toppings. No known toxicity. GRAS.

**ALLYL ISOTHIOCYANATE.** A naturally occurring agent in mustard, horseradish, and onion used in meat and spice flavorings for beverages, ice cream, ices, candy, condiments, meat, and pickles. Colorless or pale yellow with a very pungent irritating odor and acrid taste. It is used also in the manufacture of war gas. Can cause blisters. Toxic.

**ALLYL MERCAPTAN.** A synthetic spice flavoring agent for beverages, ice cream, ices, candy, baked goods, condiments, and meats. No known toxicity.

**4-ALLYL-2-METHOXYPHENOL.** See Eugenol.

**ALLYL NONANOATE.** A synthetic fruit and wine flavoring agent for beverages, ice cream, ices, candy, baked goods, and meats. No known toxicity.

**ALLYL OCTANOATE.** A synthetic pineapple flavoring agent for beverages, ice cream, ices, candy, baked goods, and gelatin desserts. No known toxicity.

**ALLYL PHENOXYACETATE. Acetate PA.** A synthetic fruit flavoring agent for beverages, ice cream, ices, candy, baked goods, and gelatin desserts. No known toxicity.

**ALLYL PHENYLACETATE.** A synthetic pineapple and honey flavoring agent for beverages, ice cream, ices, candy, and baked goods. No known toxicity.

**ALLYL PROPIONATE.** A synthetic pineapple flavoring agent for beverages, ice cream, ices, candy, and baked goods. No known toxicity.

**ALLYL SORBATE.** A synthetic fruit flavoring agent for beverages, ice cream, ices, candy, baked goods, and gelatin desserts. No known toxicity.

**ALLYL SULFHYDRATE.** See Allyl Mercaptan.

**ALLYL SULFIDE.** A synthetic fruit and garlic flavoring agent for beverages, ice cream, ices, baked goods, candy, condiments, and meats. Occurs naturally in garlic and horseradish. Produces irritation of the eyes and respiratory tract. Readily absorbed through the skin. Acute exposure can cause unconsciousness. Long-term exposure can cause liver and kidney damage.

**ALLYL UNDECYLENATE.** See Allyl 10-Undecenoate.

**ALLYL TIGLATE.** A synthetic fruit flavoring agent for beverages, ice cream, ices, candy, and baked goods. No known toxicity.

**ALLYL 10-UNDECENOATE.** A synthetic fruit flavoring agent for beverages, ice cream, candy, and baked goods. No known toxicity.

*p*-**ALLYLANISOLE.** See Estragole.

**ALLYLTHIOL.** See Allyl Mercaptan.

**4-ALLYLVERATROLE.** See Eugenyl Methyl Ether.

**ALMOND. Bitter Oil.** A flavoring agent from the ripe seed of a small tree grown in Italy, Spain, and France. Colorless or slightly yellow, strong almond odor, and mild taste. Used in cherry and almond flavorings for beverages, ice cream, ices, candy, baked goods, gelatin desserts, chewing gum, and maraschino cherries. Used also in the manufacture of liqueurs and perfumes. It is distilled to remove hydrocyanic acid (Prussic acid), which is very toxic. Nontoxic without the hydrocyanic acid. GRAS.

**ALOE EXTRACT.** From the leaves of various plants grown in Curacao, Dutch West Indies, and South Africa. Used in bitters, vermouth, and spice flavorings for beverages (2,000 ppm) and alcoholic drinks. It has been used as a cathartic but was found to cause severe intestinal cramps and sometimes kidney damage.

**ALTHEA ROOT. Marshmallow Root.** A natural flavoring substance from a plant grown in Europe, Asia, and the U.S. The dried root is used in strawberry, cherry, and root beer flavorings for beverages. The boiled root is used as a demulcent to soothe mucous membranes; the roots, leaves, and flowers are used externally as a poultice. Nontoxic.

**ALUM.** A colorless, odorless, crystalline, water-soluble solid used in packaging. It is also called aluminum potassium sulfate, common alum, potash alum, and potassium alum. A double sulfate of aluminum and ammonium potassium, it is also employed to harden gelatin, size paper, or waterproof fabrics; in medicine, an astringent and styptic. It has a low toxicity in experimental animals, but ingestion of 30 grams (one ounce) has killed adult humans. Concentrated solutions have caused breakdown of gum tissues, kidney damage, and fatal intestinal bleeding. Liquid alum has been found by Penn State researchers to be capable of removing over 99 percent of phosphates from waste water effluent. GRAS when used in packaging only.

**ALUMINUM AMMONIUM SULFATE.** Odorless, colorless crystals with a strong astringent taste. Used in purifying drinking water; in baking powders; as a buffer and neutralizing agent in milling; and in the cereal industries. Used also for fireproofing and in the manufacture of vegetable glue and artificial gems. In medicine, it is an astringent and styptic (stops bleeding). Ingestion of large amounts may cause burning in mouth and pharynx, vomiting, and diarrhea. The final report to the FDA of the Select Committee on GRAS Substances stated in 1980 that it should continue its GRAS status with no limitations other than good manufacturing practices.

**ALUMINUM CALCIUM SILICATE.** Anticaking agent used so that it is 2 percent of table salt. Used also in vanilla powder to prevent caking. Essentially harmless when given orally. GRAS.

**ALUMINUM HYDROXIDE.** An alkali used as a leavening agent in the production of baked goods. It is also used in antiperspirants and dentifrices and as a gastric antacid but it can cause constipation. The final report to the FDA of the Select Committee on GRAS Substances stated in 1980 that it should continue its GRAS status for packaging only with no limitations other than good manufacturing practices.

**ALUMINUM NICOTINATE.** Used as a source of niacin in special diet foods, also as a medication to dilate blood vessels and to combat fat. Tablets of 625 milligrams are a complex of aluminum nicotinate, nicotinic acid, and aluminum hydroxide. Side effects are flushing, rash, and gastrointestinal distress when taken in large doses.

**ALUMINUM OLEATE.** A yellow, thick, acidic mass practically insoluble in water. Used in packaging, as lacquer for metals, in waterproofing, and for thickening lubricating oils. Low toxicity. The final report to the FDA of the Select Committee on GRAS Substances stated in 1980 that it should continue its GRAS status for packaging only with no limitations other than good manufacturing practices.

**ALUMINUM PALMITATE.** A whitish-yellow mass or powder, practically insoluble in water or alcohol, used in packaging. Also used to thicken petroleum, in waterproofing, and for glazing paper and leather. No known toxicity. The final report to the FDA of the Select Committee on GRAS Substances stated in 1980 that it should continue its GRAS status for packaging only with no limitations other than good manufacturing practices.

**ALUMINUM PHOSPHIDE.** Used to fumigate processed foods, the FDA requires that processors aerate the finished food for 48 hours before it is offered to the consumer. It further warns that under no condition should the formulation containing aluminum phosphide be used so that it or its unreacted residues will come in contact with any processed food. Reacts with moist air to produce the highly toxic phosphine. Residues of phosphine in or on processed food may not exceed .01 parts per million, according to the FDA. Phosphine may cause pain in the region of the diaphragm, a feeling of coldness, weakness, vertigo, shortness of breath, bronchitis, edema, lung damage, convulsions, coma, and death.

**ALUMINUM POTASSIUM SULFATE.** Colorless, odorless, hard, transparent crystals or powder with a sweet antiseptic taste used for clarifying sugar, and as a firming agent and carrier for bleaching agents. It is used in the production of sweet and dill pickles, cereal, flours, bleached flours, and cheese. Ingestion of large quantities may cause burning in the mouth and throat and stomach distress. The final report to the FDA of the Select Committee on GRAS Substances stated in 1980 that it should continue its GRAS status with no limitations other than good manufacturing practices.

**ALUMINUM SODIUM SULFATE.** Firming agent and carrier for bleaching agents. For other uses, see Aluminum Potassium Sulfate. The final report to the FDA of the Select Committee on GRAS Substances stated in 1980 that it should continue its GRAS status with no limitations other than good manufacturing practices.

**ALUMINUM STEARATE.** Hard, plasticlike material used in waterproofing fabrics, thickening lubricating oils, and as a chewing gum base component and a defoamer component used in processing beet sugar and yeast. No known toxicity.

**ALUMINUM SULFATE. Cake Alum. Patent Alum.** Firming agent that occurs as a white powder or crystals in the earth. Odorless, with a sweet, mildly astringent taste. Used in producing sweet and dill pickles and as a modifier for food starch. Also used in tanning leather, sizing paper, waterproofing for antiperspirants, agricultural pesticides, antiseptics, and detergents. Low in toxicity. The final report to the FDA of the

Select Committee on GRAS Substances stated in 1980 that it should continue its GRAS status with no limitations other than good manufacturing practices.

**AMARANTH.** Red No. 2 banned by the FDA in 1976. The ban was reaffirmed in 1980.

**AMBERGRIS.** Concretion from the intestinal tract of the sperm whale found floating in tropical seas or on shore. A waxy grayish mass, it is about 80 percent cholesterol and is used as a fixative for delicate odors in perfumery. In food, used in berry, fruit, rum, spice, and vanilla flavorings for beverages, ice cream, ices, candy, and baked goods. No known toxicity. GRAS.

**AMBRETTE.** A natural flavoring agent from the seed of the hibiscus plant, clear yellow to amber as a liquid, with a musky odor. Seed used in berry and floral flavorings for beverages, ice cream, ices, candy, baked goods. The tincture is used in black walnut and vanilla flavorings for the same products and in cordials. The seed oil is used in fruit flavoring for beverages, ice cream, candy, and baked goods. No known toxicity. GRAS.

**AMERICAN DILL SEED OIL.** See Dill.

**AMES TEST.** In the early 1970s, Dr. Bruce Ames, a biochemist at the University of California at Berkeley, developed a simple test using common bacteria that reveals whether a chemical is a mutagen. The test can be done quickly and is relatively inexpensive. Mutagens act by changing the genetic material that is transferred to daughter cells when cell division occurs. Carcinogens also act by fouling up the genetic material within a cell. Almost all chemicals known to be carcinogenic have also been shown to be mutagenic in the Ames Test.

**AMINE OXIDES.** Surfactants derived from ammonia (*see both*).

**AMINO ACIDS.** The body's building blocks, from which proteins are constructed. Of the twenty-two known amino acids, eight cannot be manufactured in the body in sufficient quantities to sustain growth and health. These eight are called "essential" because they are necessary to maintain good health. A ninth, histidine, is thought to be necessary for growth only in childhood. Certain amino acid deficiencies appear to have tumor-suppressing action. The amino acids of protein foods are separated by digestion and go into a general pool from which the body takes the ones it needs to synthesize its own personal proteins. A diet deficient in cystine (*see*) was reported to inhibit the induction of leukemia in mice. Spontaneous mammary carcinoma in female mice was inhibited by lysine-deficient or cystine-deficient diets. The tumor-suppressing action may be due to the effect on the body's immune system. One theory is that the lack of amino acids may lower the defenses of the tumor against the body's own defenses or alter the metabolism of cancer-causing agents.

**AMMONIA.** A liquid obtained by blowing steam through incandescent coke. It is used in the manufacture of surfactants, in permanent waves (cold) and hair bleaches, and in cleaning preparations. It is also used in the manufacture of explosives and synthetic fabrics. It is extremely toxic when inhaled in concentrated vapors and is irritating to the eyes and mucous membranes.

**AMMONIUM ALGINATE.** A stabilizer and water retainer. The final report to the FDA of the Select Committee on GRAS Substances stated in 1980 that there is no evidence in the available information that it is a hazard to the public when used as it is now and it should continue its GRAS status with limitations on amounts that can be added to food. See Alginates.

**AMMONIUM BICARBONATE.** An alkali used as a leavening agent in the production of baked goods, confections, and cacao products. The shiny, hard crystals or mass, with a faint odor of ammonia, do not combine with acids. Used also in soothing baths, in compost heaps to accelerate decomposition, as an expectorant, and to relieve flatulence. Nontoxic. The final report to the FDA of the Select Committee on GRAS Substances stated in 1980 that it should continue its GRAS status with no limitations other than good manufacturing practices.

**AMMONIUM CARBONATE.** The final report to the FDA of the Select Committee on GRAS Substances stated in 1980 that it should continue its GRAS status with no limitations other than good manufacturing practices. See Ammonium Bicarbonate.

**AMMONIUM CHLORIDE.** Colorless, odorless crystals or white powder used as a yeast food and dough conditioner in bread, rolls, buns, and so on. Saline in taste and incompatible with alkalies. Industrially employed in freezing mixtures, batteries, dyes, safety explosives, and in medicine as an expectorant, urinary acidifier, and diuretic; keeps snow from melting on ski slopes. Can cause nausea, vomiting, and acidosis in doses of 0.5 to 1 gram. The final report to the FDA of the Select Committee on GRAS Substances stated in 1980 that it should continue its GRAS status for packaging only with no limitations other than good manufacturing practices.

**AMMONIUM CITRATE.** The salt of citric acid (*see*), it is a natural constituent of plants and animals and dissolves easily in water, releasing free acid. Used as a sequestrant, flavor enhancer, and as a firming agent. The final report to the FDA of the Select Committee on GRAS Substances stated in 1980 that it should continue its GRAS status with no limitations other than good manufacturing practices.

**AMMONIUM HYDROXIDE.** An alkali and cacao product. See uses for Ammonium Bicarbonate. The final report to the FDA of the Select Committee on GRAS Substances stated in 1980 that it should continue its GRAS status for packaging only with no limitations other than good manufacturing practices.

**AMMONIUM ISOVALERATE.** A synthetic butter, nut, and cheese flavoring agent for baked goods and syrups. No known toxicity.

**AMMONIUM PHOSPHATE. Monobasic and Dibasic.** White, odorless, salty crystals or powders, used as acidic constituents of baking powder. They are used as buffers, leavening agents, and bread, roll, and bun improvers up to 10 percent of product. Used in brewing industry. Also used in fireproofing, purifying sugar, in yeast cultures, dentifrices, and fertilizers. Monobasic is used as baking powder with sodium bicarbonate. Medically used for their saline action. They have a diuretic effect (reducing body water) and they make urine more acid. Nontoxic. The final report to the FDA of the Select Committee on GRAS Substances stated in 1980 that it should continue its GRAS status with no limitations other than good manufacturing practices.

**AMMONIUM SULFATE.** A yeast food, dough conditioner, and buffer in bakery products. Colorless, odorless, white crystals or powder. Industrial uses in freezing mixtures, fireproofing fabrics, tanning, and fertilizers. Used also in the production of caramel. Medically it has been employed to prolong analgesia. No known toxicity. The final report to the FDA of the Select Committee on GRAS Substances stated in 1980 that it should continue its GRAS status with no limitations other than good manufacturing practices. See use for Ammonium Phosphate.

**AMMONIUM SULFIDE.** A synthetic spice flavoring agent for baked goods and condiments. Also used to apply patina to bronze and in film developers. May evolve into toxic hydrogen sulfide and a fatality has been reported from use of ammonium sulfide "permanent wave" lotion.

**AMYL ACETATE.** See Isoamyl Acetate.

**AMYL ALCOHOL.** A synthetic berry, chocolate, apple, banana, pineapple, liquor, and rum flavoring agent for beverages, ice cream, ices, candy, baked goods, gelatin desserts, and chewing gum. Occurs naturally in cocoa and oranges. Highly toxic and narcotic. Ingestion of 30 milligrams has killed humans. Smells like camphor. Inhalation causes violent coughing.

**AMYL ALDEHYDE.** See Valeraldehyde.

**AMYL BUTYRATE.** A synthetic flavoring agent, colorless, with a strong apricot odor. Occurs naturally in cocoa. Used in raspberry, strawberry, butter, butterscotch, fruit, apple, apricot, banana, cherry, grape, peach, pineapple, and vanilla flavorings for beverages, ice cream, ices, candy, baked goods, gelatin desserts, puddings, chewing gum, and cherry syrup. Also used in perfume compositions. No known toxicity.

**AMYL CAPRATE.** See Cognac Oil.

**AMYL FORMATE. Formic Acid.** A synthetic flavoring agent, colorless, with a plumlike odor. Used in strawberry, apple, apricot, banana, cherry, peach, plum, nut, and walnut flavorings for beverages, ice cream, ices, candy, baked goods, and chewing gum. Occurs naturally in apples. See Formic Acid for toxicity.

**AMYL 2-FUROATE.** A synthetic rum and maple flavoring agent for beverages, candy, baked goods, and condiments. No known toxicity.

**AMYL HEPTANOATE.** A synthetic lemon, coconut, fruit, and nut flavoring agent for beverages, ice cream, ices, candy, baked goods, gelatin desserts, puddings, and chewing gum. No known toxicity.

**AMYL HEXANOATE.** A synthetic citrus, chocolate, apple, grape, pineapple, honey, and liquor flavoring agent for beverages, ice cream, ices, candy, baked goods, gelatin desserts, puddings, and chewing gum. No known toxicity.

**2-AMYL-5 (OR 6)-KETO-1, 4-DIOXAME.** A synthetic fruit flavoring agent for beverages, ice cream, ices, candy, baked goods, and shortening. No known toxicity.

**AMYL OCTANOATE.** Occurs naturally in apples. A synthetic chocolate, fruit, and liquor flavoring agent for beverages, ice cream, ices, candy, baked goods, and gelatin desserts. No known toxicity.

**α-AMYL β-PHENYLACROLEIN BUXINE.** See α-Amylcinnamaldehyde.

**AMYL VINYL CARBINOL.** See 1-Octen-3-ol.

**α-AMYLASE.** An enzyme prepared from hog pancreas used in flour to break down starch into smaller sugar molecules. Then, in turn, the enzymes produced by yeast in the dough again split these sugar molecules to form carbon dioxide gas, which causes the dough to rise. Used medically to combat inflammation. Nontoxic.

**α-AMYLCINNAMALDEHYDE.** A synthetic agent, yellow, with a strong floral odor of jasmine, used in strawberry, apple, apricot, peach, and walnut flavorings for beverages, ice cream, ices, candy, baked goods, gelatin desserts, and chewing gum. Very susceptible to oxidation by air. No known toxicity.

**α-AMYLCINNAMALDEHYDE DIMETHYL ACETAL.** A synthetic

fruit flavoring agent for beverages, ice cream, candy, and baked goods. No known toxicity.

**α-AMYLCINNAMYL ACETATE.** A synthetic chocolate, fruit, and honey flavoring agent for beverages, ice cream, ices, candy, baked goods, and chewing gum. No known toxicity.

**α-AMYLCINNAMYL ALCOHOL.** A synthetic chocolate, fruit, and honey flavoring agent for beverages, ice cream, ices, candy, baked goods, and chewing gum. No known toxicity.

**α-AMYLCINNAMYL FORMATE.** A synthetic chocolate, fruit, maple, and nut flavoring agent for beverages, ice cream, ices, candy, baked goods, and chewing gum. No known toxicity.

**α-AMYLCINNAMYL ISOVALERATE.** A synthetic chocolate, fruit, grape, and nut flavoring agent for beverages, candy, ice cream, ices, baked goods, and chewing gum. No known toxicity.

**AMYLOPECTIN.** The outer, almost insoluble portion of the starch granules. It forms a paste with water. Waxy corn starches are particularly high in amylopectins.

**AMYLOSE.** Starches commonly processed from plants contain 18 to 27 percent amylose. It is the inner, relatively soluble portion of starch granules. Corn starch solutions often form opaque gels after cooking and cooling; this is because of the presence of amylose. It is used as a dispersing and mixing agent for oleoresins. Nontoxic.

**AMYRIS OIL. Sandalwood Oil.** The volatile oil obtained from a gummy wood and used as a flavoring agent in chewing gum and candy. It is a clear, pale yellow viscous liquid with a distinct odor of sandalwood. No known toxicity.

**ANCHUSIN EXTRACT.** See Alkanet Root.

**ANETHOLE.** Occurs naturally in anise, fennel, and star anise, with a strong smell and sweet taste. Chief constituent of star anise. Used in fruit, honey, licorice, anise, liquor, nut, root beer, sarsaparilla, spice, vanilla, wintergreen, and birch beer flavorings for beverages, ice cream, ices, candy, baked goods, chewing gum (1,500 ppm) and liquors (1,400 ppm). Intestinal stimulant in colic, also an expectorant, and used in perfumes, soaps, dentifrices. Applied to the skin it causes blisters and scaling. Inflammation of the mouth after use of a denture cream containing anethole was reported. GRAS.

**ANETHUM GRAVEOLENS L.** See Dill.

**ANGELICA.** Grown in Europe and Asia, the aromatic seeds, leaves, stems, and roots have been used as a medicine for flatus (gas), to increase sweating, and to reduce body water. The *root oil* is used in fruit, gin, and rum flavorings for beverages, ice cream, ices, candy, baked goods, gelatin desserts, chewing gum, and liquors. The *root extract* is used in berry, liquor, wine, maple, nut, walnut, and root beer flavorings for the same foods, up to baked goods, plus syrups. The *seed extract* is used in berry, fruit, maple, walnut, and spice flavorings for beverages, candy, baked goods, syrups, and condiments. The *seed oil* is used for fruit and gin flavoring for beverages, ice cream, ices, candy, baked goods, gelatin desserts, and liquors. The *stem oil* is used for fruit flavoring for the same foods as is seed oil, excepting liquors. Angelica can induce sensitivity to light. GRAS.

**ANGOSTURA.** Flavoring agent from the bark of trees, grown in Venezuela and Brazil. Unpleasant musty odor and bitter aromatic taste. The light yellow liquid extract is used in bitters, liquor, root beer, and spice flavorings for beverages and liquors (1,700 ppm). Formerly used to lessen fever. No known toxicity. GRAS.

**ANHYDRIDE.** A residue resulting from water being removed from a compound, for example, acetic anhydride (*see*). Anhydrous describes a substance that contains no water.

**ANISE. Anise Seed.** Dried ripe fruit of Asia, Europe, and the U.S. Used in licorice, anise, pepperoni, sausage, spice, and vanilla flavorings for beverages, ice cream, ices, candy, baked goods, condiments (5,000 ppm), and meats (1,200 ppm). The *oil* is used for butter, caramel, licorice, anise, rum, sausage, nut, root beer, sarsaparilla, spice, vanilla, wintergreen, and birch beer flavorings for the same foods as above excepting condiments but including chewing gum (3,200 ppm) and liquors. Sometimes used to break up intestinal gas. Nontoxic. GRAS. See Star Anise.

**ANISIC ALCOHOL.** See Anisyl Alcohol.

**ANISOLE.** A synthetic agent with a pleasant odor used in licorice, root beer, sarsaparilla, wintergreen, and birch beer flavorings for beverages, ice cream, ices, candy, and baked goods. Used also in perfumes. No known toxicity.

**ANISYL ACETATE.** A synthetic berry, chocolate, cocoa, fruit, and vanilla flavoring agent for beverages, ice cream, ices, candy, baked goods, gelatin desserts, and chewing gum. No known toxicity.

**ANISYL ALCOHOL.** A synthetic chocolate, cocoa, fruit, licorice, and vanilla flavoring agent for beverages, ice cream, ices, candy, baked goods, and gelatin desserts. Found naturally in vanilla. No known toxicity.

**ANISYL BUTYRATE.** A synthetic fruit and licorice flavoring agent for beverages, ice cream, ices, candy, and baked goods. No known toxicity.

**ANISYL FORMATE. Formic Acid.** A synthetic raspberry, fruit, licorice, and vanilla flavoring agent for beverages, ice cream, ices, baked goods, and gelatin desserts. Found naturally in currant and vanilla. See Formic Acid for toxicity.

**ANISYL METHYL KETONE.** See 1-(*p*-Methoxyphenyl)-2-Propanone.

**ANISYL PHENYLACETATE.** A synthetic honey flavoring agent for beverages, ice cream, ices, candy, and baked goods. No known toxicity.

**ANISYL PROPIONATE.** Occurs naturally in quince, apple, banana, cherry, peach, and pineapple. A raspberry, cherry, and licorice flavoring agent for beverages, ice cream, ices, candy, baked goods, and gelatin desserts. No known toxicity.

**ANNATTO. Extract and Seed.** A vegetable dye from the pulp surrounding the seeds of the tropical annatto tree. Its yellow to peach coloring goes into such dairy products as butter, cheese, cottage cheese, and buttermilk in addition to margarine, beverages, ice cream, ices, baked goods, cake mixes, and breakfast cereals. It is used also to color such meat-product casings as bologna and frankfurters. A spice flavoring for beverages, ice cream, baked goods (2,000 ppm), margarine, breakfast cereals (2,000 ppm), and baked goods. No known toxicity.

**ANTHOCYANINS.** Intensely colored, water-soluble pigments responsible for nearly all the reds and blues of flowers and other plant parts. Such color, which is dissolved in plant sap, is markedly affected by the acidity and alkalinity of substances: red at low pH (*see*) and blue at higher pH values. There are about 120 known anthocyanins, including those obtained from grapes, cranberries, cherries, and plums. They can be used to color acid compounds such as wines and cranberry juice cocktail. No known toxicity.

**ANTICAKING AGENTS.** These keep powders and salt free-flowing, such as with calcium phosphates (*see*) in instant breakfast drinks and other soft drink mixes.

**ANTIOXIDANTS.** Substances added to food to keep oxygen from changing the food's color or flavor. Apples, for instance, will turn brown when exposed to air, and fats will become rancid after exposure. Among the most widely used antioxidants are butylated hydroxyanisole (BHA) and butylated hydroxytoluene (BHT) (*see both*).

**APPLE ACID.** See Malic Acid.

**APRICOT KERNEL. Persic Oil.** A natural cherry flavoring agent for beverages, ice cream, ices, candy, baked goods, and soups. No known toxicity. GRAS.

**ARABINOGALACTAN.** A polysaccharide extracted with water from larch wood. Used in the minimum quantity required to be effective as an emulsifier, stabilizer, binder, or bodying agent in essential oils, nonnutritive sweeteners, nonstandard dressings, flavors, and puddings. On the FDA priority list of additives to be studied for mutagenic, teratogenic, subacute, and reproductive effects.

**ARAMANTH.** See FD and C Red No. 2.

**ARGININE. L and DL Forms.** An essential amino acid (*see*), strongly alkaline, given for liver deficiency. The FDA wants further information on the nutrient, which plays an important role in the production of urea in excretion. GRAS.

**ARHEOL.** See Sandalwood Oil, Yellow.

**ARNOTTA EXTRACT.** See Annatto Extract.

**ARNOTTA SEED.** See Annatto Seed.

**ARROWROOT STARCH.** From the rhizome of *Maranta arundinacea,* a plant of tropical America. It is used in the diet of babies and invalids because it is easy to digest. The final report to the FDA of the Select Committee on GRAS Substances stated in 1980 that it should continue its GRAS status with no limitations other than good manufacturing practices.

**ARTIFICIAL.** In foods, the term follows the standard meaning: a substance not duplicated in nature. A flavoring, for instance, may have all the natural ingredients but it must be called artificial if it has no counterpart in nature.

**ASAFETIDA. Devil's Dung.** A natural flavoring extracted from the roots of several plants grown in Iran, Turkestan, and Afghanistan. The *fluid extract* is used in sausage, onion, and spice flavorings for beverages, ice cream, ices, candy, baked goods, meat, condiments, and soups. The *gum* is used in onion and spice flavorings for beverages, ice cream, ices, candy, baked goods, and seasonings. The *oil* is used for spice flavoring in candy, baked goods, and condiments. Asafetida has a bitter taste, an offensive charcoal odor, and is particularly used in India and Iran as a condiment. It has been used medically as an expectorant and to break up intestinal gas. No known toxicity. GRAS.

**ASCORBATE. Calcium and Sodium.** Antioxidants used in concentrated milk products, cooked, cured, or pulverized meat food products, and in the pickle in which pork and beef products are cured or packed. Nontoxic.

**ASCORBIC ACID. Vitamin C.** A preservative and antioxidant used in frozen fruit, particularly sliced peaches, frozen fish dip, dry milk, beer and ale, flavoring oils, apple juice, soft drinks, fluid milk, candy, artificially sweetened jellies and preserves, canned mushrooms, cooked, cured, pulverized meat food products, pickle in which beef or pork is cured or packed (75 ounces of Vitamin C per 100 gallons). It is an antiscurvy vitamin used in fruit juices, frozen concentrated drinks, grape juice, orangeade, and carbonated drinks. Vitamin C is essential for normal teeth, bones, and blood vessels and may play a part in immunity, but that is still controversial and being researched. The recommended daily requirements are 50 to 60 milligrams for adults, 35 to 45 for children. The white or slightly yellow powder darkens when exposed to air. Reasonably stable when it remains dry in air but deteriorates rapidly when exposed to air in solution. Nobel Laureate Linus Pauling caused a run on Vitamin C in 1970 by endorsing it as a cold medicine. Although his theories were not widely accepted by the medical community, a great deal of work is now in progress studying Vitamin C and immunity. Vitamin C is known to affect the excretion of medications such as barbiturates and to make them more toxic. Pharmaceutically incompatible with sodium salicylate, sodium nitrate, theobromine, and methenamine. The final report to the FDA of the Select Committee on GRAS Substances stated in 1980 that it should continue its GRAS status with no limitations other than good manufacturing practices.

**ASCORBYL PALMITATE.** A derivative of ascorbic acid (*see*) used as a preservative and antioxidant for candy. Like ascorbic acid, prevents rancidity, browning of cut apples and other fruit, used in meat curing. Nontoxic. The final report to the FDA of the Select Committee on GRAS Substances stated in 1980 that it should continue its GRAS status with no limitations other than good manufacturing practices.

**ASPARTAME.** A compound prepared from aspartic acid and phenylalanine (*see both*), with about 200 times the sweetness of sugar, discovered during routine screening of drugs for the treatment of ulcers. The G. D. Searle Company sought FDA approval in 1973. The FDA approved it in 1974, but objections that aspartame might cause brain damage led to a stay, or legal postponement, of that approval. Another problem arose. An FDA investigation of records of animal studies conducted for Searle drug approvals and for aspartame raised questions. The FDA arranged for an independent audit, which took more than two years and concluded that the aspartame studies and results were authentic. The agency then organized an expert board of inquiry and the members concluded that the evidence did not support the charge that aspartame might kill clusters of brain cells or cause other damage. However, persons with phenylketonuria, or PKU, must avoid protein foods such as meat that contain phenylalanine—one of two components of aspartame. The board did, however, recommend that aspartame not be approved until further long-term animal testing could be conducted to rule out a possibility that aspartame might cause brain tumors. The FDA's Bureau of Foods reviewed the study data already available and concluded that the board's concern was unfounded. Aspartame was approved for use as a tabletop sweetener in certain dry foods on October 22, 1981.

In 1984 news reports fueled by the announcement that the Arizona Department of Health Services was testing soft drinks containing aspartame to see if it deteriorated into toxic levels of methyl alcohol under storage conditions created alarm. The Arizona Health Department acted after the director of the Food Sciences and Research Laboratory at Arizona State submitted a study alleging that higher than normal temperatures could lead to a dangerous breakdown in the chemical composition. The author checked with representatives of the Food and Drug Administration. They said that there are higher levels of methyl alcohol in regular fruit juices, and as far as the agency was concerned, the fears about decomposition products were unfounded.

**ASPARTIC ACID. DL and L forms.** A nonessential amino acid (*see*) occurring in animals and plants, especially young sugar cane and sugar beet molasses, but synthesized for commercial use as a supplement. The FDA is seeking further information. GRAS.

**ASPERGILLUS.** A genus of fungi. It contains many species of molds, some of which are very toxic. *Aspergillus flavus* is a form with yellow spores, which produces the antibiotic aspergillic acid. An *Aspergillus flavus-Oryzae Group* of mold has been cleared by the U.S. Department of Agriculture's Meat Inspection Division to soften tissues of beef cuts, to wit: "Solutions containing water, salt, monosodium glutamate, and approved proteolytic enzymes applied or injected into cuts of beef shall not result in a gain of more than 3 percent above the weight of the untreated product." It is also used in bakery products such as bread, rolls, and buns. Toxicity is unknown but because of the use of the fungi-antibiotic and monosodium glutamate, allergic reactions would certainly be possible.

**ATTAR OF ROSES.** See Rose Bulgarian.

**AUBEPINE LIQUID.** See *p*-Methoxybenzaldehyde.

**AZO DYES.** A large category of colorings used in both the food and cosmetic industries, the dyes are characterized by the way they combine with nitrogen. They are made from diazonium compounds and phenol, and usually contain a mild acid such as citric or tartaric acid. Among the foods in which they are used are "penny" candies, caramels and chews, Life Savers, fruit drops, filled chocolates (but not pure chocolate); soft drinks, fruit drinks, and ades; jellies, jams, marmalades, stewed fruit sauces, fruit gelatins, fruit yogurts; ice cream, pie fillings, vanilla, butterscotch, and chocolate puddings, caramel custard, whips, dessert sauces such as vanilla, and cream in powdered form; bakery goods (except plain rolls), crackers, cheese puffs, chips, cake and cookie mixes, waffle/pancake mixes, macaroni and spaghetti (certain brands); mayonnaise, salad dressings, catsup (certain brands), mustard, ready-made salads with dressings, rémoulade, béarnaise, and hollandaise sauces, as well as sauces such as curry, fish, onion, tomato, and white cream; mashed rutabagas, purees, packaged soups and some canned soups; canned anchovies, herring, sardines, fish balls, caviar, cleaned shellfish. Azo dyes can cause allergic reactions, particularly hives.

**AZODICARBON AMIDE.** A bleaching and maturing agent for flour, yellow to orange red, a crystalline powder, practically insoluble in water. Used in amounts up to 45 ppm. The FDA wants further study of this chemical for both short-term and long-term effects.

# B

**BACTERIAL CATALASE.** A catalase is an enzyme in plant and animal tissues. It exerts a chemical reaction that converts hydrogen peroxide into water and oxygen. Derived from bacteria by a pure culture fermentation process, bacterial catalase may be used safely, according to the FDA, in destroying and removing hydrogen peroxide that has been used in the manufacture of cheese—providing "the organism *Micrococcus lysodeikticus* from which the bacterial catalase is to be derived, is demonstrated to be nontoxic and non-pathogenic." The organism is removed from the bacterial catalase prior to the use of the catalase, the catalase to be used in an amount not in excess of the minimum required to produce its intended effect. No known toxicity.

**BAKING POWDER.** In baking, any powders used as a substitute for yeast, usually a mixture of sodium bicarbonate, starch, as a filler, and a harmless acid such as tartaric. Cream of tartar is often used as the necessary acid. Nontoxic.

**BAKING SODA.** A common name for sodium bicarbonate (*see*).

**BALM OIL.** A natural fruit and liquor flavoring agent for beverages, ice cream, ices, candy, and baked goods. The balm leaves extract also is used in fruit flavors for beverages. Nontoxic. GRAS.

**BALSAM, PERU.** Peruvian balsam, a natural liquid extracted from a variety of evergreens. Used in strawberry, chocolate, cherry, grape, brandy, rum, maple, walnut, coconut, spice, and vanilla flavoring for beverages, ice cream, ices, candy, baked goods, gelatin desserts, chewing gum, and syrups. Dark brown, with a pleasant aromatic odor and a bitter, persistent aftertaste. Used also in the manufacture of chocolate. Applied to the skin as a stimulant for wounds and ulcers, and to remove scabs. Peruvian balsam *oil* is used in berry, coconut, fruit, rum, maple, and vanilla flavoring for beverages, ice cream, ices, candy, and baked goods. Balsam *fir oil* is a natural pineapple, lime, and spice flavoring for beverages, ice cream, ices, candy, baked goods, and gelatin desserts. Balsam *fir oleoresin* is a natural fruit and spice flavoring for beverages, ice cream, ices, candy, and baked goods. Fir balsam is yellowish green, thick, transparently liquid, with a pinelike smell, and a bitter aftertaste. It is used in the manufacture of fine lacquers. Balsam is mildly antiseptic and may be slightly irritating to the skin. Practically nontoxic upon ingestion.

**BARLEY FLOUR.** A cereal grass cultivated since prehistoric times. Used in the manufacture of malt beverages and as a breakfast food. It is used also as a demulcent (to soothe) in cosmetics. No known toxicity.

**BASES.** Alkalies, such as ammonium hydroxide (*see*), used to control the acidity-alkalinity balance of food products. See pH.

**BASIL. Sweet Basil.** An herb having spikes of small white flowers and aromatic leaves used as seasoning. A natural flavoring distilled from the flowering tops of the plant. Slightly yellow, liquid, with a spicy odor. Used in sausage and spice flavorings for beverages, candy, ice cream, baked goods, condiments, and meats. The *oleoresin* is used in spice flavorings for baked goods and condiments. The *oil* is used in loganberry, strawberry, orange, rose, violet, cherry, honey, licorice, basil, muscatel, meat, and root beer flavorings for beverages, ice cream, ices, candy, baked goods. No known toxicity. GRAS.

**BAY, SWEET.** A natural flavoring native to a Mediterranean plant with stiff, glossy, fragrant leaves. Used in vermouth, sausage, and spice flavorings for beverages, ice cream, ices, candy, baked goods, condiments, and meats. The *oil,* from the laurel, is used in fruit and spice flavorings for beverages, ice cream, ices, candy, baked goods, chewing gum, and condiments. No known toxicity.

**BAY LEAVES.** The West Indian extract is a natural flavoring used in vermouth and spice flavorings for beverages, ice cream, ices, candy, baked goods, meats, and soups. The *oil* is used in fruit, liquor, and bay flavorings for beverages, ice cream, ices, candy, baked goods, condiments, and meats. The *oleoresin* (*see*) is used in sausage flavoring for meats and soups. No known toxicity.

**BEEF TALLOW.** See Tallow Flakes. GRAS for packaging.

**BEESWAX. Yellow Wax.** From the honeycomb of the bee. Used as a candy glaze and polish. Yellowish, soft to brittle, with a honeylike odor. Practically insoluble in water, it is used also in the manufacture of wax paper, candles, artificial fruit, and shoe polish. Formerly employed in the treatment of diarrhea, it has been utilized as a repository for slow-release medicines. See Bleached Beeswax. Nontoxic. The final report to the FDA of the Select Committee on GRAS Substances stated in 1980 that it should continue its GRAS status with no limitations other than good manufacturing practices.

**BEESWAX, BLEACHED. White Wax.** Yellow wax bleached and purified, from the honeycomb of the bee. Remains yellowish white, is solid, somewhat translucent and fairly insoluble in water. Differs slightly in taste from yellow beeswax. Used in fruit and honey flavorings for beverages, ice cream, ices, baked goods, and honey. See Yellow Beeswax for medical uses. Nontoxic. The final report to the FDA of the Select Committee on GRAS Substances stated in 1980 that it should continue its GRAS status with no limitations other than good manufacturing practices.

**BEET. Juice and Powder.** Vegetable dye used to color dairy products. Listed for food use in 1967. No known toxicity.

**BENTONITE.** A clarifying agent derived from clays from the Midwest and Canada. It forms a highly viscous suspension or gel. Used in wine, and it has been prescribed as a bulk laxative and base for many dermatologic formulas. The final report to the FDA of the Select Committee on GRAS Substances stated in 1980 that it should continue its GRAS status with no limitations other than good manufacturing practices.

**BENZALDEHYDE.** Artificial essential oil of almond with an almond-like odor used in berry, butter, coconut, apricot, cherry, peach, liquor, brandy, rum, almond, pecan, pistachio, spice, and vanilla flavoring. Occurs naturally in cherries, raspberries, tea, almonds, bitter oil, cajeput oil, cassia bark. Used in beverages, ice cream, ices, candy, baked goods, chewing gum, and cordials. Narcotic in high concentrations and may cause skin rash. Produces central nervous system depression and convulsions. Fatal dose is estimated to be 2 ounces. GRAS.

**BENZALDEHYDE DIMETHYL ACETAL.** A synthetic agent used in fruit, cherry, nut, and almond flavorings for beverages, ice cream, ices, candy, baked goods, gelatin, puddings, and alcoholic beverages. See Benzaldehyde for toxicity.

**BENZALDEHYDE GLYCERYL ACETAL.** A synthetic agent used in fruit, cherry, nut, and almond flavorings for beverages, ice cream, ices, candy, baked goods, and chewing gum. See Benzaldehyde for toxicity.

**BENZALDEHYDE PROPYLENE GLYCOL ACETAL.** A synthetic agent used in fruit, cherry, nut, and almond flavorings for beverages, ice cream, ices, candy, baked goods, gelatin, and puddings. See Benzaldehyde for toxicity.

**BENZENECARBONAL.** See Benzaldehyde.

**BENZENECARBOXYLIC ACID.** See Benzoic Acid.

**BENZENEMETHYLAL.** See Benzaldehyde.

**BENZILIDENE ACETONE.** See 4-Phenyl-3-Buten-2-One.

**BENZOATE OF SODA.** See Sodium Benzoate.

**1,2-BENZODIHYDROPYRONE.** See Dihydrocoumarin.

**BENZOE.** See Benzoin.

**BENZOIC ACID.** A preservative that occurs in nature in cherry bark, raspberries, tea, anise, and cassia bark. First described in 1608 when it was found in gum benzoin. Used in chocolate, lemon, orange, cherry, fruit, nut, and tobacco flavorings for beverages, ice cream, ices, candy, baked goods, icings, and chewing gum. Also used in margarine. Also an antifungal agent. Used as a chemical preservative and as a dietary supplement up to .1 percent. Mild irritant to skin, eyes, and mucous membranes, and reported to cause allergic reactions. Listed by the FDA as GRAS in a reevaluation of safety in 1976. In 1980, the final report to the FDA of the Select Committee on GRAS Substances stated that it should continue its GRAS status with no limitations other than good manufacturing practices.

**BENZOIC ALDEHYDE.** See Benzaldehyde.

**BENZOIN. Gum Benjamin. Gum Benzoin.** Any of several resins containing benzoic acid (*see*), obtained as a gum from various trees. Used as a preserving ointment for fumigating, in perfumes and cosmetics as a compound tincture of benzoin, as a skin protectant and respiratory inhalant. The resin is used as a flavoring agent in chocolate, cherry, rum, spice, and vanilla for beverages, ice cream, ices, candy, baked goods, gelatin desserts, and chewing gum. Benzoin also is a natural flavoring agent for butterscotch, butter, fruit liquor, and rum. Nontoxic. It was tested by the National Cancer Institute and found not to be a cancer-causing agent in rats and mice.

**BENZOPHENONE.** A synthetic agent used in berry, butter, fruit, apricot, peach, nut, and vanilla flavorings in beverages, ice cream, ices, candy, and baked goods. Its persistent roselike odor makes a good fixative for heavy perfumes, especially when used in soaps. Used also in the manufacture of pesticides, antihistamines, and hypnotics. No known toxicity.

**2,3-BENZOPYRROLE.** See Indole.

**BENZOYL EUGENOL.** See Eugenyl Benzoate.

**BENZOYLBENZENE.** See Benzophenone.

**BENZOYL PEROXIDE.** A bleaching agent for flours, blue cheese, Gorgonzola, and milk. A catalyst for hardening certain fiberglass resins. May explode when heated. Reported to be a skin allergen. Has been used topically for burns and poison ivy (as paste).

**BENZYL ACETATE. Acetic Acid.** A synthetic raspberry, strawberry, butter, violet, apple, cherry, banana, and plum flavoring agent for beverages, ice cream, ices, candy, baked goods, chewing gum, and gelatin desserts. Colorless liquid, with a floral odor. If ingested, can cause gastrointestinal irritation, vomiting, diarrhea. Irritating to skin, eyes, and respiratory tract.

**BENZYL ACETOACETATE.** A synthetic berry and fruit flavoring agent for beverages, ice cream, ices, candy, baked goods, gelatin desserts, and chewing gum. See Benzyl Acetate for toxicity.

**BENZYL ACETYL ACETATE.** See Benzyl Acetoacetate.

**BENZYL ALCOHOL.** A flavoring that is a constituent of jasmine, hyacinth, and other plants. Faint, sweet odor, and burning taste. Occurs naturally in raspberries and tea. Used in synthetic blueberry, loganberry, raspberry, orange, floral, rose, violet, fruit, cherry, grape, honey, liquor, muscatel, nut, walnut, root beer, and vanilla flavorings for beverages, ice cream, ices, candy, baked goods, gelatin desserts, and chewing gum. Ingestion of large doses can cause vomiting, diarrhea, and central nervous system depression. Irritating and corrosive to the skin and mucous membranes. Used as a solvent in perfumes, as a local anesthetic, and topical antiseptic.

**BENZYL BUTYL ETHER.** Synthetic fruit flavoring agent for beverages, ice cream, ices, candy, baked goods, gelatin desserts, and puddings. No known toxicity.

**BENZYL BUTYRATE. Butyric Acid.** A synthetic flavoring agent, colorless, liquid, with a plumlike odor. Used in loganberry, raspberry, strawberry, butter, apricot, peach, pear, liquor, muscatel, cheese, and nut flavorings for beverages, ice cream, ices, candy, baked goods, gelatin desserts, and chewing gum. No known toxicity.

**BENZYL CARBINOL.** See Phenethyl Alcohol.

**BENZYL CINNAMATE.** A synthetic flavoring agent, white to pale yellow, solid, with a sweet, balsamic odor. Used in raspberry, chocolate, apricot, cherry, peach, pineapple, plum, prune, honey, liquor, and rum flavorings for beverages, ice cream, ices, candy, baked goods, gelatin desserts, and chewing gum. Employed in perfumes. No known toxicity.

**BENZYL DIMETHYL CARBINYL ACETATE.** See $\alpha,\alpha$-Dimethylphenethyl Acetate.

**BENZYL DIMETHYL CARBINYL BUTYRATE.** See $\alpha,\alpha$-Dimethylphenethyl Butyrate.

**BENZYL DIMETHYL CARBINYL FORMATE.** See $\alpha,\alpha$-Dimethylphenethyl Formate.

**BENZYL 2,3-DIMETHYLCROTONATE.** A synthetic fruit and spice flavoring agent for beverages, ice cream, ices, candy, and baked goods.

**BENZYL DIPROPYL KETONE.** See 3-Benzyl-4-Heptanone.

**BENZYL DISULFIDE.** A synthetic coffee and caramel flavoring agent for baked goods, beverages, ice cream, ices, and candy. No known toxicity.

**BENZYL ETHYL ETHER.** A synthetic fruit flavoring agent for beverages, ice cream, ices, candy, and baked goods. Aromatic odor. No known toxicity. Probably narcotic in high concentrations.

**BENZYL FORMATE. Formic Acid.** A synthetic chocolate, apricot, cherry, peach, pineapple, plum, prune, honey, and liquor flavoring agent for beverages, ice cream, ices, candy, baked goods, and chewing gum. Pleasant, fruity odor. Most esters of this type are narcotic in high concentrations. See Formic Acid for toxicity.

**3-BENZYL-4-HEPTANONE.** Synthetic fruit flavoring agent for beverages, ice cream, ices, candy, and baked goods. No known toxicity.

**BENZYL o-HYDROXYBENZOATE.** See Benzyl Salicylate.

**BENZYL ISOAMYL ALCOHOL.** See α-Isobutylphenyl Alcohol.

**BENZYL ISOBUTYL CARBINOL.** See α-Isobutylphenethyl Alcohol.

**BENZYL ISOBUTYRATE.** A synthetic strawberry and fruit flavoring agent for beverages, ice cream, ices, candy, and baked goods. No known toxicity.

**BENZYL ISOEUGENOL.** A synthetic spice and banana flavoring agent for beverages, ice cream, ices, candy, and baked goods. No known toxicity.

**BENZYL ISOVALERATE.** A synthetic raspberry, apple, apricot, banana, cherry, pineapple, walnut, and cheese flavoring agent for beverages, ice cream, ices, candy, baked goods, gelatin desserts, and chewing gum. No known toxicity.

**BENZYL MERCAPTAN.** Synthetic coffee flavoring agent for beverages, ice cream, ices, candy, and baked goods. No known toxicity.

**BENZYL METHOXYETHYL ACETAL.** Synthetic fruit and cherry flavoring agent for beverages, ice cream, ices, candy, and baked goods. No known toxicity.

**BENZYL METHYL TIGLATE.** See Benzyl 2,3-Dimethylcrotonate.

**BENZYL PHENYLACETATE.** A synthetic butter, caramel, fruit, and honey flavoring agent for beverages, ice cream, ices, candy, baked goods, and toppings. A colorless liquid with a sweet, floral odor, it occurs naturally in honey. No known toxicity.

**BENZYL β-PHENYLACRYLATE.** See Benzyl Cinnamate.

**BENZYL PROPIONATE.** A synthetic flavoring substance, colorless, liquid, with a sweet fruity odor. Used in berry, apple, banana, grape, pear, and pineapple flavorings for beverages, ice cream, ices, candy, baked goods, chewing gum, and icings. No known toxicity.

**BENZYL SALICYLATE. Salicylic Acid.** An almost colorless liquid with a faint, sweet odor, used in floral and peach flavorings for beverages, ice cream, ices, candy, and baked goods. Also used as a fixer in perfumes and sun-screen lotions. As with other salicylates it may interact adversely with such medications as antidepressants and anticoagulants, and may cause allergic reactions.

**BENZYLACETIC ACID.** See 3-Phenylpropionic Acid.

**BENZYLACETONE.** See 4-Phenyl-3-Buten-2-One.

**BENZYLETHYL ALCOHOL.** See 3-Phenyl-1-Propanol.

**1-BENZYLOXY (β-METHOXY) ETHOXY ETHANE.** See Benzyl Methoxyethyl Acetal.

**BENZYLPROPYL ACETATE.** See α,α-Dimethylphenethyl Acetate.

**BENZYLPROPYL ALCOHOL.** See α,α-Dimethylphenethyl Alcohol.

**BENZYLPROPYL CARBINOL.** See α-Propylphenethyl Alcohol.

**BENZYLTHIOL.** See Benzyl Mercaptan.

**BERGAMOL.** See Linalyl Acetate.

**BERGAMOT. Bergamot Orange.** A natural flavoring extracted from the rind of the fruit of a small, spiny tree. Used in strawberry, lemon, orange, tangerine, cola, floral, banana, grape, peach, pear, pineapple, liquor, spice, and vanilla flavorings for beverages, ice cream, ices, candy, baked goods, gelatin desserts, chewing gum, and icings. The oil is used in perfume. May cause sensitivity to light. GRAS.

**BETA-APO-8'-CAROTENAL.** Coloring agent for solid or semisolid foods. Nontoxic.

**BETA CAROTENE.** A precursor of Vitamin A, it has been shown in animal studies and in human epidemiological studies to protect against the induction of tumors. It has less serious side effects than Vitamin A and was given to 22,000 physicians as part of a five-year study to determine whether aspirin could protect against heart disease and beta carotene against tumors. It is used to color food and is nontoxic.

**BETA-CITRAURIN.** Excellent raw material for the extraction of carotenoids (*see* Carotene), or orange coloring. Found in tangerine and orange peels. Soluble in alcohol.

**BETAINE.** Occurs in common beets and in many vegetables as well as animal substances. Used as a coloring and as a dietary supplement and in the manufacture of resins. Has been employed medically to treat muscle weakness. No known toxicity.

**BETAINE, ANHYDROUS.** See Betaine.

**BHA.** See Butylated Hydroxyanisole.

**BHT.** See Butylated Hydroxytoluene.

**BIACETYL.** See Diacetyl.

**BIOFLAVINOIDS. Vitamin P Complex.** Citrus-flavored compounds needed to maintain healthy blood vessel walls. Widely distributed among plants, especially citrus fruits and rose hips. Usually taken from or—ange and lemon rinds and used as a reducing (*see*) agent. No known toxicity.

**BIOTIN. Vitamin B Factor. Vitamin H.** An essential nutrient vital for growth and manufactured in the body. It is present in minute amounts in every living cell, but the richest source is in kidney and pancreas cells and in yeast and milk. Cancer cells have more biotin than do normal cells. It acts as a coenzyme in the formation of certain essential fatlike substances, and plays a part in reactions involving carbon dioxide. It is needed for healthy circulation and red blood cells. There is no official minimum daily requirement, but a diet of 150 to 300 milligrams of biotin is considered adequate. The final report to the FDA of the Select Committee on GRAS Substances stated in 1980 that it should continue its GRAS status with no limitations other than good manufacturing practices.

**BIRCH. Sweet Oil and Tar Oil.** A flavoring agent from the bark and wood of deciduous trees common in the Northern Hemisphere. The oil is obtained by distillation. It is a clear, dark brown liquid with a strong leatherlike odor. Birch *sweet oil* is used in synthetic strawberry, pineapple, maple, nut, root beer, sarsaparilla, spice, wintergreen, and birch beer flavorings for beverages, ice cream, ices, candy, baked goods, gelatins, puddings (4,300 ppm), and syrups. Birch *tar oil,* which is refined, is used in chewing gum, and has also been used for preserving leather and wood and for treating skin diseases. No known toxicity.

**BITTER ASH EXTRACT.** See Quassia Extract.

**BITTERWOOD EXTRACT.** See Quassia Extract.

**BIXIN. Norbixin.** The active ingredients of annatto, both carotenoid-like compounds, but with five times the coloring power of carotene, and with better stability. They impart a yellow coloring to food. See Annatto.

**BLACK CUTCH EXTRACT.** See Catechu Extract.

**BLACKBERRY BARK EXTRACT.** A natural flavoring agent extracted from the woody plant. Used in berry, pineapple, grenadine, root beer, sarsaparilla, wintergreen, and birch beer flavorings for beverages, ice cream, candy, baked goods, and liquors (10,000 ppm). No known toxicity.

**BLACKSTRAP MOLASSES.** Obtained from processed sugar cane, it has the lowest carbohydrate content of all molasses and is rich in iron.

**BLACKTHORN BERRIES.** See Sloe Berries.

**BLATTERALKOHOL.** See 3-Hexen-1-ol.

**BLEACHING AGENTS.** Used by many industries, particularly in flour milling, to make dough rise faster. Certain chemical qualities, which pastry chefs call "gluten characteristics," are needed to make an elastic, stable dough. Such qualities are acquired during aging but in the process, flour oxidizes, that is, combines with oxygen, and loses its natural gold color. Although mature flour is white, it possesses the qualities bakers want. But proper aging costs money and makes the flour more susceptible to insects and rodents, according to food manufacturers. Hence, the widespread use of bleaching and maturing agents.

**BLOOM INHIBITOR.** Bloom is an "undesirable effect" caused by the migration of cocoa fat from the cocoa fibers to the chocolate's surface. Chocolate that has bloomed has a gray-white appearance. Non-bloomed chocolate has a bright, shiny surface, with a rich appearance. The bloom inhibitor—a surfactant (*see*) such as sorbitan or lecithin (*see both*)—by controlling the size of the chocolate crystals reduces the tendency of the fat to mobilize.

**BLUE.** See FD and C Blue.

**BOIS DE ROSE.** The volatile oil used as a flavoring agent, which is obtained by steam distillation from the chipped wood of the tropical rosewood tree. The oil is colorless to pale yellow, with a slight camphor odor. Used in citrus, floral, fruit, meat, and spice flavorings for beverages, ice cream, ices, candy, baked goods, and chewing gum. No known toxicity. GRAS.

**BOLETIC ACID.** See Fumaric Acid.

**BORIC ACID.** See Boron Sources.

**BORNEO CAMPHOR.** See Borneol.

**BORNEOL.** A flavoring agent found naturally in coriander, ginger oil, oil of lime, rosemary, strawberries, thyme, citronella, and nutmeg. It has a peppery odor and burning taste. Used as a synthetic nut or spice flavoring for beverages, ice cream, ices, candy, baked goods, syrup, and chewing gum. Smells like camphor, and is used in perfumery. Can cause nausea, vomiting, convulsions, confusion, and dizziness. It has a toxicity similar to camphor.

**BORNYL ACETATE.** It may be obtained from various pine needle oils. Strong piney odor. As a yarrow herb and iva herb extract, it is used as a synthetic fruit and spice flavoring agent for beverages, ice cream, ices, candy, baked goods, syrups, gelatin desserts, puddings, and chewing gum. Toxicity may be similar to borneol (*see*).

**BORNYL FORMATE. Formic Acid.** A synthetic fruit flavoring agent for beverages, ice cream, ices, candy, baked goods, and syrups. See Formic Acid for toxicity.

**BORNYL ISOVALERATE.** A synthetic flavoring agent with a camphorlike smell used in fruit flavoring for beverages, ice cream, candy, baked goods, and syrups. Also used medicinally as a sedative. No known toxicity.

**BORNYL VALERATE.** A synthetic fruit flavoring agent for beverages, ice cream, ices, candy, and baked goods. No known toxicity.

**BORNYVAL.** See Bornyl Isovalerate.

**BORON SOURCES. Boric Acid. Sodium Borate.** Boron occurs in the earth's crust (in the form of its compounds, not the metal) and borates are widely used as antiseptics even though toxicologists warn about possible adverse reactions. Boric acid and sodium borate are astringents and antiseptics. Borates are absorbed from mucous membranes and can cause symptoms such as gastrointestinal bleeding, skin rash, central nervous system stimulation. The adult lethal dose is 30 grams (1 ounce). Infants and young children are more susceptible. Boron is used as a diet supplement up to 1 milligram per day. Cleared for use by the FDA in modified hops extract up to 310 ppm.

**BORONIA, ABSOLUTE.** A synthetic violet and fruit flowering agent extracted from a plant. Used for beverages, ice cream, ices, candy, baked goods. No known toxicity.

**BOSWELLIA SPECIES.** See Olibanum Oil.

**BRAN.** The outer indigestible shell of cereal grain that is usually removed before the grain is ground into flour. It provides bulk and fiber.

**BRASSICA ALBA.** See Mustard.

**BREWERS' YEAST.** Originally used by beer brewers, it is a good source of B vitamins and protein. It can cause allergic reactions.

**BRILLIANT BLUE.** See FD and C Blue No. 1.

**BROMATE.** *Calcium* bromate is a maturing agent and dough conditioner in bromated flours and bromated whole wheat flour. *Potassium* bromate is a bread improver. Sugar contaminated with potassium bromate caused a food poisoning outbreak in New Zealand. The lethal dose is not certain, but 2 to 4 ounces of a 2 percent solution causes serious poisoning in children. Death in animals and man apparently is due to kidney failure, but central nervous system problems have been reported.

**BROMELIN. Bromelain.** A protein-digesting and milk-clotting enzyme found in pineapple. Used for tenderizing meat, chill-proofing beer, and as an anti-inflammatory medication. "Solutions consisting of water, salt, monosodium glutamate, and approved proteolytic enzymes, applied or injected into cuts of beef shall not result in a gain of more than 3 percent above the weight of the untreated product." No known toxicity.

**BROMINATED VEGETABLE OILS.** Bromine, a heavy, volatile, corrosive, nonmetallic liquid element, added to vegetable oil or other oils. Dark brown or pale yellow, with a bland or fruity odor. These high-density oils are blended with low-density essential oils to make them easier to emulsify. Used largely in soft drinks, citrus-flavored beverages, ice cream, ices, and baked goods. The FDA has them on the "suspect list." See Bromate for toxicity.

**BROOM EXTRACT.** See Genet, Absolute.

**BUCHU LEAF OIL.** A natural flavoring agent from a South African plant. Used in berry, fruit, chocolate, mint, and spice flavorings for beverages, ice cream, ices, candy, baked goods, condiments, and liquors. Has been used as a urinary antiseptic and mild diuretic. No known toxicity.

**BUFFER.** Usually a solution whose acidity-alkalinity is relatively constant and unaffected by the addition of comparatively large amounts of acid or alkali. Frequently a buffer consists of a weak acid mixed with the sodium salt of the weak acid and is frequently used to control acidity in soft drinks. A typical buffer solution would be hydrochloric acid (*see*) and sodium hydroxide (*see*).

**BUTADIENE-STYRENE COPOLYMER.** A component for a chewing gum base. Butadiene is produced largely from petroleum gases and is used in the manufacture of synthetic rubber. It may be irritating to the skin and mucous membranes and narcotic in high concentrations. Styrene, obtained from ethyl benzene, is an oily liquid with a penetrating odor. It has the same uses and toxicity.

**BUTADIENE STYRENE RUBBER. Latex.** A chewing gum base. No known toxicity.

**BUTANAL.** See Butyraldehyde.

**BUTANDIONE.** See Diacetyl.

**BUTANE. Methylsulfonal. Bioxiran. Dibutadiene Dioxide.** Butane is a natural gas that occurs in petroleum and in refinery cracking products. It is the raw material for motor fuels and is used in the manufacture of synthetic rubber. It may be narcotic in high concentrations. It caused tumors when injected under the skin of mice in 1,900-milligram doses per kilogram of body weight, when injected into the abdomens of rats in 38-milligram doses per kilogram of body weight, and when inhaled by mice in doses of 3,400 milligrams per kilogram of body weight. It has been determined by the National Institute of Occupational Safety and Health to be an animal carcinogen. The final report to the FDA of the Select Committee on GRAS Substances stated in 1980 that it should continue its GRAS status with no limitations other than good manufacturing practices.

**1,4-BUTANEDICARBOXYLIC ACID.** See Adipic Acid.

**BUTANOIC ACID.** See Butyric Acid.

**1-BUTANOL.** See Butyl Alcohol.

**2,3-BUTANOLONE.** See Acetoin.

*(trans)*-**BUTENEDIOIC ACID.** See Fumaric Acid.

**BUTOXYPOLYETHYLENE.** A synthetic antifoaming agent used in beet sugar manufacture. No known toxicity.

**BUTTERS. Acids, Esters, and Distillate.** Butter *acids* are synthetic butter and cheese flavoring agents for beverages, ice cream, ices, candy (2,800 ppm), and baked goods. Butter *esters* are synthetic butter, caramel, and chocolate flavoring agents for beverages, ice cream, ices, baked goods, toppings, and popcorn (1,200 ppm). Butter *starter distillate* is a synthetic butter flavoring agent for ice cream, ices, baked goods, and shortening (12,000 ppm). No known toxicity.

**BUTYL ACETATE.** A synthetic flavoring agent, a clear liquid with a strong, fruity odor, prepared from acetic acid and butyl alcohol. Used in raspberry, strawberry, butter, banana, and pineapple flavorings for beverages, ice cream, ices, candy, baked goods, gelatin desserts, and chewing gum. An irritant, which may cause conjunctivitis (pink eye). A central nervous system depressant and in high doses it is narcotic.

**BUTYL ACETOACETATE.** A synthetic berry and fruit flavoring agent for beverages, ice cream, candy, and baked goods. No known toxicity.

**BUTYL ALCOHOL.** A synthetic butter, cream, fruit, liquor, rum, and whiskey flavoring agent for beverages, ice cream, ices, candy, baked goods, cordials, and cream. Occurs naturally in apples and raspberries. Used as a solvent for waxes, fats, resins, and shellac. May cause irritation of the mucous membranes, contact dermatitis, headache, dizziness, and drowsiness.

**BUTYL ALDEHYDE.** See Butyraldehyde.

**BUTYL ANTHRANILATE.** A synthetic grape, mandarin, and pineapple flavoring agent for beverages, ice cream, ices, candy, and baked goods. No known toxicity.

**BUTYL BUTYRATE.** A colorless, synthetic flavoring agent prepared from butyl alcohol, with a fruity odor. Used in berry, butter, apple, banana, peach, pineapple, liquor, Scotch, and nut flavoring for beverages, ice cream, ices, candy, baked goods, gelatin desserts, and chewing gum (1,500 ppm). In high concentrations may be irritating and narcotic.

**BUTYL BUTYRYLLACTATE.** A synthetic flavoring agent, colorless, liquid, with a buttery odor. Used in butterscotch, fruit, nut, and vanilla flavorings for beverages, ice cream, ices, candy, and baked goods. No known toxicity.

*α*-**BUTYL CINNAMALDEHYDE.** A synthetic fruit, nut, spice, and cinnamon flavoring agent for beverages, ice cream, ices, candy, and baked goods. No known toxicity.

**BUTYL CINNAMATE.** A synthetic chocolate, cocoa, and fruit flavoring agent for beverages, ice cream, ices, candy, baked goods, and liquors. No known toxicity.

**BUTYL 2-DECENOATE.** A synthetic apricot and peach flavoring agent for beverages, ice cream, ices, candy, and chewing gum (2,000 ppm). No known toxicity.

**BUTYL DECYLENATE.** See Butyl 2-Decenoate.

**BUTYL DODECANOATE.** See Butyl Laurate.

**BUTYL ETHYL MALONATE.** A synthetic fruit and apple flavoring agent for beverages, ice cream, ices, candy, and baked goods. No known toxicity.

**BUTYL FORMATE. Formic Acid.** A synthetic fruit, plum, liquor, and rum flavoring agent for beverages, ice cream, ices, candy, gelatin desserts, and baked goods. See Formic Acid for toxicity.

**BUTYL HEPTANOATE.** A synthetic fruit and liquor flavoring agent for beverages, ice cream, ices, candy, and baked goods. No known toxicity.

**BUTYL HEXANOATE.** A synthetic butter, butterscotch, pineapple, and rum flavoring agent for beverages, ice cream, ices, candy, and baked goods. No known toxicity.

**BUTYL *p*-HYDROXYBENZOATE. Butyl Paraben. Butyl *p*-Oxybenzoate.** Almost odorless, small colorless crystals or a white powder used as an antimicrobial preservative. No known toxicity.

**BUTYL ISOBUTYRATE.** A synthetic raspberry, strawberry, butter, banana, and cherry flavoring agent for beverages, ice cream, ices, candy, baked goods, and chewing gum (2,000 ppm). No known toxicity.

**BUTYL ISOVALERATE.** A synthetic chocolate and fruit flavoring agent for beverages, baked goods, ice cream, ices, candy, puddings, and gelatin desserts. No known toxicity.

**2-BUTYL-5 (or 6) -KETO-1,4-DIOXANE.** A synthetic fruit flavoring for beverages, ice cream, ices, candy, baked goods, and shortenings. No known toxicity.

**BUTYL LACTATE.** A synthetic butter, butterscotch, caramel, and fruit flavoring agent for beverages, ice cream, ices, candy, and baked goods. No known toxicity.

**BUTYL LAURATE.** A synthetic fruit flavoring agent for beverages, ice cream, ices, candy and baked goods. No known toxicity.

**BUTYL LEVULINATE.** A synthetic butter, fruit, and rum flavoring agent for beverages, ice cream, ices, candy, and baked goods. No known toxicity.

**BUTYL PARASEPT.** See Butyl *p*-Hydroxybenzoate.

**BUTYL PHENYLACETATE.** Synthetic butter, honey, caramel, chocolate, rose, fruit, and nut flavoring agent for beverages, ice cream, ices, candy, baked goods, gelatin desserts, and puddings. No known toxicity.

**BUTYL PROPIONATE.** A synthetic butter, rum butter, fruit, and rum flavoring agent for beverages, ice cream, ices, candy, and baked goods. May be an irritant.

**BUTYL RUBBER.** A synthetic rubber used as a chewing gum base component. No known toxicity.

**BUTYL SEBACATE.** See Dibutyl Sebacate.

**BUTYL STEARATE.** A synthetic antifoaming agent used in the production of beet sugar. Also a synthetic banana, butter, and liquor flavoring agent for beverages, ice cream, ices, candy, baked goods, chewing gum, and liqueurs. No known toxicity.

**BUTYL SULFIDE.** A synthetic floral, violet, and fruit flavoring agent for beverages, ice cream, ices, candy, and baked goods. No known toxicity.

**BUTYL 10-UNDECENOATE.** A synthetic butter, apricot, cognac, and nut flavoring agent for beverages, ice cream, ices, candy, baked goods, chewing gum, icing, and liquor. No known toxicity.

**BUTYL VALERATE.** A synthetic butter, fruit, and chocolate flavoring agent for beverages, baked goods, ice cream, ices, candy, puddings, and gelatin desserts. No known toxicity.

**BUTYLATED HYDROXYANISOLE (BHA).** A preservative and antioxidant used in many products, including beverages, chewing gum, ice cream, ices, candy, baked goods, gelatin desserts, soup bases, potatoes, glacéed fruits, potato flakes, sweet potato flakes, dry breakfast cereals, dry yeast, dry mixes for desserts and beverages, lard, shortening, unsmoked dry sausage, and in emulsions for stabilizers for shortenings. It is a white, or slightly yellow, waxy solid with a faint, characteristic odor. Insoluble in water. Total content of antioxidants is not to exceed .02 percent of fat or oil content of food; allowed up to 1,000 ppm in dry yeast; 200 ppm in shortenings; 50 ppm in potato flakes; and 50 ppm with BHT (butylated hydroxytoluene) in dry cereals. Can cause allergic reactions. BHA affects the liver and kidney functions (the liver detoxifies it). BHA may be more rapidly metabolized than BHT (*see*) and in experiments at Michigan State University it appeared to be less toxic to the kidneys of living animals than BHT. The final report to the FDA of the Select Committee on GRAS Substances stated in 1980 that while no evidence in the available information on it demonstrates a hazard to the public at current use levels, uncertainties exist, requiring that additional studies be conducted. GRAS status continues while tests on BHA are being completed and evaluated.

**BUTYLATED HYDROXYMETHYLPHENOL.** A new antioxidant, a nearly white, crystalline, solid, with a faint characteristic odor. Insoluble in water and propylene glycol; soluble in alcohol. No known toxicity but the formula, 4-hydroxymethyl-2,6-di-*tert*-butylphenol, contains phenol, which is very toxic.

**BUTYLATED HYDROXYTOLUENE (BHT).** An antioxidant employed in many foods. Used as a chewing gum base, added to potato and sweet potato flakes, and dry breakfast cereals, an emulsion stabilizer for shortenings, used in enriched rice, animal fats, and shortenings containing animal fats. White, crystalline, solid, with a faint characteristic odor. Insoluble in water. Total content of antioxidants in fat or oils not to exceed .02 percent. Allowed up to 200 ppm in emulsion stabilizers for shortenings, 50 ppm in dry breakfast cereals and potato flakes. Used also as an antioxidant to retard rancidity in frozen fresh pork sausage and freeze-dried meats up to .01 percent based on fat content. Can cause allergic reactions. Loyola University scientists reported on April 14, 1972, that pregnant mice fed a diet consisting of one half of one percent of BHT (or BHA, butylated hydroxyanisole) gave birth to offspring that frequently had chemical changes in the brain and subsequent abnormal behavior patterns. BHT and BHA are chemically similar but BHT may be more toxic to the kidney than BHA (*see*), according to researchers at Michigan State University. The Select Committee of the Federation of American Societies for Experimental Biology, which advises the FDA on additives, recommended further studies to determine "the effects of BHT at levels now present in foods under conditions where steroid hormones or oral contraceptives are being ingested." They said the possibility that BHT may convert other ingested substances into toxic or cancer-causing agents should be investigated. BHT is prohibited as a food additive in England. The FDA is pursuing further study of BHT. GRAS.

**1, 3-BUTYLENE GLYCOL.** A clear, colorless, viscous liquid with slight taste. A solvent and humectant for natural and synthetic flavorings except where government standards preclude such use. It has a similar toxicity to ethylene glycol (*see*) which, when ingested, may cause transient stimulation of the central nervous system, then depression, vomiting, drowsiness, coma, respiratory failure, and convulsions; renal damage may proceed to uremia and death. One of the few humectants not on the GRAS list, although efforts to place it there are under way.

**BUTYLPARABEN.** Widely used in food and cosmetics as an antifungal preservative, it is the ester of butyl alcohol and *p*-hydroxybenzoic acid (*see both*). No known toxicity.

**BUTYRALDEHYDE.** A synthetic flavoring agent found naturally in coffee and strawberries. Used in butter, caramel, fruit, liquor, brandy, and nut flavorings for beverages, ice cream, ices, candy, baked goods, alcoholic beverages, and icings. Used also in the manufacture of rubber accelerators, synthetic resins, and plasticizers. May be an irritant and narcotic.

**BUTYRIC ACID.** A clear, colorless liquid present in butter at 4 to 5 percent with a strong penetrating rancid-butter odor. Butter, butterscotch, caramel, fruit, and nut flavoring agent for beverages, ice cream, ices, candy, baked goods, gelatin desserts, puddings, chewing gum, and margarine. Found naturally in apples, butter acids, geranium, rose oil, grapes, strawberries, and wormseed oil. It has a low toxicity but can be a mild irritant. GRAS.

**BUTYRIC ALDEHYDE.** See Butyraldehyde.

**BUTYRIN.** See (tri-) Butyrin.

**(tri-) Butyrin.** A synthetic flavoring agent found naturally in butter. Butter flavoring for beverages, ice cream, ices, candy (1,000 ppm), baked goods, margarine, and puddings. No known toxicity.

**BUTYROIN.** See 5-Hydroxy-4-Octanone.

**BUTYRONE.** See 4-Heptanone.

**BUXINE.®** See α-Amylcinnamaldehyde.

**BUXINOL.** See α-Amylcinnamyl Alcohol.

# C

**CACAO SHELL.** Cocoa shells of the seeds of trees grown in Brazil, Central America, and most tropical countries. Weak chocolatelike odor and taste, thin and peppery, with a reddish-brown color. Used in the manufacture of caffeine (*see*); also theobromine, which occurs in chocolate products and is used as a diuretic and nerve stimulant. Occasionally causes allergic reactions from handling. GRAS.

**CACHOU EXTRACT.** See Catechu Extract.

**CACTUS ROOT EXTRACT.** See Yucca.

**CADINENE.** A general fixative that occurs naturally in juniper oil and pepper oil. It has a faint, pleasant smell. Used in candy, baked goods (1,200 ppm), and chewing gum (1,000 ppm). No known toxicity.

**CAFFEINE. Guaranine. Methyltheobromine. Theine. 1,3,7-Trimethyl-2, 6-Dioxopurine.** A white odorless powder with a bitter taste. It occurs naturally in coffee, cola, guarana paste, maté-leaves, tea, and kola nuts. Obtained as a byproduct of caffeine-free coffee. Used as a flavor in cola and root beer beverages. A central nervous system, heart, and respiratory stimulant. Can cause nervousness, insomnia, irregular heartbeat, noises in ear, and, in high doses, convulsions. Can alter blood sugar release and uptake by liver. Caffeine crosses the placental barrier. Because of its capability to cause birth defects in rats, the FDA proposed regulations to request new safety studies and to encourage the manufacture and sale of caffeine-free colas. One regulation would make the food industry's continued use of caffeine as an added ingredient in soft drinks and other foods conditional upon its funding of studies of caffeine's effects on children and the unborn. Under present regulations, a soft drink, except one artificially sweetened, must contain caffeine if it is to be labeled as "cola" or "pepper" and the FDA wants soda producers to be able to use this name when caffeine is not used. The FDA has asked for studies on the long-term effects of the additive to determine whether it may cause cancer or birth defects. The final report to the FDA of the Select Committee on GRAS Substances stated in 1980 that while no evidence in the available information on it demonstrates a hazard to the public at current use levels, uncertainties exist, requiring that additional studies be conducted. GRAS status continues while tests are being conducted.

**CAJEPUT OIL.** A spice flavoring from the cajeput tree native to Australia. The leaves yield an aromatic oil. Used for beverages, ice cream, ices, candy, and baked goods. No known toxicity.

**CAJEPUTENE.** See *d*-Limonene.

**CAJEPUTOL.** See Eucalyptol.

**CALCIUM ACETATE.** Present in acetic acid, it is used as a sequestrant (*see*). A white amorphous powder that has been used medicinally as a source of calcium, it is used in the manufacture of acetic acid and acetone and in dyeing, tanning, and curing skins as well as a corrosion inhibitor in metal containers. Low oral toxicity. The final report to the FDA of the Select Committee on GRAS Substances stated in 1980 that it should continue its GRAS status with no limitations other than good manufacturing practices.

**CALCIUM ACID PHOSPHATE.** See Calcium Phosphate.

**CALCIUM ALGINATE.** A stabilizer, thickener, and texturizer. See Alginates.

**CALCIUM ASCORBATE.** A preservative and antioxidant prepared from ascorbic acid (Vitamin C) and calcium carbonate (*see*). Used in concentrated milk products; in cooked, cured, or pulverized meat products; in pickles in which pork and beef products are cured and packed (up to 75 ounces per 100 gallons). See Ascorbic Acid for toxicity. The final report to the FDA of the Select Committee on GRAS Substances stated in 1980 that it should continue its GRAS status with no limitations other than good manufacturing practices.

**CALCIUM BROMATE.** A maturing agent and dough conditioner used in bromated flours. See Bromate.

**CALCIUM CARBONATE.** A tasteless, odorless powder that occurs naturally in limestone, marble, and coral. Used as a white food dye, and alkali to reduce acidity in wine up to 2.5 percent, a neutralizer for ice cream and in cream syrups up to .25 percent, in confections up to .25 percent, and in baking powder up to 50 percent. Employed as a carrier for bleaches. Also used in dentrifices as a tooth polisher, in deodorants as a filler, in depilatories as a filler, and in face powder as a buffer. A gastric antacid and antidiarrhea medicine, it may cause constipation. Female mice were bred after a week on diets supplemented with calcium carbonate at 220 and 880 times the human intake of this additive. At all dosage levels, the first and second litters of newly weaned mice were lower in weight and number, and mortality was increased. The highest level caused heart enlargement. Supplementing the maternal diet with iron prevented this, so the side effects were attributed to mineral imbalance due to excessive calcium intake. In humans, 500 milligrams per kilogram of body weight was fed to ulcer victims for three weeks. The amount ingested was 145 times the normal amount ingested as an additive. Some patients developed an excess of calcium in the blood and suffered nausea, weakness, and dizziness.

**CALCIUM CHLORIDE.** White, hard, odorless grains, which absorb water. Used as a firming agent for sliced apples and other fruit, in apple pie mix, as a jelly ingredient, in certain cheeses to aid coagulation, in artificially sweetened fruit jelly, and in canned tomatoes. Used also to preserve wood, fireproof materials, in automobile antifreeze, and as a dust control on unpaved roads. Replaces the body's electrolytes, reduces body water, combats allergies, and is urinary acidifier. May cause stomach upset and heart irregularities. The final report to the FDA of the Select Committee on GRAS Substances stated in 1980 that it should continue its GRAS status for packaging only with no limitations other than good manufacturing practices.

**CALCIUM CITRATE.** A fine, white, odorless powder prepared from citrus fruit. Used as a buffer to neutralize acids in confections, jellies, and jams, and in saccharine at the rate of 3 ounces per 100 pounds of the artificial sweetener. It is also used to improve the baking properties of flour. See Citrate Salts for toxicity. The final report to the FDA of the Select Committee on GRAS Substances stated in 1980 that it should continue its GRAS status with no limitations other than good manufacturing practices.

**CALCIUM DISODIUM (EDTA).** A preservative and sequestrant (*see both*), white, odorless, crystalline powder, with a faint, salty taste. Used in canned and carbonated soft drinks for flavor retention; in canned white potatoes and cooked canned clams for color retention; in crab meat to retard struvite (crystal) formation; in dressings as a preservative; in cooked and canned dried lima beans for color retention; in fermented malt beverages to prevent gushing; in mayonnaise and oleomargarine as a preservative; in processed dried pinto beans for color retention; and in sandwich spreads as a preservative. Used medically as a chelating agent to detoxify poisoning by lead and other heavy metals. May cause intestinal upsets, muscle cramps, kidney damage, and blood in urine. On the FDA priority list of food additives to be studied for mutagenic, teratogenic, subacute, and reproductive effects.

**CALCIUM GLUCONATE.** Odorless, tasteless, white crystalline granules, stable in air. Used as a buffer, firming agent, sequestrant. It is soluble in water. May cause gastrointestinal and cardiac disturbances. The final report to the FDA of the Select Committee on GRAS Substances stated in 1980 that it should continue its GRAS status with no limitations other than good manufacturing practices.

**CALCIUM DI-L-GLUTAMATE.** Salt of glutamic acid (*see*). A flavor enhancer and salt substitute. Almost odorless white powder. The FDA says that it needs further study.

**CALCIUM GLYCEROPHOSPHATE.** A fine, white, odorless, nearly tasteless powder used in dentrifices, baking powder, and as a food stabilizer and dietary supplement. A component of many over-the-counter nerve-tonic foods. Administered medicinally for numbness and debility. See Calcium Sources. The final report to the FDA of the Select Committee on GRAS Substances stated in 1980 that it should continue its GRAS status with no limitations other than good manufacturing practices.

**CALCIUM 5'-GUANYLATE.** Flavor potentiator. Odorless white crystals or powder having a characteristic taste. See Flavor Potentiators.

**CALCIUM HEXAMETAPHOSPHATE.** An emulsifier, sequestering agent, and texturizer used in breakfast cereals, angel food cake, flaked fish (prevents struvite), ice cream, ices, milk, bottled beer, reconstituted lemon juice, puddings, processed cheeses, artificially sweetened jellies and preserves, potable water supplies to prevent scale formation and corrosion, and in pickle for curing hams. No known toxicity. The final report to the FDA of the Select Committee on GRAS Substances stated in 1980 that it should continue its GRAS status with no limitations other than good manufacturing practices.

**CALCIUM HYDROXIDE. Calcium Hydrate. Slaked Lime.** An alkali, a white powder with slightly bitter taste. Used as a firming agent for various fruit products, as an egg preservative, in water treatment, and for dehairing hides. It is also used in mortar, plaster, cement, and other building materials, and medically as a topical astringent. Calcium sucrate or saccharate (which is used to standardize the potassium iodide of iodized table salt, reduces the acidity in wine, and is a sour cream neutralizer) is made up of 3 parts sugar to 1 part calcium hydroxide. No known toxicity. The final report to the FDA of the Select Committee on GRAS Substances stated in 1980 that it should continue its GRAS status with no limitations other than good manufacturing practices.

**CALCIUM HYPOCHLORITE.**  A germicide and sterilizing agent, the active ingredient of chlorinated lime, used in the curd washing of cottage cheese, in sugar refining, as an oxidizing and bleaching agent, and as an algae killer, bactericide, deodorant, disinfectant, and fungicide. Sterilizes fruit and vegetables by washing in a 50 pecent solution. Under various names, dilute hypochlorite is found in homes as laundry bleach and household bleach. Occasionally cases of poisoning occur when people mix household hypochlorite solution with various other household chemicals, which causes the release of poisonous chlorine gas. As with other corrosive agents, calcium hypochlorite's toxicity depends upon its concentration. It is highly corrosive to skin and mucous membranes. Ingestion may cause pain and inflammation of the mouth, pharynx, esophagus, and stomach, with erosion particularly of the mucous membranes of the stomach.

**CALCIUM HYPOPHOSPHITE.**  Crystals or powder that is slightly acid in solution, and practically insoluble in alcohol. It is a corrosion inhibitor and has been used as a dietary supplement in veterinary medicine. The final report to the FDA of the Select Committee on GRAS Substances stated in 1980 that it should continue its GRAS status with no limitations other than good manufacturing practices.

**CALCIUM 5′-INOSINATE.**  See Inosinate.

**CALCIUM IODATE.**  White, odorless, or nearly odorless powder used as a dough conditioner and oxidizing agent in bread, rolls, and buns. It is a nutritional source of iodine in foods such as table salt, and used also as a tropical disinfectant and as a deodorant. Low toxicity, but may cause allergic reactions.

**CALCIUM LACTATE.**  White, almost odorless crystals or powder, used as a buffer and as such is a constituent of baking powders and is employed in confections; also used in dentrifices and as a yeast food and dough conditioner. In medical use, given for calcium deficiency; may cause gastrointestinal and cardiac disturbances. The final report to the FDA of the Select Committee on GRAS Substances stated in 1980 that it should continue its GRAS status with no limitations other than good manufacturing practices.

**CALCIUM OXIDE. Quicklime. Burnt Lime.** A hard, white or grayish white odorless mass or powder that is used as a yeast food and dough conditioner for bread, rolls, and buns. It is also an alkali for neutralizing dairy products (including ice cream mixes) and alkalizes sour cream, butter, and confections, and is used in the processing of tripe. Industrial uses are for bricks, plaster, mortar, stucco, dehairing hides, fungicides, insecticides, and for clarification of beet and cane sugar juices. A strong caustic, it may severely damage skin and mucous membranes. See Calcium Sources. The final report to the FDA of the Select Committee on GRAS Substances stated in 1980 that it should continue its GRAS status with no limitations other than good manufacturing practices.

**CALCIUM PANTOTHENATE. Pantothenic Acid Calcium Salt.** A B-complex vitamin, pantothenate is a white, odorless powder, with a sweetish taste and bitter aftertaste. Pantothenic acid occurs everywhere in plant and animal tissue, and the richest common source is liver; jelly of the queen bee contains 6 times as much. Rice bran and molasses are other good sources. Acid derivatives sold commercially are synthesized. See *d*-Pantothenamide. Biochemical defects from lack of calcium pantothenate may exist undetected for some time, but eventually manifest themselves as tissue failures. The calcium chloride double salt of calcium pantothenate has been cleared for use in foods for special dietary uses. The final report to the FDA of the Select Committee on GRAS Substances stated in 1980 that it should continue its GRAS status with no limitations other than good manufacturing practices.

**CALCIUM PHOSPHATE. Dibasic, Monobasic, and Tribasic.** White, odorless powders used as yeast foods, dough conditioners, and firming agents. *Tribasic* is an anticaking agent used in table salt, powdered sugar, malted milk powder, condiments, puddings, meat, dry-curing mixtures, cereal flours, and vanilla powder. It is tasteless. Used as a gastric antacid, mineral supplement, and a clarifying agent for sugars and syrups. *Dibasic* is used to improve bread, rolls, buns, cereal flours; a carrier for bleaching; used as a mineral supplement in cereals, in dental products, and in fertilizers. *Monobasic* is used in bread, rolls, and buns, artificially sweetened fruit jelly, canned potatoes, canned sweet peppers, canned tomatoes, and as a jelling ingredient. Employed in fertilizer as an acidulant, in baking powders, and in wheat flours as a mineral supplement. Nontoxic. The final report to the FDA of the Select Committee on GRAS Substances stated in 1980 that it should continue its GRAS status with no limitations other than good manufacturing practices. See Calcium Salts.

**CALCIUM PHYTATE.** Used as a sequestrant (*see*). When 300 milligrams per kilogram of body weight was fed to rats as a diet supplement, it successfully provided calcium for bone deposition, and the animals remained healthy. The final report to the FDA of the Select Committee on GRAS Substances stated in 1980 that it should continue its GRAS status with no limitations other than good manufacturing practices.

**CALCIUM PROPIONATE.** A preservative. White crystals or crystalline solid with the faint odor of propionic acid. Mold and rope inhibitor in bread and rolls; used in poultry stuffing, chocolate products, processed cheese, cakes and cupcakes, and artificially sweetened fruit jelly and preserves. Has been used as an antifungal medication for the skin. The final report to the FDA of the Select Committee on GRAS Substances stated in 1980 that it should continue its GRAS status with no limitations other than good manufacturing practices.

**CALCIUM PYROPHOSPHATE.** A fine, white, odorless, tasteless powder, used as a nutrient, buffer, and neutralizing agent. It is also an abrasive in dentifrices, a feed supplement, and a compound used in ceramic ware. No known toxicity. The final report to the FDA of the Select Committee on GRAS Substances stated in 1980 that it should continue its GRAS status with no limitations other than good manufacturing practices. See Calcium Sources.

**CALCIUM 5'-RIBONUCLEOTIDES.** Flavor potentiators (*see*), in odorless, white crystals or powder, with a characteristic taste. See Inosinates.

**CALCIUM SALTS: Acetate, Chloride, Citrate, Diacetate, Gluconate, Phosphate (Monobasic), Phytate, Sulfate.** Emulsifier salts used in evaporated milk and frozen desserts. Also in enriched bread. Firming agent in potatoes and canned tomatoes. May be gastric irritants, but they have little oral toxicity. See separate listing for Calcium Sulfate and Calcium Phosphate. GRAS.

**CALCIUM SALTS OF FATTY ACIDS.** Used as binders and anticaking agents in foods.

**CALCIUM SILICATE.** An anticaking agent, white or slightly cream-colored, free-flowing powder. Up to 5 percent in baking powder and 2 percent of table salts. Absorbs water. Constituent of lime glass and cement, used in road construction. Practically nontoxic orally, except that inhalation may cause irritation of the respiratory tract. On the FDA list of additives that need further study for mutagenic, teratogenic, subacute, and reproductive effects. The final report to the FDA of the Select Committee on GRAS Substances stated in 1980 that it should continue its GRAS status with no limitations other than good manufacturing practices.

**CALCIUM SORBATE.** A preservative and fungus preventative used in beverages, baked goods, chocolate syrups, soda-fountain syrups, fresh fruit cocktail, tangerine purée (sherbet base), salads (potato, macaroni, cole slaw, gelatin), cheesecake, pie fillings, cake, cheese in consumer-size packages, and artificially sweetened jellies and preserves. No known toxicity. The final report to the FDA of the Select Committee on GRAS Substances stated in 1980 that it should continue its GRAS status with no limitations.

**CALCIUM SOURCES (harmless calcium salts): Carbonate, Citrate, Glycerophosphate, Oxide, Phosphate, Pyrophosphate, Sulfate (see all).** Calcium is a mineral supplement for breakfast cereals, white cornmeal, infant dietary formula, enriched flour, enriched bromated flour (*see* Bromate), enriched macaroni, noodle products, self-rising flours, enriched farina, cornmeal, and corn grits, and enriched bread and rolls. Calcium is a major mineral in the body. It is incompletely absorbed from the gastrointestinal tract when in the diet so its absorption is enhanced by calcium normally present in intestinal secretions. Vitamin D is also required for efficient absorption of calcium. Recommended daily requirements for adult females is 1.5 grams, for adult males 1.2 grams, and for children .8 gram. Calcium and phosphorus are the major constituents of teeth and bones. The ratio of calcium to phosphorus in cow's milk is approximately 1.2 to 1. In human milk the ratio is 2 to 1. The final report to the FDA of the Select Committee on GRAS Substances stated in 1980 that it should continue its GRAS status with no limitations other than good manufacturing practices.

**CALCIUM STEARATE.** Prepared from limewater (*see*), it is an emulsifier used in hair grooming products, a coloring agent, and it is used in waterproofing. Nontoxic. The final report to the FDA of the Select Committee on GRAS Substances stated in 1980 that it should continue its GRAS status with no limitations other than good manufacturing practices.

**CALCIUM STEARYL-2-LACTYLATE.** A free-flowing, white powder dough conditioner in yeast-leavened bakery products and prepared mixes for yeast-leavened bakery products. Also a whipping agent in dried, liquid, and frozen egg whites. On the FDA list of additives requiring further safety information. No known toxicity.

**CALCIUM SULFATE. Plaster of Paris.** A fine, white to slightly yellow odorless, tasteless powder used as a firming agent and yeast food and dough conditioner. Utilized in brewing and other fermentation industries, in Spanish-type sherry, as a jelling ingredient, in cereal flours, as a carrier for a bleaching agent, in bread, rolls, and buns, in blue cheese and

Gorgonzola cheese, artificially sweetened fruit, jelly, canned potatoes, canned sweet peppers, and canned tomatoes. Used also in creamed cottage cheese as an alkali, and employed industrially in cement, wall plaster, and insecticides. Because it absorbs moisture and hardens quickly, its ingestion may result in intestinal obstruction. Mixed with flour, it has been used to kill rodents. See Calcium Salts. GRAS.

**CALENDULA.** Dried flowers of marigolds, grown in Southern Europe and in gardens everywhere. Used as a natural flavoring agent. See Marigold, Pot, for foods in which used. Formerly used to soothe inflammation of skin and mucous membranes. No known toxicity. GRAS.

**CALORIE.** A unit used to express the heat output of an organism and the fuel or energy value of food. The amount of heat required to raise the temperature of one gram of water from 14.5 to 15.5 degrees C. at atmospheric pressure.

**2-CAMPHANOL.** See Borneol.

**CAMPHENE.** A synthetic spice and nutmeg flavoring agent for beverages, ice cream, ices, candy, and baked goods. Occurs naturally in calamus oil, citronella, ginger, lemon oil, mandarin oil, myrtle, petitgrain oil, and juniper berries. No known toxicity.

*d*-CAMPHOR. Occurs naturally in basil, ho oil, iva herb extract, and zedoary-bark extract. It is a synthetic mint flavoring agent for ice cream, ices, candy, baked goods, and condiments. No known toxicity.

**CAMPHOR, JAPANESE WHITE OIL. Camphor Tree.** Distilled from trees at least fifty years old grown in China, Japan, Formosa, Brazil, and Sumatra. Camphor tree is used in spice flavorings for beverages, baked goods, and condiments. It is also used in embalming fluid, as a preservative in cosmetics, in the manufacture of explosives, in lacquers, as a moth repellent, and topically (as a counterirritant) in liniments, cold medications, and anesthetics. Camphor ingestion may cause vertigo, mental confusion, delirium, clonic convulsions, coma, respiratory failure, and death. Salts of any kind are incompatible and should not be added to camphor water. Camphor is readily absorbed from all sites of administration. Ingestion of 2 grams generally produces dangerous effects in an adult. Ingestion by pregnant women has caused fetal death.

**CANANGA OIL.** A natural flavor extract obtained by distillation from the flowers of the tree. Light to deep yellow liquid, with a harsh, floral odor. Used in cola, fruit, spice, and ginger ale flavoring for beverages, ice cream, ices, candy, and baked goods. No known toxicity. GRAS.

**CANE SUGAR.** See Sucrose.

**CANTHAXANTHINE.** A colorant from edible mushrooms, crustaceans, trout and salmon, and tropical birds. It produces a pink to red color when used in foods. FAO/WHO said that up to 25 milligrams per kilogram of body weight is acceptable. It is exempt from certification.

**CAPERS.** A natural flavoring from the spiny shrub. The picked flower bud is used as a condiment for sauces and salads. No known toxicity. GRAS.

**CAPRALDEHYDE.** See Decanal.

**CAPRIC ACID.** See Decanoic Acid.

**CAPRIC ALDEHYDE.** See Decanal.

**CAPRINALDEHYDE.** See Decanal.

**CAPROALDEHYDE.** See Hexanal.

**CAPROIC ACID.** See Hexanoic Acid.

**CAPROIC ALDEHYDE.** See Hexanal.

**CAPRONIC ETHER ABSOLUTE.** See Ethyl Hexanoate.

**CAPRYLIC ACID.** An oily liquid with a rancid taste made by the oxidation of octanol (*see*). It is a fatty acid that occurs in sweat, fusel oil, in the milk of cows and goats, and in palm and coconut oil. Used as a preservative and in the manufacture of dyes. Cleared for use as a synthetic flavoring. No known toxicity. The final report to the FDA of the Select Committee on GRAS Substances stated in 1980 that it should continue its GRAS status with no limitations other than good manufacturing practices.

**CAPSANTHIN.** Coloring from paprika (*see*).

**CAPSICUM. African Chillies. Cayenne Pepper. Tabasco Pepper.** The dried fruit of a tropical plant used as a natural spice and ginger ale flavoring for beverages, ice cream, ices, candy, and baked goods; also meats and sauces. The *oleoresin* form is used in sausage, spice, ginger ale, and cinnamon flavorings for beverages, candy, baked goods, chewing gum, meats, and condiments. Used internally as a digestive stimulant. Irritating to the mucous membranes, it can produce severe diarrhea and gastritis. GRAS.

**CAPSORUBIN.** Coloring from paprika (*see*).

**CARAMEL.** A chemically ill-defined group of material produced by heating carbohydrates. Burnt sugar with a pleasant, slightly bitter taste, the caramel is distinguished by the method of manufacture. It is usually made by heating sugar or glucose and adding small quantities of alkali or a trace of mineral acid during heating. Caramel color prepared by an ammonia process has been associated with blood toxicity in rats. Because of this, the joint FAO/WHO Expert Committee on Food Additives temporarily removed the acceptable daily intake for ammonia-made caramel. It was found to inhibit the metabolism of $B_6$ in rabbits. Caramel is used as brown coloring in ice cream, baked goods, soft drinks, confections. As a flavoring, it is used in strawberry, butter, butterscotch, caramel, chocolate, cocoa, cola, fruit, cherry, grape, birch beer, liquor, rum, brandy, maple, black walnut, walnut, root beer, spice, ginger, ginger ale, vanilla, and cream soda beverages, (2,200 ppm), ice cream, candy, baked goods, syrups (2,800 ppm), and meats (2,100 ppm). The FDA gave caramel priority for testing its mutagenic, teratogenic, subacute, and reproductive effects. The final report to the FDA of the Select Committee on GRAS Substances, however, stated in 1980 that it should continue its GRAS status with no limitations other than good manufacturing practices.

**CARAWAY.** The dried ripe seeds of a plant common to Europe and Asia and cultivated in England, Russia, and the U.S. Volatile, colorless to pale yellow liquid. Used as a liquor flavoring for beverages, ice cream, ices, baked goods (10,000 ppm), and condiments; also as a spice in baking. The *oil* is used in grape licorice, anisette, kummel, liver, sausage, mint, caraway, and rye flavorings for beverages, ice cream, ices, candy, baked goods, chewing gum, meats, condiments, and liquors. A mild carminative from 1 to 2 grams to break up intestinal gas. No known toxicity. GRAS.

**CARBON BLACK.** Several forms of artificially prepared carbon or charcoal, including animal charcoal, furnace black, channel (gas) black, lampblack, activated charcoal. Animal charcoal is used as a black coloring in confectionery. Activated charcoal is used as an antidote for ingested poisons and as an absorbent in diarrhea. The others have industrial uses. Carbon black, which was not subject to certification (*see*) for coloring by the FDA, was reevaluated and then banned in 1976. It was found in tests to contain a cancer-causing byproduct that was released during dye manufacture. It can no longer be used in candies such as licorice and in jelly beans, or in drugs or cosmetics.

**CARBON DIOXIDE.** Colorless, odorless, noncombustible gas with a faint acid taste. Used as a pressure-dispensing agent in gassed creams (pressure-dispensed whipped cream). Also used in the carbonation of beverages and as dry ice for refrigeration in the frozen food industry. Used on stage to produce harmless smoke or fumes. May cause shortness of breath, vomiting, high blood pressure, and disorientation. The final report to the FDA of the Select Committee on GRAS Substances stated in 1980 that it should continue its GRAS status with no limitations other than good manufacturing practices.

**CARBONATE, POTASSIUM.** See Potassium Carbonate.

**CARBONATE, SODIUM.** See Sodium Carbonate.

**CARBONYL IRON.** Iron which has been processed with carbon and oxygen. Used as a coloring. See Iron Sources. The final report to the FDA of the Select Committee on GRAS Substances stated in 1980 that there is no evidence in the available information that it is a hazard to the public when used as it is now and it should continue in GRAS status with limitations on amounts that can be added to food.

**CARBOXYMETHYLCELLULOSE. Sodium.** Made from cotton by-products, it occurs as a white powder or in granules. A synthetic gum used in bath preparations, beauty masks, dentifrices, hair-grooming aids, hand creams, rouge, shampoos, and shaving creams. It is also used as an emulsifier; as a stabilizer in ice cream, beverages, and other foods; medicinally as a laxative or antacid; and as a foaming agent. It has been shown to cause cancer in animals when ingested. Its toxicity on the skin is unknown. The final report to the FDA of the Select Committee on GRAS Substances stated in 1980 that it should continue its GRAS status with no limitations other than good manufacturing practices.

**CARDAMOM. Grains of Paradise.** A natural flavoring agent from the dried ripe seeds of trees common to India, Ceylon, and Guatemala. Used in butter, chocolate, liquor, spice, and vanilla flavorings for beverages, ice cream, ices, candy, baked goods (1,700 ppm), meats, and condiments (900). The seed *oil* is used in chocolate, cococa, coffee, cherry, liquor, liver, sausage, root beer, sarsaparilla, cardamom, ginger ale, vanilla, and cream soda flavorings for beverages, ice cream, candy, baked goods, meats, chewing gum, condiments, liquors, pickles, and curry powder. It is a mild carminative (breaks up intestinal gas). No known toxicity.

**CARMINE. Cochineal.** A crimson pigment derived from a Mexican species of scale insect (*Coccus cacti*) that feeds on various species of cacti. The dye is used in red apple sauce, confections, baked goods, meats, and spices. It was involved in an outbreak of salmonellosis (an intestinal infection), which killed one infant in a Boston hospital, and made twenty-two other patients seriously ill. Carmine, used in the diagnostic solution to test the digestive organs, was found to be the infecting agent. Also used as a lake (*see* FD and C Lakes).

**CARMINIC ACID. Natural Red 4.** Coloring matter, the essential constituent of carmine (*see*). Used in color photography and as a pigment for artists; also as a bacterial stain and for coloring food products. Not subject to certification of dye batch by the FDA.

**CARNAUBA WAX.** A candy glaze and polish from the dried exudate of the leaves and buds of a South American palm tree. The crude wax is yellow or dirty green, brittle, and very hard. It is used in many polishes and varnishes, and when mixed with other waxes, makes then harder and gives them more luster. Used in cosmetic materials such as depilatories and deodorant sticks; in the last stage in tablet coating. Skin sensitization or irritation seems infrequent. On the FDA list for further study for mutagenic, teratogenic, subacute, and reproductive effects. The final report to the FDA of the Select Committee on GRAS Substances stated in 1980 that there were insufficient relevant biological and other studies upon which to base an evaluation of it when it is used as a food ingredient.

**CAROB BEAN.** See Gum, Carob Bean.

**CAROTENE. Provitamin A. Beta Carotene.** Found in all plants and in many animal tissues, it is the chief yellow coloring matter of carrots, butter, and egg yolk. Extracted as red crystals or crystalline powder, it is used as a vegetable dye in butter, margarine, shortening, skimmed milk, buttermilk, and cottage cheese. It is also used to manufacture Vitamin A and is a nutrient added to skimmed milk, vegetable shortening, and margarine at the rate of 5,000 to 13,000 USP units per pound. Insoluble in water, acids, and alkalies. Too much carotene in the blood (exceeding 200 micrograms per 100 milliliters of blood) can lead to carotinemia—a pale yellow-red pigmentation of the skin that may be mistaken for jaundice. It is a benign condition and withdrawal of carotene from the diet cures it. The final report to the FDA of the Select Committee on GRAS Substances stated in 1980 that it should continue its GRAS status with no limitations other than good manufacturing practices.

**CARRAGEENAN CHONDRUS EXTRACT. Irish Moss Derivative.** Seaweed-like odor; gluey, salty taste. Used as a stabilizer and emulsifier in chocolate products, chocolate-flavoring drinks, chocolate milk, gassed cream (pressure-dispensed whipped), syrups for frozen products, confections, evaporated milk, cheese spreads and cheese foods, ice cream, frozen custard, sherbets, ices, French dressing, artificially sweetened jellies and jams. Completely soluble in hot water and not coagulated by acids. Salts of carrageenan, an extract of Irish moss, a mixture of two or more of the ammonium, calcium, potassium, or sodium salts, are used in beverages, baked goods, puddings, jelly, and syrups, and are used also as a demulcent to soothe mucous membrane irritation. The use of Irish moss in food and medicine has been known in Ireland for hundreds of years. Its use in the United States began in 1835, but really became common during World War II as a replacement for Japanese Isinglass (agar-agar). Carageenan stimulated the formation of fibrous tissue when injected subcutaneously into the guinea pig. When a single dose of it dissolved in saline was injected into the subcutaneous tissue of rats, it caused malignant tumors after approximately two years. Its cancer-causing ability may be that of a foreign body irritant, because upon administration to rats and mice at high levels in their diet it did not appear to induce tumors, although survival of the animals for this period was not good. The final report to the FDA of the Select Committee on GRAS Substances stated in 1980 that while no evidence in the available information on it demonstrates a hazard to the public at current use levels, uncertainties exist, requiring that additional studies be conducted. GRAS status continues while tests are being completed and evaluated.

**CARROT OIL.** A natural flavoring. The volatile oil is obtained by steam distillation from the crushed seeds of a widely cultivated plant. Light yellow to amber liquid, with a pleasant odor. Used in violet, fruit, rum, and spice flavorings for beverages, ice cream, ices, candy, baked goods, gelatin desserts, puddings, condiments, and soups. Nontoxic. GRAS.

**CARVACROL.** A colorless to pale yellow liquid with a pungent, spicy odor, related to thymol, but more toxic. It is found naturally in oil of origanum, dittany of crete oil, oregano, lovage oil, marjoram, and savory. It is a synthetic flavoring used in citrus, fruit, mint, and spice flavorings for beverages, ice cream, ices, candy, baked goods, and condiments. It is used as a disinfectant and is corrosive; one gram by mouth can cause respiratory and circulatory depression and cardiac failure leading to death.

**CARVACRYL ETHYL ETHER.** A synthetic spice flavoring agent for beverages, ice cream, ices, candy, and baked goods. No known toxicity.

**CARVEOL.** A synthetic mint, spearmint, spice, and caraway flavoring agent for beverages, ice cream, ices, candy, and baked goods. Found naturally in caraway and grapefruit. No known toxicity.

**CARVOL.** See *d*- or *l*-Carvone.

**4-CARVOMENTHENOL.** A synthetic citrus and spice flavoring agent for beverages, ice cream, ices, candy, and baked goods. Occurs naturally in cardamom oil, juniper berries. No known toxicity.

***d*- or *l*-CARVONE. Carvol.** *d*-Carvone is usually prepared by distillation from caraway seed and dillseed oil. It is colorless to light yellow, with an odor of caraway. *l*-Carvone occurs in several essential oils. It may be isolated from spearmint oil or synthesized commercially from *d*-limonene. It is colorless to pale yellow, with the odor of spearmint. Carvol is a synthetic liquor, mint, and spice flavoring agent for beverages, ice cream, ices, candy, baked goods, and liqueur. Used also in perfumery and soaps. No known toxicity. GRAS.

**CARVYL ACETATE.** A synthetic mint flavoring agent for beverages, ice cream, ices, candy, and baked goods. No known toxicity.

**CARVYL PROPIONATE.** A synthetic mint flavoring agent for beverages, ice cream, ices, candy, and baked goods. No known toxicity.

**CARYOPHYLLENE ACETATE.** A general fixative that occurs in many essential oils, especially in clove oil. Colorless, oily, with a clovelike odor. Used in beverages, ice cream, ices, candy, baked goods, and chewing gum. Practically insoluble in alcohol. No known toxicity.

**β-CARYOPHYLLENE.** A synthetic spice flavoring. Occurs naturally in cloves, black currant buds, yarrow herb, grapefruit, allspice, and black pepper. The liquid smells like oil of cloves and turpentine. Used for beverages, ice cream, ices, candy, baked goods, chewing gum, and condiments. No known toxicity.

**CARYOPHYLLENE ALCOHOL.** A flavoring that occurs in many essential oils, especially in clove oil. Colorless, oily, with a clovelike odor. Used as a synthetic mushroom flavoring for baked goods and condiments. No known toxicity.

**CASCARA, BITTERLESS EXTRACT.** A natural flavoring derived from the dried bark of a plant grown from northern Idaho to northern California. Used in butter, caramel, maple, and vanilla flavorings for beverages, ice cream, ices, and baked goods. Also used as a laxative. The freshly dried bark causes vomiting, and must be dried for a year before use, when the side effect has disappeared. It has a bitter taste and its laxative effect is due to its ability to irritate the mucosa of the large intestine.

**CASCARILLA BARK.** A natural flavoring agent obtained from the bark of a tree grown in Haiti, the Bahamas, and Cuba. The dried bark extract is added to smoking tobacco for flavoring and used in bitters and spice flavorings for beverages. The *oil,* obtained by distillation, is light yellow to amber, with a spicy odor. It is used in cola, fruit, root beer, and spice flavorings for beverages, ice cream, ices, candy, baked goods, and condiments. Cascarilla has no known toxicity. GRAS.

**CASEIN. Ammonium Caseinate. Calcium Caseinate. Potassium Caseinate. Sodium Caseinate.** The principal protein of cow's milk, without odor or taste. Used as a texturizer for ice cream, frozen custard, ice milk, fruit sherbets, and in special diet preparations. Also used in the manufacture of plastic, adhesives, and paints. Nontoxic. The final report to the FDA of the Select Committee on GRAS Substances stated in 1980 that it should continue its GRAS status for packaging only with no limitations other than good manufacturing practices.

**CASHOO EXTRACT.** See Catechu Extract.

**CASSIA.** A flavoring from a tropical Asian tree used in bitters, fruit, liquor, meat, root beer, sarsaparilla, and spice flavorings for beverages, ice cream, candy, and baked goods (3,000 ppm). No known toxicity.

**CASSIA BARK. Padang or Batavia.** GRAS. See Cassia Bark, Chinese.

**CASSIA BARK, CHINESE.** A natural flavoring extract from cultivated trees. Used in cola, root beer, and spice flavorings for beverages, ice cream, ices, candy, and baked goods. The bark *oil* is used in berry, butter, chocolate, lemon, coffee, cola, cherry, peach, rum, peppermint, pecan, root beer, cassia, ginger ale, and cinnamon flavorings for beverages, ice cream, ices, baked goods, chewing gum, meats, and condiments. The *buds* are used in spice flavorings for beverages. Cassia bark can cause inflammation and erosion of the gastrointestinal tract. GRAS.

**CASSIE, ABSOLUTE.** A natural flavoring from the flowers of the acacia plant. Used in blackberry, violet, vermouth, and fruit flavorings for beverages, ice cream, ices, candy, baked goods, and gelatin desserts. No known toxicity.

**CASSIS.** See Currant Buds, Absolute.

**CASTOR OIL.** A flavoring, pale yellow and viscous, obtained from castor oil plant seeds. Slightly acrid, sometimes nauseating taste. Used in butter and nut flavorings for beverages, ice cream, ices, candy, and baked goods. Also a release and anti-sticking agent in hard candy products. The raw material is a constituent of embalming fluid, a cathartic, and a topical emollient. It can produce pelvic congestion and induce abortions.

**CASTOREUM EXTRACT.** A natural plant extract used in gooseberry, raspberry, tutti-frutti, rum, wine, black walnut, and vanilla flavorings for beverages, ices, ice cream, candy, chewing gum, condiments, and toppings. The *liquid* is used in loganberry, raspberry, orange, balsam, rose, violet, cherry, grape, honey, rum, muscatel, whiskey, and vanilla flavorings for beverages, ice cream, ices, candy, baked goods, gelatin desserts, chewing gum, and toppings. No known toxicity. GRAS.

**CATALASE.** An enzyme from bovine liver used in milk, for making cheese, and for the elimination of peroxide. It is used also in combination with glucose oxidase for treatment of food wrappers to prevent oxidative deterioration of food.

**CATECHU EXTRACT. Black Cutch Extract. Cachou Extract. Cashoo Extract. Pegu Catechu Extract.** Flavoring extract prepared from the heartwood of acacia catechu (*see* Acacia) grown in India, Sri Lanka, and Jamaica. Used in bitters, fruit, and drum flavorings for beverages, ice cream, ices, candy, baked goods, and chewing gum. Used also for staining wood and dyeing fabrics. The *powder* is used in fruit, rum, and spice flavorings for beverages, ice cream, candy, baked goods, and chewing gum. Incompatible with iron compounds, gelatin, lime water, and zinc sulfate. Catechu has been used as an astringent in diarrhea. No known toxicity.

**CAYENNE PEPPER. Pepper, Red.** A condiment made from the pungent fruit of the plant. Used in sausage and pepper flavorings for beverages, ice cream, ices, candy, condiments, meats (910 ppm), and soups. Reported to retard growth of Mexicans and South Americans and Spanish who eat a great deal of these peppers. Rats fed the ingredient of pepper, a reddish-brown liquid called capsaicin, used in flavoring vinegar and pickles, were stunted in growth.

**CEDAR LEAF OIL.** The volatile oil is a natural flavoring obtained by steam distillation from the fresh leaves of a variety of evergreen trees. It is a colorless to yellow liquid, with a sagelike odor. Used in fruit and spice flavorings for beverages, ice cream, ices, candy, baked goods, meats, and liquors. Has been used to produce abortion, sometimes with fatal results. Similar toxicity to camphor (*see*). May cause sensitivity to light.

**CEDRO OIL.** See Lemon Oil.

**CELERY SEED.** A yellowish to greenish brown liquid, having a pleasant aromatic odor, distilled from the dried ripe fruit of the plant grown in southern Europe. *Celery seed* is used in sausage and celery flavorings for beverages (1,000 ppm), baked goods, condiments (2,500 ppm), soups, meats, and pickles. *Celery seed extract* is used in celery, meat, and spice flavorings for beverages, ice cream, ices, candy, baked goods (1,900 ppm), condiments, meats, and soups. *Celery seed solid extract* is used in celery, maple, meat, and spice flavorings for beverages, candy, baked goods, condiments, and maple syrup. *Celery seed oil* is used in fruit, honey, maple, sausage, nut, root beer, spice, vanilla, and cream soda flavorings for beverages, ice cream, ices, candy, baked goods, chewing gum, condiments, meats, soups, and pickles. Celery seed may cause a sensitivity to light. GRAS.

**CELLULOSE ACETATE.** Obtained by treating cellulose with a food starch modifier, it is insoluble in water, alcohol, and ether. Used in the manufacture of rubber and celluloid substitutes, airplane dopes, varnishes, and lacquer. No known toxicity. The final report to the FDA of the Select Committee on GRAS Substances stated in 1980 that it should continue its GRAS status for packaging only with no limitations other than good manufacturing practices.

**CETONE D.** See Methyl $\beta$-Naphthyl Ketone.

**CETONE V.** See Allyl $\alpha$-Ionone.

**CETYL ALCOHOL.** See 1-Hexadeconal.

**CETYLIC ACID.** See Palmitic Acid.

**CEYLON CINNAMON.** See Cinnamon.

**CEYLON CINNAMON LEAF OIL.** See Cinnamon Leaf Oil.

**CHAMOMILE. Camomile.** Roman, English, or Hungarian flowers; English chamomile *oil* is used as a natural flavoring in chocolate, fruit, and liquor flavorings for beverages, ice cream, ices, candy, and baked goods. Roman chamomile *extract* is a natural flavoring in berry, fruit, vermouth, maple, spice, and vanilla flavorings for the same foods as above. Roman chamomile *oil* is used in chocolate, fruit, vermouth, and spice flavorings for beverages, ice cream, ices, candy, baked goods, gelatin desserts, and liquors. Hungarian chamomile *oil* is used in chocolate, fruit, and liquor flavorings for beverages, ice cream, ices, candy, baked goods, chewing gum, and liquors. Chamomile may cause vomiting. GRAS.

**CHECKERBERRY EXTRACT.** See Wintergreen.

**CHECKERBERRY OIL.** See Wintergreen.

**CHERRY LAUREL OIL.** A fruit and nut flavoring from the cultivated European shrub. Used in baked goods, Maraschino cherries, and extracts.

**CHERRY BARK (WILD) EXTRACT.** A natural flavoring extracted from a variety of cherry trees and used in berry, chocolate, cola, cherry, peach, wild cherry, liquor, nut, root beer, and vanilla flavorings for beverages, ice cream, ices, candy, baked goods, gelatin desserts, puddings, syrups, and liquors (800 ppm). No known toxicity.

**CHERRY PIT EXTRACT.** A natural flavoring extracted from the pits of sweet and sour cherries used in cherry flavoring for beverages, ice cream, and ices. No known toxicity.

**CHERRY PLUM.** Source of purplish red color. See Anthocyanins.

**CHERVIL.** A natural flavoring extracted from an aromatic Eurasian plant and used in spice flavorings for beverages, ice cream, ices, baked goods, and condiments. No known toxicity. GRAS.

**CHICLE.** The gummy, milky resin obtained from trees grown in Mexico and Central America. Rubberlike and quite soft at moderate temperatures. Used in the manufacture of chewing gum, insulation, and waterproofing. No known toxicity.

**CHICORY EXTRACT.** A natural flavor extract from a plant, usually with blue flowers and leaves. Used in butter, caramel, chocolate, coffee, maple, nut, root beer, sarsaparilla, vanilla, wintergreen, and birch beer flavorings for beverages, ice cream, candy, and baked goods. The root of the plant is dried, roasted, and ground for mixing with coffee. No known toxicity.

**CHILTE.** A chewing gum base component of vegetable origin. No known toxicity.

**CHINA BARK EXTRACT.** See Quillaja.

**CHINESE CINNAMON.** See Cinnamon.

**CHINESE CINNAMON LEAF OIL.** See Cinnamon Leaf Oil.

**CHIVES.** A member of the onion family, native to Eurasia. The leaves are used for a seasoning. No known toxicity. GRAS.

**CHLORINE DIOXIDE.** Flour bleacher and oxidizing agent. A yellow to reddish yellow gas, with an unpleasant odor, highly irritating and corrosive to the skin and mucous membranes of respiratory tract. Reacts violently with organic materials. It can kill.

**CHLORINE GAS.** Flour bleaching agent and an aging and oxidizing agent. Also used in water purification. Found in the earth's crust, it is a greenish-yellow gas with a suffocating odor. A powerful irritant, dangerous to inhale, and lethal. Thirty ppm will cause coughing. The chlorine used in drinking water often contains carcinogenic carbon tetrachloride, a contaminant formed during the production process. Chlorination has also been found to sometimes form undesirable "ring" compounds in water, such as toluene, xylene, and the suspected carcinogen stryrene—they have been observed in both the drinking water and waste-water plants in the Midwest.

**CHLORITE.** See Calcium Hypochlorite.

**CHLOROPHYLL.** The green coloring matter of plants which plays an essential part in the photosynthesis process. It impairs a greenish color to certain fats and oils, notably olive and soybean oils. Most of the green coloring is removed during the processing of oils. No known toxicity.

**CHLORTETRACYCLINE. Aureomycin. Biomycin. Biomitsin.** A preservative, an antibiotic, used in a dip for uncooked poultry. One of the reasons for increased resistance to antibiotics in patients is believed to be the widespread use of antibiotics in food animals. In 1969, the British restricted the veterinary use of antibiotics. In 1972, an FDA-appointed committee to study the use of antibiotics in animals recommended curbs on use. Many strains of bacteria are now known to be resistant to tetracycline. The use of this antibiotic has caused permanent discoloration of the permanent teeth in children given the drug prior to the eruption of their second teeth. The drug can also cause skin rash, gastrointestinal upsets, and inflammations in the ano-genital area.

**CHOLIC ACID.** A colorless or white crystalline powder that occurs in the bile of most vertebrates and is used as an emulsifying agent in dried egg whites and as a choleretic to regulate the secretion of bile. Bitter taste; sweetish aftertaste. No known toxicity.The final report to the FDA of the Select Committee on GRAS Substances stated in 1980 that it should continue its GRAS status with no limitations other than good manufacturing practices.

**CHOLINE BITARTRATE.** A dietary supplement included in the B complex and found in the form of a thick syrupy liquid in most animal tissue. It is necessary to nerve function and fat metabolism and can be manufactured in the body but not at a sufficient rate to meet health requirements. Dietary choline protects against poor growth, fatty liver, and renal damage in many animals. Choline deficiency has not been demonstrated in man but the National Academy of Sciences lists 500 to 900 milligrams per day as sufficient for the average man. The final report to the FDA of the Select Committee on GRAS Substances stated in 1980 that it should continue its GRAS status with no limitations other than good manufacturing practices.

**CHOLINE CHLORIDE. Ferric Choline Citrate.** A dietary supplement with the same function as choline bitartrate (*see*). The final report to the FDA of the Select Committee on GRAS Substances stated in 1980 that it should continue its GRAS status with no limitations other than good manufacturing practices.

**CINCHONA BARK, RED.** A natural flavoring from the bark of a South American tree used in bitters, fruit, rum, vermouth, and spice flavorings for beverages, ice cream, ices, candy, liquors, and bitters (1,000 ppm). Yellow cinchona bark is a natural flavoring from the bark of a species of South American tree used in bitters, fruit, and vermouth flavorings for liquors and bitters. The yellow *extract* is used as a bitters flavoring for beverages. Cinchona is grown also in Java and India and at one time was used as an antimalarial. May rarely cause allergies.

**CINENE.** See *d*-Limonene.

**CINEOLE.** See Eucalyptol.

**CINNAMAL.** See Cinnamaldehyde.

**CINNAMALDEHYDE. Cinnamic Aldehyde.** A flavoring, a yellowish oily liquid with a strong odor of cinnamon, the chief ingredient of the oil of cinnamon. Found naturally in cassia bark, cinnamon bark, and cinnamon root. Used in cola, apple, cherry, liquor, rum, nut, pecan, spice, cinnamon, vanilla, and cream soda flavorings for beverages, ice cream, ices, candy, baked goods, chewing gum (4,900 ppm), condiments, and meats. Also used in perfume industry. An irritant, especially in undiluted form. Can cause inflammation and erosion of gastrointestinal tract. GRAS.

**CINNAMALDEHYDE ETHYLENE GLYCOL ACETAL. Cinncloval.** Spice, cassia, cinnamon, and clove flavorings for beverages, ice cream, ices, candy, baked goods, and condiments. See Cinnamaldehyde for toxicity.

**CINNAMEIN.** See Benzyl Cinnamate.

**CINNAMIC ACID.** A cherry, honey, spice, cassia, and cinnamon flavoring agent for beverages, ice cream, ices, candy, baked goods, and chewing gum. Occurs naturally in cassia bark, strawberries, and vanilla. Used medicinally to combat intestinal worms. Main use is in the perfume industry. No known toxicity.

**CINNAMIC ALCOHOL.** See Cinnamyl Alcohol.

**CINNAMIC ALDEHYDE.** See Cinnamaldehyde.

**CINNAMON (CEYLON, CHINESE, SAIGON).** Dried bark of culti-vated trees. Used in bitters, cola, apple, plum, vermouth, sausage, eggnog, cinnamon, and vanilla flavorings for beverages, ices, ice cream, candy (4,-000 ppm), baked goods (1,900 ppm), condiments, meats, and apple but-ter. Used to break up intestinal gas and as an antidiarrheal. See Cinnamaldehyde for toxicity. GRAS.

**CINNAMON BARK. Extract and Oil.** From the dried bark of culti-vated trees. The *extract* is used in cola, eggnog, root beer, cinnamon, and ginger ale flavorings for beverages, ice cream, baked goods, condiments, and meats. The *oil* is used in berry, cola, cherry, rum, root beer, cinna-mon, and ginger ale flavorings for beverages, condiments, and meats. Can be a skin sensitizer in humans and cause mild phototoxicity.

**CINNAMON LEAF OIL.** A volatile oil obtained by steam distillation from cinnamon leaves. Used in cola, apricot, rum, root beer, cinnamon, and ginger ale flavorings for beverages, ice cream, ices, candy, baked goods, chewing gum, gelatin desserts, condiments, pickles, and sliced fruits. No known toxicity.

**CINNAMYL ACETATE.** A synthetic flavoring, colorless to slightly yellow, liquid, with a sweet floral odor. Occurs naturally in cassia bark. Used in berry, apple, apricot, cherry, grape, peach, pineapple, cinnamon, and vanilla flavorings for beverages, ice cream, ices, candy, baked goods, condiments, and chewing gum. No known toxicity.

**CINNAMYL ALCOHOL.** A synthetic flavoring, white to slightly yel-low, liquid, with a balsamic odor. Occurs naturally in storax, balsam Peru, and cinnamon leaves. Used in raspberry, strawberry, apricot, peach, plum, prune, grape, liquor, brandy, nut, black walnut, spice, and cinnamon flavorings for beverages, ice cream, candy, baked goods, chewing gum, gelatin desserts, and brandy. Also used in perfumery and as a deodorant. No known toxicity.

**CINNAMYL ANTHRANILATE.** A synthetic flavoring, reddish-yel-low powder with a fruity taste. Used in cherry, grape, honey, and vanilla flavorings for beverages, ice cream, ices, candy, baked goods, gelatin des-serts, and chewing gum. In experiments testing for cancer-causing agents, cinnamyl anthranilate was the only one of 41 additives that caused lung tumors in mice. It was banned on May 25, 1982, for use in foods because it caused cancerous tumors at the site of injection in rats and mice.

**CINNAMYL BENZOATE.** A synthetic butter, caramel, and fruit fla-voring agent for beverages, ice cream, ices, candy, baked goods, condi-ments, and chewing gum. No known toxicity.

**CINNAMYL BUTYRATE.** A synthetic citrus, orange, and fruit flavor-ing agent for beverages, ice cream, ices, candy, baked goods, and gelatin desserts. No known toxicity.

**CINNAMYL CINNAMATE.** A synthetic fruit flavoring agent for beverages, ice cream, ices, candy, baked goods. No known toxicity.

**CINNAMYL FORMATE. Formic Acid.** A synthetic flavoring, colorless to yellow liquid, with a faint cinnamon odor. Used in banana, cherry, pear, and spice flavorings for beverages, ice cream, ices, candy, baked goods, and chewing gum. See Formic Acid for toxicity.

**CINNAMYL ISOBUTYRATE.** A synthetic strawberry, citrus, apple, banana, grape, peach, pear, and pineapple flavoring agent for beverages, ice cream, ices, candy, baked goods, gelatin desserts, chewing gum, and toppings. No known toxicity.

**CINNAMYL ISOVALERATE.** A synthetic flavoring, colorless to yellow liquid, with a spicy, fruity, floral odor. Used in strawberry, chocolate, apple, apricot, cherry, grape, maple nut, nut, spice, peach, pineapple, and plum flavorings for beverages, ice cream, ices, candy, baked goods, gelatin desserts, and chewing gum. No known toxicity.

**CINNAMYL PHENYLACETATE.** A synthetic chocolate, honey, and spice flavoring agent for beverages, ice cream, ices, candy, and baked goods. No known toxicity.

**CINNAMMYL PROPIONATE.** A synthetic flavoring, colorless to yellow liquid, with a fruity-floral odor. Used in berry, apple, chocolate, currant, grape, peach, pear, and pineapple flavorings for beverages, ice cream, ices, candy, baked goods, gelatin desserts, and chewing gum. No known toxicity.

**CINNCLOVAL.** See Cinnamaldehyde Ethylene Glycol Acetal.

**CIRE D'ABEILLE, ABSOLUTE.** See Beeswax, Bleached.

**CITRAL.** A flavoring agent, light, oily, with a strong lemon odor. Occurs naturally in grapefruit, orange, peach, ginger, oil of lemon, oil of lime. Either isolated from citral oils or made synthetically. Used in strawberry, lemon, lime, orange, apple, cherry, grape, spice, ginger, and vanilla flavorings for beverages, ice cream, ices, candy, baked goods, and chewing gum. Used also in the synthesis of Vitamin A. Causes discoloration of white soaps. No known toxicity. GRAS.

**CITRAL DIMETHYL ACETAL.** A synthetic citrus, lemon, and fruit flavoring agent for beverages, ice cream, ices, candy, fruit, and chewing gum. No known toxicity.

**CITRAL DIETHYL ACETAL.** A synthetic citrus flavoring agent for beverages, ice cream, ices, candy, and condiments. No known toxicity.

**CITRATE, CALCIUM.** See Calcium Citrate.

**CITRATE, ISOPROPYL.** See Isopropyl Citrate.

**CITRATE, MONOGLYCERIDE.** See Monoglyceride Citrate.

**CITRATE SALTS.** Softening agents for cheese spreads; emulsifier salts to blend pasteurized processed cheeses and cheese foods. Citrates may interfere with the results of laboratory tests including tests for pancreatic function, abnormal liver function, and blood alkalinity-acidity.

**CITRATE, SODIUM.** See Sodium Citrate.

**CITRATE, STEARYL.** See Stearyl Citrate.

**CITRIC ACID.** One of the most varied additives. Used in the United States for nearly a century. Colorless or white, with a strong acid taste. Widely distributed in plant and animal tissues and fluids, it is produced commercially from the fermentation of crude sugars. It is also extracted from citrus fruits and occurs naturally in coffee and peaches. It is a fruit flavoring for beverages (2,500 ppm), ice cream, ices, candy (4,300 ppm), baked goods, and chewing gum (3,600 ppm). Citric acid is used to neutralize lye employed in peeling vegetables, as an adjuster of acid-alkalinity in fruit juices, wines, jams, jellies, jelly candies, canned fruit, carbonated beverages, frozen fruit, canned vegetables, frozen dairy products, cheese spreads, sherbet, confections, canned figs, dried egg white, mayonnaise, salad dressing, fruit butter, preserves, and fresh beef blood. Employed in curing meats, for firming peppers, potatoes, tomatoes, and lima beans and to prevent off-flavors in fried potatoes. Removes trace metals and brightens color in various commercial products. It has also been used to dissolve urinary bladder stones, and as a mild astringent. No known toxicity. The final report to the FDA of the Select Committee on GRAS Substances stated in 1980 that it should continue its GRAS status with no limitations other than good manufacturing practices.

**CITRIDIC ACID.** See Aconitic Acid.

**CITROFLEX A-4.** See Tributyl Acetylcitrate.

**CITRONELLA OIL.** A natural flavoring extract from fresh grass grown in Sri Lanka. It consists of about 60 percent geraniol (*see*), 15 percent citronellol (*see*), and 10 to 15 percent camphene (*see*). Almost colorless, with a pleasant odor. Used in citrus, fruit, and ginger ale flavorings for beverages, ice cream, ices, candy, baked goods. Has been used in perfumes and as an insect repellent. Can cause vomiting when ingested, cyanosis, convulsions, damage to intestinal mucosa, and, when taken in sufficient amounts, death. GRAS.

**CITRONELLAL.** A synthetic flavoring agent. The chief constituent of citronella oil (*see*). Also found in lemon and lemon grass oils. Colorless liquid, with an intense lemon-rose odor. Used in citrus, lemon, fruit, cherry, and spice flavorings for beverages, ice cream, ices, candy, baked goods, gelatin desserts, and chewing gum. A mild irritant. See Citronella Oil for toxicity.

**CITRONELLOL.** A synthetic flavoring. Obtained from citronellal or geraniol, geranium rose oil, or citronella oil (*see all*). Colorless liquid, with a roselike odor. The *d* form is more oily and is the major ingredient of rhodinol (*see*). Used in berry, citrus, cola, fruit, rose, and floral flavorings for beverages, ice cream, ices, candy, baked goods, gelatin desserts, and chewing gum. See Citronella Oil for toxicity.

**CITRONELLOXY ACETALDEHYDE.** A synthetic floral, rose, and fruit flavoring agent for beverages, ice cream, ices, candy, and baked goods. See Citronella Oil for toxicity.

**CITRONELLYL ACETATE.** A synthetic flavoring agent, colorless liquid, with a fruity odor. Used in lemon, rose, apricot, banana, grape, pear, and raisin flavorings for beverages, ice cream, ices, candy, baked goods, gelatin desserts, and chewing gum. A major ingredient of rhodinyl acetate (*see*). No known toxicity.

**CITRONELLYL BUTYRATE.** A synthetic flavoring, colorless liquid, with a strong fruit-rose odor. Used in cola, floral, rose, apple, pineapple, plum, prune, and honey flavorings for beverages, ice cream, ices, candy, baked goods, gelatin desserts, and chewing gum. A major ingredient of rhodinyl butyrate (*see*). No known toxicity.

**CITRONELLYL FORMATE. Formic Acid.** A synthetic flavoring, colorless liquid, with a strong fruity odor. Used in orange, apple, apricot, peach, plum, and honey flavorings for beverages, ice cream, ices, candy, baked goods, and chewing gum. A major ingredient of rhodinyl formate (*see*). See Formic Acid for toxicity.

**CITRONELLYL ISOBUTYRATE.** A synthetic flavoring, colorless liquid, with a rose-fruit odor. Used in raspberry, strawberry, floral, rose, and grape flavorings for beverages, ice cream, ices, candy, baked goods, and gelatin desserts. A major ingredient of rhodinyl isobutyrate (*see*). No known toxicity.

**CITRONELLYL PHENYLACETATE.** A synthetic butter, caramel, rose, fruit, and honey flavoring agent for beverages, ice cream, ices, candy, and baked goods. A major ingredient of rhodinyl phenylacetate (*see*). No known toxicity.

**CITRONELLYL PROPIONATE.** A synthetic flavoring, colorless liquid, with a rose-fruit odor. Used in lemon and fruit flavorings for beverages, ice cream, ices, candy, baked goods, and chewing gum. A major ingredient of rhodinyl propionate (*see*). No known toxicity.

**CITRONELLYL VALERATE.** A synthetic fruit flavoring used in beverages, ice cream, ices, candy, and baked goods. No known toxicity.

**CITRUS BIOFLAVONOIDS.** Vitamin P complex, a nutrient supplement up to one gram per day. Occur naturally in plant coloring and in the tonka bean; also in lemon juice. High concentrates can be obtained from all citrus fruits, rose hips, and black currants. Commercial methods extract rinds of oranges, tangerines, lemons, limes, kumquats, and grape-fruits. P vitamin is related to healthy blood vessels and skin. At one time it was thought to prevent colds.

**CITRUS PEEL EXTRACT.** A natural flavor extract from citrus fruits used in bitters, lemon, lime, orange, vermouth, beer, and ginger ale flavorings for beverages, ice cream, ices, candy, and baked goods. No known toxicity. GRAS.

**CITRUS RED NO. 2. Monoazo.** Used only for coloring orange skins that are *not* intended for processing, and that meet minimum maturity standards established by or under laws of the states in which the oranges are grown. Oranges colored with Citrus Red No. 2 are not supposed to bear more than 2 ppm of the color additive calculated on the weight of the whole fruit. Citrus Red No. 2 toxicity is far from determined even though, theoretically, consumers would not ingest the dye because they peel the orange before eating. The 2-naphthol constituent of the dye if ingested in quantity can cause eye lens clouding, kidney damage, vomiting, and circulatory collapse. Application to the skin can cause peeling, and deaths have been reported after application to the skin. See FD and C Colors.

**CIVET, ABSOLUTE.** Flavoring derived from the unctuous secretion from the receptacles between the anus and genitalia of both male and female civet cats. Semisolid, yellowish to brown, with an unpleasant, acrid, bitter taste. Used in raspberry, butter, caramel, grape, and rum flavorings for beverages, ice cream, ices, candy, baked goods, gelatin desserts, and chewing gum. A fixative in perfumery. No known toxicity.

**CLARIFICATION.** Removal from liquid of small amounts of suspended matter, for example, the removal of particles and traces of copper and iron from vinegar and certain beverages.

**CLARIFYING AGENT.** See Clarification.

**CLARY. Clary Sage.** A natural extract of an aromatic herb grown in Southern Europe and cultivated widely in England. The herb is a vermouth and spice flavoring agent in vermouth (500 ppm). Clary *oil* is used in butter, black cherry, grape, licorice, vermouth, wine, root beer, birch beer, spice, vanilla, and cream soda flavorings for beverages, ice cream, ices, candy, baked goods, condiments, and vermouth. No known toxicity. GRAS.

**CLAY. Kaolin. China Clay.** Used to clarify liquids (see Clarification) and as a filler for paper. Also used in the manufacture of porcelain and pottery, as an emollient, and as a poultice and gastrointestinal adsorbent. Nontoxic. The final report to the FDA of the Select Committee on GRAS Substances stated in 1980 that it should continue its GRAS status for packaging with no limitations other than good manufacturing practices.

**CLOVE BUD EXTRACT.** A natural flavor extract from the pungent, fragrant, reddish-brown dried flower buds of a tropical tree. Used in berry, fruit, meat, root beer, and spice flavorings for beverages, ice cream, ices, candy, baked goods, condiments, and meats. Cloves are used also as a dental analgesic and germicide. They may cause intestinal upsets. Rats poisoned with clove oil have shown paralysis of hind legs and jaws, with prostration and eventually death. The FDA has given toxicity studies of clove additives top priority. GRAS.

**CLOVE BUD OIL.** The volatile, colorless or pale yellow oil obtained by steam distillation from the dried flower buds of a tropical tree. A characteristic clove odor and taste. Used in raspberry, coffee, cola, banana, cherry, peach, plum, rum, sausage, eggnog, pecan, root beer flavorings for beverages, ice cream, ices, candy, baked goods, gelatin desserts, chewing gum (1,800 ppm), condiments, meats, liquors, spiced fruit (830 ppm), and jelly. See Clove Bud Extract for toxicity. The final report to the FDA of the Select Committee on GRAS Substances stated in 1980 that it should continue its GRAS status with no limitations other than good manufacturing practices.

**CLOVE BUD OLEORESIN.** A natural resinous, viscous flavoring extract from the tree that produces clove buds. Used in fruit, meat, and spice flavorings for meat. See Clove Bud Extract for toxicity.

**CLOVE LEAF OIL.** The volatile pale yellow oil obtained by steam distillation of the leaves of the tropical tree that produces clove buds. Used in loganberry, cherry, root beer, sarsaparilla, and cinnamon flavorings for beverages, ice cream, ices, candy, baked goods, gelatin desserts, condiments, meats, pickles, and apple butter. See Clove Bud Extract for toxicity. The final report to the FDA of the Select Committee on GRAS Substances stated in 1980 that it should continue its GRAS status with no limitations other than good manufacturing practices.

**CLOVE STEM OIL.** The volatile yellow to light brown oil obtained by steam distillation from the dried stems of the tropical tree that produces clove buds. Characteristic odor and taste of cloves. Used in berry, cherry, root beer, ginger ale, and ginger beer flavorings for beverages, ice cream, ices, candy, baked goods, and condiments. See Clove Bud Extract for toxicity. The final report to the FDA of the Select Committee on GRAS Substances stated in 1980 that it should continue its GRAS status with no limitations other than good manufacturing practices.

**CLOVER.** An herb, a natural flavoring extract, from a plant characterized by three leaves and flowers in dense heads. Used in fruit flavoring for beverages, ice cream, ices, candy, and baked goods. May cause a sensitivity to light. GRAS.

**COBALT SOURCES: Carbonate, Chloride, Gluconate, and Sul-**

**fate.** Cobalt is a metal occurring in the earth's crust. It is gray, hard, and magnetic. All here are used as a mineral supplement at the rate of 1 milligram per day. Excess administration can produce an overproduction of red blood cells plus toxic symptoms in the gastrointestinal tract. GRAS.

**COCA LEAF EXTRACT (DECOCAINIZED).** Flavoring from the dried leaves of cocaine-containing plants grown in Bolivia, Brazil, Peru, and Java. Used in bitters and cola flavoring for beverages, ices, ice cream, and candy. Once a central nervous system stimulant. No known toxicity. GRAS.

**COCHINEAL.** See Carmine.

**COCONUT OIL (REFINED).** A white semisolid highly saturated fat expressed from the kernels of the coconut palm. Used in chocolate, candies, in baking, instead of lard, and in self-basting turkeys. Believed to be a precursor of hardening of the arteries. No known toxicity. The final report to the FDA of the Select Committee on GRAS Substances stated in 1980 that it should continue its GRAS status for packaging with no limitations other than good manufacturing practices.

**COGNAC OIL. Wine Yeast Oil.** The volatile oil obtained from distillation of wine, with the characteristic aroma of cognac. *Green cognac oil* is used as a flavoring for beverages, ice cream, candy, baked goods, chewing gum, condiments, liquors. *White cognac oil,* which has the same constituents as green oil, is used in berry, cherry, grape, brandy, and rum flavorings for beverages, ice cream, ices, candy, baked goods, and gelatin desserts. No known toxicity. GRAS.

**COLLOIDAL SILICON DIOXIDE.** Practically insoluble in water. A free-flowing agent in salt, seasoned salt, and sodium bicarbonate. Also included in vitamin products, dietary products, spices, meat-curing compounds, flavoring powders, dehydrated honey, dehydrated molasses, and dehydrated nondiastatic malt. Percentages range from 1 percent in salt, to 2 percent in dehydrated products. Prolonged inhalation of the silicon dust can cause fibrosis of the lungs. Increases susceptibility to tuberculosis. Chemically and biologically inert when ingested. See Silicon Dioxide.

**COLORING.** More than 90 percent of the food colorings now in use are manufactured, frequently from coal-tar colors. The coal-tar derivatives need to be certified, which means that batches of the dyes are chemically tested and approved by the FDA. As more and more food colors are banned, interest has grown in color derived from natural sources such as carotene (*see*) from carrots, which is used to color margarine, and beet juice, which provides a red color for some foods. See FD and C Colors for information on the synthetics now in use.

**COLORS.** See FD and C Colors.

**COPPER. Gluconate, Sulfate.** One of the earliest known metals. Used as a mineral supplement. An essential nutrient for all mammals. Naturally occurring or experimentally produced copper deficiency in animals leads to a variety of abnormalities, including anemia, skeletal defects, and muscle degeneration. Copper deficiency is extremely rare in man. The body of an adult contains from 75 to 150 milligrams of copper. Concentrations are highest in the brain and liver and heart. A copper intake of 2 milligrams per day appears to maintain a balance in adults. An ordinary diet provides 2 to 5 milligrams daily. Copper itself is nontoxic, but soluble copper salts, notably copper sulfate, are highly irritating to the skin and mucous membranes and cause serious vomiting. Copper salts include copper carbonate, chloride, gluconate, hydroxide, orthophosphate, oxide, pyrophosphate, and sulfate. The final report to the FDA of the Select Committee on GRAS Substances stated in 1980 that it should continue its GRAS status with no limitations other than good manufacturing practices.

**CORIANDER.** The dried ripe fruit of a plant grown in Asia and Europe. Colorless or pale yellow liquid with the characteristic odor and taste of coriander. Used as a natural flavoring agent in raspberry, bitters, fruit, meat, spice, ginger ale, and vanilla flavorings for beverages, ice cream, candy, baked goods (880 ppm), condiments, meats (1,300 ppm), and liquors (1,000 ppm). The *oil* is used in blackberry, raspberry, chocolate, coffee, cola, fruit, liquor, sausage, root beer, spice, ginger ale, and vanilla flavorings for beverages, ice cream, ices, candy, baked goods, chewing gum, condiments, meats, and liquors. Coriander is used as a weak medication (up to 1 gram) to break up intestinal gas. No known toxicity. GRAS.

**CORN DEXTRIN®. Dextri-Maltose.** A white or yellow powder obtained by enzymatic action of barley malt on corn flours, and used as a modifier or thickening agent in milk and milk products. Nontoxic. The final report to the FDA of the Select Committee on GRAS Substances stated in 1980 that it should continue its GRAS status for packaging with no limitations other than good manufacturing practices.

**CORN SILK.** Used as a natural flavoring extract. The final report to the FDA of the Select Committee on GRAS Substances stated in 1980 that there were insufficient relevant biological and other studies upon which to base an evaluation of it when it is used as a food ingredient. It remains GRAS.

**CORN SUGAR.** See Corn Syrup.

**CORN SYRUP. Corn Sugar. Dextrose.** Used in maple, nut, and root beer flavorings for beverages, ice cream, ices, candy, and baked goods.

Corn syrup is used for envelopes, stamps, sticker tapes, ale, aspirin, bacon, baking mixes, powders, beer, bourbon, breads, breakfast cereals, pastries, candy, carbonated beverages, catsups, cheeses, cereals, chop suey, chow mein, confectioners' sugar, cream puffs, fish products, ginger ale, hams, jellies, processed meats, peanut butter, canned peas, plastic food wraps, sherbet, whiskey, and American wines. May cause allergies. The final report to the FDA of the Select Committee on GRAS Substances stated in 1980 that there is no evidence in the available information that it is a hazard to the public when used as it is now and it should continue in GRAS status with limitations on amounts that can be added to food.

**CORNSTARCH.** Many containers are powdered with cornstarch to prevent sticking. The dietetic grade is marketed as Maizena®, Mondamin®. It is an absorbent dusting powder and a demulcent for irritated colons. May cause allergic reactions such as inflamed eyes, stuffy nose, and perennial hay fever. The final report to the FDA of the Select Committee on GRAS Substances stated in 1980 that it should continue its GRAS status with no limitations other than good manufacturing practices.

**CORPS PRALINE.** See Maltol.

**COSTMARY. Virgin Mary.** A natural flavoring derived from an herb native to Asia. Its yellow aromatic flowers are shaped like buttons. Used as a pot herb and salad plant. Infrequently used today as a flavoring in beer and ale. Regarded as sacred to the Virgin Mary. No known toxicity.

**COSTUS ROOT OIL.** The volatile oil obtained by steam distillation from the dried roots of an herb. Light yellow to brown viscous liquid, with a persistent violetlike odor. A natural fruit and vanilla flavoring for beverages, ice cream, ices, candy, baked goods, and gelatin desserts. No known toxicity.

**COTTONSEED FLOUR.** Cooked, partly defatted and toasted flour used for pale yellow coloring. Sometimes used to make gin. The *oil* is used in most salad oils and oleomargarines and most mayonnaises and salad dressings. Lard compounds and lard substitutes are made with cottonseed oil. Sardines and other smoked seafood may be packed in it. Most commercial fried products such as potato chips and doughnuts are fried in cottonseed oil, and restaurants almost universally use it for cooking. Candies, particularly chocolates, often contain this oil and it is used to polish fruits at stands. It is known to cause allergies and because it is used in a wide variety of products without notice, it may be hard to avoid.

**COTTONSEED OIL.** See Cottonseed Flour.

**COUCH GRASS.** See Dog Grass Extract.

**CRANBERRY JUICE CONCENTRATE.** Bright red coloring from the juice of the red acid berry, produced by any of several plants of the genus *Vaccinium* grown in the United States and Europe. Food manufacturers may substitute this natural coloring for the synthetic reds that were banned. No known toxicity.

**CRANBERRY POMACE.** Source of natural red coloring. See Anthocyanins.

**CREAM OF TARTAR.** See Tartrate.

**CREOSOL.** See 2-Methoxy-4-Methylphenol.

***p*-CRESOL.** A synthetic nut and vanilla flavoring agent. Obtained from coal tar. It occurs naturally in tea, and is used in beverages, ice cream, ices, candy, and baked goods. It is more powerful than phenol and less toxic. Phenol is an extremely toxic acid obtained from coal tar which has many industrial uses, including use as a disinfectant for toilets and as an anesthetic.

**4-CRESOL.** See *p*-Cresol.

***o*-CRESYL ACETATE.** See *o*-Tolyl Acetate.

***p*-CRESYL ACETATE.** See *p*-Tolyl Acetate.

**CRETAN DITTANY.** See Dittany of Crete.

**CROCETIN.** Yellow coloring from saffron (*see*).

**CROCUS EXTRACT.** See Saffron.

**CRYPTOXANTHIN.** A natural yellow coloring from corn and marigolds. See Xanthophyll.

**CUBEBS. Tailed Pepper. Java Pepper.** The mature, unripe, sun-dried fruit of a perennial vine grown in South Asia, Java, Sumatra, the Indies, and Sri Lanka. It has a strong, spicy odor and is used in fruit flavoring for beverages (800 ppm). The volatile *oil* is obtained by steam distillation from the fruit and is colorless to light green with the characteristic spicy odor and a slightly acrid taste. It is used in berry, fruit, and ginger flavorings for beverages, ice cream, candy, baked goods, condiments, and meats. Java pepper was formerly used to stimulate healing of mucous membranes. The fruit has been used as a stimulant and diuretic and sometimes is smoked in cigarettes. No known toxicity.

**CUMALDEHYDE.** See Cuminaldehyde.

**CUMIN. Cummin.** A natural flavoring obtained from the seeds of an Old World plant. Used in spice and sausage flavorings for baked goods (2,500 ppm), condiments (3,900 ppm), and meats. A volatile *oil,* light yellow to brown, with a strong, disagreeable odor, is distilled from the plant. It is used in berry, fruit, sausage, and spice flavorings for beverages, ice cream, ices, candy, chewing gum, baked goods, condiments, meats, and pickles. No known toxicity. GRAS.

**CUMINAL.** See Cuminaldehyde.

**CUMINALDEHYDE.** The constituent of eucalyptus, myrrh, cassia, cumin, and other essential oils, it is a synthetic flavoring used in berry, fruit, and spice flavorings for beverages, ice cream, ices, candy, baked goods, chewing gum, and condiments. Used in perfumery. No known toxicity.

**CUMINIC ALDEHYDE.** See Cuminaldehyde.

**CUPRIC CHLORIDE.** See Copper.

**CUPRIC OXIDE.** See Copper.

**CUPRIC SULFATE.** See Copper.

**CUPROUS IODIDE.** The final report to the FDA of the Select Committee on GRAS Substances stated in 1980 that it should continue its GRAS status with no limitations other than good manufacturing practices. See Iodine Sources.

**CURAÇAO PEEL EXTRACT.** A natural flavoring extracted from a plant native to the Caribbean island. Used in orange and liquor flavorings for beverages (1,700 ppm). GRAS.

**CURAÇAO PEEL OIL.** Obtained from the plant and used in berry, lime, orange, and liquor flavorings for beverages, ice cream, ices, candy, baked goods. No known toxicity.

**CURCUMIN.** The orange-yellow colorant derived from tumeric (*see*) and used as a natural food coloring. It does not require certification because it is a natural product but the Expert Committee on Food Additives of the FDA recommended that the acceptable daily intake of curcumin (and tumeric) be limited to 0 to 0.5 milligrams per kilogram of body weight.

**CURING AGENTS.** These include salt, nitrites (*see*), and other compounds used to stabilize color, give flavor, and/or preserve.

**CURRANT BUDS, ABSOLUTE.** A natural flavoring from a variety of small raisins grown principally in Greece. Used in fruit, berry, and raspberry flavorings for beverages, ice cream, ices, candy, and baked goods. No known toxicity.

**CYANOCOBALAMIN.** See Vitamin $B_{12}$.

**CYANODITHIOIMIDOCARBONATE, DISODIUM.** Bacteria-killing component in the processing of sugar cane. Many organic cyano compounds are decomposed in the body to yield highly toxic cyanide.

**CYCLAMATES. Sodium Cyclamate and Calcium Cyclamate.** Artificial sweetening agents about 30 times as sweet as refined sugar, removed from the market September 1, 1969, because they were found to cause bladder cancer in rats. At the time 175 million Americans were swallowing cyclamates in significant doses in many products ranging from chewing gum to soft drinks.

**CYCLOHEXANEACETIC ACID.** A synthetic butter and fruit flavoring agent for beverages, ice cream, ices, candy, and baked goods. Cyclo-

hexane in high concentrations may act as a narcotic and a skin irritant.
**CYCLOHEXANEETHYL ACETATE.** A synthetic fruit and honey flavoring agent for beverages, ice cream, candy, and baked goods. See Cyclohexaneacetic Acid for toxicity.

**CYCLOHEXYL ANTHRANILATE.** A synthetic apple, banana, and grape flavoring agent for beverages, ice cream, ices, candy, baked goods, and gelatin desserts. Some cyclohexyl compounds are irritating to the skin.

**CYCLOHEXYL BUTYRATE.** A synthetic strawberry, apple, apricot, banana, and peach flavoring agent for beverages, ice cream, ices, candy, baked goods, and gelatin desserts. See Cyclohexyl Anthranilate for toxicity.

**CYCLOHEXYL CINNAMATE.** A synthetic apple, apricot, peach, and prune flavoring agent for beverages, ice cream, ices, candy, and baked goods. See Cyclohexyl Anthranilate for toxicity.

**CYCLOHEXYL FORMATE. Formic Acid.** A synthetic cherry flavoring for beverages, ice cream, ices, candy, and baked goods. See Formic Acid and Cyclohexyl Anthranilate for toxicity.

**CYCLOHEXYL ISOVALERATE.** A synthetic strawberry and apple flavoring agent for beverages, ice cream, ices, candy, and baked goods. See Cyclohexyl Anthranilate for toxicity.

**CYCLOHEXYL PROPIONATE.** A synthetic fruit flavoring for beverages, ice cream, ices, candy, baked goods, and gelatin desserts. See Cyclohexyl Anthranilate for toxicity.

**CYCLOPENTADECANOLIDE.** See ω-Pentadecalactone.

**CYCLOTENE.** See Methylcyclopentenolone.

**CYMENE.** See p-Cymene.

**p-CYMENE.** A synthetic flavoring, a volatile hydrocarbon solvent occurring naturally in anise star, coriander, cumin, mace oil, oil of mandarin, and origanum oil. Used in citrus and spice flavorings for beverages, ice cream, ices, candy, baked goods, chewing gum, and condiments. Ingestion may cause a burning sensation in the mouth and stomach, nausea, vomiting, salivation, headache, giddiness, vertigo, confusion, and coma. Contact with liquid may cause blisters of the skin and inflammation of mucous membranes.

**CYMOL.** See p-Cymene.

**CYMOPHENOL.** See Carvacrol.

**CYSTEINE. L-form.** An essential amino acid (*see*) derived from hair. Soluble in water, used in bakery products as a nutrient. Use allowed up to .009 part for each 100 parts of flour. Has been used to promote wound healing. On the FDA list of additives to be studied. GRAS.

**CYSTINE. L and DL forms.** Nonessential amino acid (*see*) found in urine and in horsehair. Colorless, practically odorless white crystals. Used as a nutrient supplement. On the FDA list for further study. GRAS.

# D

**DANDELION ROOT, EXTRACT.** A natural extract from the dandelion plant, cultivated as a lawn weed in North America and native to Eurasia. Dandelion coffee is made from the dried roots of the plant. The *root* extract is used in bitters, butter, caramel, floral, fruit, root beer, and vanilla flavorings for beverages, ice cream, ices, candy, and baked goods. The *fluid* extract is used in butter, caramel, fruit, maple, and vanilla flavorings for beverages, ice cream, ices, candy, and baked goods. There is no known toxicity from ingestion of dandelions.

**DAUCUS CAROTA.** See Carrot Oil.

**DAVANA OIL.** A plant extract used in fruit flavoring for beverages, ice cream, ices, candy, baked goods, and chewing gum. No known toxicity.

**γ-DECALACTONE.** A synthetic flavoring agent, colorless, with a fruity odor, used in citrus, orange, coconut, and fruit flavorings for beverages, ice cream, ices, baked goods, and gelatin desserts. No known toxicity.

**δ-DECALACTONE.** A synthetic flavoring agent. Occurs naturally in butter, cream, and milk. Colorless, with a fruity odor. Used in coconut and fruit flavorings for beverages, ice cream, ices, candy, baked goods, and toppings. No known toxicity.

**DECANAL.** A synthetic flavoring agent. Occurs naturally in oranges, sweet orange peel, sweet mandarin oil, grapefruit oil, orris, and coriander. Colorless to light yellow, with a definite fatlike odor that becomes florallike when diluted. Used in berry, citrus, lemon, orange, fruit, and honey flavorings for beverages, ice cream, ices, candy, baked goods, gelatin desserts, and chewing gum. No known toxicity. GRAS.

**DECANAL DIMETHYL ACETAL.** A synthetic citrus, liquor, brandy, and cognac flavoring agent for beverages, ice cream, ices, candy, baked goods, gelatin desserts, puddings, and alcoholic beverages. No known toxicity. GRAS.

**DECANOIC ACID.** A synthetic flavoring agent. Occurs naturally in anise, butter acids, oil of lemon, and oil of lime. Used in butter, coconut, fruit, liquor, whiskey, and cheese flavorings for beverages, ice cream, ices, baked goods, candy, gelatin desserts, puddings, and shortenings. No known toxicity.

**1-DECANOL.** A synthetic flavoring agent. Occurs naturally in sweet orange and ambrette seed. Used in butter, lemon, orange, coconut, and fruit flavorings for beverages, ice cream, ices, candy, baked goods, and chewing gum. No known toxicity.

**DECANYL ACETATE.** See Decyl Acetate.

**2-DECENAL.** A synthetic fruit flavoring for beverages, ice cream, ices, candy, and baked goods. No known toxicity.

**DECENALDEHYDE.** See 2-Decenal.

**DECYL ACETATE.** A synthetic berry, orange, apple, peach, plum, and honey flavoring agent for beverages, ice cream, ices, candy, baked goods, gelatin desserts, and chewing gum. No known toxicity.

**DECYL ALCOHOL.** See 1-Decanol.

**DECYL BUTYRATE.** A synthetic citrus and fruit flavoring agent for beverages, ice cream, ices, candy, and baked goods. No known toxicity.

**DECYL PROPIONATE.** A synthetic citrus and fruit flavoring agent used in beverages, ice cream, ices, candy, and baked goods. No known toxicity.

**DECYLIC ACID.** See Decanoic Acid.

**DECYLIC ALCOHOL.** See 1-Decanol.

**DEFATTED.** Meaning the fat has been partly or totally removed from a product. If partly removed there is no minimum percentage set by the Food and Drug Administration.

**DEFATTED COTTONSEED OIL.** From cottonseed flour (*see*) with the fat removed.

**DEFOAMER. Antifoamer. Foam Inhibitor.** Any number of surface active agents (*see*), such as liquid glycerides (*see*), which are used to control the amount of foam produced in the processing of baked goods, coffee whiteners, candies, milk products, jams, jellies, and fruit juices. They remove the "head" from processed drinks, such as orange and pineapple juice.

**DEHYDRATED.** With the water removed.

**DEHYDROACETIC ACID.** See Sodium Dehydroacetate.

**DEMULCENT.** A soothing, usually thick oily or creamy substance used to relieve pain in inflamed or irritated mucous surfaces. The gum acacia, for instance, is used as a demulcent.

**DENATURANT.** A substance that changes another substance's natural qualities or characteristics. For example, denatonium benzoate is added to the alcoholic content in cosmetics to make it undrinkable.

**DESOXYCHOLIC ACID.** An emulsifying agent, white, crystalline, powdered, almost insoluble in water. Used in dried egg whites up to .1 percent. No known toxicity. The final report to the FDA of the Select Committee on GRAS Substances stated in 1980 that it should continue its GRAS status with no limitations other than good manufacturing practices.

**DEXTRAN.** A term applied to polysaccharides produced by bacteria growing on sugar. Used as a foam stabilizer for beer, in soft-center confections, and as a substitute for barley malt. It has also been used as a plasma expander for emergency treatment of shock. Has caused cancer in laboratory rats. The final report to the FDA of the Select Committee on GRAS Substances stated in 1980 that there is no evidence in the available information that it is a hazard to the public when used as it is now and it should continue its GRAS status with limitations on amounts that can be added to food.

**DEXTRIN. British Gum. Starch Gum.** White or yellow powder produced from starch. Used as a foam stabilizer for beer, a diluting agent for dry extracts and pills, in polishing cereals, for preparing emulsions and dry bandages, for thickening industrial dye pastes, and in matches, fireworks, and explosives. No known toxicity. The final report to the FDA of the Select Committee on GRAS Substances stated in 1980 that it should continue its GRAS status with no limitations other than good manufacturing practices.

**DEXTROSE.** The final report to the FDA of the Select Committee on GRAS Substances stated in 1980 that there is no evidence in the available information that it is a hazard to the public when used as it is now and it should continue its GRAS status with limitations on amounts that can be added to food. See Corn Syrup.

**DHC.** See Dihydrochalcones.

**DIACETYL.** A flavoring agent that occurs naturally in cheese, cocoa, pears, coffee, raspberries, strawberries, angelica root, coffee extract, and cooked chicken, but usually prepared by a special fermentation of glucose. It is a yellowish-green liquid. Used as a carrier for aroma of butter, vinegar, and coffee. Also used in blueberry, raspberry, strawberry, butter, buttermilk, butterscotch, caramel, chocolate, coffee, fruit, cheese, cherry, liquor, rum, wine, nut, almond, spice, ginger ale, vanilla, and cream soda flavorings for beverages, ice cream, ices, candy, baked goods, gelatin desserts, chewing gum, and shortening. Cleared by U.S. Department of Agriculture (Meat Inspection Division) to flavor oleomargarine in "amounts sufficient for the purpose." No known toxicity. GRAS.

**DIACETYL TARTARIC OF MONOGLYCERIDES AND DIGLYCERIDES.** An emulsifying agent used to improve volume and uniformity in bakery products up to 20 percent by weight of the combination of such a preparation and the shortening. The final report to the FDA of the Select Committee on GRAS Substances stated in 1980 that it should continue its GRAS status with no limitations other than good manufacturing practices.

**DIALLYL DISULFIDE.** See Allyl Disulfide.

**DIALLYL SULFIDE.** See Allyl Sulfide.

**DIASMOL.** See 1,3-Nonanediol Acetate (mixed esters).

**DIATOMACEOUS EARTH. Infusorial Earth. Kieselguhr.** A porous and relatively pure form of silica formed from fossil remains of diatoms—one-celled algae with shells. Inert when ingested. Used in dentifrices, as a clarifying agent, as an absorbent for liquids because it can absorb about four times its weight in water, used as a buffer and for acid-proofing food packaging. The dust can cause lung damage after long exposure to high concentrations. The final report to the FDA of the Select Committee on GRAS Substances stated in 1980 that it should continue its GRAS status for packaging with no limitations other than good manufacturing practices.

**DIBENZYL ETHER.** A synthetic fruit and spice flavoring agent for beverages, ice cream, ices, candy, baked goods, and chewing gum. No known toxicity.

**DIBENZYL KETONE.** See 1,3-Diphenyl-2-Propanone.

**4,4-DIBUTYL-γ-BUTYROLACTONE.** A synthetic butter, coconut, and nut flavoring agent for ice cream, candy, ices, and baked goods. No known toxicity.

**DIBUTYL SEBACATE. Sebacic Acid.** A synthetic fruit flavoring agent usually obtained from castor oil and used for beverages, ice cream, ices, candy, and baked goods. No known toxicity.

**DIBUTYL SULFIDE.** See Butyl Sulfide.

**DIETHYL PYROCARBONATE (DEP).** A fermentation inhibitor in still wines, beer, and orange juice added before or during bottling at a level not to exceed 200 to 500 parts per million. DEP was widely used because it supposedly did its job of preserving and then decomposed within 24 hours. However, instead of disappearing, it reacted with the ammonia in beverages to form urethane, according to University of Stockholm researchers. They said that DEP caused urethane concentrations of 0.1 to 0.2 milligrams per liter in orange juice and approximately 1 milligram per liter in white wine and beer. Since 1943 urethane has been identified as a cancer-causing agent. The FDA had not required listing of DEP on the label and therefore did not know how many beverages were actually treated with this additive. The FDA banned the use of DEP in 1976.

**DIETHYL MALATE. Malic Acid.** A synthetic apple and rum flavoring agent for beverages, ice cream, ices, candy, baked goods, gelatin, and puddings. No known toxicity.

**DIETHYL MALONATE.** A synthetic berry, fruit, apple, grape, peach, and pear flavoring agent for beverages, ice cream, candy, and baked goods. No known toxicity.

**DIETHYL SEBACATE. Sebacic Acid.** A synthetic butter, coconut, apple, melon, peach, and nut flavoring agent for beverages, ice cream, ices, candy, baked goods, gelatin desserts, and chewing gum. No known toxicity.

**DIETHYL SUCCINATE.** A synthetic raspberry, butter, orange, and grape flavoring agent for beverages, ice cream, ices, candy, and baked goods. No known toxicity.

**DIETHYL TARTRATE.** See Tartaric Acid.

**DIETHYLSTILBESTROL (DES). Stilbestrol.** A synthetic estrogen fed to cattle and poultry to "fatten them." A proven carcinogen, hormonal in nature, according to the FDA, which has given top priority to the study of the safety of DES. The FDA stipulates a zero tolerance for the compound after a proper withdrawal period. In 1971, three Harvard scientists linked DES to a rare form of vaginal cancer in the daughters of women who had taken DES during pregnancy. An estimated 100,000 to 150,000 head of cattle containing residues of the hormone are apparently getting to market. The European Common Market, Italy, and Sweden have forbidden the use of DES in cattle.

**DIGLYCERIDES. Emulsifiers.** See Glycerides.

**2,3-DIHYDRO-3-OXO-BENZISOSULFONAZOLE.** See Saccharin.

**DIHYDROACARVEOL.** A synthetic flavoring agent occurring naturally in black pepper. Used in liquor, mint, spice, and caraway flavorings for beverages, ice cream, candy, baked goods, and alcoholic beverages. No known toxicity.

**DIHYDROANETHOLE.** See *p*-Propyl Anisole.

**DIHYDROCARVYL ACETATE. Acetic Acid.** A synthetic berry, fruit, mint, and spice flavoring agent for beverages, ice cream, ices, candy, baked goods, and condiments. No known toxicity.

**DIHYDROCHALCONES (DHC).** A new class of intensely sweet compounds—about 1,500 times sweeter than sugar—obtained by a simple chemical modification of naturally occurring bioflavonoids (*see*). Hydrogenation (*see*) of naringin and neohesperidin (the predominant bitter constituents in grapefruit and Seville orange rind) provides the intensely sweet dihydrochalcones. DHCs are seemingly safe. There have not been any reports, thus far, of side effects in either multigeneration feeding studies or in long-term feeding trials. The disadvantage is that they cannot be easily reproduced in the laboratory so supplies are dependent on natural sources. A more serious problem is that the intense, pleasant sweetness of DHCs is slow in onset, with considerable lingering taste, which renders them unsuitable for many food uses. Approval to use DHCs in toothpaste and chewing gum is pending. Food scientists are now trying to find derivatives and analogs of DHCs to overcome the slow onset and lingering factor in the natural compound.

**DIHYDROCOUMARIN.** A synthetic flavoring agent occurring naturally in tonka bean, oil of lavender, and sweet clovers. Used in butter, caramel, coconut, floral, fruit, cherry, liquor, rum, nut, root beer, spice, cinnamon, vanilla, cream soda, and tonka flavorings for beverages, ice cream, ices, candy, baked goods, gelatin desserts, puddings, and chewing gum. Prolonged feeding has revealed a possible trend toward liver injury.

**2,3-DIKETOBUTANE.** See Diacetyl.

**DILAURYL THIODIPROPIONATE.** An antioxidant, white, crystalline flakes with a sweet odor, in general food use to extend shelf life. In fat or oil up to .02 percent. The final report to the FDA of the Select Committee on GRAS Substances stated in 1980 that there is no evidence in the available information that it is a hazard to the public when used as it is now and it should continue its GRAS status with limitations on amounts that can be added to food.

**DILL.** A natural flavoring agent from a European herb bearing a seed-like fruit. Used in sausage and spice flavorings for baked goods (4,800 ppm), condiments, meats, and pickles (8,200 ppm). Also used in medicine. Can cause sensitivity to light. The final report to the FDA of the Select Committee on GRAS Substances stated in 1980 that it should continue its GRAS status with no limitations other than good manufacturing practices.

**DILL OIL.** The volatile oil obtained from the crushed, dried seeds or fruits of the herb. Slightly yellow, with a caraway odor and flavor. Used in strawberry, fruit, sausage, and dill flavorings for beverages, ice cream, ices, baked goods, gelatin desserts, chewing gum, condiments, meats, liquors, and pickles. The final report to the FDA of the Select Committee on GRAS Substances stated in 1980 that it should continue its GRAS status with no limitations other than good manufacturing practices. See Dill for toxicity.

**DILLSEED. Indian Dill.** The volatile oil from a variety of dill herbs. Obtained by steam distillation. Light yellow, with a harsh carawaylike odor. Used in rye flavorings for baked goods, condiments, and meats. The final report to the FDA of the Select Committee on GRAS Substances stated in 1980 that it should continue its GRAS status with no limitations other than good manufacturing practices. See Dill for toxicity.

***m*-DIMETHOXYBENZENE. Resorcinol.** A synthetic fruit, nut, and vanilla flavoring agent for beverages, ice cream, candy, and baked goods. Used on the skin as a bactericidal and fungicidal ointment. Has the same toxicity as phenol (extremely toxic), but causes more severe convulsions.

***p*-DIMETHOXYBENZENE.** A synthetic raspberry, fruit, nut, hazel nut, root beer, and vanilla flavoring agent for beverages, ice cream, ices, candy, and baked goods. See above for toxicity.

**3,4-DIMETHOXYBENZENECARBONAL.** See Veratraldehyde.

**DIMETHYL BENZYL CARBINOL.** See α,α-Dimethylphenethyl Alcohol.

**DIMETHYL ETHER PROTOCATECHUALDEHYDE.** See Veratraldehyde.

**DIMETHYL ETHER RESORCINOL.** A benzene derivative, originally obtained from certain resins but now usually synthesized. See *m*-Dimethoxybenzene.

**2,6-DIMETHYL-5-HEPTENAL.** A synthetic fruit flavoring for beverages, ice cream, ices, candy, baked goods, gelatin desserts, and chewing gum. No known toxicity.

**3,7-DIMETHYL-7-HYDROXYOCTANAL.** See Hydroxycitronellal.

**DIMETHYL KETONE.** See Diacetyl.

**2,6-DIMETHYL OCTANAL.** A synthetic melon flavoring agent for beverages, ice cream, ices, candy, and baked goods. No known toxicity.

**3,7-DIMETHYL-1-OCTANOL.** A synthetic flavoring, colorless, with a sweet roselike odor. Used in floral, rose, and fruit flavorings for beverages, ice cream, ices, candy, and baked goods. No known toxicity.

**DIMETHYL PHENETHYL CARBINYL ACETATE.** See 2-Methyl-4-Phenyl-2-Butyl Acetate.

**DIMETHYL POLYSILOXANE. Antifoam A.** An antifoaming agent for use in processing foods in "amounts reasonably required to inhibit foaming." Used as a chewing gum base, in molasses, soft drinks, sugar distillation, skimmed milk, wine fermentation, syrups, soups, rendered fats, and curing solutions. Not to exceed 10 ppm in nonalcoholic beverages. No known toxicity.

**DIMETHYL RESORCINOL.** See *m*-Dimethoxybenzene.

**DIMETHYL SUCCINATE. Succinic Acid.** A synthetic fruit flavoring agent for beverages, ice cream, ices, candy, baked goods, and chewing gum. No known toxicity.

**DIMETHYL SULFIDE.** See Methyl Sulfide.

**α,α-DIMETHYLBENZYL ISOBUTYRATE.** A synthetic fruit flavoring for beverages, ice cream, ices, candy, and baked goods. No known toxicity.

**DIMETHYLGLYOXAL.** See Diacetyl.

**DIMETHYLKETOL.** See Acetoin.

**2,4-DIMETHYLACETOPHENONE.** A synthetic grape, vanilla, and cream soda flavoring agent for beverages, ice cream, ices, candy, baked goods, and liquor. No known toxicity.

**α,α-DIMETHYLPHENETHYL ACETATE. Acetic Acid.** A synthetic cherry and honey flavoring agent for beverages, ice cream, ices, candy, baked goods, and chewing gum. No known toxicity.

**α,α-DIMETHYLPHENETHYL ALCOHOL.** A synthetic fruit flavoring agent for beverages, ice cream, ices, candy, baked goods, chewing gum, jellies, and gelatin desserts. No known toxicity.

**α,α-DIMETHYLPHENETHYL BUTYRATE. Butyric Acid.** A synthetic fruit flavoring for beverages, ice cream, ices, candy, baked goods, puddings, and gelatins. No known toxicity.

**α,α-DIMETHYLPHENETHYL FORMATE. Formic Acid.** A synthetic spice flavoring for beverages, ice cream, ices, and candy. See Formic Acid for toxicity.

**2,6-DINITRO-3-METHOXY-1-METHYL-4-TERT-BUTYL-BENZENE.** See Musk; Ambrette.

**DIOCTYL SODIUM SULFOSUCCINATE.** A waxlike solid, or dissolved in a solution it is used as a wetting agent in industrial, pharmaceutical, cosmetic, and food applications. In foods and beverages it is used as a dispersing and solubilizing agent for gums, cocoa, and various hard-to-wet materials. Also a wetting agent in the cleaning of fruits, vegetables, and leafy plant material. Used in nonalcoholic beverages and sherbets at a rate not to exceed .5 percent of the weight of such ingredients. It is a stool softener in laxatives. Conjunctival irritation may result from use in ophthalmic preparations.

**DIOXYMETHYLENE PROTOCATECHUIC ALDEHYDE.** See Piperonal.

**DIPENTENE.** See d-Limonene.

**DIPHENYL KETONE.** See Benzophenone.

**1,3-DIPHENYL-2-PROPANONE.** A synthetic fruit, honey, and nut flavoring agent for beverages, ice cream, ices, candy, and baked goods. No known toxicity.

**DIPOTASSIUM PHOSPHATE.** A sequestrant, a white grain, very soluble in water. Used as a buffering agent to control the degree of acidity in antifreeze solutions and in the preparation of nondairy powdered coffee creams and in cheeses up to 3 percent by weight of cheese. It is a saline cathartic. No known toxicity. GRAS.

**DIPROPYL DISULFIDE.** A synthetic flavoring agent. Colorless, insoluble in water. Occurs naturally in onion. Used in imitation onion flavoring for pickle products and baked goods. No known toxicity.

**DIPROPYL KETONE.** See 4-Heptanone.

**DISODIUM CYANODITHIOMIDOCARBONATE.** Bacteria-killing component in the processing of sugar cane. Any substance that releases the cyanide ion can cause poisoning. Sodium cyanide is one of the swiftest poisons known.

**DISODIUM GUANYLATE.** A flavor intensifier believed to be more effective than sodium inosinate and sodium glutamate. It is the disodium salt of 5′-guanylic acid, widely distributed in nature as a precursor of RNA and DNA. Can be isolated from certain mushrooms. No known toxicity.

**DISODIUM 5′-INOSINATE.** Flavor potentiator (*see*), odorless and colorless, or white crystal or powder, with a characteristic taste. See Inosinate.

**DISODIUM PHOSPHATE (DIBASIC).** A sequestrant (*see*) used in evaporated milk, up to .1 percent by weight of finished product; in macaroni and noodle products at not less than .5 percent nor more than 1 percent. It is used an an emulsifier up to 3 percent by weight in specified cheeses. Cleared by the U.S. Department of Agriculture's Meat Inspection Department to prevent cooked-out juices in cured hams, pork shoulders and loins, canned hams, chopped hams, and bacon (5 percent in the pickling and 5 percent injected into the product). Used as a buffer to adjust acidity in chocolate products, beverages, sauces, and toppings, enriched farina. Incompatible with alkaloids. It is a mild saline cathartic and has been used in phosphorous deficiency treatment. It may cause mild irritation to the skin and mucous membranes, and can cause purging. GRAS.

**DISODIUM 5′RIBONUCLEOTIDES.** Flavor potentiators (*see*), odorless, in white crystals or powder, having a characteristic taste. See Inosinate.

**DISTARCH PHOSPHATE.** A modified starch (*see*) commonly used in baby foods. The final report to the FDA of the Select Committee on GRAS Substances stated in 1980 that there is no evidence in the available information that it is a hazard to the public when used as it is now and it should continue its GRAS status with limitations on amounts that can be added to food.

**DISTARCH PROPANOL.** A modified starch. The final report to the FDA of the Select Committee on GRAS Substances stated in 1980 that while no evidence in the available information on it demonstrates a hazard to the public at current use levels, uncertainties exist, requiring that additional studies be conducted. GRAS status continues while tests are being completed and evaluated.

**DISTILLED ACETYLATED MONOGLYCERIDES.** Food emulsifiers and binders in nutrient capsules and tablets to make them palatable; also food-coating agents. Use is "at level not in excess of the amount reasonably required to produce the intended effect." Cleared by the U.S.D.A. Meat Inspection Department as an emulsifier for shortening. No known toxicity.

**DITTANY OF CRETE.** A natural flavoring extracted from a small herb grown in Crete. Used in spice flavorings for beverages and baked goods. No known toxicity.

**γ-DODECALACTONE.** A synthetic flavoring, colorless, with a coconut odor that becomes butterlike in low concentrations. Used in butter, butterscotch, coconut, fruit, maple, and nut flavorings for beverages, ice cream, ices, candy, baked goods, gelatin desserts, puddings, and jellies. No known toxicity.

**δ-DODECALACTONE.** A synthetic flavoring. Occurs naturally in butter, cream, and milk. Used in butter, fruit, and pear flavorings for candy, baked goods, oleomargarine, and toppings. Not to exceed 20 ppm in oleomargarine. No known toxicity.

**DODECANOIC ACID.** See Lauric Acid.

**2-DODECENAL.** A synthetic flavoring agent occurring naturally in oranges. Used in citrus flavoring for beverages, ice cream, ices, candy, and baked goods. No known toxicity.

**DODECOIC ACID.** See Lauric Acid.

**DOG GRASS EXTRACT.** A natural flavoring extract used in maple flavoring for beverages, ice cream, ices, candy, and baked goods. Derives its name from the fact that it is eaten by sick dogs. No known toxicity for humans. GRAS.

**DRACO RUBIN EXTRACT.** See Dragon's Blood Extract.

**DRAGON'S BLOOD EXTRACT.** The resinous secretion of the fruit of trees grown in Sumatra, Borneo, and India. Almost odorless and tasteless and available in the form of red sticks, pieces, or cakes. Makes a bright crimson powder. Used in bitters flavoring for beverages. Also used to color lacquers and varnishes. No known toxicity.

**DRAYLIS ACID.** See Benzoic Acid.

**DRIED SORGHUM GRAIN SYRUP.** A corn syrup substitute produced from the starch of sorghum grain. See Sorghum.

**DRIED YEAST.** A dietary source of folic acid. Used to enrich farina, cornmeals, corn grits, and bakery products. Dried yeast is cleared for use in food provided the total folic acid content of the yeast does not exceed .04 milligram per gram of yeast. Nontoxic.

**DRY MILK, NONFAT.** See Nonfat Dry Milk.

**DULSE.** A natural flavoring extract from red seaweed. Used as a food condiment. No known toxicity. GRAS.

# E

**ELDER FLOWERS.** A natural flavoring from the small white flowers of a shrub or small tree. Used in fruit, wine, and spice flavorings for beverages, ice cream, ices, candy, baked goods, and wine. The leaves, shoot, and bark can cause nausea, vomiting, and diarrhea. GRAS.

**ELEMI.** An oily resin derived from the tropical trees. The *gum* is used in fruit flavoring for beverages, ice cream, ices, candy, and baked goods. The *oil* is used in citrus, fruit, vermouth, and spice flavorings for beverages, ice cream, ices, candy, baked goods, and soups. The *resins* are used industrially for making varnishes and inks. No known toxicity.

**ELETTERIA CARDAMOMUM.** See Cardamom.

**EMOLLIENT.** A substance which has a soothing, softening effect on the skin.

**EMULSIFIERS.** Widely used additives used to stabilize a mixture and to ensure consistency. They make chocolate more mixable with milk and keep puddings from separating. One of the most widely used emulsifiers is lecithin (*see*) and another is polysorbate 60 (*see*). Di- and mono-glycerides (*see both*) are also used in many products.

**EMULSION.** An emulsion is a mixture of two or more normally non-mixable liquids shaken so thoroughly together as to appear homogenized, for example, as is done with salad dressing. Most oils form emulsions with water.

**ENRICHED.** A food term indicating that the original nutrients removed during the processing of a particular product have been restored, at least in part.

**ENZYMATICALLY HYDROLYZED PROTEIN.** Enzymes are used to break down the protein in solution. The final report to the FDA of the Select Committee on GRAS Substances stated in 1980 that it should continue its GRAS status with no limitations other than good manufacturing practices.

**EPICHLOROHYDRIN.** A modifier for food starches that the FDA permits to be used up to a level of 0.3 percent in starch. It is also used as a solvent for cosmetic resins and nitrocellulose and in the manufacture of varnishes, lacquers, and cements for celluloid articles. A colorless liquid with an odor resembling chloroform, it is a strong skin irritant. There may be 50,000 workers exposed to epichlorohydrin, according to OSHA. A two-year study of workers who had been exposed to the substance for six months or more before January 1966 showed an increase in the incidence of cancer. Chronic exposure is known to cause kidney damage in humans A 30-minute exposure to ambient air concentrations of 8,300 ppm was lethal to mice. Poisoned animals showed cyanosis, muscular relaxation or paralysis, convulsions, and death. Germany regulates it as a known carcinogen.

**1,8-EPOXY-*p*-MENTHANE.** See Eucalyptol.

**EQUISETIC ACID.** See Aconitic Acid.

**ERIGERON CANADENSIS.** See Erigeron Oil.

**ERIGERON OIL. Horseweed. Fleabane Oil.** Derived from the leaves and tops of a plant grown in the northern and central United States. Used in fruit and spice flavorings for beverages, ice cream, ices, candy, baked goods, and sauces. No known toxicity.

**ERIODICTYON CALIFORNICUM.** See Yerba Santa Fluid Extract.

**ERYTHORBIC ACID. Isoascorbic Acid.** White, slightly yellow crystals, which darken on exposure to light. An antioxidant used in pickling brine at a rate of 7.5 ounces per 100 gallons; in meat products at the rate of ¾ ounce per hundred pounds; in beverages; baked goods; cured cuts and cured pulverized products to accelerate color fixing in curing, to ¾ ounce per 100 pounds. Isoascorbic acid contains one-twentieth of the Vitamin C activity of ascorbic acid (*see*). Nontoxic. The final report to the FDA of the Select Committee on GRAS Substances stated in 1980 that it should continue its GRAS status with no limitations other than good manufacturing practices.

**ERYTHROSINE.** See FD and C Red No. 3.

**ERYTHROXYLON COCA.** See Coca Leaf Extract (Decocainized).

**ESSENCE.** An extract of a substance that retains its fundamental or most desirable properties in concentrated form, such as a flavoring or fragrance.

**ESSENTIAL OIL.** The oily liquid obtained from plants through a variety of processes. The essential oil usually has the taste and smell of the original plant. Essential oils are called volatile because most of them are easily vaporized. The two theories offered for calling such oils essential are (1) the oils were believed essential to life and (2) that they were the "essence" of the plant. A teaspoon may cause illness in an adult and less than an ounce may kill.

**ESTRAGOLE.** A colorless to light yellow oily liquid occurring naturally in anise, anise star, basil, estragon oil, and pimento oil. Used as a synthetic fruit, licorice, anise, and spice flavoring agent for beverages, ice cream, ices, baked goods, chewing gum, and condiments. No known toxicity. GRAS.

**ESTRAGON. Tarragon.** A flavoring agent from the oil of leaves of a plant native to Eurasia and used in fruit, licorice, liquor, root beer, and spice flavorings for beverages, ice cream, ices, candy, baked goods, condiments, meats, and liquors. GRAS.

**ETHANAL.** See Acetaldehyde; Heptanal.

**ETHANOIC ACID.** See Acetic Acid.

**ETHANOL.** An alcohol used as a solvent in candy, candy glaze, beverages, ice cream, ices, baked goods, liquors, sauces, and gelatin desserts. See Ethyl Alcohol for toxicity. GRAS.

**ETHANTHALDEHYDE.** See Heptanal.

**ETHANTHIC ALCOHOL.** See Heptyl Alcohol.

**ETHANTHYL ALCOHOL.** See Heptyl Alcohol.

**ETHONE.** See 1-(*p*-Methoxyphenyl)-1-Penten-3-One.

**ETHANOLAMINES.** Widely used as surfactants (*see*), these are compounds—monoethanolamine, diethanolamine, and triethanolamine—that have low melting points. They are colorless and solid and readily absorb water to form viscous liquids. They are soluble in both water and alcohol. Ethanolamines have an ammonia smell and are strong bases (*see*). Used in cosmetics, soaps, and detergents, they are popular emulsifying agents in foods. Very large quantities are required for a lethal oral dose in mice (2,149 milligrams per kilogram of body weight). They have been used medicinally as sclerosal agents for varicose veins and can be irritating to the skin if very alkaline.

**ETHOVAN.** See Ethyl Vanillin.

*p*-**ETHOXYBENZALDEHYDE.** A synthetic fruit and vanilla flavoring agent for beverages, ice cream, ices, candy, and baked goods. No known toxicity.

**ETHOXYLATE.** An ethyl (*see*) and oxygen compound is added to an additive to make it less or more soluble in water, depending upon the mixture. Ethoxylate acts as an emulsifier.

**ETHOXYLATED MONO- AND DI-GLYCERIDES.** Dough conditioners in bread used to increase the volume of the loaf. See Glycerols.

**ETHYL ACETATE. Acetic Acid.** A clear, volatile, flammable liquid with a fruity odor, occurring naturally in apples, bananas, grape juice (Concord), grapes, pineapple, raspberries, and strawberries. It is employed as a synthetic flavoring agent in blackberry, raspberry, strawberry, butter, lemon, apple, banana, cherry, grape, peach, pineapple, brandy, muscatel, rum, whiskey, mint, almond, and cream soda flavorings for beverages, ice cream, ices, baked goods, chewing gum, gelatins, puddings, and liquor. Industrially used in solvents, varnishes, and artificial leather. It is a mild local irritant and central nervous system depressant. Used medically to break up intestinal gas and as a stimulant to revive persons who have fainted. Its vapor is irritating. GRAS.

**ETHYL ACETOACETATE. Acetoacetic Ester.** A synthetic flavoring that occurs naturally in strawberries. Pleasant odor. Used in loganberry, strawberry, apple, apricot, cherry, peach, liquor, and muscatel flavorings for beverages, ice cream, ices, candy, baked goods, chewing gum, and gelatin desserts. Moderately irritating to skin and mucous membranes.

**ETHYL ACETONE.** See 2-Pentanone.

**ETHYL 2-ACETYL-3-PHENYLPROPIONATE.** A synthetic fruit flavoring agent for beverages, ice cream, ices, and candy. No known toxicity.

**ETHYL ACONITATE. Aconitic Acid.** A synthetic fruit, liquor, and rum flavoring agent for beverages, ice cream, ices, candy, baked goods, and gelatin deserts. No known toxicity.

**ETHYL ACRYLATE.** A synthetic flavoring agent that occurs naturally in pineapple and raspberries. Used in fruit, liquor, and rum flavorings for beverages, ice cream, candy, baked goods, and chewing gum. Also used in the manufacture of water-resistant paint, paper coating, and leather finishes. Highly irritating to the eyes, skin, and mucous membranes and may cause lethargy and convulsions if concentrated vapor is inhaled. The final report to the FDA of the Select Committee on GRAS Substances stated in 1980 that it should continue its GRAS status with no limitations other than good manufacturing practices.

**ETHYL ALCOHOL.** Contains ethanol (*see*), grain alcohol, and neutral spirits and is used as a solvent in candy glaze, beverages, ices, ice cream, candy, baked goods, liquors, sauces, and gelatin desserts. It is rapidly absorbed through the gastric and intestinal mucosa. For ingestion, within a few minutes, the fatal dose in adults is considered to be one and one half to two pints of whiskey (40 to 55 percent ethyl alcohol). It was approved in 1976 for use in pizza crusts to extend handling and storage life.

**ETHYL *p*-ANISATE.** A synthetic flavoring agent, colorless to slightly yellow, liquid, with a light fruity smell. Used in berry, fruit, grape, licorice, anise, liquor, rum, and vanilla flavorings for beverages, ice cream, ices, candy, and baked goods. No known toxicity.

**ETHYL ANTHRANILATE.** A synthetic flavoring agent, clear, colorless to amber liquid, with an odor of orange blossoms. Used in berry, mandarin, orange, floral, jasmine, neroli, fruit, grape, peach, and raisin flavorings for beverages, ice cream, ices, candy, baked goods, gelatin desserts, and chewing gum. No known toxicity.

**ETHYL BENZENECARBOXYLATE.** See Ethyl Benzoate.

**ETHYL BENZOATE. Ethyl Benzenecarboxylate.** A synthetic flavoring agent, almost insoluble in water, with a pleasant odor. Used in currant, raspberry, strawberry, fruit, cherry, grape, liquor, nut, walnut, and vanilla flavorings for beverages, ice cream, ices, candy, baked goods, gelatin desserts, chewing gum, and liquors. No known toxicity.

**ETHYL BENZOYLACETATE.** A synthetic fruit flavoring agent for beverages, ice cream, ices, candy, and baked goods. It becomes yellow when exposed to light. Pleasant odor. No known toxicity.

**ETHYL BENZYL ACETOACETATE.** See Ethyl 2-Acetyl-3-Phenyl-propionate.

**α-ETHYL BENZYL BUTYRATE.** A synthetic fruit flavoring agent for beverages, ice cream, ices, candy, and baked goods. No known toxicity.

**2-ETHYL BUTYL ACETATE.** A synthetic fruit flavoring agent for beverages, ice cream, ices, and candy. No known toxicity.

**ETHYL BUTYL KETONE.** See 3-Heptanone.

**ETHYL BUTYRATE. Butyric Acid.** A synthetic flavoring agent, colorless, with a pineapple odor. Found naturally in apples and strawberries. In alcoholic solution it is known as pineapple oil. Used in blueberry, raspberrry, strawberry, butter, caramel, cream, orange, banana, cherry, grape, peach, pineapple, rum, walnut, and eggnog flavorings for beverages, ice cream, ices, candy, baked goods, gelatins, puddings, and chewing gum (1,400 ppm). No known toxicity. GRAS.

**ETHYL CAPRATE.** See Cognac Oil.

**ETHYL CAPRYLATE.** See Cognac Oil.

**ETHYL CARVACROL.** See Carvacryl Ethyl Ether.

**ETHYL CELLULOSE.** White granules prepared from wood pulp or chemical cotton and used as a binder and filler in dry vitamin preparations up to 35 percent; chewing gum up to .025 percent, and in confectionery up to .012 percent. Also used in the manufacture of plastics and lacquers. No known toxicity. The final report to the FDA of the Select Committee on GRAS Substances stated in 1980 that it should continue its GRAS status for packaging with no limitations other than good manufacturing practices.

**ETHYL CINNAMATE. Cinnamic Acid.** An almost colorless, oily liquid with a faint cinnamon odor, used as a synthetic flavoring in raspberry, strawberry, cherry, grape, peach, plum, spice, cinnamon, and vanilla flavorings for beverages, ice cream, ices, candy, baked goods, gelatin desserts, and chewing gum. Also a fixative for perfumes. No known toxicity.

**ETHYL CITRATE.** A bitter, oily sequestrant used in dried egg whites. No known toxicity. See Sequestrants.

**ETHYL CYCLOHEXANEPROPIONATE.** A synthetic pineapple flavoring agent for beverages, ice cream, ices, candy, and baked goods. No known toxicity.

**ETHYL DECANOATE. Decanoic Acid.** A synthetic flavoring occurring naturally in green and white cognac oils. Used in strawberry, cherry, grape, pineapple, liquor, brandy, cognac, and rum flavorings for beverages, ice cream, ices, candy, baked goods, gelatin desserts, and liquors. No known toxicity.

**ETHYL DODECANOATE.** See Ethyl Laurate.

**ETHYL FORMATE. Formic Acid.** A colorless, flammable liquid with a distinct odor occurring naturally in apples and coffee extract. Used as a yeast and mold inhibitor and as a fumigant for bulk and packaged raisins and dried currants; fungicide for cashew nuts, cereals, tobacco, and dried fruits. Also a synthetic flavoring agent for blueberry, raspberry, strawberry, butter, butterscotch, apple, apricot, banana, cherry, grape, peach, plum, pineapple, tutti-frutti, brandy, rum, sherry, and whiskey flavorings for beverages, ice cream, ices, candy, baked goods, liquor, gelatin, and chewing gum. Irritating to the skin and mucous membranes, and in high concentrations it is narcotic. The final report to the FDA of the Select Committee on GRAS Substances stated in 1980 that it should continue its GRAS status with no limitations other than good manufacturing practices. See Formic Acid for further toxicity.

**ETHYL 2-FURANPROPRIONATE.** A synthetic raspberry, apple, cherry, and pineapple flavoring agent for beverages, ice cream, ices, candy, and baked goods. No known toxicity.

**ETHYL FURYLPROPIONATE.** See Ethyl 2-Furanpropionate.

**4-ETHYL GUAIACOL.** A synthetic coffee and fruit flavoring agent for beverages, ice cream, ices, and gelatin desserts. No known toxicity.

**ETHYL HEPTANOATE.** A synthetic flavoring agent, colorless, with a fruity, winelike odor and taste, and a burning aftertaste. Used in blueberry, strawberry, butter, butterscotch, coconut, apple, cherry, grape, melon, peach, pineapple, plum, vanilla, cheese, nut, rum, brandy, and cognac flavorings for beverages, ice cream, ices, candy, baked goods, gelatin desserts, chewing gum, and liqueurs. No known toxicity.

**2-ETHYL-2-HEPTENAL.** A synthetic pineapple flavoring agent for beverages and candy. No known toxicity.

**ETHYL HEXADECANOATE.** See Ethyl Palmitate.

**ETHYL 2,4-HEXADIENOATE.** See Ethyl Sorbate.

**ETHYL HEXANOATE.** A synthetic flavoring agent that occurs naturally in apples, pineapples, and strawberries. Used in fruit, rum, nut, and cheese flavorings for beverages, ice cream, ices, candy, baked goods, gelatin desserts, chewing gum, and jelly. No known toxicity.

**ETHYL α-HYDROXYPROPIONATE.** See Ethyl Lactate.

**ETHYL ISOBUTYRATE. Isobutyric Acid.** A synthetic strawberry, fruit, cherry, and butter flavoring agent for beverages, ice cream, ices, candy, baked goods, gelatin desserts, and toppings. No known toxicity.

**ETHYL ISOVALERATE. Isovaleric Acid.** A synthetic flavoring agent used in alcoholic solution for pineapple flavoring for beverages, ice cream, ices, candy, baked goods, gelatin desserts, and chewing gum. No known toxicity.

**ETHYL LACTATE. Lactic Acid.** A synthetic flavoring agent, colorless, with a characteristic odor. Used in strawberry, butter, butterscotch, coconut, grape, rum, maple, cheese, and nut flavorings for beverages, ice cream, candy, baked goods, gelatin deserts, chewing gum (3,100 ppm), syrup, and brandy (1,000 ppm). Used also as a solvent for cellulose acetate and nitrocellulose, which are used in the manufacture of explosives. No known toxicity.

**ETHYL LAURATE.** A synthetic flavoring agent, colorless, oily, with a light, fruity odor. Insoluble in water; very soluble in alcohol. Used in berry, coconut, fruit, grape, liquor, cognac, rum, nut, spice, nutmeg, and cheese flavorings for beverages, ice cream, ices, candy, baked goods, gelatin desserts, chewing gum, and liqueurs. No known toxicity.

**ETHYL LEVULINATE. Levulinic Acid.** A synthetic apple flavoring agent for beverages, ice cream, ices, candy, and baked goods. No known toxicity.

**ETHYL MALATE.** See Diethyl Malate.

**4-ETHYL-2-METHOXYPHENOL.** See 4-Ethyl Guaiacol.

**ETHYL *trans*-2-METHYL-2-BUTENOATE.** See Ethyl Tiglate.

**ETHYL 2-METHYLBUTYRATE.** A synthetic fruit flavoring agent for beverages, ice cream, ices, and candy. No known toxicity.

**ETHYL 3-METHYL-3-PHENYLGLYCIDATE. Strawberry Aldehyde.** A synthetic berry, loganberry, raspberry, strawberry, coconut, fruit, cherry, grape, pineapple, liquor, and wine flavoring agent for beverages, ice cream, ices, candy, baked goods, gelatin, pudding, and chewing gum. Caused growth retardation in rats, particularly males, and testicular atrophy. Females showed paralysis of hindquarters and deterioration of muscles. GRAS.

**ETHYL MYRISTATE.** A synthetic coconut, fruit, honey, and cognac flavoring agent for beverages, ice cream, ices, candy, baked goods, and liqueurs. No known toxicity.

**ETHYL NITRITE. Sweet Spirit of Niter. Spirit of Nitrous Ether.** A synthetic flavoring agent, colorless or yellowish liquid with a characteristic odor and a burning, sweetish taste. Used in strawberry, cherry, pineapple, liquor, brandy, and rum flavorings for beverages, ice cream, ices, candy, baked goods, chewing gum, syrup, and icings. It may cause methemoglobinemia, in which oxygen is diminished in the red blood cells, low blood pressure, and, when it is in a high concentration, narcosis.

**ETHYL NONANOATE. Nonanoic Acid.** A synthetic fruit and rum flavoring agent for beverages, ice cream, ices, candy, baked goods, gelatin desserts, chewing gum, icings, and liqueurs. No known toxicity.

**ETHYL 2-NONYNOATE.** A synthetic berry, fruit and melon flavoring agent for beverages, ice cream, ices, candy, and baked goods. No known toxicity.

**ETHYL OCTANOATE. Octanoic Acid.** A synthetic flavoring agent that occurs naturally in both cognac green and cognac white oils. Used in strawberry, butter, citrus, apple, pineapple, rum, nut, and cheese flavorings for beverages, ice cream, ices, candy, baked goods, gelatin desserts, and chewing gum. No known toxicity.

**ETHYL OCTYNE CARBONATE.** See Ethyl 2-Nonynoate.

**ETHYL OLEATE. Oleic Acid.** A synthetic flavoring agent, yellowish, oily, insoluble in water. Used in butter and fruit flavorings for beverages, ice cream, ices, candy, baked goods, gelatin desserts, and puddings. No known toxicity.

**ETHYL 3-OXOBUTANOATE.** See Ethyl Acetoacetate.

**ETHYL OXYHYDRATE.** See Rum Ether.

**ETHYL PALMITATE. Ethyl Hexadecanoate.** A synthetic butter and rum flavoring agent for ice cream, ices, candy, and baked goods. No known toxicity.

**ETHYL PHENYLACETATE. Phenylacetic Acid.** A synthetic flavoring agent, colorless or nearly colorless liquid, with a pleasant odor. Used in butter, honey, apricot, and cherry flavorings for beverages, ice cream, ices, candy, baked goods, and syrups. No known toxicity.

**ETHYL PHENYLACRYLATE.** See Ethyl Cinnamate.

**ETHYL 4-PHENYLBUTYRATE.** A synthetic fruit flavoring agent for beverages and candy. No known toxicity.

**ETHYL 3-PHENYLGLYCIDATE.** A synthetic berry, strawberry, fruit, and cherry flavoring agent for beverages, ice cream, ices, candy, baked goods, and gelatin desserts. No known toxicity.

**ETHYL 3-PHENYLPROPENOATE.** See Ethyl Cinnamate.

**ETHYL 3-PHENYLPROPIONATE.** A synthetic fruit flavoring agent for beverages, ice cream, ices, candy, and baked goods. No known toxicity.

**ETHYL 1-PROPENE-1,2,3-TRICARBOXYLATE.** See Ethyl Aconitate.

**ETHYL PROPIONATE. Propionic Acid.** A synthetic flavoring agent, colorless, transparent liquid, with a fruity odor. Occurs naturally in apples. Used in butter, fruit, and rum flavorings for beverages, ice cream, ices, candy, baked goods, gelatin desserts, and chewing gum (1,100 ppm). No known toxicity.

**ETHYL PYRUVATE. Pyruvic Acid.** A synthetic chocolate, fruit, rum, maple, and spice flavoring agent for beverages, ice cream, ices, candy, and baked goods. No known toxicity.

**ETHYL SALICYLATE. Salicylic Ether.** A synthetic flavoring agent that occurs naturally in strawberries, and has a pleasant odor. Used in fruit, root beer, sassafras, and wintergreen flavorings for beverages, ice cream, ices, candy, baked goods, chewing gum, gelatins, and puddings. At one time it was given medically to rheumatics. May interact with harmful results with medications such as anticoagulants, antidepressants, and medications for cancer such as Methotrexate. May cause allergic reaction in persons allergic to salicylates (*see*).

**ETHYL SEBACATE.** See Diethyl Sebacate.

**ETHYL SORBATE.** A synthetic fruit flavoring agent for beverages, ice cream, ices, candy, and baked goods. No known toxicity.

**ETHYL TETRADECANOATE.** See Ethyl Myristate.

**ETHYL TIGLATE. Tiglic Acid.** A synthetic raspberry, strawberry, pineapple, and rum flavoring agent for beverages, ice cream, ices, candy, and baked goods. No known toxicity.

**ETHYL 10-UNDECENOATE.** A synthetic coconut, fruit, cognac, and nut flavoring agent for beverages, ice cream, ices, candy, baked goods, and liquor. No known toxicity.

**ETHYL VALERATE. Valeric Acid.** A synthetic butter, apple, apricot, peach, and nut flavoring agent for beverages, ice cream, ices, candy, baked goods, gelatin desserts, and chewing gum. No known toxicity.

**ETHYL VANILLIN.** Colorless flakes with a stronger odor and taste than vanillin (*see*). Used as a synthetic flavoring in raspberry, strawberry, butter, butterscotch, caramel, rum butter, chocolate, cocoa, citrus, coconut, macaroon, cola, fruit, cherry, grape, honey, liquor, muscatel, rum, maple, nut, pecan, root beer, vanilla, and cream soda for beverages, ice cream, ices, candy, baked goods, gelatin desserts, puddings, chewing gum, imitation vanilla extract (28,000 ppm), liquor, icings, and toppings. Also used in perfumery. Caused mild skin irritaton in humans. In rats, it produced a reduction in growth rate and heart, kidney, liver, lung, spleen, and stomach injuries. GRAS.

**ETHYLACETIC ACID.** See Butyric Acid.

**2-ETHYLBUTYRALDEHYDE.** A synthetic chocolate flavoring agent for beverages, ice cream, ices, candy, and baked goods. No known toxicity.

**2-ETHYLBUTYRIC ACID.** A synthetic fruit, nut, and walnut flavoring agent for beverages, ice cream, ices, candy, and baked goods. No known toxicity.

**ETHYLENE DICHLORIDE (EDC). Dutch Liquid. 1,2-Dichloroethane. Ethylene Chloride.** Derived from the action of chlorine on ethylene, it is a solvent used in spice oleoresins (*see*) up to .005 percent, and for fats, oils, waxes, gums, and resins (*see*). Used in making tobacco extract. It burns with a smoky flame. Has a pleasant odor and sweet taste, but its vapors are irritating. Deaths due to liver and kidney injury following ingestion of large amounts (30 to 70 grams) have been reported. Clouding of the eyes, hemorrhages, and destruction of the adrenal cortex have been reported in humans and dogs. Annual production in the United States is now estimated at about 10 billion pounds—the sixteenth largest of all chemicals. EDC has been found in human milk and in the exhaled breath of nursing mothers who were exposed to the chemical. In carcinogenesis testing by the National Cancer Institute, this compound caused stomach cancers, vascularized (bloody) cancers of multiple organs, and cancers beneath the skin in male rats. Female rats exposed to EDC developed mammary cancers—in some high-dose animals as early as the twentieth week of the study. The chemical also caused breast cancers as well as uterine cancers in female mice and respiratory-tract cancers in both male and female mice.

**ETHYLENE OXIDE-METHYL FORMATE MIXTURE.** A mold and yeast control agent in dried and glacéed fruits. Ethylene oxide is highly irritating to the mucous membranes and eyes. High concentrations may cause pulmonary edema. Inhalation of methyl formate vapor produces nasal and eye irritation, retching, narcosis, and death from pulmonary irritation. Exposure to 1 percent vapor for 2½ hours or 5 percent vapor for ½ hour is lethal.

**ETHYLENEDIAMINE.** Colorless, clear, thick, and strongly alkaline. A component of a bacteria-killing agent in processing sugar cane. Also used as a solvent for casein (*see*), albumin, and shellac. Has been used as a urinary acidifier. May be irritating to the skin and mucous membranes and has been known to cause sensitization leading to asthma and allergic skin rashes.

**ETHYLENEDIAMINETETRAACETATE (EDTA).** A sequestrant (*see*) used in carbonated beverages. EDTA salts are used in crab meat (cooked and canned) to retard struvite (crystal) formation and promote color retention. It is also used in nonstandardized dressings. A chelating agent, EDTA is on the FDA list to be studied for possible harmful effects. It may cause errors in a number of laboratory tests including those for calcium, carbon dioxide, nitrogen, and muscular activity. According to a summary of the National Cancer Institute's tests of EDTA, when it was fed to rats and mice for two years, a variety of tumors occurred among test and control animals of both species, but the test did not indicate that any of the tumors observed in the animals were attributable to EDTA.

*trans*-1,2-ETHYLENEDICARBOXYLIC ACID. See Fumaric Acid.

**ETHYLFORMIC ACID.** See Propionic Acid.

**EUBATUS, RUBUS.** See Blackberry Bark Extract.

**EUCALYPTOL. Eucalyptus Oil.** A synthetic flavoring that occurs naturally in allspice, star anise, basil, bay and bay leaf extract, cajaput oil, calamus and calamus oil, caraway, laurel leaf oil, peppermint oil, and pimento oil. Eucalyptus oil is 70–80 percent active eucalyptol. Eucalyptol is used in mint flavorings for beverages, ice cream, ices, candy, baked goods, and chewing gum. Fatalities have followed ingestion of doses as small as 3 to 5 milliliters and recovery has occurred after doses as large as 20 to 30 milliliters. Symptoms of poisoning are epigastric burning with nausea, weakness, water retention, and delirium.

**EUCALYPTUS OIL. Dinkum Oil.** Volatile oil from the fresh leaves of an Australian dwarfish tree, cultivated in southern U.S. Colorless or pale yellow, smells like camphor, and has a pungent, spicy, cooling taste. Used in fruit, mint, root beer, spice, and ginger ale flavoring for beverages, ice cream, ices, candy, baked goods, and liquors. Has been used as an expectorant, vermifuge, and local antiseptic. As little as 1 milliliter has caused coma. Fatalities have followed doses as small as 3.5 milliliters. Symptoms include epigastric burning, with nausea. Symptoms have been reported to occur as long as two hours after ingestion.

**EUCHEUMA COTTONI EXTRACT.** A stabilizing and thickening agent in foods. Used in dairy products to suspend particles and for gelling. No known toxicity. See Hydrogenation.

**EUGENOL.** The main constituent of such natural sources as carnation, cinnamon leaf, and clove oils. Colorless to pale yellow liquid with a strong odor of cloves; spicy pungent taste. Darkens and thickens upon exposure to air. Used as a defoamer in yeast production, in the manufacture of vanilla, and in perfumery. It is a synthetic fruit, nut, and spice flavoring agent for beverages, ice cream, ices, candy, baked goods, gelatin desserts, chewing gum, meats (2,000 ppm), and condiments. Acts as a local antiseptic and anesthetic when applied topically to control a toothache. When ingested in an aqueous emulsion, it can cause vomiting and gastric secretion of mucin (stomach cells). Toxicity is similar to phenol, which is highly toxic. Death in laboratory animals given eugenol is due to vascular collapse. GRAS.

**EUGENYL ACETATE. Acetic Acid.** A synthetic berry, fruit, mint, spice, and vanilla flavoring agent for beverages, ice cream, ices, candy, baked goods, chewing gum, and condiments. No known toxicity.

**EUGENYL BENZOATE.** A synthetic fruit and spice flavoring agent for beverages, ice cream, ices, candy, and baked goods. No known toxicity.

**EUGENYL FORMATE. Formic Acid.** A synthetic spice flavoring agent used in condiments. See Formic Acid for toxicity.

**EUGENYL METHYL ETHER.** A synthetic raspberry, strawberry, fruit, spice, clove, and ginger flavoring agent for beverages, ice cream, ices, candy, baked goods, and jellies. No known toxicity.

**EVERNIA FURFURACEA.** See Oak Moss, Absolute.

**EVERNIA PRUNASTIC.** See Oak Moss, Absolute.

**EXALTOLIDE.** See $\omega$-Pentadecalactone.

**EXTRACT.** The solution that results from passing alcohol or an alcohol-water mixture through a substance. Examples would be the alcohol-water mixtures of vanilla, orange, or lemon extracts found in bottles among the spices and flavorings on the supermarket shelf.

# F ———————————————

**FARNESOL.** A flavoring agent that occurs naturally in ambrette seed, star anise, linden flowers, oil of musk seed, oils of citronella, rose, lemon grass, and balsam. Used in berry, apricot, banana, cherry, melon, peach, citrus, fruit, raspberry, and strawberry flavorings for beverages, ice cream, ices, baked goods, candy, and gelatin desserts. Also used in perfumery to emphasize the odor of sweet floral perfumes, such as lilac. No known toxicity.

**FAT.** The most concentrated source of food energy and very necessary to health. Fat deposits provide insulation and protection for body structure as well as a storehouse for energy. Food fats are carriers of fat-soluble vitamins and include certain essential unsaturated fatty acids (*see*). *Saturated fats* contain only single-bond carbon linkages and are the least active chemically. They are usually solid at room temperature. Most animal fats are saturated. The common saturated fats are acetic, butyric, caproic, caprylic, capric, lauric, myristic, palmitic, stearic, arachidic, behenic. Butterfat, coconut oil, and peanut oil are high in saturated fats. *Unsaturated fats* contain one or more double-bond carbon linkages and are usually liquid at room temperature. Vegetable oils and fish oils most frequently contain unsaturated fats. Among the unsaturated fats are caproleic, lauroleic, myristoleic, palmitoleic, oleic, petroselinic, vaccenic, linoleic, linolenic, elaeosstearic, gadoleic, arachidonic, erucic.

**FATTY ACIDS.** One or any mixture of liquid and solid acids, capric, caprylic, lauric, myristic, oleic, palmitic, and stearic. In combination with glycerin they form fat. Necessary for normal growth and skin. Commercially, used chiefly for making soaps and detergents. In foods they are used as emulsifiers, general food binders, lubricants, and defoamer components in the processing of beet sugar and yeast. *Polyglycerol esters* of fatty acids are prepared from edible fats, oils, corn, cottonseed, palm fruit, peanut, safflower, and soybean oils, lard, and tallow. Used as emulsifiers and defoaming agents in beet sugar and yeast production, and as lubricant binders and components in the manufacture of other food additives. Fatty acid *salts* (one or more of the aluminum, ammonium, calcium, magnesium, potassium, and sodium salts of all of the above fatty acids) are used as emulsifiers, binders, and anticaking agents. A *free fatty acid* (FFA) is the uncombined fatty acid present in a fat. Some raw oils may contain as much as 3 percent FFA. These are removed in the refining process and refined fats and oils ready for use as foods usually have extremely low FFA content. No known toxicity.

**FD AND C COLORS (Food Drug and Cosmetic Colors).** A color additive is a term to describe any dye, pigment, or other substance capable of coloring a food, drug, or cosmetic on any part of the human body. In 1900, there were more than 80 dyes used to color food. There were no regulations and the same dye used to color clothes could also be used to color candy. In 1906, the first comprehensive legislation for food colors was passed. There were only seven colors which, when tested, were shown to be composed of known ingredients which demonstrated no known harmful effects. Those colors were orange, erythrosine, ponceau 3R, amaranth, indigotine, naphthol yellow, and light green. A voluntary system of certification for batches of color dyes was set up. In 1938, new legislation was passed, superseding the 1906 act. The colors were given numbers instead of chemical names and every batch *had* to be certified. There were 15 food colors in use at the time. In 1950, children were made ill by certain coloring used in candy and popcorn. These incidents led to the delisting of FD and C Orange No. 1, Orange No. 2, and FD and C Red No. 32. Since that time, because of experimental evidence of possible harm, Red 1, Yellows 1, 2, 3, and 4 have also been delisted. Violet 1 was removed in 1973. In 1976, one of the most widely used of all colors, FD and C Red No. 2, was removed because it was found to cause tumors in rats. In 1976 Red No. 4 was banned for coloring maraschino cherries (its last use) and carbon black was also banned at the same time because it contains a cancer-causing agent. Earlier, in 1960, scientific investigations were required by law to determine the suitability of all colors in use for permanent listing. Citrus Red No. 2 (limited to 2 ppm) for coloring orange skins has been permanently listed; Blue No. 1, Red No. 3, Yellow No. 5, and Red No. 40 are permanently listed but without any restrictions. The other food coloring additives are still on the "temporary list." In 1959, the Food and Drug Administration approved the use of "lakes," in which the dyes have been mixed with alumina hydrate to make them insoluble. See FD and C Lakes. The safety of colors in food is now being questioned by the FDA and regulatory agencies in other countries as well as the World Health Organization. There are inconsistencies in safety data and in the banning of some colors which, in turn, affects international commerce.

**FD AND C BLUE NO. 1. Brilliant Blue.** A coal-tar derivative, it is used as a coloring in bottled soft drinks, gelatin desserts, ice cream, ices, dry drink powders, candy, confections, bakery products, cereals, and puddings. It may cause allergic reactions. It will produce malignant tumors at the site of injection in rats. On the FDA permanent list of color additives. Rated 1A for toxicology (completely vegetable). Carcinogen suspected. See FD and C Colors.

**FD AND C BLUE NO. 2. Indigotine. Indigo Carmine.** A dark-blue powder almost always containing sodium chloride or sulfate. Easily faded by light. Used in bottled soft drinks, bakery products, cereals, candy, confections, and dry drink powders. Also used as a dye in kidney tests and in testing milk. The World Health Organization gives it a toxicology rating of B—available data not entirely sufficient to meet requirements acceptable for food use. Permanently listed in 1983. See FD and C Colors.

**FD AND C CITRUS RED NO. 2.** Found in 1960 to damage internal organs and to be a weak cancer-causing agent. Used to color orange skins. The World Health Organization said the color has been shown to cause cancer and that toxicological data available were inadequate to allow the determination of a safe limit; they recommended that it not be used as a food color. The FDA ruled on October 28, 1971 that results of several rodent studies and one dog study using both oral and injected Citrus Red No. 2 showed either no adverse effect or no adverse effect levels. No abnormalities in urinary bladders were reported. The FDA noted that a paper presented in 1965 by the University of Otega Medical School reported a significant level of urinary bladder cancers in rodents fed the dye for up to 24 months. The FDA said that since slides of the tissues in photographs were not yet available for examination, and since there has been no confirmation of the studies, "the listing of Citrus Red 2 should remain unchanged until the Otega results can be confirmed by examination." See FD and C Colors.

**FD AND C GREEN NO. 1. Guinea Green B.** A dull, dark green powder used as coloring in bottled soft drinks. The certified color industry did not apply for the extension of this color because of small demand for its use, so it was automatically deleted from the list of color additives in 1966. Rated E by the World Health Organization, meaning it was found to be harmful and not to be used in food. See FD and C Colors.

**FD AND C GREEN NO. 2. Light Green S.F. Yellow.** Coloring used in bottled soft drinks. Because of lack of demand for this color, the certified color industry did not petition for extension and it was automatically deleted in 1966. It produces tumors at the site of injection under the skin of rats. See FD and C Colors.

**FD AND C GREEN NO. 3. Fast Green.** Used as coloring matter in mint-flavored jelly, frozen desserts, gelatin desserts, candy, confections, baking products, and cereals. Has been suspected of being a sensitizer in the allergic. On the FDA permanent list of approved color additives. Produces malignant tumors at the site of injection when introduced under the skin of rats. The World Health Organization gives it a toxicology rating of 1A, meaning completely acceptable. See FD and C Colors.

**FD AND C LAKES. Aluminum or Calcium Lakes.** Lakes are pigments prepared by combining FD and C colors with a form of aluminum or calcium, which makes the colors insoluble. Aluminum and calcium lakes are used in confection and candy products and for dyeing egg shells and other products that are adversely affected by water. See FD and C colors for toxicity.

**FD and C RED NO. 2. Amaranth.** Formerly one of the most widely used food and cosmetic colorings, it was removed from the market by the FDA in January 1976. It is a dark, reddish brown powder that turns bright red when mixed with fluid. A monoazo color (a dye made from diazonium and phenol), it was used in cereals, maraschino cherries, and desserts. The safety of this dye was questioned by American scientists for more than twenty years. Two Russian scientists found that FD and C Red No. 2 prevented some pregnancies and caused some stillbirths in rats. The FDA ordered manufacturers using the color to submit data on all food, drug, and cosmetic products containing it. Controversial tests at the FDA's Center for Toxicological Research in Arkansas showed that in high doses Red No. 2 caused a statistically significant increase in a variety of cancers in female rats. Red No. 2 was then banned in the United States in 1976 but not in Canada. See FD and C Colors.

**FD AND C RED NO. 3. Erythrosine.** A coal-tar derivative, it is used in canned fruit cocktail, fruit salad, cherry pie mix (up to .01 percent), maraschino cherries, gelatin desserts, ice cream, sherbets, candy, confectionery products, bakery products, cereals, and puddings. It is on the permanent list of color additives. It was reported in 1981 by NIH researchers that Red No. 3 may interfere with the neurotransmitters in the brain. Suspected carcinogen. See FD and C Colors.

**FD AND C RED NO. 4.** Banned by the FDA in 1964 when it was shown to damage the adrenal glands and bladders of dogs, the agency relented and put it on the provisional list for use in maraschino cherries. It is still in use in some drugs and cosmetics. It is a coal-tar dye. The World Health Organization gives it a rating of 4 E meaning it has been found to be harmful and should not be used in food. Banned in all foods in 1976 because experiments showed it caused urinary bladder polyps and atrophy of the adrenal glands. It was also banned in orally taken drugs but is still permitted in cosmetics for external use only. See FD and C Colors.

**FD and C RED NO. 40. Allura Red AC.** The newest and last general-purpose red coloring used in American foods, cosmetics, and drugs. It is an artificial dye produced by Allied Chemical and rapidly replaced the banned dye Red. No. 2. Although Red No. 40 was given a "permanent safety rating" by the FDA after 1971 laboratory tests conducted by Allied, the dye has since been banned as a potential carcinogen (1973).

**FD AND C VIOLET NO. 1.** Used as coloring matter in gelatin desserts, ice cream, sherbets, carbonated beverages, dry drink powders, candy, confections, bakery products, cereals, puddings, and as the dye used for the Department of Agriculture's meat stamp. A Canadian study in 1962 showed the dye caused cancer in 50 percent of the rats fed the dye in food. The FDA did not consider this valid evidence since the exact nature of the dye used could not be determined and all records and specimens are lost and not available for study. Furthermore, previous and subsequent studies have not confirmed evidence of Violet 1 causing cancer in rats. However, a two-year study with dogs did show noncancerous lesions on the dog's ears after being fed Violet 1. The FDA again felt the study was not adequate but that the ear lesions did appear to be dye-related and that perhaps two years may be too short a period to determine their eventual outcome. The FDA ruled on October 28, 1971, that Violet 1 should remain provisionally listed pending the outcome of a new dog study to be started as soon as possible and to last seven years. The FDA finally banned the use of Violet 1 in 1973. In 1976, however, the U.S. Department of Agriculture found that Violet 1 was still being used as a "denaturant" on carcasses, meats, and food products. The USDA ruled that any such use of mixing Violet 1 with any substance intended for food use will cause the final products to be "adulterated." See FD and C Colors.

**FD AND C YELLOW NO. 5. Tartrazine.** A coal-tar derivative, it is used as a coloring in prepared breakfast cereals, imitation strawberry jelly, bottled soft drinks, gelatin desserts, ice cream, sherbets, dry drink powders, candy, confections, bakery products, spaghetti, and puddings. Causes allergic reactions in persons sensitive to aspirin. The certified color industry petitioned for permanent listing of this color in February 1966, with no limitations other than good manufacturing practice. However, in February 1966, the FDA proposed the listing of this color with a maximum rate of use of 300 ppm in food. The color industry had objected to the limitation. Yellow No. 5 was thereafter permanently listed as a color additive without restrictions. Rated 1A by the World Health Organization—acceptable in food. It is estimated that half the aspirin-sensitive people plus 47,000 to 94,000 other individuals in the nation are sensitive to this dye. It is used in about 60 percent of both over-the-counter and prescription drugs. Efforts were made to ban this color in over-the-counter pain relievers, antihistamines, oral decongestants, and prescription antiinflammatory drugs. Aspirin-sensitive patients have been reported to develop life-threatening asthmatic symptoms when ingesting Yellow No. 5. When used in a food product, it is supposed to be listed by name since 1981. See FD and C Colors.

**FD AND C YELLOW NO. 6. Monoazo. Sunset Yellow FCF.** A coaltar dye used as coloring matter in carbonated beverages, gelatin desserts, dry drink powders, candy and confectionery products that do not contain oils and fats, bakery products, cereals, puddings, and tablets. May cause allergic reactions. Rated 1A by the World Health Organization—acceptable in food. On the FDA provisional list of approved color additives. See FD and C Colors.

**FENCHOL.** See Fenchyl Alcohol.

*d*-**FENCHONE.** A synthetic flavoring occurring naturally in common fennel (*see*). It is an oily liquid with a camphor smell and practically insoluble in water. Used in berry, liquor, and spice flavorings for beverages, ice cream, ices, candy, baked goods, and liquors. Used medically as a counterirritant.

**FENCHYL ALCOHOL.** A synthetic berry, lime, and spice flavoring agent in beverages, ice cream, ices, candy, and baked goods. No known toxicity.

**FENNEL.** A natural flavor extract from the dried ripe fruit of a variety of cultivated plants grown in Southern Europe and Western Asia. Colorless with the characteristic fennel taste. *Common fennel* is used as a sausage and spice flavoring for beverages, baked goods, condiments, and meats. *Sweet fennel* has the same function but includes ice cream, ices, candy. *Sweet fennel oil* is used in raspberry, fruit, licorice, anise, rye, sausage, root beer, sarsaparilla, spice, wintergreen, and birch beer flavorings for beverages, ice cream, ices, candy, baked goods, gelatin desserts, condiments, meats, and liquors. May cause a sensitivity to light.

**FENUGREEK. Greek Hay.** A natural flavoring from an annual herb grown in Southern Europe, North Africa, and India for the seeds used in making curry. Fenugreek is a butter, butterscotch, maple, black walnut, and spice flavoring agent for beverages, ice cream, candy, baked goods, condiments, meats, and syrups. The *extract (see)* is a butter, butterscotch, caramel, chocolate, coffee, fruit, maple, meat, black walnut, walnut, root beer, spice, and vanilla flavoring agent for beverages, ice cream ices, candy, baked goods, puddings, chewing gum, condiments, meats, syrups, pickles, liquors, and icings. The *oleoresin (see)* is a fruit, maple, and nut flavoring agent for beverages, ice cream, ices, candy, baked goods, puddings, and syrups. No known toxicity.

**FERRIC CHOLINE CITRATE.** See Iron Sources.

**FERRIC ORTHOPHOSPHATE.** See Iron Sources.

**FERRIC PHOSPHATE.** The final report to the FDA of the Select Committee on GRAS Substances stated in 1980 that there is no evidence in the available information that it is a hazard to the public when used as it is now and it should continue its GRAS status with limitations on the amounts that can be added to the food. See Iron Sources.

**FERRIC PYROPHOSPHATE.** See Iron Sources.

**FERRIC SODIUM PYROPHOSHATE.** The final report to the FDA of the Select Committee on GRAS Substances stated in 1980 that there is no evidence in the available information that it is a hazard to the public when used as it is now and it should continue its GRAS status with limitations on the amounts that can be added to food. See Iron Sources.

**FERROUS FUMARATE.** See Iron Sources.

**FERROUS GLUCONATE. Gluconic Acid. Iron Salt. Iron Gluconate. Ferronicum.** Used for food coloring, it is a yellowish gray. It is also used as a flavoring agent and to treat iron-deficiency anemia. It may cause gastrointestinal disturbances. When painted on mouse skin in 2,600-milligram doses per kilogram of body weight, it causes tumors.

**FERROUS LACTATE. Lactic Acid. Iron Salt. Iron Lactate.** Greenish-white crystals that have a slightly peculiar odor. It is derived from the interaction of calcium lactate with ferrous sulfate, or the direct action of lactic acid on iron filings. It is used as a food additive and dietary supplement. Causes tumors when injected under the skin of mice.

**FERROUS SULFATE.** See Iron Sources.

**FERULA ASSAFOETIDA.** See Asafetida.

**FIBER.** Commonly termed "bulk"—the indigestible carbohydrates, including cellulose, hemicellulose, and gums. Fiber is added to food to reduce calorie content, as a thickening agent, and a stabilizer. If an apple a day keeps the doctor away, it may be because of the fiber content. Scientists have suspected that the high intestinal cancer rate in the United States may be linked to the 80 percent decrease of consumption of fiber in the average diet during the past century. Essentially, there are three classes of fiber found in the fruit, leaves, stems, seeds, flowers, and roots of different plants. The first class is the insoluble cellulose found in the plant-cell wall. Some of the other polysaccharides constitute a second class and are also found in the cell wall (hemicellulose and pectic polyerms), in the endosperm of seeds (mucilages), or in the plant's surface (gums). The third class, the lignins, are noncarbohydrates that infiltrate and contribute to the death of the plant cell, which then becomes part of the woody reinforcing plant structure.

Enzymes from a number of the more than 400 kinds of bacteria in the human colon are capable of digesting many components of plant fiber. Doctors have found that the water-holding capacity of some fibers may be helpful in treating colon disease. The fiber's bile absorption properties might be used in modifying cholesterol metabolism. Plant fibers are also capable of binding trace metals and bile acids. These properties modify the action of the gut contents. Fibers pass through the gut somewhat like a sponge, probably altering metabolism in the intestine. The fibers appear to protect intestinal cells by removing foreign substances, such as carcinogens produced by charbroiling. Increased fiber consumption has been recommended for relief of some symptoms of diverticular disease, irritable bowel syndrome, and constipation.

**FICIN.** An enzyme occurring in the latex of tropical trees. A buff-colored powder with an acrid odor. Absorbs water. Concentrated and used as a meat tenderizer. Ten to twenty times more powerful than papain tenderizers. Used to clot milk, as a protein digestant in the brewing industry, and as a chillproofing agent in beer. Also, in cheese as a substitute for rennet in the coagulation of milk; and for removing casings from sausages. Can cause irritation to the skin, eyes, and mucous membranes and in large doses can cause purging.

**FILLED MILK.** A combination of skim milk and vegetable oil to replace milk fat. Usually has the same amount of protein and calories as whole milk. Used as a milk substitute. It often contains the high cholesterol fatty acids (*see*) of coconut oil. Nontoxic.

**FINOCHIO.** See Fennel.

**FISH OIL (HYDROGENATED).** A fatty oil from fish or marine mammals used in soapmaking. The final report to the FDA of the Select Committee on GRAS Substances stated in 1980 that it should continue its GRAS status for food packaging with no limitations other than good manufacturing practices.

**FIXATIVE.** A chemical which reduces the tendency of an odor or flavor to vaporize. Patchouly, for instance, fixes the flavor of cola beverages and undecyl aldehyde fixes citrus flavors.

**FLAVOR POTENTIATORS.** One of the newest and fastest growing categories of additives, potentiators enhance the total seasoning effect, generally without contributing any taste or odor of their own. They are effective in minute doses—in parts per million or even less. A potentiator produces no identifiable effect itself but exaggerates one's response. They alter the response of the sensory nerve endings on the tongue and in the nose. The first true potentiators in the United States were the 5'-nucleotides, which are derived from a natural seasoning long in use in Japan: small flakes of dry bonito (a tuna-like fish) are often added to modify and improve the flavor of soups, and from bonito a 5'-nucleotide, disodium inosinate (*see*), has been isolated and identified as a flavor potentiator. Another 5'-nucleotide is disodium guanylate (*see*), one of the newer additives on the market, which gives one a sensation of "fullness" and "increased viscosity" when eating. The product is advertised as being able to give diners a sense of "full-bodied flavor" when ingesting a food containing it.

**FLAVORING COMPOUND.** A flavoring composed of two or more substances. The substances may be natural or synthetic and they are usually closely guarded secrets. Normally, a flavoring compound is complete, that is, it is added to a food without any additional flavorings being necessary. A strawberry flavoring compound, for example, may contain 28 separate ingredients before it is complete.

**FLAVORINGS.** There are more than 2,000 flavorings added to foods, of which approximately 500 are natural and the rest synthetic. This is the largest category of additive. Lemon and orange are examples of natural flavorings, while benzaldehyde and methyl salicylate (*see both*) are examples from the laboratory.

**FLAXSEED.** The seed of the flax plant may be "hidden" in cereals and milk of cows fed flaxseed. It is also in flaxseed tea and the laxative Flaxolyn. It is a frequent allergen when ingested, inhaled, or in direct contact. Flaxseed is the source of linseed oil.

**FLEABANE OIL. Oil of Canada Fleabane. Erigeron Oil.** The pale yellow volatile oil from a fresh flowering herb. It takes its name from its supposed ability to drive away fleas. Used in fruit and spice flavorings for beverages, ice cream, ices, candy, baked goods, and sauce. No known toxicity.

**FLORENCE FENNEL.** See Fennel.

**FLUORINE SOURCES: Calcium Fluoride; Hydroflurosilicic Acid; Potassium Fluoride; Sodium Fluoride and Sodium Silicofluoride.** All have been used in the fluoridation of water. Fluorides cross the placental barrier and the effects on the fetus are unknown. New clinical evidence shows that kidney disturbance sometimes is due to the amount of fluoride it contributes to the blood.

**FOAM INHIBITOR.** An antifoaming agent such as dimethyl polysiloxane (*see*) used in chewing gum bases, soft drinks, and fruit juices to keep them from foaming. See Defoamer.

**FOAMING AGENT.** Used to help whipped topping peak when it is being whipped with cold milk. A commonly added foaming agent is sodium caseinate (*see*).

**FORMIC ETHER.** See Ethyl Formate.

**FORTIFIED.** Fortification of food refers to the addition of nutrients, such as Vitamin C to breakfast drinks and Vitamin D to milk. It actually increases the nutritional values of the original food.

**FRANKINCENSE.** Aromatic gum resin obtained from African and Asian trees and used chiefly as incense. For food use, see Olibanum Oil.

**FRUCTOSE. Fructopyranose, Beta-D.** A sugar occurring naturally in a large number of fruits and honey. It is the sweetest of the foodstuffs. It is also used as a medicine, preservative, common sugar, and to prevent sandiness in ice cream. Researchers at the General Clinical Research Center at the University of Colorado School of Medicine in Denver report that fructose is absorbed in the gastrointestinal tract more slowly than sugars like sucrose, which contain glucose. As a result, even though the body converts some fructose to glucose, 80 to 90 percent of the sugar is absorbed intact, and there is only a slight increase in blood glucose levels immediately after consumption. Fructose can be up to two times sweeter than sucrose. Recent advances in enzyme technology have made it possible to produce fructose on a commercial scale.

**FUMARIC ACID.** White, odorless, derived from many plants and essential to vegetable and animal tissue respiration; prepared industrially. An acidulant used as a leavening agent and a dry acid for dessert powders and confections (up to 3 percent). Also as apple, peach, and vanilla flavoring agent for beverages, baked goods (1,300 ppm), and gelatin desserts (3,600 ppm). Used in baked goods as an antioxidant and as a substitute for tartaric acid (*see*). No known toxicity. GRAS.

**2-FURALDEHYDE.** See Furfural.

**2-FURANACROLEIN.** See Furyl Acrolein.

**FURCELLERAN. Sodium, Calcium, Potassium, and Ammonium Salts.** Extracted from red seaweed grown in Northern European waters. The processed gum is a white, odorless powder soluble in water. Used as an emulsifier, stabilizer, and thickener in foods. It is a natural colloid and gelling agent. Also used in puddings and jams, in products for diabetics, as a carrier for food preservatives, and in bactericides. It is also used in over-the-counter drugs for weight reducing and toothpastes. On the FDA list of additives to be studied for mutagenic, teratogenic, subacute, and reproductive effects.

**FURFURAL.** Artificial ant oil. A synthetic flavoring that occurs naturally in angelica root oil, apples, coffee, peaches, skim milk (heated), oils of lime and lavender. Used in butter, butterscotch, caramel, coffee, fruit, brandy, rum, rye, molasses, nut, and cassia flavorings for beverages, ice cream, ices, candy, gelatin desserts, syrups (the biggest user: up to 30 ppm), and spirits. Used also as a solvent, insecticide, and fungicide. It irritates mucous membranes and acts on the central nervous system. Causes tearing and inflammation of eyes and throat irritation. Ingestion or absorption of .06 grams produces a persistent headache. Used continually, it leads to nervous disturbances and eye disorders (including photosensitivity).

**FURFURYL ACETATE. Acetic Acid.** A synthetic raspberry, fruit, spice, and ginger ale flavoring agent for beverages, ice cream, ices, candy, baked goods, and chewing gum. No known toxicity.

**FURFURYL ALCOHOL.** A synthetic flavoring obtained mainly from corncobs and roasted coffee beans. Has a faint burning odor and a bitter taste. Used in butter, butterscotch, caramel, coffee, fruit, and brandy flavorings for beverages, ice cream, ices, baked goods, and spirits. Also, an industrial solvent and wetting agent. It is poisonous.

**FURFURYL MERCAPTAN.** A synthetic flavoring that occurs naturally in coffee and is used in chocolate, fruit, coffee, and nut flavorings for beverages, ice cream, ices, candy, baked goods, gelatin desserts, and icings. No known toxicity.

**2-FURFURYLIDENE BUTYRALDEHYDE.** A synthetic fruit, liquor, rum, nut, and spice flavoring agent for beverages, ice cream, ices, candy, and baked goods. No known toxicity.

**FURYL ACETONE.** See (2-Furyl)-2-Propanone.

**FURYL ACROLEIN.** A synthetic coffee, fruit, cassia, and cinnamon flavoring agent for beverages, ice cream, ices, candy, baked goods, gelatin desserts, and puddings. No known toxicity.

**4-(2-FURYL)-3-BUTEN-2-ONE.** A synthetic nut, almond, and spice flavoring agent for beverages, ice cream, ices, candy, baked goods, and gelatin desserts. No known toxicity.

**(2-FURYL)-2-PROPANONE.** A synthetic fruit flavoring agent for ice cream, ices, candy, and baked goods. No known toxicity.

**FUSEL OIL (REFINED).** A synthetic flavoring that occurs naturally in cognac oil. It is also a product of carbohydrate fermentation to produce ethyl alchol (*see*) and varies widely in composition. Used in grape, brandy, cordial, rum, rye, Scotch, whiskey, and wine flavorings for beverages, ice cream, ices, candy, baked goods, chewing gum, gelatin desserts, puddings, and liquor. Commercial amyl alcohol (*see*), its major ingredient, is more toxic than ethyl alcohol, and as little as 30 milliliters has caused death. Smaller amounts can cause methemoglobinuria (blood cells in the urine) and kidney damage.

**GALANGAL ROOT. East Indian Root. Chinese Ginger.** The pungent, aromatic *oil* of the galangal root is a bitters, vermouth, spice, and ginger ale flavoring agent for beverages. The *extract* is a bitters, fruit, liquor, spice, and ginger ale flavoring agent for beverages, ice cream, ices, candy, baked goods, bitters, and liquors. Related to true ginger, it was formerly used in cooking and in medicine to treat colic. No known toxicity. GRAS.

**GALBANUM OIL.** A yellowish to green or brown aromatic bitter gum resin from an Asiatic plant used as incense. The *oil* is a fruit, nut, and spice flavoring for beverages, ice cream, ices, candy, and baked goods. The *resin* is a berry, fruit, nut, and spice flavoring for beverages, ice cream, ices, candy, baked goods, and condiments. Has been used medicinally to break up intestinal gas and as an expectorant. No known toxicity.

**GALLIC ACID.** See Propyl Gallate.

**GALLOTANNIC ACID.** See Tannic Acid.

**GAMBIR CATECHU.** See Catechu Extract.

**GAMBIR GUM.** See Catechu Extract.

**GARDEN ROSEMARY OIL.** See Rosemary.

**GARDENOL.** See α-Methylbenzyl Acetate.

**GARLIC OIL.** Yellow liquid with a strong odor, obtained from the crushed bulbs or cloves of the plant. Used in fruit and garlic flavorings for beverages, ice cream, ices, candy, baked goods, chewing gum, and condiments. Has been used medicinally to combat intestinal worms. Reevaluated and found to be GRAS by the FDA's committee of experts in 1976.

**GAS.** A combustion product from the controlled combustion in air of butane, propane, or natural gas. It is used for removing or displacing oxygen in the processing, storage, or packaging of citrus products, vegetable fats, vegetable oils, coffee, and wine. No known toxicity when used in packaging.

**GELATIN.** A food thickener and stabilizer. A protein obtained by boiling animal skin, tendons, ligaments, or bones with water. Nutritionally, it is an incomplete protein lacking the amino acid tryptophan, and containing small amounts of other amino acids (*see*). It is colorless, or slightly yellow, and tasteless, and absorbs cold water 5 to 10 times its weight. Employed as a base for fruit gelatins, puddings, and chocolate milk, as well as chocolate-flavored beverages, cream (10 percent), and confections. It is an ingredient in cream cheese, Neufchâtel cheese, cheese spreads, cheese snacks, ice cream, frozen custard, fruit sherbet, and water ices. Used medicinally to treat malnutrition and brittle fingernails and as a blood plasma extender in treatment of shock. No known toxicity. The final report to the FDA of the Select Committee on GRAS Substances stated in 1980 that it should continue its GRAS status with no limitations other than good manufacturing practices.

**GENET, ABSOLUTE.** A natural flavoring from flowers used in fruit and honey flavorings for beverages, ice cream, ices, candy, baked goods, and chewing gum. The extract is a raspberry and fruit flavoring for beverages. No known toxicity.

**GENTIAN ROOT EXTRACT.** The yellow or pale bitter root of Central and Southern European plants used in angostura, chocolate, cola, fruit, vermouth, maple, root beer, and vanilla flavorings for beverages, ice cream, ices, candy, and liquors. It has been used as a bitter tonic. No known toxicity.

**GERANIAL.** See Citral.

**GERANIUM ROSE OIL.** Derived from the leaves of Southern African geranium herbs and rose petals added. Used in strawberry, lemon, cola, geranium, rose, violet, cherry, honey, rum, brandy, cognac, nut, vanilla, spice, and ginger ale flavorings for beverages, ice cream, ices, candy, baked goods, gelatin desserts, chewing gum, and jelly. A geranium root derivative has been used as an astringent and to treat chronic diarrhea in dogs. No known toxicity. GRAS.

**GERANIOL.** A synthetic flavoring agent that occurs naturally in apples, bay leaves, cherries, coriander, grapefruit, oranges, tea, ginger, mace oil, and the oils of lavender, lavandin, lemon, lime, mandarin, and petitgrain. Sweet rose odor, and used in compounding artificial attar of roses in perfumery. A berry, lemon, rose, apple, cherry, peach, honey, root beer, cassia, cinnamon, ginger ale, and nutmeg flavoring for beverages, ice cream, ices, baked goods, candy, gelatin desserts, chewing gum, and toppings. Whereas no specific toxicity information is available, deaths have been reported from ingestion of unknown amounts of citronella oil (*see*), which is 93 percent geraniol; gastric mucosa was found to be severely damaged. GRAS.

**GERANYL ACETATE. Acetic Acid.** A synthetic flavoring agent that occurs naturally in oil of lavender and oil of lemon. A colorless liquid, with a flowery odor. Used in berry, lemon, orange, floral, apple, grape, peach, pear, honey, spice, and ginger ale flavorings for beverages, ice cream, ices, candy, baked goods, gelatin desserts, chewing gum, and syrup. No known toxicity but it is obtained from geraniol (*see*).

**GERANYL ACETOACETATE.** A synthetic fruit flavoring agent for beverages, ice cream, ices, candy, and baked goods. See Geranyl Acetate for toxicity.

**GERANYL BENZOATE. Benzoic Acid.** A synthetic flavoring agent, slightly yellowish liquid, with a floral odor. Used in floral and fruit flavorings for beverages, ice cream, ices, baked goods, and candy. See Geranyl Acetate for toxicity.

**GERANYL BUTYRATE. Butyric Acid.** A synthetic flavoring, colorless, liquid, with a rose or fruit odor. Used in berry, citrus, fruit, apple, cherry, pear, and pineapple flavorings for beverages, ice cream, ices, baked goods, gelatin desserts, and chewing gum. See Geranyl Acetate for toxicity.

**GERANYL FORMATE. Formic Acid.** A synthetic flavoring, colorless to pale yellow liquid, with a fresh, leafy, rose odor. Used in berry, citrus, apple, apricot, and peach flavorings for beverages, ice cream, ices, candy, baked goods, gelatins, puddings, and chewing gum. See Geranyl Acetate for toxicity.

**GERANYL HEXANOATE. Hexanoic Acid.** A synthetic citrus and pineapple flavoring agent for beverages, ice cream, ices, candy, and baked goods. See Geranyl Acetate for toxicity.

**GERANYL ISOBUTYRIC ACID. Isobutyric Acid.** A synthetic floral, rose, apple, pear, and pineapple flavoring agent for beverages, ice cream, ices, candy, baked goods, gelatin desserts, puddings, and chewing gum. See Geranyl Acetate for toxicity.

**GERANYL ISOVALERATE.** A synthetic berry, lime, apple, peach, and pineapple flavoring agent for beverages, ice cream, ices, candy, and baked goods. See Geranyl Acetate for toxicity.

**GERANYL PHENYLACETATE. Phenylacetic Acid.** A synthetic flavoring, yellow liquid, with a honey-rose odor. Used in fruit flavorings for beverages, ice cream, ices, candy, baked goods, and chewing gum. See Geranyl Acetate for toxicity.

**GERANYL PROPIONATE. Propionic Acid.** A synthetic flavoring, almost colorless liquid, with a fruity-floral scent. Occurs naturally in oil of lavender. Used in berry, geranium, apple, pear, pineapple, and honey flavorings for beverages, ice cream, ices, candy, baked goods, gelatin desserts, and chewing gum. See Geranyl Acetate for toxicity.

**GHATTI GUM. Indian Gum.** The gummy exudate from the stems of a plant abundant in India and Ceylon. Used as an emulsifier and in butter, butterscotch and fruit flavorings for beverages. Has caused an occasional allergy, but when ingested in large amounts, it has not caused obvious distress. The FDA's reevaluation in 1976 found the gum was GRAS if used at the rate of 0.2 percent for alcoholic beverages and 0.1 percent for all other food categories. In pharmaceutical preparations one part ghatti usually replaces two parts acacia (*see*). The final report to the FDA of the Select Committee on GRAS Substances stated in 1980 that there is no evidence in the available information that it is a hazard to the public when used as it is now and it should continue its GRAS status with limitations on amounts that can be added to food.

**GINGER.** Derived from the rootlike stem of plants cultivated in all tropical countries, it is used in apple, plum, sausage, eggnog, pumpkin, ginger, ginger ale, and ginger beer flavorings for beverages, ice cream, ices, baked goods (2,500 ppm), and meats. The *extract* is used for cola, sausage, root beer, ginger, ginger ale, and ginger beer flavorings for beverages, ice cream, ices, candy, baked goods, condiments, and meats. The *oil* is used in root beer and ginger ale flavorings for the same products. Likewise the *oleoresin,* which is a ginger flavoring. Ginger has been used to break up intestinal gas and colic. No known toxicity. GRAS.

**GINSENG.** Root of the ginseng plant grown in China, Korea, and the United States. It produces a resin, a sugar starch, glue, and a volatile oil. Ginseng has a sweetish, licorice-like taste and is widely used in Ori— ental medicines as an aromatic bitter and tonic. It is used in American cosmetics to soothe the skin and in foods as a flavoring. No known toxicity.

**GLUCOMANNAN.** A powder extracted from the roots of the konjac plant. The promoters claim that the powder, taken in a capsule before meals, absorbs liquid and swells in the stomach to form a gel and reduces hunger. The FDA was asked to approve it as GRAS but refused to do so unless scientific data were submitted.

**GLUCONATE. Calcium and Sodium.** A sequestrant (*see*) derived from glucose, a sugar. Odorless, tasteless. Used as a buffer for confections and a firming agent for tomatoes and apple slices. Sodium gluconate is also used as a nutrient and dietary supplement. The final report to the FDA of the Select Committee on GRAS Substances stated in 1980 that it should continue its GRAS status with no limitations other than good manufacturing practices.

**GLUCONIC ACID.** A light, amber liquid with the faint odor of vinegar, produced from corn. It is water-soluble and used as a dietary supplement and as a sequestrant (*see*). The magnesium salt of gluconic acid has been used as an antispasmodic. No known toxicity. GRAS.

**GLUCONO-DELTA-LACTONE.** An acid with a sweet taste; fine, white, odorless. It is used as a leavening agent, in jelly powders and soft-drink powders where dry food acid is desired. Used in the dairy industry to prevent milk stone, and by breweries to prevent beer stone, and is also a component of many cleaning compounds. Cleared by the U.S. Department of Agriculture's Meat Inspection Division for use at 8 ounces for each 100 pounds of cured, pulverized meat or meat food product to speed up the color-fixing process and to reduce the time required for smoking. No specific data on toxicity.

**GLUCOSE.** Occurs naturally in blood, grape, and corn sugars. A source of energy for plants and animals. Sweeter than sucrose, glucose syrup is used to flavor sausage, hamburger, meat loaf, luncheon meat, chopped or pressed ham. It is also used as an extender in maple syrup. It is used medicinally for nutritional purposes and in the treatment of diabetic coma. No known toxicity.

**GLUTAMATE. Ammonium and Monopotassium.** Salt of glutamic acid. Used to impart meat flavor to foods and to enhance other natural food flavors and to improve the taste of tobacco. The final report to the FDA of the Select Committee on GRAS Substances stated in 1980 that there is no evidence in the available information that it is a hazard to the public when used as it is now and it should continue its GRAS status with limitations on the amount that can be added to food.

**GLUTAMIC ACID.** A white, practically odorless, free-flowing crystalline powder, a nonessential amino acid (*see*) usually manufactured from vegetable protein. A salt substitute, it has been used to treat epilepsy and to correct low stomach acid. It is used to impart meat flavor to foods. Glutamic acid with hydrochloride (*see* Hydrochloric Acid) is used to improve the taste of beer, and is also used as a salt substitute. The final report to the FDA of the Select Committee on GRAS Substances stated in 1980 that there is no evidence in the available information that it is a hazard to the public when used as it is now and it should continue its GRAS status with limitations on the amount that can be added to food.

**GLUTARAL. Glutaraldehyde.** An amino acid (*see*) that occurs in green sugar beets, and used as a flavor enhancer. It has a faint, agreeable odor. See Glutaric Acid.

**GLUTARIC ACID. Pentanedioic Acid.** A crystalline fatty acid (*see*) that occurs in green sugar beets, meat, and in crude wood. Very soluble in alcohol and ether. It is used as an emulsifier. No known toxicity.

**GLUTEN.** A mixture of proteins present in wheat flour, obtained as an extremely sticky yellowish-gray mass by making a dough and then washing out the starch. It consists almost entirely of two proteins, gliadin and glutelin, the exact proportions of which depend upon the variety of wheat. Contributes to the porous and spongy structure of bread. No known toxicity.

**(MONO) GLYCERIDE CITRATE.** Aids the action of and helps dissolve antioxidant formulations for oils and fats, such as shortenings for cooking. No known toxicity.

**GLYCERIDES, DISTILLED.** Food emulsifiers and binders in nutrient capsules and tablets; food-coating agent up to 5 percent of compound.

**GLYCERIDES. Monoglycerides, Diglycerides, and Monosodium Glycerides of Edible Fats and Oils.** Emulsifying and defoaming agents. Used in bakery products to maintain "softness," in beverages, ice cream, ices, ice milk, milk, chewing gum base, shortening, lard, oleomargarine, confections, sweet chocolate, chocolate, rendered animal fat, and whipped toppings. The diglycerides are on the FDA list of food additives to be studied for possible mutagenic, teratogenic, subacute, and reproductive effects. The final report to the FDA of the Select Committee on GRAS Substances stated in 1980 that it should continue its GRAS status with no limitations other than good manufacturing practices.

**GLYCERIN. Glycerol.** A sweet (about .6 times as cane sugar), warm-tasting substance which absorbs water from the air. Obtained from oils and fats as a byproduct in the manufacture of soaps and fatty acids. Used as a humectant in tobacco and in marshmallows, pastilles, and jellylike candies; as a solvent for colors and flavors; as a bodying agent in combination with gelatins and edible gums; as a plasticizer in edible coatings for meat and cheese. It is used, too, in beverages, confectionery, baked goods, chewing gum, gelatin desserts, meat products, soda-fountain fudge. Also used in perfumery and as an emollient for the skin, and in suppositories for constipation. In concentrated solution it is irritating to the mucous membranes. Contact with strong oxidizing agent such as chromium trioxide, potassium chlorate, or potassium permanganate (*see*) may produce an explosion. The final report to the FDA of the Select Committee on GRAS Substances stated in 1980 that it should continue its GRAS status with no limitations other than good manufacturing practices.

**GLYCEROL.** See Glycerin.

**GLYCEROL ESTER OF WOOD ROSIN.** Made from refined, pale yellow-colored wood rosin and food grade glycerin (*see*). A hard, pale, amber-colored resin, it is used as a chewing gum base and as a beverage stabilizer. No known toxicity.

**GLYCERYL ABIETATE.** A density adjuster for citrus oil used in the preparation of alcoholic beverages and still and carbonated fruit drinks. Also cleared as a plasticizing material in chewing gum base. No known toxicity.

**GLYCERYL LACTOOLEATE AND LACTOPALMITATE OF FATTY ACIDS.** Food emulsifiers used in shortening where free and combined lactic acid does not exceed 1.75 percent of shortening plus additive. They add calories but are considered nontoxic. The final report to the FDA of the Select Committee on GRAS Substances stated in 1980 that they should continue their GRAS status with no limitations other than good manufacturing practices.

**GLYCERYL MONO- AND DI-ESTERS.** Manufactured by reacting edible glycerides with ethylene oxide. These are used as defoamers in yeast production. No known toxicity. The final report to the FDA of the Select Committee on GRAS Substances stated in 1980 that it should continue its GRAS status with no limitations other than good manufacturing practices.

**GLYCERYL TRIACETATE.** See (tri-) Acetin. GRAS.

**GLYCERYL TRIBUTYRATE.** See (tri-) Butyrin.

**GLYCOHOLIC ACID.** A product of mixing cholic acid with glycine, it is the chief ingredient of bile in vegetarian animals. It is used as an emulsifying agent for dried egg whites up to .1 percent. No known toxicity. The final report to the FDA of the Select Committee on GRAS Substances stated in 1980 that it should continue its GRAS status with no limitations other than good manufacturing practices.

**GLYCYRRHIZA AND GLYCYRRHIZA EXTRACT.** See Glycyrrhizin, Ammoniated.

**GLYCYRRHIZIN, AMMONIATED.** Licorice. Product of dried roots from the Mediterranean region used in licorice, anise, root beer, wintergreen, and birch beer flavorings for beverages, candy, and baked goods. Also used as a demulcent and expectorant and as a drug vehicle. The final report to the FDA of the Select Committee on GRAS Substances stated in 1980 that there is no evidence in the available information that it is a hazard to the public when used as it is now and it should continue in GRAS status with limitations on amounts that can be added to food. Cases have been reported of avid licorice eaters who develop high blood pressure. See Licorice.

**GRAINS OF PARADISE.** Pungent aromatic seeds of a tropical African plant of the ginger family. It is a natural flavoring used in fruit, ginger, ginger ale, and pepper flavorings for beverages, ice cream, ices, and candy. No known toxicity.

**GRAMINIS.** See Dog Grass Extract.

**GRAPE POMACE.** Source of natural red and blue colorings. See Anthocyanins.

**GRAPEFRUIT OIL.** The oil obtained by expression from the fresh peel of the grapefruit citrus Paradise. It is a yellow, sometimes reddish liquid used in grapefruit, lemon, lime, orange, and peach flavorings for beverages, ice cream, ices, candy, baked goods, gelatin desserts, chewing gum (1,500 ppm), and toppings. No known toxicity. GRAS.

**GRAPESKIN EXTRACT. Enocianina.** A purple-red liquid extracted from the residue of grapes pressed for use in grape juice and wine. Used for coloring in still and carbonated drinks and ales, beverage bases, and alcoholic beverages. Regarding the spraying of grapes, specifications by the FDA restrict pesticide residues to not more than 10 ppm lead and not more than 1 ppm arsenic.

**GREEN.** See FD and C Green (No. 1, 2, 3).

**GUAIAC WOOD EXTRACT.** A gum resin used in fruit and rum flavorings for beverages, ice cream, ices, candy, and baked goods. The *oil* is a raspberry, strawberry, rose, fruit, honey, ginger, and ginger ale flavoring for beverages, ice cream, candy, baked goods, gelatin desserts, and chewing gum. Formerly used to treat rheumatism. No known toxicity.

**GUAIACYL ACETATE.** A synthetic berry flavoring agent for beverages, ice cream, ices, candy, baked goods, gelatin, and chewing gum. No known toxicity.

**GUAIYL ACETATE. Guaiac Wood Acetate.** A synthetic tobacco and fruit flavoring agent for beverages, ice cream, ices, baked goods, and chewing gum. No known toxicity.

**GUAIYL PHENYLACETATE.** A synthetic berry, coffee, honey, tobacco, and smoke flavoring agent for beverages, ice cream, ices, candy, baked goods, and toppings. No known toxicity.

**GUAR GUM. Guar Flour.** From ground nutritive seed tissue of plants cultivated in India. A free-flowing powder, it is used as a stabilizer for frozen fruit, icings, glazes, and fruit drinks and as a thickener for hot and cold drinks. Has 5 to 8 times the thickening power of starch. Also, a binder for meats, confections, baked goods, cheese spreads, cream cheese, ice cream, ices, French dressing, and salad dressing. Keeps tablet formulations from disintegrating, and is used in lotions, creams, and toothpastes; employed as a bulk laxative, appetite suppressant, and to treat peptic ulcer. The FDA's reevaluation in 1976 found guar gum to be GRAS if used as a stabilizer, thickener, and firming agent at .35 percent in baked goods; 1.2 percent in breakfast cereals; 2.0 percent in fats and oils; 1.2 percent in gravies; 1.0 percent in sweet sauces, toppings, and syrups; and 2.0 percent in processed vegetables and vegetable juices. The final report to the FDA of the Select Committee on GRAS Substances stated in 1980 that there is no evidence in the available information that it is a hazard to the public when used as it is now and it should continue its GRAS status with limitations on amounts that can be added to food.

**GUARANA GUM.** The dried paste consisting mainly of crushed seed from a plant grown in Brazil. Contains about 4 percent caffeine. Used in cola flavorings for beverages and candy. See Caffeine for toxicity.

**GUARANINE.** See Caffeine.

**GUAVA.** Extracted from the fruit of a small, shrubby American tree widely cultivated in warm regions. The fruit is sweet, sometimes acid, globular, and yellow. It is used to flavor jelly. No known toxicity. GRAS.

**GUINEA GREEN B.** See FD and C Green No. 1.

**GUM.** True plant gums are the dried exudates from various plants obtained when the bark is cut or other injury is suffered. Gums are soluble in hot or cold water, and sticky. Today, the term gum, both for natural and synthetic sources, usually refers to water-soluble thickeners. Water-insoluble thickeners are referred to as resins. Gums are also used as emulsifiers, stabilizers, and suspending agents. No known toxicity.

**GUM, CAROB BEAN.** A thickener and stabilizer derived from the carob plant and used in chocolate milk, chocolate-flavored beverages, gassed cream (aerosol whipped cream), syrups for frozen products, confections, cream cheese, Neufchâtel cheese, ice cream, frozen custard, fruit sherbet, water ices, French dressing, and artificially sweetened jellies and preserves. Carob flour is an absorbent-demulcent in diarrhea. On the FDA list of additives for short-term study of mutagenic, teratogenic, subacute, and reproductive effects. See Locust Bean Gum. GRAS.

**GUM ACACIA.** See Acacia.

**GUM ARABIC.** See Acacia.

**GUM BENJAMIN.** See Benzoin.

**GUM BENZOIN.** See Benzoin.

**GUM GHATTI.** See Ghatti Gum.

**GUM GUAIAC.** Resin from the wood of the Guaiacum. Brown or greenish brown. Used as an antioxidant in edible fats or oils, beverages, rendered animal fat, or a combination of such fats and vegetable fats. It was formerly used in the treatment of rheumatism and other chronic diseases. No known toxicity. The final report to the FDA of the Select Committee on GRAS Substances stated in 1980 that it should continue its GRAS status with no limitations other than good manufacturing practices.

**GUM TRAGACANTH.** The dried gummy exudation from plants

found in Iran, Asia Minor, and Syria. A thickener and stabilizer, odorless, and with a gluelike taste. Used in fruit jelly, ornamental icings, fruit sherbets, water ices, salad dressing, French dressing, confections, and candy. Also employed in compounding drugs and pastes. One of the oldest known natural emulsifiers, its history predates the Christian era by hundreds of years; it has been recognized in the U.S. Pharmacopoeia since 1820. It has a long shelf life and is resistant to acids. Aside from occasional allergic reactions, it can be ingested in large amounts with little harm except for diarrhea, gas, or constipation. When reevaluated it was found to be GRAS in the following percentages: .2 for baked goods; .7 percent in condiments and relishes; 1.3 in fats and oils; .8 percent in gravies and sauces; .2 percent in meat products; .2 percent in processed fruits; and .1 percent in all other categories.

# H

**HAW BARK. Black Extract.** Extract of the fruit of a hawthorn shrub or tree. Used in butter, caramel, cola, maple, and walnut flavorings for beverages, ice cream, ices, candy, and baked goods. Has been used as a uterine antispasmodic. No known toxicity.

**HEDEONA OIL.** See Pennyroyal Oil.

**HELIOTROPINE.** See Piperonal.

**HELIOTROPYL ACETATE.** See Piperonyl Acetate.

**HELIUM.** This colorless, odorless, tasteless gas is used as propellant for foods packed in pressurized containers. No known toxicity. The final report to the FDA of the Select Committee on GRAS Substances stated in 1980 that it should continue its GRAS status with no limitations other than good manufacturing practices.

**HEMLOCK OIL. Spruce Oil.** A natural flavoring extract from North American or Asian nonpoisonous hemlock. Used in fruit, root beer, and spice flavorings for beverages, ice cream, ices, candy, baked goods, gelatin puddings, and chewing gum. No known toxicity.

**HENDECANAL.** See Undecanal.

**HENDECEN-9-OL.** See 9-Undecanal.

**10-HENDECENYL ACETATE.** See 10-Undecen-1-yl Acetate.

**γ-HEPTALACTONE.** A synthetic coconut, nut, and vanilla flavoring agent for beverages, ice cream, ices, candy, and baked goods. No known toxicity.

**HEPTALDEHYDE.** See Heptanal.

**HEPTANAL. Heptyl Aldehyde.** A synthetic flavoring agent, colorless to slightly yellow, with a penetrating fruity odor. Obtained by distilling castor oil. Used in citrus, apple, melon, cognac, rum, and almond flavorings for beverages, ice cream, ices, candy, baked goods, and liqueurs. No known toxicity.

**HEPTANAL DIMETHYL ACETAL.** A synthetic fruit, melon, and mushroom flavoring agent for beverages, ice cream, ices, candy, baked goods, and condiments. No known toxicity.

**HEPTANAL GLYCERYL ACETAL.** A synthetic mushroom flavoring agent for beverages, ice cream, ices, candy, and baked goods. No known toxicity.

**2, 3-HEPTANEDIONE.** A synthetic raspberry, strawberry, butter, fruit, rum, nut, and cheese flavoring agent for beverages, ice cream, ices, candy, baked goods, and chewing gum. No known toxicity.

**1-HEPTANOL.** A synthetic flavoring agent, liquid, and miscible with alcohol and ether. See Heptyl Alcohol for use.

**2-HEPTANONE.** A synthetic flavoring agent, liquid, with a penetrating odor, used to give a "peppery" smell to such cheeses as Roquefort. Used in berry, butter, fruit, and cheese flavorings for beverages, ice cream, ices, candy, baked goods, and condiments (25 ppm). Used also in perfumery. Found naturally in oil of cloves and in cinnamon bark oil. The lethal concentration in air for rats is 4,000 ppm. In high doses it is narcotic, and a suspected irritant to human mucous membranes.

**3-HEPTANONE.** A synthetic melon flavoring agent for beverages, ice cream, ices, candy, and baked goods. See 2-Heptanone, which is a similar compound.

**4-HEPTANONE.** A synthetic strawberry and fruit flavoring agent for beverages, ice cream, ices, candy, baked goods, and gelatin desserts. See 2-Heptanone, which is a similar compound.

**HEPTYL ACETATE.** A synthetic berry, banana, melon, pear, and pineapple flavoring agent for beverages, ice cream, ices, candy, and baked goods. No known toxicity.

**HEPTYL ALCOHOL. 1-Heptanol.** A synthetic flavoring agent, colorless, with a fatty citrus odor, used in fruit flavorings for beverages, ice cream, ices, candy, and baked goods. No known toxicity.

**HEPTYL ALDEHYDE.** See Heptanal.

**HEPTYL BUTYRATE. Butyric Acid.** A synthetic raspberry, floral, violet, apricot, melon, and plum flavoring agent for beverages, ice cream, ices, candy, baked goods. No known toxicity.

**γ-HEPTYL BUTYROLACTONE.** See γ-Undecalactone.

**HEPTYL ISOBUTYRATE.** A synthetic coconut, apricot, peach, pineapple, and plum flavoring agent for beverages, ice cream, ices, candy, and baked goods. No known toxicity.

**HEPTYLPARABEN.** A preservative. See Parabens.

**HEXADECANOIC ACID.** See Palmitic Acid.

**1-HEXADECANOL. Cetyl Alcohol.** A synthetic chocolate flavoring agent for ice cream, ices, and candy. No known toxicity.

**ω-6-HEXADECENLACTONE. Ambrettolide. 6-Hexadecenolide.** A synthetic fruit flavoring agent for beverages, ice cream, ices, candy, baked goods, gelatin desserts, and chewing gum. No known toxicity.

**6-HEXADECENOLIDE.** See ω-6-Hexadecenlactone.

**HEXADECYLIC ACID.** See Palmitic Acid.

**2,4-HEXADIENOATE.** See Allyl Sorbate.

**HEXAHYDROPYRIDENE.** See Piperidine.

**HEXAHYDROTHYMOL.** See Menthol.

**γ-HEXALACTONE.** A synthetic butter, fruit, honey, and vanilla flavoring agent for beverages, ice cream, ices, candy, and baked goods. No known toxicity.

**HEXALDEHYDE.** See Hexanal.

**HEXANAL. Hexaldehyde. Hexoic Aldehyde.** A synthetic flavoring agent occurring naturally in apples, coffee, cooked chicken, strawberries, tea, and tobacco leaves (oils). Used in butter, fruit, honey, and rum flavorings for beverages, ice cream, ices, candy, baked goods, gelatin desserts, and chewing gum. No known toxicity.

**1-HEXANAL.** See Hexyl Alcohol.

**2,3-HEXANDIONE.** A synthetic strawberry, butter, citrus, banana, pineapple, rum, and cheese flavoring agent for beverages, ice cream, ices, candy, and baked goods. No known toxicity.

**HEXANE.** A colorless volatile liquid derived from distillation of petroleum and used as a solvent for spice oleoresins (*see*). Also used in low-temperature thermometers instead of mercury, usually with a blue or red dye. It is a mild central nervous system depressant which may be irritating to the respiratory tract.

**HEXANEDIOIC ACID.** See Adipic Acid.

**HEXANOIC ACID.** A synthetic flavoring agent that occurs naturally in apples, butter acids, cocoa, grapes, oil of lavender, oil of lavandin, raspberries, strawberries, and tea. Used in butter, butterscotch, chocolate, fruit, rum, pecan, and cheese flavorings for beverages, ice cream, ices, candy, baked goods, chewing gum, and condiments. No known toxicity.

**2-HEXEN-1-OL.** A synthetic flavoring that occurs naturally in grapes; similar in compound to 3-Hexen-1-ol (*see*). Used in fruit and mint flavorings for beverages, ice cream, ices, candy, and baked goods. No known toxicity.

**3-HEXEN-1-OL. Leaf Alcohol. Blatteralkohol.** A synthetic flavoring that occurs naturally in leaves of odoriferous plants and in grapefruit, raspberries, and tea. Strong odor. Used in fruit and mint flavorings for beverages, ice cream, ices, candy, and baked goods. No known toxicity.

**2-HEXEN-1-YL ACETATE.** A synthetic fruit flavoring agent for beverages, ice cream, ices, candy, and baked goods. No known toxicity.

**2-HEXENAL.** A synthetic berry and fruit flavoring agent that occurs naturally in apples and strawberries and is used for beverages, ice cream, ices, candy, and baked goods. No known toxicity.

*cis*-**3-HEXENAL.** A synthetic fruit flavoring agent for beverages, ice cream, ices, and candy. No known toxicity.

**2-HEXENOIC ACID.** See Methyl 2-Hexenoate.

**HEXOIC ACID.** See Hexanoic Acid.

**HEXOIC ALDEHYDE.** A synthetic berry, apple, pear, and pineapple flavoring agent for beverages, ice cream, ices, candy, baked goods, and chewing gum. No known toxicity. See Hexanal.

**HEXYL ACETATE. Acetic Acid. Hexyl Ester.** A synthetic berry, apple, pear, and pineapple flavoring agent for beverages, ice cream, ices, candy, baked goods, and chewing gum. No known toxicity.

**2-HEXYL-4-ACETOXYTETRAHYDROFURAN.** A synthetic fruit flavoring agent for beverages, ice cream, ices, candy, and baked goods. No known toxicity.

**HEXYL ALCOHOL. 1-Hexanol.** A synthetic flavoring agent that occurs naturally in apples, oil of lavender, strawberries, and tea. Used in berry, coconut, and fruit flavorings for beverages, ice cream, ices, candy, baked goods, and gelatin desserts. Also used as a solvent. No known toxicity. GRAS.

**HEXYL ESTER.** See Hexyl Acetate.

**HEXYL FORMATE. Formic Acid.** A synthetic raspberry and fruit flavoring agent for beverages, ice cream, ices, candy, and baked goods. See Formic Acid for toxicity.

**HEXYL 2-FUROATE.** A synthetic coffee, maple, and mushroom flavoring agent for candy and condiments. No known toxicity.

**HEXYL HEXANOATE. Hexanoic Acid.** A synthetic fruit flavoring agent for beverages, ice cream, ices, candy, and baked goods. No known toxicity.

**2-HEXYL-5 (or 6)-KETO-1, 4-DIOXANE.** A synthetic cream flavoring agent for beverages, ice cream, ices, candy, baked goods, and margarine. No known toxicity.

**HEXYL OCTANOATE. Octanoic Acid.** A synthetic fruit flavoring agent for beverages and puddings. No known toxicity.

**HEXYL PROPRIONATE. Proprionic Acid.** A synthetic fruit flavoring agent for beverages, ice cream, ices, candy, and baked goods. No known toxicity.

**α-HEXYLCINNAMALDEHYDE.** A synthetic flavoring, pale yellow liquid, with a jasminelike odor. Used in berry, fruit, and honey flavorings for beverages, ice cream, ices, candy, baked goods, and gelatin desserts. No known toxicity.

**HEXYLENE GLYCOL DIACETATE.** See 1, 3-Nonanediol Acetate (mixed esters).

**2-HEXYLIDENE CYCLOPENTANONE.** A synthetic fruit flavoring agent for beverages, ice cream, ices, candy, and baked goods. No known toxicity.

**HICKORY BARK EXTRACT.** A natural flavoring extract from the hickory nut tree and used in butter, caramel, rum, maple, nut, spice, tobacco, and smoke flavorings for beverages, ice cream, ices, candy, baked goods, condiments, and liquors. No known toxicity. GRAS.

**HIGH AMYLOSE CORNSTARCH.** Cornstarch that has been treated with enzymes to make it sweeter.

**HIGH FRUCTOSE CORN SYRUP.** Corn syrup (*see*) that has been treated with enzymes to make it sweeter.

**HIPBERRY EXTRACT.** See Rose Hips Extract.

**HISTIDINE. L and DL forms.** One of the basic, essential amino acids (*see*), used as a nutrient. Soluble in water. (L-Histidine is the natural form). Histidine is on the FDA list of additives that need further study. GRAS.

**HOPS.** Carefully dried pineconelike fruit of the hop grown in Europe, Asia, and North America. Light yellow to greenish, oily, bitter, with an aromatic odor. Used especially in beer brewing and in fruit and root beer flavorings for beverages. A *solid extract* is used in bitters, fruit, and root beer flavorings for beverages, ice cream, ices, candy, and baked goods. Hops *oil* is used in raspberry, grape, whiskey, and spice flavorings for beverages, ice cream, ices, candy, baked goods, chewing gum, and condiments. Hops at one time were thought to be a sedative. No known toxicity. GRAS.

**HOREHOUND EXTRACT. Hoarhound.** A flavoring extracted from a mintlike plant cultivated in Europe, Asia, and the United States. It has a very bitter taste and is used in maple, nut, and root beer flavorings for beverages, ice cream, ices, candy, and baked goods. It is also a bitter tonic and expectorant. No known toxicity.

**HORSEMINT LEAVES EXTRACT.** A flavoring extract from any of several coarse, aromatic plants, grown from New York to Florida, and from Texas to Wisconsin. Used in fruit flavorings for beverages (600 ppm). Formerly used as an aromatic stimulant and to break up intestinal gas. No known toxicity.

**HORSERADISH.** A condiment ingredient utilizing the grated root from the tall, coarse, white-flowered herb native to Europe. Often combined with vinegar or other ingredients. Contains ascorbic acid (*see*) and acts as a urinary antiseptic. No known toxicity. GRAS.

**HUMECTANT.** A substance used to preserve the moisture content of materials. For example, glycerin (*see*), which is used to preserve moisture in confections and tobaccos.

**HYACINTH, ABSOLUTE.** A natural flavoring from the very fragrant common flower native to the Mediterranean. It is used in chewing gum. The bulb can cause severe gastrointestinal symptoms.

**HYACINTHIN.** See Phenylacetaldehyde.

**HYDRATROPALDEHYDE.** See 2-Phenylpropionaldehyde.

**HYDRATROPALDEHYDE DIMETHYL ACETAL.** See 2-Phenyl-propionaldehyde Dimethyl Acetal.

**HYDROCHLORIC ACID.** An acid used as a modifier for food starch, in the manufacture of sodium glutamate (*see*) and gelatin, for the conversion of cornstarch to syrup (0.012 percent), and to adjust the pH (acid-alkalinity balance) in the brewing industry (0.02 percent). Concentrated solutions may cause severe burns, permanent eye damage, and skin rash. Inhalation of the fumes causes choking and inflammation of the respiratory tract; ingestion may corrode the mucous membranes, esophagus, and stomach, and cause diarrhea. Circulatory collapse and death can occur. The final report to the FDA of the Select Committee on GRAS Substances stated in 1980 that it should continue its GRAS status with no limitations other than good manufacturing practices.

**HYDROCINNAMIC ACID.** See 3-Phenylpropionic Acid.

**HYDROGEN PEROXIDE.** A preservative and bacteria killer for milk and cheese and a bleaching and oxidizing agent and modifier of food starch. Bleaches tripe and butter; used in the treatment of eggs before drying and in cheddar and Swiss cheeses. Because it is a strong oxidizer, undiluted it can cause burns of the skin and mucous membranes. In 1980, the Japanese notified the World Health Organization that hydrogen peroxide was suspect as a cancer-causing agent. It was widely used in Japanese fish cakes. The noodles were dipped in dilute hydrogen peroxide for disinfection. The fish meat and raw flour were also mixed with hydrogen peroxide. In laboratory rats, it was discovered that at the sixty-fifth week, the lining of the duodenum was thickened but no cancers occurred. The Japanese Welfare Ministry decided that hydrogen peroxide is safe for food when it is entirely decomposed and that the food should not contain any residual.

**HYDROGENATED TALLOW.** A component used in the production of beet sugar and yeast in amounts to inhibit foaming. See Hydrogenation. No known toxicity. The final report to the FDA of the Select Committee on GRAS Substances stated in 1980 that it should continue its GRAS status with no limitations other than good manufacturing practices.

**HYDROGENATED TALLOW ALCOHOL.** See Hydrogenated Tallow, which has the same uses. The final report to the FDA of the Select Committee on GRAS Substances stated in 1980 that it should continue its GRAS status with no limitations other than good manufacturing practices.

**HYDROGENATION.** The adding of hydrogen gas under high pressure to liquid oils. It is the most widely used chemical process in the edible fat industry. Used in the manufacture of margarine and shortening and in the extraction of petrol from coal. In the food industry its primary use is to convert liquid oils to semisolid fats, Crisco, for example, at room temperature. It retards rancidity in the compound and improves color. Usually, the higher the amount of hydrogenation, the lower the unsaturation in the fat and the less the possibility of flavor degradation due to rancidity. Hydrogenated oils still contain some unsaturated components which are susceptible to rancidity. Therefore, the addition of antioxidants is still necessary.

**HYDROLYZED.** Subject to hydrolysis or turned partly into water. Hydrolysis is derived from the Greek *hydro,* meaning "water," and *lysis,* meaning "a setting free." It occurs as a chemical process in which the decomposition of a compound is brought about by water, resolving into simpler compounds. Hydrolysis also occurs in the digestion of foods. The proteins in the stomach react with water in an enzyme reaction to form peptones, peptides, and amino acids.

**HYDROLYZED VEGETABLE PROTEIN (HVP).** A flavor enhancer used in soup, beef, and stew gravy. On the GRAS list, but the Select Committee of the Federation of American Societies for Experimental Biology (FASEB) advised the FDA that hydrolyzed vegetable protein contains dicarboxylic amino acid (a building block of the protein that affects growth, when used at present levels in strained and junior baby foods). They said that the effects of this substance on children should be studied further; the effects on adults of vegetable and animal protein hydrozylates demonstrate "no current hazard," but FASEB voiced uncertainties about future consumption levels for those products and recommended further studies.

**HYDROQUINONE DIMETHYL ETHER.** See *p*-Dimethoxybenzene.

*p*-**HYDROXY BENZOATE.** See Propylparabens.

*p*-HYDROXYBENZOIC ACID. A preservative and fungicide. See Benzoic Acid for toxicity.

3-HYDROXY-2-BUTANONE. See Acetoin.

2-HYDROXY-*p*-CYMENE. See Carvacrol.

5-HYDROXY-4-OCTANONE. A synthetic butter, butterscotch, fruit, cheese, and nut flavoring agent for beverages, ice cream, ices, candy, and baked goods. No known toxicity.

HYDROXY PROPYLMETHYL CELLULOSE CARBONATE. Prepared from wood pulp or cotton by treatment with methyl chloride. Used as a substitute for water-soluble gums, to render paper greaseproof, and as a thickener. The final report to the FDA of the Select Committee on GRAS Substances stated in 1980 that there is no evidence in the available information that it is a hazard to the public when used as it is now and it should continue its GRAS status with limitations on amounts that can be added to food.

*o*-HYDROXYBENZALDEHYDE. See Salicylaldehyde.

*p*-HYDROXYBENZYL ACETONE. See 4-(*p*-Hydroxyphenyl)-2-Butanone.

*p*-HYDROXYBENZYL ISOTHIOCYANATE. A derivative of mustard oil used in flavoring. The final report to the FDA of the Select Committee on GRAS Substances stated in 1980 that it should continue its GRAS status with no limitations other than good manufacturing practices.

2-HYDROXYCAMPHANE. See Borneol.

HYDROXYCITRONELLAL. **Laurine®**. A synthetic flavoring, colorless liquid, with a sweet lily odor. Used in berry, citrus, linden, violet, and cherry flavorings for beverages, ice cream, ices, candy, baked goods, gelatin desserts, and chewing gum. No known toxicity.

HYDROXYCITRONELLAL DIETHYL ACETAL. A synthetic citrus and fruit flavoring agent for beverages, ice cream, ices, candy, and baked goods. No known toxicity.

HYDROXYCITRONELLAL DIMETHYL ACETAL. A synthetic flavoring, colorless liquid, with a light floral odor. Used in fruit and cherry flavorings for beverages, ice cream, ices, candy, and baked goods. No known toxicity.

HYDROXYCITRONELLOL. A synthetic lemon, floral, and cherry flavoring agent for beverages, ice cream, ices, candy, baked goods, gelatin desserts, and chewing gum. No known toxicity.

HYDROXYLATE. The process in which an atom of hydrogen and an atom of oxygen are introduced into a compound to make the compound more soluble.

**HYDROXYLATED LECITHIN.** An emulsifier and antioxidant used in baked goods, ice cream, and margarine. According to the Food and Agricultural Organization/World Health Organization Expert Committee on Food Additives, the safety of hydroxylated lecithin (*see* Lecithin) has not been adequately established. It has been cleared by the EDA for use as a food emulsifier.

**HYDROXYPROPYL STARCH, HYDROXYPROPYL STARCH OXIDIZED, AND HYDROXYPROPYL DISTARCHPHOS-PHATE.** These are all modified starches. The final report to the Select Committee on GRAS Substances stated in 1980 that while no evidence in the available information on these starches demonstrates a hazard to the public when they are used at levels that are now current and in the manner now practiced, uncertainties exist requiring that additional studies should be conducted. GRAS status continues while tests are being completed and evaluated.

**4-HYDROXYUNDECANOIC ACID. γ-LACTONE.** See γ-Undecalactone.

**HYPNONE.** See Acetophenone.

**4-(*p*-HYDROXYPHENYL)-2-BUTANONE.** A synthetic fruit flavoring for beverages, ice cream, ices, candy, baked goods, gelatin desserts, and chewing gum. No known toxicity.

**HYPO.** Prefix from the Greek meaning "under" or "below," as in hypoacidity—acidity in a lesser degree than is usual or normal.

**HYSSOP.** A synthetic flavoring from the aromatic herb. Used in bitters. The *extract* is a liquor flavoring for beverages, ice cream, ices, and liquors. The *oil* is a liquor and spice flavoring for beverages, ice cream, ices, candy, baked goods, and liquors. GRAS.

# I

**IMITATION FLAVOR.** A flavor containing any portion of nonnatural materials. For instance, unless a strawberry flavoring is made entirely from strawberries, it must be called imitation. When a processor fails to use all the standard ingredients in mayonnaise, he must call it salad dressing.

**IMITATION MILK.** Contains no milk derivatives. Usually contains water, sugar, and vegetable fat. A source of protein (such as soy bean) with various additive flavorings. Imitation milk contains 1 percent protein compared to 3.5 percent in whole cow's milk.

**IMMORTELLE EXTRACT.** A natural flavoring extract from a red-flowered tropical tree. The name derives from the French *immortel*— "immortal" or "everlasting." Used in raspberry, fruit, and liquor flavoring for beverages, ice cream, ices, baked goods, candy, gelatin desserts, and chewing gum. GRAS.

**INDIAN GUM.** See Ghatti Gum.

**INDIAN TRAGACANTH.** See Karaya Gum.

**INDIGO CARMINE.** See FD and C Blue No. 2.

**INDOLE.** A synthetic flavoring agent, white, lustrous, flaky, with an unpleasant odor, occurring naturally in jasmine oil and orange flowers. Also extracted from coal tar and feces; in highly dilute solutions the odor is pleasant, and it has been used in perfumery. Used in raspberry, strawberry, bitters, chocolate, orange, coffee, violet, fruit, nut, and cheese flavorings for beverages, ice cream, ices, candy, baked goods, and gelatin desserts. The lethal dose in dogs is 60 milligrams per kilogram of body weight.

**INOSINATE.** A salt of inosinic acid used to intensify flavor, as with sodium glutamate (*see*). Inosinic acid is prepared from meat extract; also from dried sardines. No known toxicity.

**INOSITOL.** A dietary supplement, a member of the Vitamin B complex. Found in plant and animal tissue. Isolated commercially from corn. Fine, white, crystalline powder, odorless, with a sweet taste, and stable in air. Also called muscle sugar. No known toxicity. The final report to the FDA of the Select Committee on GRAS Substances stated in 1980 that it should continue its GRAS status with no limitations other than good manufacturing practices.

**INVERT SUGAR. Inversol. Nulomoline. Colorose.** A mixture of 50 percent glucose and 50 percent fructose. It is sweeter than sucrose. Commercially produced by "inversion" of sucrose. Honey is mostly invert sugar. Invert sugar is used in confectionery and in brewing. Like glycerin (*see*) it holds in moisture and prevents drying out. Used medicinally in intravenous solutions. No known toxicity. The final report to the FDA of the Select Committee on GRAS Substances stated in 1980 that there is no evidence in the available information that it is a hazard to the public when used as it is now and it should continue its GRAS status with limitations on amounts that can be added to food.

**IODINE SOURCES: Calcium Iodate, Cuprous Iodide, Potassium Iodate, and Potassium Iodide.** Iodine occurs in solid earth crust. It is an integral part of the thyroid hormones which have important metabolic roles, and is an essential nutrient for man. Iodine deficiency leads to thyroid enlargement or goiter. Nutritionists have found that the most efficient way to add iodine to the diet is through the use of iodized salt. The

FDA has ordered all table salts to specify whether the product contains iodide. However, many commercially prepared food items do not contain iodized salt. Iodized salt contains up to .01 percent; dietary supplements contain .16 percent. Cuprous and potassium iodides are used in table salts; potassium iodide is in some drinking water; and potassium iodate is used in animal feeds. Dietary iodine is absorbed from the intestinal tract, and man's main sources are from food and water. Seafoods are good sources, and dairy products may be good sources if the cows eat enriched grain. Adult daily iodine requirement is believed to be 110 to 150 milligrams. Growing children and pregnant or lactating women may need more. Iodine has been found to cause allergic reaction in susceptible people. The final report to the FDA of the Select Committee on GRAS Substances stated in 1980 that it should continue its GRAS status with no limitations other than good manufacturing practices.

**IONONE. Irisone.®** A flavoring agent that occurs naturally in Boronia, an Australian shrub; colorless to pale yellow, with an odor reminiscent of cedarwood or violets. $\alpha$-Ionone is used in blackberry, loganberry, raspberry, citrus, orange, floral, fruit, cherry, spice, and vanilla flavorings for beverages, ice cream, ices, candy, baked goods, gelatin desserts, chewing gum, and icings. $\beta$-Ionone is used in blackberry, berry, loganberry, raspberry, strawberry, floral, violet, fruit, cherry, grape, pineapple, liquor, muscatel, nut, and pistachio flavorings for beverages, ice cream, ices, candy, baked goods, gelatin desserts, chewing gum, and maraschino cherries. It may cause allergic reactions.

**IRIS FLORENTINA.** See Orris.

**IRISH MOSS DERIVATIVE.** See Carrageenan Chondrus Extract.

**$\alpha$-IRISONE.®** See Ionone, $\alpha$-Ionone.

**$\beta$-IRISONE.®** See Ionone, $\beta$-Ionone.

**IRON.** It is an essential mineral element and occurs widely in foods, especially organ meats such as liver, red meats, poultry, and leafy vegetables. The principal foods to which iron or iron salts are added are enriched cereals and some beverages, including milk, poultry stuffing, cornmeal, corn grits, and bread. Iron ammonium citrate is an anticaking agent in salt. Iron-choline citrate is cleared for use as a source of iron in foods for special dietary use. Iron peptonate, a combination of oxide and peptone, is made soluble by the presence of sodium citrate and is used in the treatment of iron-deficiency anemia. The recommended daily allowance for children and adults is from .2 milligram to 1.0 milligram and 18 milligrams per day for pregnant women. Iron is potentially toxic in all its forms.

**IRON CAPRYLATE, IRON LINOLEATE, IRON NAPHTHENATE,**

**AND IRON TALLATE.** All are used in packaging. Iron naphthenate was said by the Select Committee on GRAS Substances to have so little known about it that there was nothing upon which to base an evaluation of it when it is used as a food ingredient. As for the others, the final report to the FDA of the Select Committee on GRAS Substances stated in 1980 that they should continue as GRAS with no limitations other than good manufacturing practices.

**IRON OXIDE.** Any of several natural or synthetic oxides of iron (iron combined with oxygen) varying in color from red-brown or black-orange to yellow. Used for dyeing eggshells and for pet food. See Iron for toxicity.

**IRON SOURCES (IRON SALTS): Ferric Choline Citrate; Ferric Orthophosphate; Ferric Phosphate; Ferric Pyrophosphate, Ferric Sodium Pyrophosphate; Ferrous Fumarate; Ferrous Gluconate; Ferrous Lactate; and Ferrous Sulfate.** Ferric phosphate is used as a food supplement, particularly in bread enrichment. Ferric pyrophosphate is a grayish-blue powder used in ceramics. Ferric sodium pyrophosphate is used in prepared breakfast cereals, poultry stuffing, enriched flours, self-rising flours, farina, cornmeal, corn grits, bread, and rolls. The final report to the FDA of the Select Committee on GRAS Substances said there were insufficient relevant biological and other studies upon which to base an evaluation of ferric sodium pyrophosphate as a food ingredient. Ferrous fumarate is used to treat iron-deficiency anemia and the Select Committee told the FDA in 1980 that there is no evidence in the available information that it is a hazard to the public when used as it is now and should continue as GRAS with limitations on amounts that can be added to food. It may cause gastrointestinal disturbances. Ferrous lactate is greenish-white with a sweet iron taste. It is affected by air and light. It is also used to treat anemia. The Select Committee also said there is no evidence in the available information that ferrous lactate is hazardous and therefore it should continue as GRAS with limitations. Ferrous sulfate is blue-green and odorless and oxidizes in air and is used as a wood preservative, weed killer, and to treat anemia. Large quantities can cause gastrointestinal disturbances. For ferric choline citrate, see Choline Chloride. Among other irons used are ferrous gluconate, ferrous fumarate, sodium ferric EDTA; sodium ferricitropyrophosphate; and ferrous citrate and ferrous ascorbate.

**α-IRONE.** A synthetic flavoring derived from the violet family and usually isolated from irises and orris oil. Light yellow, slightly viscous. Used in berry, raspberry, strawberry, floral, violet, and fruit flavorings for beverages, ice cream, ices, candy, baked goods, and chewing gum. Also used in perfumery. See Orris Root Extract for toxicity.

**IRRADIATED ERGOSTEROL.** See Vitamin $D_2$.

**ISO.** Greek for "equal." In chemistry, it is a prefix added to the name of one compound to denote another composed of the same kinds and numbers of atoms but different from each other in structural arrangement.

**ISOAMYL ACETATE.** A synthetic flavoring agent that occurs naturally in bananas and pears. Colorless; pearlike odor and taste. Used in raspberry, strawberry, butter, caramel, coconut, cola, apple, banana, cherry, grape, peach, pear, pineapple, rum, cream soda, and vanilla flavorings for beverages, ice cream, ices, candy, baked goods, gelatin desserts, and chewing gum (2,700 ppm). Also used in perfuming shoe polish among other industrial uses. Exposure to 950 ppm for one hour has caused headache, fatigue, substernal pressure, and irritation of mucous membranes.

**ISOAMYL ACETOACETATE.** A synthetic fruit and apple flavoring agent for beverages, ice cream, ices, candy, and baked goods. No known toxicity.

**ISOAMYL ALCOHOL.** A synthetic flavoring agent that occurs naturally in apples, cognac, lemons, peppermint, raspberry, strawberry, and tea. Used in chocolate, apple, banana, brandy, and rum flavorings for beverages, ice cream, ices, candy, baked goods, gelatin desserts, chewing gum, and brandy. A central nervous system depressant. Vapor exposures have caused marked irritation of the eyes, nose, and throat, and headache. Amyl alcohols are highly toxic, and ingestion has caused human deaths from respiratory failure. Isoamyl alcohol may cause heart, lung, and kidney damage.

**ISOAMYL BENZOATE.** A synthetic berry, apple, cherry, plum, prune, liquor, rum, and maple flavoring agent for beverages, ice cream, ices, candy, gelatin desserts, baked goods, and chewing gum. Also used in perfumery and cosmetics. No known toxicity.

**ISOAMYL CINNAMATE.** A synthetic strawberry, butter, caramel, chocolate, cocoa, fruit, peach, pineapple, and honey flavoring agent for beverages, ice cream, candy, and baked goods. No known toxicity.

**ISOAMYL FORMATE. Formic Acid.** A synthetic flavoring agent, colorless, liquid, with a fruity smell. Used in strawberry, apple, apricot, banana, peach, and pineapple flavorings for beverages, ice cream, candy, baked goods, gelatin desserts, and chewing gum. See Formic Acid for toxicity.

**ISOAMYL 2-FURANBUTYRATE.** A synthetic chocolate, coffee, fruit, and whiskey flavoring agent for beverages, ice cream, ices, candy, baked goods, and gelatin. No known toxicity.

**ISOAMYL 2-FURANPROPIONATE.** A synthetic chocolate, coffee, fruit, and whiskey flavoring agent for beverages, ice cream, ices, candy, and baked goods. No known toxicity.

**α-ISOAMYL FURFURYLACETATE.** See Isoamyl 2-Furanpropionate.

**α-ISOAMYL FURFURYLPROPIONATE.** See Isoamyl 2-Furanbutyrate.

**ISOAMYL ISOBUTYRATE.** A synthetic fruit and banana flavoring agent for beverages, ice cream, ices, candy, baked goods, gelatin desserts, puddings, and chewing gum (2,000 ppm). Used in manufacture of artificial rum and fruit essences. No known toxicity.

**ISOAMYL ISOVALERATE.** A synthetic flavoring agent, clear, colorless, liquid, with an apple odor. Occurs naturally in bananas and peaches. Used in raspberry, strawberry, apple, apricot, banana, cherry, peach, pineapple, honey, rum, walnut, vanilla, and cream soda flavorings for beverages, ice cream, ices, candy, baked goods, gelatin desserts, puddings, chewing gum, jellies, and liqueurs. No known toxicity.

**ISOAMYL LAURATE.** A synthetic fruit and liquor flavoring agent for beverages, ice cream, ices, candy, and baked goods. No known toxicity.

**ISOAMYL NONANOATE.** A synthetic fruit, cognac, and rum flavoring agent for beverages, ice cream, ices, candy, and baked goods. No known toxicity.

**ISOAMYL OCTANOATE.** A synthetic chocolate, fruit, and liquor flavoring agent for beverages, ice cream, ices, candy, baked goods, and gelatin desserts. No known toxicity.

**ISOAMYL PHENYLACETATE.** A synthetic butter, chocolate, cocoa, peach, honey, licorice, and anise flavoring agent for beverages, ice cream, ices, candy, baked goods, toppings, and gelatin deserts. No known toxicity.

**ISOAMYL PYRUVATE.** A synthetic fruit, rum, and maple flavoring agent for beverages, ice cream, ices, candy, and baked goods. No known toxicity.

**ISOAMYL SALICYLATE.** A synthetic flavoring agent, colorless, liquid, with a pleasant odor. Used in root beer and fruit flavorings for beverages, ice cream, ices, candy, and baked goods. Also used in perfumery and soaps. See Salicylic Acid for toxicity.

**ISOBORNEOL.** A synthetic fruit and spice flavoring agent for beverages, ice cream, ices, candy, baked goods, and chewing gum. See Borneol for toxicity.

**ISOBORNYL ACETATE.** A synthetic fruit flavoring for beverages, ice cream, ices, candy, baked goods, and gelatin. No known toxicity.

**ISOBUTYL ACETATE.** A synthetic flavoring agent, clear, colorless liquid, with a fruity odor. Used in raspberry, strawberry, butter, banana, and grape flavorings for beverages, ice cream, ices, candy, baked goods, gelatin desserts, chewing gum, and icings. May be mildly irritating to mucous membranes and in high concentrations it is narcotic.

**ISOBUTYL ACETOACETATE.** A synthetic berry and fruit flavoring agent for beverages, ice cream, ices, candy, and baked goods. See Isobutyl Acetate for toxicity.

**ISOBUTYL ANTHRANILATE.** A synthetic mandarin, cherry, and grape flavoring agent for beverages, ice cream, ices, candy, baked goods, and chewing gum (1,700 ppm). No known toxicity.

**ISOBUTYL BENZOATE.** A synthetic berry, cherry, plum, and pineapple flavoring agent for beverages, ice cream, ices, candy, and baked goods. No known toxicity.

**ISOBUTYL BUTYRATE.** A synthetic berry, apple, banana, pineapple, liquor, and rum flavoring agent for beverages, ice cream, ices, candy, baked goods, puddings, and liquor. No known toxicity.

**ISOBUTYL 2-FURANPROPIONATE.** A synthetic berry and pineapple flavoring agent for beverages, ice cream, ices, candy, baked goods, gelatin desserts, chewing gum, and icings. No known toxicity.

**ISOBUTYL HEXANOATE.** A synthetic apple and pineapple flavoring agent for beverages, ice cream, ices, baked goods, and chewing gum. No known toxicity.

**ISOBUTYL ISOBUTYRATE.** A synthetic strawberry, butter, fruit, banana, and liquor flavoring agent in beverages, ice cream, ices, candy, baked goods, gelatin desserts, puddings, and liquor. No known toxicity.

**ISOBUTYL PHENYLACETATE.** A synthetic butter, caramel, chocolate, fruit, honey, and nut flavoring agent for beverages, ice cream, ices, candy, baked goods, puddings, and maraschino cherries. No known toxicity.

**ISOBUTYL PROPIONATE.** A synthetic strawberry, butter, peach, and rum flavoring agent for beverages, ice cream, candy, and baked goods. Used in the manufacture of fruit essences. No known toxicity.

**ISOBUTYL SALICYLATE.** A synthetic flavoring agent, colorless liquid, with an orchid odor. Used in fruit and root beer flavorings for beverages, ice cream, ices, candy, and baked goods. See Salicylic Acid for toxicity.

**ISOBUTYLENE-ISOPYRENE COPOLYMER.** A chewing-gum base. Isobutylene is used to produce antioxidants for foods, food supplements, and packaging. Vapors may cause asphyxiation.

**α-ISOBUTYLPHENETHYL ALCOHOL.** A synthetic butter, caramel, chocolate, fruit, and spice flavoring agent for beverages, ice cream, ices, candy, baked goods, liqueurs, and chocolate. See Isoamyl Alcohol for toxicity.

**ISOBUTYRALDEHYDE.** A synthetic flavoring agent which occurs naturally in soy sauce, tea, tobacco, and coffee. It has a pungent odor. Used in berry, butter, caramel, fruit, liquor, and wine flavorings for beverages, ice cream, ices, candy, baked goods, and liquor. No known toxicity.

**ISOBUTYRIC ACID.** A synthetic flavoring agent which occurs naturally in bay, bay leaves, parsley, and strawberries. It has a pungent odor. Used in butter, butterscotch, fruit, liquor, rum, cheese, nut, vanilla, and cream soda flavorings for beverages, ice cream, ices, candy, baked goods, chewing gum, and margarine. It is a mild irritant.

**ISOEUGENOL.** A synthetic flavoring agent, pale yellow, viscous, with a floral odor. Occurs naturally in mace oil. Used in mint, fruit, spice, cinnamon, and clove flavorings for beverages, ice cream, ices, baked goods, chewing gum (1,000 ppm), and condiments. Used in the manufacture of vanillin (*see*). No known toxicity.

**ISOEUGENYL ACETATE.** A synthetic berry, fruit, and spice flavoring agent for beverages, ice cream, ices, candy, baked goods, and chewing gum. No known toxicity.

**ISOEUGENYL ETHYL ETHER.** A synthetic flavoring agent, white crystals with a spicy, clovelike odor. Used in fruit and vanilla flavorings for beverages, ice cream, ices, candy, and baked goods. No known toxicity.

**ISOEUGENYL FORMATE.** A synthetic spice flavoring agent used in condiments. See Formic Acid for toxicity.

**ISOEUGENYL METHYL ETHER.** A synthetic raspberry, strawberry, cherry, and clove flavoring agent for beverages, ices, ice cream, candy, baked goods, gelatin desserts, and chewing gum. No known toxicity.

**ISOEUGENYL PHENYLACETATE.** A synthetic fruit, honey, and spice flavoring agent for beverages, ice cream, ices, candy, and baked goods. No known toxicity.

**ISOLATE.** In chemistry, a chemical or material obtained from a natural substance. For example, citral can be isolated from lemon oil or orange oil; geraniol can be isolated from the oil of geranium and oil of citronella. An extract, on the other hand, is a solution obtained by passing alcohol or an alcohol and water mixture through a substance.

**ISOLEUCINE. L and DL forms.** An essential component in human nutrition. It is a product of almost every protein but is not synthesized in the human body. Isolated commercially from beet sugar. The FDA has asked for a further study of this nutrient. GRAS.

**ISOPROPYL CITRATE.** A sequestrant and antioxidant agent used in oleomargarine and salad oils. See Citrate Salts for toxicity. The final report to the FDA of the Select Committee on GRAS Substances stated in 1980 that it should continue its GRAS status with no limitations other than good manufacturing practices.

**ISOPROPYL FORMATE. Formic Acid.** A synthetic berry and melon flavoring agent for beverages, ice cream, candy, and baked goods. See Formic Acid for toxicity.

**ISOPROPYL HEXANOATE.** A synthetic pineapple flavoring agent for beverages, ice cream, ices, candy, and baked goods. No known toxicity.

**ISOPROPYL ISOBUTYRATE.** A synthetic pineapple flavoring agent for beverages, ice cream, ices, candy, and baked goods. No known toxicity.

**ISOPROPYL ISOVALERATE.** A synthetic pineapple and nut flavoring agent for beverages, ice cream, ices, candy, and baked goods. No known toxicity.

**ISOPROPYL PHENYLACETATE.** A synthetic butter, caramel, and honey flavoring agent for beverages, ice cream, ices, candy, and baked goods. No known toxicity.

**ISOVINYL FORMATE. Formic Acid.** A synthetic fruit flavoring agent for beverages, ice cream, ices, candy, and baked goods. See Formic Acid for toxicity.

**ISOVINYL PROPIONATE.** See Isovinyl Formate.

# J

**JAPAN WAX. Japan Talow. Sumac Wax.** Derived from a species of *Rhus* by boiling the fruit in water. It is a pale yellow solid with a tallow-like rancid odor and contains 10 to 15 percent palmatin and other glycerides (*see*). It is used in candles, as a substitute for beeswax, and in food packaging. The final report to the FDA of the Select Committee on GRAS Substances stated in 1980 that there were insufficient relevant biological and other studies upon which to base an evaluation of it when it is used as a food ingredient. It remains GRAS for packaging.

**JASMINE. Oil and Spiritus (alcoholic solution).** The oil is extracted from a tropical shrub and is used in raspberry, strawberry, floral, and cherry flavorings for beverages, ice cream, ices, candy, baked goods, gelatin desserts, chewing gum, and jelly. The *spiritus* is used in blackberry, strawberry, and fruit flavorings for beverages, ice cream, ices, candy, baked goods, gelatin, and cherries. No known toxicity.

**JASMONYL.** See 1,3-Nonanediol Acetate.

**JUNIPER. Extract, Oil, and Berries.** A flavoring from the dried ripe fruit of trees grown in Northern Europe, Asia, and North America. The greenish yellow *extract* is used in liquor, root beer, sarsaparilla, wintergreen, and birch beer flavorings for beverages, ice cream, ices, candy, and baked goods. The *oil* is used in berry, cola, pineapple, gin, rum, whiskey, root beer, ginger, and meat flavorings for beverages, ice cream, ices, candy, baked goods, gelatin desserts, chewing gum, meats, and liquors. The *berries* are used in gin flavoring for condiments and liquors. Juniper is used also in fumigating, and was formerly a diuretic for reducing body water. No known toxicity. GRAS.

# K

**KADAYA.** See Karaya Gum.

**KAOLIN. China Clay.** A white-burning aluminum silicate which, due to its purity, has a high fusion point and is the most refractory of all clays. It is found in the Southeastern United States, England, and France and is used as a coating for paper, in ceramics, as a catalyst carrier, in cosmetics, and as an anticaking agent in food. It is also used in dietary supplements. The final report to the FDA of the Select Committee on GRAS Substances stated in 1980 that it should continue its GRAS status with no limitations other than good manufacturing practices. See also Clay.

**KARAYA GUM. Kadaya. Katilo. Kullo. Kuterra. Sterculia. Indian Tragacanth. Mucara.** The dried exudate of a tree found in India. The finely ground white powder is used in gelatins and in gumdrops, prepared ices, and ice cream, and as a filler for lemon custard. Also a citrus and spice flavoring agent for beverages, ice cream, ices (1,300 ppm), candy, baked goods, meats, toppings (3,500 ppm), and emulsions (18,000 ppm). Used instead of the more expensive gum tragacanth (*see*) and in bulk laxatives. Reevaluated by the FDA in 1976 and found to be GRAS in the following percentages: .3 for frozen dairy desserts and mixes; .02 percent for milk products; .9 percent for soft candy; and .002 for all other food categories.

**KATILO.** See Karaya Gum.

**KAUTSCHIN.** See *d*-Limonene.

**KELP. Brown Algae.** Used as seasoning or flavoring and to provide iodine when used in dietary foods. It has many minerals that are associated with sea water and, as a result, is very high in sodium. The Japanese report that kelp reduced normal thyroid function, probably because of its iodine content. The FDA has also reported that high levels of arsenic have been found in people who eat a lot of kelp as a vegetable. The final report to the FDA of the Select Committee on GRAS Substances stated in 1980 that it should continue its GRAS status with no limitations other than good manufacturing practices.

**KENTONAROME.** See Methylcyclopentenolone.

**KETONE C-7.** See 2-Heptanone.

**2-KETOPROPIONALDEHYDE.** See Pyruvaldehyde.

**α-KETOPROPIONIC ACID.** See Pyruvic Acid.

**KOLA NUT EXTRACT. Guru Nut.** A natural extract from the brownish seed, about the size of a chestnut, produced by trees in Africa, West Indies, and Brazil. Contains caffeine (*see*). Used in butter, caramel, chocolate, cocoa, coffee, cola, walnut, and root beer flavorings for beverages, ice cream, ices, candy, and baked goods. Has been used to treat epilepsy. GRAS.

**KRAMERIA EXTRACT.** See Rhatany Extract.

**KULLO.** See Karaya Gum.

**KUTEERAL.** See Karaya Gum.

# L

**LABDANUM. Absolute, Oil, and Oleoresin.** A synthetic flavoring agent, a volatile oil obtained by steam distillation from gum extracted from shrubs. Golden yellow, viscous, with a strong balsamic odor. The *absolute* is used in raspberry, fruit, and vanilla flavorings for beverages, ice cream, ices, candy, baked goods, gelatin desserts, and chewing gum. The *oil* is used in fruit and spice flavorings for beverages, ice cream, ices, candy, and baked goods. The *oleoresin* (*see*) is used in fruit and vanilla flavorings for beverages, ice cream, ices, candy, and baked goods. No known toxicity.

**LACTIC ACID. Butyl Lactate. Ethyl Lactate.** A colorless, nearly odorless liquid which occurs in sour milk as the result of lactic-acid bacteria; also found in molasses, due to partial conversion of sugars, in apples and other fruits, tomato juice, beer, wines, opium, ergot, foxglove, and other plants. It is produced commercially by fermentation of whey, cornstarch, potatoes, and molasses. Used as an acidulant in beverages, candy, olives, dried egg whites, cottage cheese, confections, bread, rolls, buns, cheese products, frozen desserts, sherbets, ices, fruit jelly, butter, preserves, jams (sufficient amounts may be added to compensate for the deficiency of fruit acidity), and in the brewing industry. Also used in infant-feeding formulas. Used in blackberry, butter, butterscotch, lime, chocolate, fruit, walnut, spice, and cheese flavorings for beverages, ice cream, ices, candy, baked goods, gelatins, puddings, chewing gum, toppings, pickles, and olives (24,000 ppm). In concentrated solution it is caustic. The final report to the FDA of the Select Committee on GRAS Substances stated in 1980 that it should continue its GRAS status with no limitations other than good manufacturing practices.

**LACTOFLAVIN.** See Riboflavin.

**LACTOSE. Milk Sugar. Saccharum Lactin. D-Lactose.** A slightly sweet tasting, colorless sugar present in the milk of mammals (humans have 6.7 percent and cows 4.3 percent). Occurs as a white powder or crystalline mass as a byproduct of the cheese industry. Produced from whey (*see*). It is inexpensive and is widely used in the food industry as a culture medium, such as in souring milk and as a humectant (*see*) and nutrient in an infant's or debilitated patient's formula. Also used as a medical diuretic and laxative. Nontoxic, but in National Cancer Institute reports, it did cause tumors when injected under the skin of mice in 50-million-gram doses per kilogram of body weight.

**LACTYLIC STEARATE.** Salt of stearic acid (*see*) used as a dough conditioner to add volume and to keep baked products soft; it makes bread less sticky. See Stearic Acid for toxicity.

**LAMINARIA.** Seaweed from which algin is extracted. See Alginates. GRAS.

**LANOLIN.** Wool fat, the secretion of the sebaceous glands of sheep, which is deposited onto the wool fibers. Chemically a wax instead of a fat. Contains about 25–30 percent water; yellowish white, slight odor. Mixes with about twice its weight of water. Used as a chewing gum base component and as a water absorbable ointment base in cosmetics. May cause allergic reactions.

**LANTANA.** See Oregano.

**LARCH GUM. Larch Turpentine. Venice Turpentine.** Oleoresin (*see*) from *Larix decidua Mill.,* grown in middle and southern Europe. A yellow, sometimes greenish, tenacious, thick liquid with a pleasant, aromatic odor, it has a hot, somewhat bitter taste. It becomes hard and brittle on prolonged exposure. It is used as a stabilizer, thickener, and texturizer. No known toxicity.

**LARD AND LARD OILS. Pork Fat and Oils.** Soft, white unctuous mass from the abdomen of hogs. It is used in the manufacture of ointments and soap and as a lubricant. It is used in packaging and in chewing gum bases. When lard was fed to laboratory animals in doses of from 2 to 25 percent of the diet, the male mice had a shortened life span and increased osteoarthritis. This was thought to be due to the large amounts of fat and not specifically to lard. The final report to the FDA of the Select Committee on GRAS Substances stated in 1980 that lard and lard oil should continue their GRAS status for packaging only with no limitations other than good manufacturing practices.

**LARIXINIC ACID.** See Maltol.

**LAUREL.** The fresh berries and leaf extract of the laurel tree. The berries are used as a flavoring for beverages and the leaf extract is a spice flavoring for vegetables. No known toxicity. GRAS.

**LAURIC ACID. Dodecanoic Acid.** A common constituent of vegetable fats, especially coconut oil and laurel oil. A white, glossy powder, insoluble in water, and used in the manufacture of miscellaneous flavors for beverages, ice cream, candy, baked goods, gelatins, and puddings. Used chiefly in the manufacture of soaps, detergents, cosmetics, and lauryl alcohol. It is a mild irritant.

**LAURINE®.** See Hydroxycitronellal.

**LAUROSTEARIC ACID.** See Lauric Acid.

**LAVANDIN OIL.** A flavoring from a hybrid related to the lavender plant, pale yellow liquid, with a camphor-lavender smell. Used in berry and citrus flavorings for beverages, baked goods, ice cream, ices, candy, and chewing gum. No known toxicity. GRAS.

**LAVENDER.** The colorless liquid extracted from the fresh, flowery tops of the plant. Smells like lavender, and used in ginger ale flavoring for beverages. Lavender *absolute* is a fruit flavoring for beverages, ice cream, ices, candy, and baked goods. Lavender *concrete* is a fruit flavoring for beverages, ice cream, ices, candy, and baked goods. Lavender *oil* is a citrus, pineapple, and ginger ale flavoring for beverages, ice cream, ices, candy, baked goods, and chewing gum. Lavender was once used to break up stomach gas. Keeps moths away from clothes. Used in fumigating and in perfumery. May cause a sensitivity to light. GRAS.

**LEAF ALCOHOL.** See 3-Hexen-1-ol.

**LEAVENING.** From the Latin *levare*, "to raise." It is a substance, such as yeast, acting to produce fermentation in dough or liquid. Leavening serves to lighten or enliven, such as baking soda when it produces a gas that lightens dough or batter.

**LECITHIN.** From the Greek, meaning "egg yolk." Found in all living organisms, plant and animal. It is a significant constituent of nerve tissue and brain substance. Composed of units of choline, phosphoric acid, fatty acids, and glycerin (*see all*). Commercially isolated from eggs, soybeans, corn, and egg yolk and used as an antioxidant in prepared breakfast cereal, candy, sweet chocolate, bread, rolls, buns, and oleomargarine. *Hydroxylated* lecithin is a defoaming component in yeast and beet sugar production. Lecithin with or without *phosphatides* (components of fat) is an emulsifier for sweet chocolate, milk chocolate, bakery products, frozen desserts, oleomargarine, rendered animal fat, or a combination of vegetable-animal fats. Nontoxic. The final report to the FDA of the Select Committee on GRAS Substances stated in 1980 that it should continue its GRAS status with no limitations other than good manufacturing practices.

**LEMON. Extract and Oil.** Lemon *extract* is used in lemon flavorings for beverages, ice cream, ices, candy, baked goods, and icings. Lemon *oil* is a blueberry, loganberry, strawberry, butter, grapefruit, lemon, lime, orange, cola, coconut, honey, wine, rum, root beer, and ginger ale flavoring for beverages, ice cream, ices, candy, baked goods, gelatin desserts, chewing gum (1,900 ppm), condiments, meats, syrups, icings, and cereals. Lemon oil is suspected of being a cancer-causing agent. GRAS.

**LEMON BALM.** See Balm Oil.

**LEMON-GRASS OIL.** Volatile oil distilled from the leaves of the lemon grasses. A natural flavoring agent used in lemon and fruit flavorings for beverages, ice cream, ices, candy, baked goods, gelatin desserts, and chewing gum. Used chiefly in perfumery. Has killed a child, and autopsy showed gastric mucosa was severely damaged.

**LEMON OIL, TERPENELESS.** A lemon, fruit, ginger, and ginger ale flavoring agent for beverages, ice cream, ices, candy, baked goods, gelatin desserts, chewing gum, and toppings. Terpene, which is removed to improve flavor, is a class of unsaturated hydrocarbons. See Lemon for toxicity.

**LEMON PEEL.** From the outer rind, the extract is used as a flavor in medicines and in beverages, confectionery, and cooking. See Lemon for toxicity.

**LEUCINE. L and DL forms.** An essential amino acid (*see*) for human nutrition, not manufactured in the body. It is isolated commercially from gluten, casein, and keratin. It has a sweet taste. The FDA says it needs further study. GRAS.

**LICORICE. Extract, Extract Powder, and Root.** Licorice *extract,* from the Mediterranean plant, is used in fruit, licorice, anise, maple, and root beer flavorings for beverages, ice cream, ices, candy, baked goods, gelatin, chewing gum (29,000 ppm), and syrups. Licorice *extract powder* is used in licorice, anise, maple, and root beer flavorings for beverages, ice cream, ices, baked goods, candy (6,500 ppm), and chewing gum (22,000 ppm). Licorice *root* is used in licorice and root beer flavorings for beverages, candy, baked goods, chewing gum (3,200 ppm), tobacco, and medicines. Some people known to have eaten licorice candy regularly and generously had raised blood pressure, headaches, and muscle weakness. The final report to the FDA of the Select Committee on GRAS Substances stated in 1980 that it should continue as GRAS with no limitations.

**LIGHT GREEN.** See FD and C Green No. 2.

**LIME OIL.** A natural flavoring extracted from the fruit of a tropical tree. Colorless to greenish. Used in grapefruit, lemon, lemon-lime, lime, orange, cola, fruit, rum, nut, and ginger flavorings for beverages, ice cream, ices, candy, baked goods, gelatin desserts, chewing gum (3,100 ppm), and condiments. *Terpeneless (see* Lemon Oil) lime oil is used in lemon, lime, lemon-lime, cola, pineapple, ginger, and ginger ale flavorings for beverages, ice cream, ices, candy, baked goods, gelatin desserts, chewing gum, and syrups. May cause sensitivity to light. GRAS.

**LIMONENE. D, L, and DL forms.** A synthetic flavoring agent that occurs naturally in star anise, buchu leaves, caraway, celery, oranges, coriander, cumin, cardamom, sweet fennel, common fennel, mace, marigold, oil of lavandin, oil of lemon, oil of mandarin, peppermint, petitgrain oil, pimento oil, orange leaf (absolute), orange peel (sweet oil), origanum oil, black pepper, peels of citrus, macrocarpa bunge, and hops oil. Used in lime, fruit, and spice flavorings for beverages, ice cream, ices, candy, baked goods, gelatin desserts, and chewing gum (2,300 ppm). A skin irritant and sensitizer. GRAS.

**LINALOE WOOD OIL.** A natural flavoring agent, colorless to yellow, with a flowery odor. Used in berry, citrus, fruit, liquor, and ginger flavorings for beverages, ice cream, ices, candy, baked goods, and liquors. No known toxicity.

**LINALOL. Linalool.** A synthetic flavoring that occurs naturally in basil, bois de rose oil, cassia, coriander, cocoa, grapefruit, grapefruit oil, oranges, peaches, tea, bay and bay-leaf extract, ginger, lavender, laurel leaves, and other oils. Colorless, with a floral odor. Used in blueberry, chocolate, lemon, lime, orange, cola, grape, peach, cardamom, nutmeg, and meat flavorings for beverages, ice cream, ices, candy, baked goods, gelatin desserts, meats, and chewing gum. Used in perfumery instead of bergamot or French lavender. No known toxicity. GRAS.

**LINALYL ACETATE.** A synthetic flavoring that occurs naturally in basil, jasmine oil, lavandin oil, lavender oil, lemon oil, peels of citrus, macrocarpa bunge, petitgrain oil, and lemon oil. Colorless, with a floral odor. Used in berry, citrus, peach, pear, and ginger flavorings for beverages, ice cream, ices, candy, baked goods, gelatin desserts, and chewing gum. Used in perfumery. No known toxicity. GRAS.

**LINALYL ANTHRANILATE.** A synthetic berry, citrus, fruit, and grape flavoring agent for beverages, ice cream, ices, candy, and baked goods. No known toxicity.

**LINALYL BENZOATE.** A synthetic flavoring, brownish yellow, with a roselike odor. Used in berry, citrus, fruit, and peach flavorings for beverages, ice cream, ices, candy, baked goods, and gelatin desserts. No known toxicity.

**LINALYL BUTYRATE.** A synthetic flavoring used in loganberry, butter, caramel, citrus, floral, rose, fruit, grape, peach, pear, pineapple, plum, honey, nut, and spice flavorings for beverages, ice cream, ices, candy, baked goods, and gelatin desserts. No known toxicity.

**LINALYL CINNAMATE.** A synthetic loganberry, floral, rose, fruit, grape, and honey flavoring agent for beverages, ice cream, ices, candy, and baked goods. No known toxicity.

**LINALYL FORMATE. Formic Acid.** A synthetic flavoring that occurs naturally in oil of lavandin. Used in berry, apple, apricot, peach, and pineapple flavorings for beverages, ice cream, ices, candy, and baked goods. See Formic Acid for toxicity.

**LINALYL HEXANOATE.** A synthetic fruit flavoring agent for beverages, ice cream, ices, candy, and baked goods. No known toxicity.

**LINALYL ISOBUTYRATE.** A synthetic flavoring, colorless, slightly yellow, with a fruity odor. Used in berry, citrus, fruit, banana, black currant, cherry, pear, pineapple, plum, nut, and spice flavorings for beverages, ice cream, ices, candy, and baked goods. No known toxicity.

**LINALYL ISOVALERATE.** A synthetic flavoring, colorless to slightly yellow, with a fruity odor. Used in loganberry, apple, apricot, peach, pear, and plum flavorings for beverages, ice cream, ices, candy, baked goods, and gelatin desserts. No known toxicity.

**LINALYL OCTANOATE.** A synthetic citrus, rose, apple, pineapple, and honey flavoring agent for beverages, ice cream, ices, candy, and baked goods. No known toxicity.

**LINALYL PROPIONATE.** A synthetic currant, orange, banana, pear, and pineapple flavoring agent for beverages, ice cream, ices, candy, baked goods, and gelatin desserts. No known toxicity.

**LINDEN FLOWERS.** A natural flavoring from the flower of the tree grown in Europe and the United States. Used in raspberry and vermouth flavorings for beverages (2,000 ppm). No known toxicity. GRAS.

**LINOLEIC ACID.** An essential fatty acid (*see*) prepared from edible fats and oils. Component of Vitamin F and a major constituent of many vegetable oils, for example, cottonseed, soybean, peanut, corn, sunflower, safflower seed, poppy seed, linseed, and perilla oils. Used in emulsifiers and vitamins. Large doses can cause nausea and vomiting. When given in large doses to rats, weight loss and progressive secondary anemia developed. The final report to the FDA of the Select Committee on GRAS

Substances stated in 1980 that it should continue its GRAS status for packaging with no limitations other than good manufacturing practices.

**LIVER-STOMACH CONCENTRATE. With intrinsic factor complex.** A dietary supplement containing Vitamin $B_{12}$ activity and folic acid. In suitable dosage, liver extract increases the number of red blood cells in persons affected with pernicious anemia. May cause allergic reactions.

**LOCUST BEAN GUM. St.-John's-Bread. Carob Bean.** A natural flavor extract from the seed of the carob tree cultivated in the Mediterranean area. The history of the carob tree dates back more than 2,000 years when the ancient Egyptians used locust bean gum as an adhesive in mummy binding. It is alleged that the "locusts [through confusion of the locusts with the carob] and wild honey" that sustained John the Baptist in the wilderness were carob beans, thus the name "St.-John's-bread." The carob *pods* are used as feed for stock today because of their high protein content. They are also eaten by some health food enthusiasts for the same purpose. They are also used as a thickener and stabilizer (*see* Gum, Carob Bean). Carob bean *extract* is used in raspberry, bitters, butter, butterscotch, caramel, chocolate, cherry, brandy, wine, maple, root beer, spice, vanilla, cream soda, and grape flavorings for beverages, ice cream, ices, candy, baked goods, gelatin desserts (600 ppm), icings, and toppings (1,000 ppm). A University of Minnesota pediatric cardiologist reported in 1981 that locust bean may lower blood cholesterol levels. Dr. James Zavoral and associates found that 28 adults and children with histories of familial hypercholesterolemia were fed food products rich in locust bean gum. Some of those included breads, cookies, crackers, and "Tater Tots." After four weeks on the special diets, their cholesterol dropped 10 percent and after six weeks, 20 percent. The final report to the FDA of the Select Committee on GRAS Substances stated in 1980 that there is no evidence in the available information that it is a hazard to the public when used as it is now and it should continue its GRAS status with limitations on amounts that can be added to the food.

**LOVAGE. Smallage.** Flavoring obtained from the root of an herb native to southern Europe. Used in bitters, maple, and walnut flavorings for beverages, ice cream, ices, candy, baked goods, and table syrups. The *extract* is used in berry, butter, butterscotch, caramel, coffee, fruit, maple, meat, black walnut, and spice flavorings for the same foods as above, plus condiments and icings. The *oil,* yellow-brown and aromatic, is used in butter, butterscotch, caramel, coffee, fruit, licorice, liquor, maple, nut, walnut, and spice flavorings for the same foods as is the extract. No known toxicity.

**LUPULIN. Hops.** A natural flavoring extract from a plant (*Humulus lupulis*) grown in Europe, Asia, and North America. Used in beer brewing. Formerly used as aromatic bitters and as a sedative. At one time in veterinary usage it was recommended for treatment of nymphomania. No known toxicity. GRAS.

**LUTEIN.** See Xanthophyll.

**LYSINE. L and DL forms.** An essential amino acid (*see*) isolated from casein (*see*), fibrin, or blood. It is used for food enrichment for wheat-based foods. Lysine improves their protein quality and results in improved growth and tissue synthesis. Employed in the fortification of specialty bread and cereal mixes up to .25 percent to .5 percent of the weight of flour. On the FDA list for further study. GRAS.

# M ————————————————————

**MACE. Oil and Oleoresin.** Obtained by steam distillation from the ripe dried seed of the nutmeg. Colorless to pale yellow, with the taste and odor of nutmeg. Used in bitters, meat, and spice flavorings for beverages, ice cream, ices, baked goods, condiments, and meats (2,000 ppm). The *oil* is used in chocolate, cocoa, coconut, cola, fruit, nut, spice, and ginger ale flavorings for beverages, ice cream, ices, candy, baked goods, chewing gum, condiments, and meats. The *oleoresin* (*see*) is used in sausage and spice flavorings for baked goods, condiments, meats, and pickles. See Nutmeg for toxicity. The final report to the FDA of the Select Committee on GRAS Substances stated in 1980 that while no evidence in the available information on it demonstrates a hazard to the public at current use levels, uncertainties exist, requiring that additional studies be conducted. GRAS status continues while tests are being completed and evaluated.

**MAGNESIUM. Magnesium Phosphate, Magnesium Sulfate, Magnesium Oxide, Magnesium Silicate, Magnesium Chloride, Magnesium Carbonate, Magnesium Cyclamate, Magnesium Stearate, and Magnesium Hydroxide.** A silver-white, light, malleable, metallic element that occurs abundantly in nature but is always found in combination in minerals, in sea and mineral waters, and in plants and animals. *Magnesium phosphate,* a white, odorless powder, and *magnesium sulfate* are used as mineral supplements for food. Recommended daily allowances, according to the National Academy of Sciences, are 40 milligrams for infants; 100 to 300 milligrams for children; 350 milligrams for adult males and females. *Magnesium sulfate* is used also as a corrective in the brewing industry and for fertilizers. *Magnesium oxide,* a white, bulky powder, is an alkali used as a neutralizer in frozen dairy products, butter, cacao products, and canned peas. *Magnesium silicate,* a fine, white, odorless and tasteless powder, is used in table salt and vanilla powder as an anticaking agent. In table salt it is limited to 2 percent. *Magnesium chloride* is used for color retention and as a firming agent in canned peas. *Magnesium carbonate,* a white powder or mass, is used as an alkali for sour cream, butter, ice cream, cacao products, and canned peas. It is also used as a drying agent and an anticaking agent. *Magnesium cyclamate* was banned in 1969 as an artificial sweetener. *Magnesium hydroxide,* a bulky, white powder, is used as an alkali in canned peas and as a drying agent and color retention agent for improved gelling in the manufacture of cheese. Toxic when inhaled. Magnesium was reevaluated by the FDA in 1976 as not harmful in presently used current levels. However, the World Health Organization's Food Committee recommends further study of *magnesium silicate* because kidney damage in dogs has been reported upon ingestion. *Magnesium carbonate, chloride, sulfate, stearate, phosphate,* and *silicate* are all GRAS, according to the final report to the FDA of the Select Committee on GRAS Substances and they should continue their GRAS status with no limitations other than good manufacturing practices.

**MALEIC HYDRAZIDE.** Regulates the growth of unwanted "suckers" on about 90 percent of the United States tobacco crop. It is also applied to 10 to 15 percent of domestic potatoes and onions to prevent sprouting after harvest. It is highly toxic to humans and has produced central nervous system disturbances and liver damage in experimental animals. It has led to liver and other tumors in some mice. However, other studies, including one done for the National Cancer Institute and published in 1969, show no carcinogenic effects from it. It has produced genetic damage in plant and animal systems, a fact that often signals a cancer-causing effect.

**MALIC ACID.** A flavoring agent and aid in aging wine; colorless crystalline compound, with a strong acid taste that occurs naturally in a wide variety of fruit, including apples, cherries, peaches, and tomatoes, and coffee, rhubarb root, and vanilla. Used as an alkali in frozen dairy products, beverages, baked goods, confections, fruit, butter, and jelly and jam preserves "in amounts sufficient to compensate for the deficiency of fruit in artificially sweetened fruit." No known toxicity. The final report to the FDA of the Select Committee on GRAS Substances stated in 1980 that it should continue its GRAS status with no limitations other than good manufacturing practices.

**MALLOW EXTRACT.** From the herb family Malvaceae, it is a moderate purplish red, paler than magenta rose. It is used in coloring and also as a source of pectin *(see)*. No known toxicity.

**MALT EXTRACT.** Extracted from barley which has been allowed to germinate, and then heated to destroy vitality, and dried. Contains diastase, dextrin, dextrose, protein bodies, and salts from barley. The extract is prepared by mixing it with water and allowing the solution to evaporate. It is used as a food adjunct, or nutrient. It is also used widely in the brewing industry. No known toxicity. GRAS.

**MALTO-DEXTRIN.** Combination of maltol (*see*) and dextrin (*see*) used as a texturizer and flavor enhancer in candies, particularly chocolate. No known toxicity. The final report to the FDA of the Select Committee on GRAS Substances stated in 1980 that it should continue its GRAS status with no limitations other than good manufacturing practices.

**MALTOL.** A white, crystalline powder with a butterscotch odor, found in the bark of young larch trees, pine needles, chicory, wood tars, and in roasted malt. It imparts a "freshly baked" odor and flavor to bread and cakes. Used as a synthetic chocolate, coffee, fruit, maple, nut, and vanilla flavoring agent for beverages, ice cream, ices, candy, baked goods, gelatin desserts, chewing gum, and jelly. No known toxicity.

**MALTOSE.** It is composed of two molecules of glucose and is found in starch and glycogen. Its colorless crystals are derived from the enzymatic action of malt extract on starch. It is soluble in water and used as a nutrient, sweetener, in culture media, and as a supplement of sugar for diabetics. It is also used in brewing and as a stabilizer. It is nontoxic but it has been reported to cause tumors when injected under the skin of mice in doses of 500 milligrams per kilogram of body weight.

**MANDARIN OIL.** Obtained by expression of the peel of a ripe mandarin orange. Clear, dark orange to reddish yellow, with a pleasant orangelike odor. It is an orange, tangerine, cherry, and grape flavoring for beverages, ice cream, ices, candy, gelatin desserts, and chewing gum. No known toxicity. GRAS.

**MANGANESE SOURCES: Manganese Acetate, Manganese Carbonate, Manganese Chloride, Manganese Citrate, Manganese Gluconate, Manganese Sulfate, Manganese Glycerophosphate, Manganese Hypophosphite, and Manganese Oxide.** A mineral supplement first isolated in 1774, it occurs in minerals and in minute quantities in animals, plants, and in water. Many forms are used in dyeing. Manganous salts are activators of enzymes and are necessary to the development of strong bones. They are used as nutrients and as dairy substitutes. Toxicity occurs by inhalation. Symptoms include languor, sleepiness, weakness, emotional disturbances, and Parkinson-like symptoms. *Manganese chloride, citrate, glycerophosphate, and hypophosphite* are all considered GRAS according to the final report of the Select Committee on GRAS Substances and should continue their GRAS status as nutrients with no limitations other than good manufacturing practices. However, *manganese oxide,* according to the Select Committee, does not have enough known about it upon which to base an evaluation when it is used as a food ingredient.

**MANNITOL.** Widespread in plants but mostly prepared from seaweed, it is a white crystalline, solid, odorless, and sweet-tasting compound. It is used as a texturizer in chewing gum and in candy up to 5 percent. It has been used as a sweetener in "sugar-free" products but has calories and carbohydrates. Used as a dusting or antisticking agent in a number of food products. When taken in excess, it can cause gastrointestinal disturbances. It may also induce or worsen kidney disease. In 1982, the FDA reported that it does not cause cancer in rats.

**MARGARINE. Oleomargarine.** A butter substitute made from animal or vegetable fats or oils. If oils are used they are "hardened" into fats by the process of hydrogenation (*see*). Skimmed milk, water, salt, coloring matter (*see* carotene), artificial flavors, lecithin (*see*), and small amounts of vitamins are usually added. By federal regulations, margarine contains at least 80 percent fat. No known toxicity.

**MARIGOLD, POT.** A natural plant extract. The oil is used in various flavorings for beverages, ice cream, ices, candy, and baked goods. No known toxicity. See Tagetes. GRAS.

**MARJORAM, POT. Sweet Marjoram.** The natural extract of the flowers and leaves of two varieties of the fragrant marjoram plant. The *oleoresin* (*see*) is used in sausage and spice flavorings for condiments and meats. The *seed* is used in sausage and spice flavorings for meats (3,500 ppm) and condiments. Sweet marjoram is used in sausage and spice flavorings for beverages, baked goods (2,000 ppm), condiments, meats, and soups. The *sweet oil* is used in vermouth, wine, and spice flavorings for beverages, ice creams, ices, candy, baked goods, and condiments. No known toxicity. GRAS.

**MARSHMALLOW ROOT.** See Althea Root.

**MATÉ. Paraguay Tea. St. Bartholomew's Tea. Jesuit's Tea.** A natural flavoring extract from small gourds grown in South America, where maté is a stimulant beverage. Among its constituents are caffeine, purines, and tannins. Used as a flavoring agent. See Caffeine and Tannic Acid for toxicity. GRAS.

**MATRICARIA. Wild Chamomile Extract.** Extract of the flower heads of *Matricaria chamomilla.* Used internally as a tonic and externally as a soothing medication for contusions and other inflammations. Also used as a soothing tea.

**MATURING AGENTS.** See Bleaching Agents.

**MELISSA.** See Balm Oil.

**MELONAL.** See 2,6-Dimethyl-5-Heptenal.

**MENADIONE. Vitamin K₃.** A synthetic with properties of vitamin K. The bright yellow crystals are insoluble in water. Used medicinally to prevent blood clotting and in food to prevent the souring of milk products. Can be irritating to mucous membranes, respiratory passages, and the skin.

**p-MENTHA-1,8-DIEN-7-OL.** A synthetic citrus, fruit, mint, and vanilla flavoring agent for beverages, ice cream, ices, candy, and baked goods. It is found naturally in caraway. Can cause skin irritation.

**MENTHOL.** A flavoring agent that occurs naturally in raspberries, peppermint and other mints, as well as betel. Usually obtained from peppermint oil. Used in butter, caramel, fruit, peppermint, and spearmint flavorings for beverages, cream, ices, candy, baked goods, chewing gum (1,100 ppm), and liquor. Also used in perfumery, cigarettes, cough drops, and nasal inhalers. It is an antipruritic and mild local anesthetic (topical dose: 0.1 percent to 2 percent in skin preparations); it can cause severe abdominal pain, nausea, vomiting, vertigo, and coma when ingested in its concentrated form. The lethal dose in rats is 2.0 grams per kilogram of body weight. GRAS.

**(d)-neo-MENTHOL.** A flavoring agent that occurs naturally in Japanese mint oil. Used in mint flavorings for beverages, ice cream, ices, candy, and baked goods. See Menthol for toxicity.

**MENTHONE.** A synthetic flavoring agent that occurs naturally in raspberries and peppermint oil. Bitter, with a slight peppermint taste. Used in fruit and mint flavorings for beverages, ice cream, ices, candy, baked goods, and chewing gum. May cause gastric distress.

**MENTHYL ACETATE.** A natural flavoring agent that occurs naturally in peppermint oil. Colorless, with a mint odor. Used in fruit, mint, and spice flavorings for beverages, ice cream, ices, candy, baked goods, and chewing gum; also in perfumes and toilet waters. No known toxicity. GRAS.

**METHANETHIOL. Methyl Mercaptan.** A pesticide and fungicide isolated from the roots of a plant. Occurs in the "sour" gas of West Texas, in coal tar, and in petroleum. Produced in the intestinal tract by action of bacteria. Found in urine after ingestion of asparagus. Its odor may cause nausea and it may be narcotic in high concentrations.

**METHIONINE.** An essential amino acid (*see*) not synthesized in the human body. It is used in special dietary foods and in animal feeds. Used in fat. Rutgers University researchers have patented a process to impregnate a carrier material with methionine for use in deep-fried cooking oil to impart a "fresh" potato or potato chip flavor to snack foods, soups, or salad dressings. On the FDA list of additives requiring further study. GRAS.

*p*-METHOXY BENZYL ACETATE. See Anisyl Acetate.

*p*-METHOXY BENZYL ALCOHOL. See Anisyl Alcohol.

2-METHOXY-4-METHYLPHENOL. Creosol. A synthetic flavoring that occurs naturally in cassie and is used in fruit, rum, nut, and clove flavorings for beverages, ice cream, ices, candy, baked goods, and liqueurs. About the same toxicity as phenol, a highly caustic, poisonous compound derived from benzene.

1-METHOXY-4-PROPENYLBENZENE. See Anethole.

2-METHOXY-4-PROPENYLPHENOL. See Isoeugenol.

METHOXYACETOPHENONE. See Acetanisole.

METHOXYBENZENE. See Anisole.

*o*-METHOXYBENZALDEHYDE. A synthetic flavoring agent that occurs naturally in cassia oil and is used in spice and cinnamon flavorings for beverages, baked goods, and chewing gum. No known toxicity.

*p*-METHOXYBENZALDEHYDE. Anisaldehyde. A synthetic flavoring agent that occurs naturally in hawthorn, fennel, oil of anise, star anise, and Tahiti vanilla beans. Used in raspberry, strawberry, butter, caramel, chocolate, apricot, cherry, peach, licorice, anise, nut, black walnut, walnut, spice, and vanilla flavorings for beverages, ice cream, ices, candy, baked goods, gelatin desserts, and chewing gum. No known toxicity.

*p*-METHOXYBENZYL FORMATE. See Anisyl Formate.

4′-METHYL ACETOPHENONE. A synthetic fruit, almond, and vanilla flavoring agent for beverages, ice cream, ices, candy, baked goods, maraschino cherries, chewing gum, and condiments. No known toxicity.

METHYL ACETATE. Acetic Acid. A synthetic flavoring agent that occurs naturally in coffee. Colorless liquid with a pleasant odor. Used in fruit, rum, and nut flavorings for beverages, ice cream, ices, candy, baked goods, gelatin desserts, puddings, and liquor. Also used industrially as a solvent for many resins and oils. May be irritating to the respiratory tract and, in high concentrations, it may be narcotic.

METHYL ACRYLATE. Transparent, elastic substance used in packaging. Practically odorless. Used also to coat paper and plastic film. Can be highly irritating to the eyes, skin, and mucous membranes. Convulsions occur if vapors are inhaled in high concentration. GRAS for packaging. The final report to the FDA of the Select Committee on GRAS Substances stated in 1980 that there were insufficient relevant biological and other studies upon which to base an evaluation of it when it is used as a food ingredient.

**METHYL AMYL KETONE.** See 2-Heptanone.

**METHYL ANISATE. Anisic Acid.** A synthetic fruit, melon, liquor, root beer, and spice flavoring agent for beverages, ice cream, ices, candy, and baked goods. No known toxicity.

**METHYL ANTHRANILATE.** A synthetic flavoring, colorless to pale yellow liquid, with a grape odor. Occurs naturally in grapes, Concord grape juice, jasmine oil, lavender oil, lemon oil, orange flowers, petitgrain oil, peels of macrocarpa bunge, and tuberose. Used in loganberry, strawberry, orange, floral, rose, violet, cherry, grape, melon, liquor, wine, and honey flavorings for beverages, ice cream, ices, candy, baked goods, gelatin desserts, chewing gum (2,200 ppm), and liqueurs. Used in perfumes. No known toxicity. GRAS.

**METHYL BENZOATE. Oil of Niobe.** A synthetic flavoring agent, colorless, transparent, with a pleasant odor. Used in fruit, liquor, rum, nut, spice, and vanilla flavorings for beverages, ice cream, ices, candy, and baked goods. Also used in perfumes. No known toxicity.

**METHYL BUTYRATE.** A synthetic flavoring agent that occurs naturally in apples. Colorless. Used in fruit and rum flavorings for beverages, ice cream, candy, and baked goods. No known toxicity.

**METHYL *p*-tert-BUTYPHENYLACETATE.** A synthetic chocolate, fruit, and honey flavoring agent for beverages, ice cream, ices, candy, and baked goods. No known toxicity.

**METHYL CINNAMATE.** A synthetic strawberry, butter, cream, cherry, grape, peach, plum, and vanilla flavoring agent for beverages, ice cream, ices, candy, baked goods, gelatin desserts, chewing gum, and condiments. See Cinnamic Acid for toxicity.

**METHYL DISULFIDE.** A synthetic onion flavoring agent for baked goods, condiments, and pickle products. No known toxicity.

**METHYL ETHYL CELLULOSE.** A foaming, aerating, and emulsifying agent prepared from wood pulp or chemical cotton. Used in vegetable-fat whipped topping. Used as a bulk laxative but absorbed from the bowel. For toxicity see Sodium Carboxymethyl Cellulose.

**METHYL GLUCOSIDE OF FATTY ACIDS OF EDIBLE COCONUT OIL.** Used in the manufacture of beet sugar and as an aid in crystallization of sucrose and dextrose. No known toxicity except that coconut oil is thought to contribute to cholesterol clogging of the arteries.

**METHYL HEPTANOATE.** A synthetic berry, grape, peach, and pineapple flavoring agent for beverages, ice cream, ices, candy, and baked goods. No known toxicity.

**6-METHYL-5-HEPTEN-2-ONE.** A synthetic flavoring agent that occurs naturally in oil of lavender and oil of lemon. Used in berry, citrus, banana, melon, pear, peach, and pineapple flavorings for beverages, ice cream, ices, candy, baked goods, and gelatin desserts. No known toxicity.

**METHYL HEXANOATE.** A synthetic pineapple flavoring agent for beverages, ice cream, ices, candy, and baked goods. No known toxicity.

**METHYL 2-HEXENOATE.** A synthetic fruit flavoring agent for beverages and candy. No known toxicity.

**METHYL-*p*-HYDROXY-BENZOATE. Methylparaben.** A preservative in beverages, baked goods, candy, and artificially sweetened jellies and preserves. Methylparaben may cause allergic skin reaction. On the FDA list of additives requiring further study. GRAS.

**METHYL ISOBUTYL KETONE.** A synthetic fruit flavoring agent for beverages, ice cream, ices, candy, and baked goods. Used as a solvent for cellulose and lacquer. Similar in toxicity to methyl ethyl ketone, which is irritating to eyes and mucous membranes, but likely more toxic. Causes intestinal upsets and central nervous system depression.

**METHYL ISOBUTYRATE.** A synthetic fruit flavoring agent for beverages, ice cream, ices, candy, and baked goods. No known toxicity.

**METHYL LAURATE.** A synthetic floral flavoring agent for beverages, ice cream, ices, candy, and baked goods. No known toxicity.

**METHYL MERCAPTAN.** A synthetic flavoring agent that occurs naturally in caseinate, cheese, skim milk, coffee, and cooked beef. Used in coffee flavoring for beverages, ice cream, ices, candy, and baked goods. See Methanethiol for toxicity.

**METHYL β-NAPHTHYL KETONE. Oranger Crystals. 2′Acetonaphthone.** A synthetic flavoring agent used in berry, strawberry, citrus, fruit, grape, and vanilla flavorings for beverages, ice cream, ices, candy, baked goods, gelatin desserts, and chewing gum. See Methyl Isobutyl Ketone for toxicity.

**METHYL NONANOATE.** A synthetic berry, citrus, pineapple, honey, and cognac flavoring agent for beverages, ice cream, ices, candy, and baked goods. No known toxicity.

**METHYL 2-NONENOATE.** A synthetic berry and melon flavoring agent for beverages, ice cream, ices, candy, and baked goods. No known toxicity.

**METHYL 2-NONYNOATE.** A synthetic berry, floral, violet, fruit, banana, and melon flavoring agent for beverages, ice cream, ices, candy, baked goods, gelatin desserts, and condiments. No known toxicity.

**METHYL OCTANOATE.** A synthetic flavoring agent that occurs naturally in pineapple. Used in pineapple and berry flavorings for beverages, ice cream, ices, candy, and baked goods. No known toxicity.

**METHYL 2-OCTYNOATE.** A synthetic flavoring agent used in berry, raspberry, strawberry, floral, violet, fruit, peach, liquor, and muscatel flavorings for beverages, ice cream, ices, candy, baked goods, gelatin desserts, chewing gum, and jellies. No known toxicity.

**4-METHYL-2-PENTANONE.** A synthetic fruit flavoring for beverages, ice cream, ices, candy, and baked goods. No known toxicity.

**2-METHYL-4-PHENYL-2-BUTYL ACETATE.** A synthetic fruit and tea flavoring agent for beverages, ice cream, ices, candy, and baked goods. No known toxicity.

**METHYL PHENYLACETATE.** A synthetic colorless flavoring with a strong odor of honey. Used in strawberry, chocolate, peach, and honey flavorings for beverages, ice cream, ices, baked goods, candy, gelatin desserts, chewing gum, and syrup. No known toxicity.

**2-METHYL-4-PHENYLBUTYRALDEHYDE.** A synthetic nut flavoring agent for beverages, ice cream, ices, candy, and baked goods. No known toxicity.

**3-METHYL-2-PHENYLBUTYRALDEHYDE.** A synthetic fruit flavoring for beverages, ice cream, ices, and candy. No known toxicity.

**METHYL 4-PHENYLBUTYRATE.** A synthetic strawberry, fruit, and honey flavoring agent for beverages, ice cream, ices, candy, and baked goods. No known toxicity.

**METHYL SALICYLATE. Salicylic Acid. Wintergreen Oil.** Found naturally in sweet birch, cassie, and wintergreen. Used in strawberry, grape, mint, walnut, root beer, sarsaparilla, spice, wintergreen, birch beer, and vanilla flavorings for beverages, ice cream, ices, candy, baked goods, chewing gum (8,400 ppm), and syrup. Used in perfumery. Ingestion of relatively small amounts may cause severe poisoning and death. The average lethal dose in children is 10 milliliters. Symptoms are nausea, vomiting, acidosis, and pulmonary edema. Salicylates interact with a number of drugs with potentially lethal combinations. Among the deadly combinations are methyl salicylate and anticoagulants, tricyclic antidepressants, the arthritis drug Indocin, and the cancer drug methotrexate. The FDA proposed that linaments and other liquid preparations containing more than 5 percent methyl salicylate be marketed in special child-resistant containers. As little as one teaspoon of methyl salicylate has been reported to be fatal.

**METHYL SILICONE.** Prepared by hydrolysis (*see* Hydrolyzed), it is used to help compounds resist oxidation. No known toxicity. See Silicones.

**METHYL SULFIDE.** A synthetic flavoring agent that occurs naturally in caseinate, cheese, coffee, coffee extract, and skim milk. Disagreeable odor. Used in chocolate, cocoa, coffee, fruit, and molasses flavorings for beverages, ice cream, ices, candy, baked goods, gelatin desserts, and syrups. Used also as a solvent for minerals. No known toxicity.

**METHYL 9-UNDECENOATE.** A synthetic citrus and honey flavoring agent for beverages, ice cream, ices, candy, and baked goods. No known toxicity.

**METHYL 2-UNDECYNOATE.** A synthetic floral and violet flavoring agent for beverages, ice cream, ices, candy, and baked goods. No known toxicity.

**METHYL VALERATE.** A synthetic flavoring agent that occurs naturally in pineapple. Used in fruit flavorings for beverages, ice cream, ices, candy, and baked goods. No known toxicity.

**2-METHYL VALERIC ACID.** A synthetic chocolate flavoring agent for candy. No known toxicity.

**METHYLACETALDEHYDE.** See Propionaldehyde.

**METHYLACETIC ACID.** See Propionic Acid.

**2-METHYLALLYL BUTYRATE.** A synthetic pineapple flavoring for beverages, ice cream, ices, candy, and baked goods. No known toxicity.

**METHYLBENZYL ACETATE.** A synthetic flavoring agent, colorless, with a gardenia odor. Used in cherry and fruit flavorings for beverages, ice cream, ices, candy, baked goods, gelatin desserts, and chewing gum. See Methyl Acetate for toxicity.

**α-METHYLBENZYL ACETATE. Acetic Acid.** A synthetic berry and fruit flavoring agent for beverages, ice cream, ices, candy, baked goods, chewing gum, and toppings. See Methyl Acetate for toxicity.

**α-METHYLBENZYL ALCOHOL.** A synthetic flavoring agent, colorless, with a hyacinth odor. Used in strawberry, rose, fruit, and honey flavorings for beverages, ice cream, ices, candy, baked goods, gelatin desserts, and chewing gum. Methyl alcohol is wood alcohol, a widely used solvent in paints, varnishes, and paint removers. Readily absorbed from the gastrointestinal tract; as little as two teaspoonfuls is considered toxic if ingested. The fatal dose lies between 2 and 8 ounces.

**α-METHYLBENZYL BUTYRATE.** A synthetic berry and fruit flavoring agent for beverages, ice cream, ices, candy, and baked goods. No known toxicity.

**α-METHYLBENZYL ISOBUTYRATE.** A synthetic fruit flavoring agent for beverages, ice cream, ices, candy, and baked goods. No known toxicity.

**α-METHYLBENZYL FORMATE. Formic Acid.** A synthetic fruit and berry flavoring agent for beverages, ice cream, ices, candy, and baked goods. See Formic Acid for toxicity.

**2-METHYLBUTYRALDEHYDE.** A synthetic flavoring agent that

occurs naturally in coffee and tea. Used in chocolate and fruit flavorings for beverages, ice cream, ices, candy, and baked goods. No known toxicity.

**3-METHYLBUTYRALDEHYDE.** A synthetic flavoring agent that occurs naturally in coffee extract, oil of lavender, and peppermint oil. Used in butter, chocolate, cocoa, fruit, and nut flavorings for beverages, ice cream, ices, candy, baked goods, and gelatin desserts. No known toxicity.

**2-METHYLBUTYRIC ACID.** A synthetic fruit flavoring agent for beverages, ice cream, ices, and candy. No known toxicity.

**METHYLCELLULOSE.** A thickening agent and stabilizer prepared from wood pulp or chemical cotton. Commercial product has a methoxyl content of 29 percent. Used as a bodying agent for beverages and canned fruits sweetened with artificial sweeteners; a thickener for kosher food products; a bulking agent for low-calorie crackers; a binder in nonwheat baked goods for nonallergic diets; a beer foam stabilizer; a condiment carrier; in food products for diabetics and low-calorie dietetic products; an edible film for food products; a leavening agent for prepared mixes; a clarifier for vinegar and beverages; in imitation jellies and jams; processed cheese; confectionery; and toppings. It is a bulk laxative. For toxicity see Sodium Carboxymethyl Cellulose. The final report to the FDA of the Select Committee on GRAS Substances stated in 1980 that there is no evidence in the available information that it is a hazard to the public when used as it is now and it should continue its GRAS status with limitations on amounts that can be added to food.

**6-METHYLCOUMARIN.** A synthetic flavoring agent used in butter, caramel, coconut, fruit, nut, root beer, and vanilla flavorings for beverages, ice cream, ices, candy, baked goods, gelatin desserts, puddings, and chewing gum. Unlike methylcoumarin, which is listed as "generally recognized as safe" by the Flavor Extract Manufacturers Association, coumarin, once widely used in foods, is banned. Prolonged feeding of coumarin causes liver injury.

**METHYLCYCLOPENTENOLONE.** A synthetic flavoring agent used in berry, butter, butterscotch, caramel, maple, hazelnut, pecan, walnut, fruit, and vanilla flavorings for beverages, ice cream, ices, candy, baked goods, gelatin desserts, chewing gum, and syrups. No known toxicity.

**5-METHYLFURFURAL.** A synthetic honey, maple, and meat flavoring agent for beverages, ice cream, ices, candy, and baked goods. No known toxicity.

*o*-**METHYLANISOLE.** A synthetic fruit and nut flavoring agent for beverages, ice cream, ices, candy, and baked goods. No known toxicity.

*p*-METHYLANISOLE. A synthetic berry, maple, black walnut, walnut, and spice flavoring agent for beverages, ice cream, ices, candy, baked goods, gelatin desserts, puddings, condiments, and syrups. No known toxicity.

**METHYLENE CHLORIDE.** A colorless liquid used as a solvent in the microencapsulation of thiamine (*see*) intended for use in both dry beverage and dry gelatin mixes. Narcotic in high concentrations.

**2-METHYLOCTANAL.** A synthetic citrus flavoring agent for beverages, ice cream, ices, candy, and baked goods. No known toxicity.

**METHYLPARABEN.** See Methyl-*p*-Hydroxy Benzoate.

**2-METHYLPENTANOIC ACID.** See 2-Methyl Valeric Acid.

**β-METHYLPHENETHYL ALCOHOL.** A synthetic berry, rose, melon, and honey flavoring agent for beverages, ice cream, ices, candy, and baked goods. Methyl alcohol is absorbed from the gastrointestinal tract. As little as two teaspoonfuls can be fatal.

**METHYLPHENYL ETHER.** See Anisole.

**METHYLPROTOCATECHUIC ALDEHYDE.** See Vanillin.

**4-METHYLQUINOLINE.** A synthetic butter, caramel, fruit, honey, and nut flavoring agent for beverages, ice cream, ices, candy, and baked goods. No known toxicity.

**METHYLTHEOBROMINE.** See Caffeine.

**2-METHYLUNDECANAL.** A synthetic flavoring agent, colorless, with a fatty odor. Used in a variety of foods. No known toxicity.

**4(*p*-METHOXYPHENYL)-2-BUTANONE.** A synthetic fruit, licorice, and anise flavoring agent for beverages, ice cream, ices, candy, baked goods, and gelatin desserts. No known toxicity.

**1-(*p*-METHOXYPHENYL)-1-PENTEN-3-ONE.** A synthetic butter, cream, fruit, maple, nut, and vanilla flavoring agent for beverages, ice cream, ices, candy, and baked goods. No known toxicity.

**1-(*p*-METHOXYPHENYL)-2-PROPANONE.** A synthetic flavoring agent that occurs naturally in star anise. Used in fruit and vanilla flavorings for beverages, ice cream, ices, candy, and baked goods. No known toxicity.

*p*-METHOXYTOLUENE. See *p*-Methylanisole.

**MEXICAN SAGE.** See Oregano.

**MILFOIL.** See Yarrow.

**MILK.** Milk may be a hidden ingredient in cream of rice, macaroni, filled candy bars, Ovaltine, Junket, prepared flours, frankfurters, and other sausages. Some people are allergic to milk. See also Nonfat Dry Milk.

**MILO STARCH.** See Modified Starch. The final report to the FDA of the Select Committee on GRAS Substances stated in 1980 that it should continue its GRAS status with no limitations other than good manufacturing practices.

**MIMOSA, ABSOLUTE.** A natural flavoring agent extracted from mimosa trees, herbs, and shrubs, which are native to warm regions and have small white or pink flowers. Used in raspberry and fruit flavorings for beverages, ice cream, ices, candy, and baked goods. No known toxicity.

**MINERAL OIL.** A distillate of petroleum used as a defoaming component in the processing of beet sugar and yeast; as a coating for fresh fruits and vegetables; a lubricant and binder for capsules and tablets supplying small amounts of flavor, spice, condiments, and vitamins. Also employed as a lubricant in food-processing equipment, a dough-divider oil, pan oil; a lubricant in meat-packing plants. It is also used in confectionery as a sealant. May inhibit absorption of digestive fats and it has a mild laxative effect.

**MODIFIED SEA SALT.** Salt derived from sea water with reduced sodium chloride content.

**MODIFIED STARCH.** Ordinary starch that has been altered chemically to modify such properties as thickening or jelling. Babies have difficulty in digesting starch in its original form. Modified starch is used in baby food on the theory that it is easier to digest. Questions about safety have arisen because babies do not have the resistance of adults to chemicals. Among chemicals used to modify starch are propylene oxide, succinic anhydride, 1-octenyl succinic anhydride, aluminum sulfate, and sodium hydroxide (*see all*). On the FDA top priority list for reevaluation.

**MOLASSES EXTRACT.** Extract of sugar cane, a thick, brown, viscid syrup. Separated from raw sugar in the successive processes of sugar manufacture and graded according to its quality. It is a natural flavoring agent for candy, baked goods, ice cream, and medicines. No known toxicity.

**MOLYBDENUM.** A dietary supplement. The dark gray powdered mineral is a trace element in animal and plant metabolism. Resembles chromium and tungsten in many of its properties. Low order of toxicity.

**MONARDA SPECIES.** See Horsemint Leaves Extract.

**MONO- AND DI-GLYCERIDES OF FATS OR OILS.** See Glycerides.

**4-MONOAMINOPHOSPHATIDE.** See Lecithin.

**MONOAMMONIUM GLUTAMATE.** See Glutamate, Ammonium.

**MONOGLYCERIDE CITRATE.** Aids the action of and helps dissolve antioxidant formulations which retard rancidity in oils and fats. See Citrate Salts for toxicity. The final report to the FDA of the Select Committee on GRAS Substances stated in 1980 that there were insufficient relevant biological and other studies upon which to base an evaluation of it when it is used as a food ingredient.

**MONOPOTASSIUM GLUTAMATE.** See Glutamate, Monopotassium.

**MONOSODIUM GLUTAMATE (MSG).** The monosodium salt of glutamic acid (*see*), one of the amino acids. Occurs naturally in seaweed, sea tangles, soybeans, and sugar beets. Used to intensify meat and spice flavorings in meats, condiments, pickles, soups, candy, and baked goods. Believed responsible for the so-called "Chinese Restaurant Syndrome" in which diners suffer from chest pain, headache, and numbness after eating a Chinese meal. Causes brain damage in young rodents and brain damage effects in rats, rabbits, chicks, and monkeys. Baby food processors removed MSG from baby food products. On the FDA list of additives needing further study for mutagenic, teratogenic, subacute, and reproductive effects. Recent studies showed that MSG administered to animals during the neonatal period resulted in reproductive dysfunction when both males and females became adults. Females treated with MSG had fewer pregnancies and smaller litters, while males showed reduced fertility. The final report to the FDA of the Select Committee on GRAS Substances stated in 1980 that while no evidence in the available information on it demonstrates a hazard to the public at current use levels, uncertainties exist requiring that additional studies be conducted. GRAS status continues while tests are being completed and evaluated.

**MONOSODIUM PHOSPHATE.** A derivative of edible fat. Used as an emulsifying agent in food products and as a buffer in prepared cereal. Cleared by the USDA's Meat Inspection Department to decrease the amounts of cooked-out juices in canned hams, pork shoulders, pork loins, chopped hams, and bacon. Monosodium phosphate is a urinary acidifier but has no known toxicity. The final report to the FDA of the Select Committee on GRAS Substances stated in 1980 that it should continue its GRAS status with no limitations other than good manufacturing practices.

**MONOSTARCH PHOSPHATE.** A modified starch (*see*). The final report to the FDA of the Select Committee on GRAS Substances stated in 1980 that there is no evidence in the available information that it is a hazard to the public when used as it is now and it should continue its GRAS status with limitations on amounts that can be added to food.

**MONOSODIUM PHOSPHATE DERIVATIVES OF DIGLYCERIDES.** Derived from edible fats or oils or edible fat-forming fatty acids and used as emulsifiers. The final report to the FDA of the Select Committee on GRAS Substances stated in 1980 that there were insufficient relevant biological and other studies upon which to base an evaluation of them when they are used as food ingredients.

**MORELLONE.** See 3-Benzyl-4-Heptanone.

**MORPHOLINE. Salt of Fatty Acid.** Coating on fresh fruits and vegetables. Broad industrial uses. A strong alkali, corrosive to the skin, irritating to the eyes and mucous membranes. May cause liver and kidney injury.

**MOSCHUS MOSCHIFERUS.** See Musk, Tonquin.

**MOUNTAIN MAPLE EXTRACT.** Extract from a tall shrub or bushy tree found in the eastern United States. Used in chocolate, malt, and maple flavoring for beverages, ice cream, ices, candy, and baked goods. No known toxicity.

**MSG.** See Monosodium Glutamate.

**MUSK.** Dried secretions from the glandular sac of a small, hornless Central Asian male deer. Musk is a brown, unctuous, smelly substance. As *musk ambrette* it is used in fruit, cherry, maple, mint, nut, black walnut, pecan, spice, and vanilla flavorings for beverages, ice cream, ices, candy, baked goods, gelatin desserts, pudding, and chewing gum. As *musk tonquin* it is used in fruit, maple, and molasses flavorings for beverages, ice cream, ices, candy, baked goods, and syrups. As *musk ketone* it is used in chewing gum and candy. Musk is also used in perfumery. No known toxicity.

**MUSTARD. Black, Brown, and Red.** Pulverized dried, ripe seeds of the mustard plant (*Brassica nigra*) grown in Europe and Asia and naturalized in the U.S. Used in mustard and spice flavorings for condiments (5,200 ppm) and meats (2,300 ppm). Used as an emetic. Has been used as a counterirritant on the skin. May cause sensitivity to light. On the FDA list of products to be studied for possible mutagenic, teratogenic, subacute, and reproductive effects. The final report to the FDA of the Select Committee on GRAS Substances stated in 1980 that it should continue its GRAS status with no limitations other than good manufacturing practices.

**MUSTARD. Yellow and White.** The pulverized dried, ripe seeds of the mustard plant (*Brassica alba*) grown in Europe and Asia and naturalized in the U.S. Used in sausage and spice flavorings for beverages, baked goods, condiments (8,200 ppm), meats, and pickles (3,800 ppm). Used as an emetic. The final report to the FDA of the Select Committee on GRAS Substances stated in 1980 that it should continue its GRAS status with no limitations other than good manufacturing practices. See Mustard, Black, for toxicity.

**MUTAGENIC.** Having the power to cause mutations. A mutation is a sudden change in the character of a gene that is perpetuated in subsequent divisions of the cells in which it occurs. It can be induced by the application of such stimuli as radiation, certain food chemicals, or pesticides. Certain food additives such as caffeine have been found to "break" chromosomes.

**MYRCENE.** A synthetic flavoring agent that occurs naturally in galbanum oil, pimenta oil, orange peel, palma rosa oil, and hop oil. Pleasant aroma. Used in fruit, root beer, and coriander flavorings for beverages, ice cream, ices, candy, and baked goods. No known toxicity.

**MYRISTALDEHYDE.** A synthetic citrus and fruit flavoring agent for beverages, ice cream, ices, candy, baked goods, and gelatin desserts. See Nutmeg for toxicity.

**MYRISTIC ACID.** A solid, organic acid which occurs naturally in butter acids (such as nutmeg butter to the extent of 80 percent), oil of lovage, coconut oil, mace oil, and cire d'abeille in palm seed fats (20 percent), and in most animal and vegetable fats; largely in sperm whale oil. Used in butter, butterscotch, chocolate, cocoa, and fruit flavorings for beverages, ice cream, ices, candy, baked goods, and gelatin desserts. Nontoxic.

**MYRISTICA FRAGRANS HOUTT.** See Mace, also Nutmeg.

**MYROXYLON.** See Balsam, Peru.

**MYRRH.** A yellow- to reddish-brown aromatic bitter gum resin from various trees. The gum is used in fruit, liquor, tobacco, and smoke flavorings for beverages, baked goods, ice cream, ices, candy, chewing gum, and soups. The oil is used in honey and liquor flavorings for beverages, ice cream, ices, candy, and baked goods. The gum resin has been used to break up intestinal gas and as a topical stimulant. Used for incense and perfume. It was one of the gifts of the Magi. No known toxicity.

# N

**N-ACETYL-L-METHIONINE.** Supplement for protein-containing foods so as to improve nutritional value. See Methionine.

**β-NAPHTHYL ANTHRANILATE. Naphthyl Anthranilate.** A synthetic fruit and grape flavoring agent for beverages, ice cream, ices, baked goods, and candy. No known toxicity.

**β-NAPHTHYL METHYL ETHER.** A synthetic berry, fruit, honey, and nut flavoring agent for beverages, ice cream, ices, chewing gum, candy, and baked goods. No known toxicity.

**NARINGIN EXTRACT.** Naringin is in the flowers, fruit, and rind of the grapefruit tree. Most abundant in immature fruit. Extracted from grapefruit peel. Used in bitters, grapefruit, and pineapple flavorings for beverages, ice cream, ices, and liquors. No known toxicity.

**NATURAL.** To be advertised as "natural," the Federal Trade Commission requires that a food may not contain synthetic or artificial ingredients and may not be more than minimally processed. For example, minimal processing includes such actions as washing or peeling fruits or vegetables; homogenizing milk; canning, bottling, and freezing food; baking bread; aging and roasting meats, and grinding nuts. It does not include processes that, in general, cannot be done in a home kitchen and involve certain types of chemicals or sophisticated technology. For example, chemically bleached foods will not qualify as minimally processed.

**NEO-DHC.** See Dihydrochalcones.

**NEOFOLIONE.** Occurs naturally in oil of lavender, orange leaf (absolute), palma rosa oil, rose, neroli, and oil of pettigrain. Used in citrus, honey, and neroli flavorings for beverages, ice cream, ices, candy, baked goods, gelatin desserts, puddings, and chewing gum. No known toxicity.

**NEOHESPERIDINE DIHYDROCHALCONE.** See Dihydrochalcones.

**NEROL.** A synthetic flavoring that occurs naturally in oil of lavender, orange leaf, palma rosa oil, rose, neroli, and oil of petitgrain. A mixture of terpene alcohol (*see* Terpene), it has a fresh, sweet, rose odor. Used as a base in perfumes, and in citrus, neroli, and honey flavorings for beverages, ice cream, ices, candy, baked goods, gelatin desserts, puddings, and chewing gum. Similar to turpentine in toxicity.

**NEROLI BIGARADE OIL.** Named for the putative discoverer, Anne Maria de la Tremoille, princess of Nerole (1670). A fragrant, pale-yellow oil obtained from the flowers of the orange tree. Used chiefly as a cologne and in other perfumes but also in berry, orange, cola, cherry, spice, and ginger ale flavorings for beverages, ice cream, ices, candy, baked goods, and chewing gum. No known toxicity. GRAS.

**NEROSOL.** See Nerol.

**NERYL ACETATE.** A synthetic citrus, fruit, and neroli flavoring agent for beverages, ice cream, ices, candy, and baked goods. No known toxicity.

**NERYL BUTYRATE.** A synthetic berry, chocolate, cocoa, citrus, and fruit flavoring agent for beverages, ice cream, ices, candy, and baked goods. No known toxicity.

**NERYL FORMATE. Formic Acid.** A synthetic berry, citrus, apple, peach, and pineapple flavoring agent for beverages, ice cream, ices, candy, and baked goods. See Formic Acid for toxicity.

**NERYL ISOBUTYRATE.** A synthetic citrus and fruit flavoring agent for beverages, ice cream, ices, candy, and baked goods. No known toxicity.

**NERYL ISOVALERATE.** A synthetic berry, rose, and nut flavoring agent for beverages, ice cream, ices, candy, and baked goods. No known toxicity.

**NERYL PROPIONATE.** A synthetic berry and fruit flavoring agent for beverages, ice cream, ices, candy, and baked goods. No known toxicity.

**NEUTRALIZING AGENT.** A substance, such as ammonium bicarbonate or tartaric acid (*see both*), used to adjust the acidity or alkalinity of certain foods. See pH.

**NIACIN. Nicotinic Acid. Nicotinamide.** White or yellow, crystalline, odorless powder. An essential nutrient necessary for the conversion of food into energy. Participates in many energy-yielding reactions and aids in the maintenance of a normal nervous system. Added to prepared breakfast cereals, peanut butter, baby cereals, enriched flours, macaroni, noodles, breads, rolls, cornmeal, corn grits, and farina. Niacin is distributed in significant amounts in liver, yeast, meat, legumes, and whole cereals. Recommended daily intake is 18 to 19 milligrams for males and 13 to 15 milligrams for females. For pregnant women the requirement is 16 milligrams. Nicotinic acid is a component of the Vitamin B complex. The final report to the FDA of the Select Committee on GRAS Substances stated in 1980 that it should continue its GRAS status with no limitations other than good manufacturing practices.

**NIACINAMIDE. Nicotinamide. Vitamin $B_3$.** See Niacin. The final report to the FDA of the Select Committee on GRAS Substances stated in 1980 that it should continue its GRAS status with no limitations other than good manufacturing practices.

**NIACINAMIDE ASCORBATE.** A complex of ascorbic acid (*see*) and niacinamide (*see*). Occurs as a yellow powder which is practically odorless but which may gradually darken on exposure to air. Used as a dietary supplement. See Niacin.

**NICKEL.** Occurs in the earth's crust. Lustrous, white, hard metal which is used as a catalyst for the hydrogenation (*see*) of fat. Nickel may cause dermatitis in sensitive individuals and ingestion of large amounts of the soluble salts may cause nausea, vomiting, diarrhea. The final report to the FDA of the Select Committee on GRAS Substances stated in 1980 that it should continue its GRAS status with no limitations other than good manufacturing practices.

**NICKEL SULFATE.** Emerald-green transparent crystals with a sweet antiseptic taste used as a mineral supplement up to 1 milligram per day. An emetic when swallowed in sufficient amounts. The lethal dose varies widely. The lethal dose in guinea pigs is 62 milligrams per kilogram.

**NICOTINAMIDE.** See Niacin.

**NICOTINIC ACID.** See Niacin.

**NITER.** See Nitrate.

**NIOSH.** National Institute of Occupational Safety and Health.

**NITRATE. Potassium and Sodium.** Potassium nitrate, also known as saltpeter and niter, is used as a color fixative in cured meats. Sodium nitrate, also called Chile saltpeter, is used as a color fixative in cured meats. Both nitrates are used in matches and to improve the burning properties of tobacco. They combine with natural stomach saliva and food substances (secondary amines) to create nitrosamines, powerful cancer-causing agents. Nitrosamines have also been found in fish treated with nitrates. Researchers at Michael Reese Medical Center's Department of Pathology in Chicago induced cancer in mice by giving single doses of one three-thousandth (0.3 microgram) of a gram of nitrosamine for each gram of the animal's weight. This is in contrast to the way other researchers have induced cancer in laboratory animals with nitrosamines, by using repeated small doses or single large doses. The tumors that developed were analogous to human liver tumors. Nitrosamines caused pancreatic cancer in hamsters, similar to human pancreatic cancers. Nitrates have caused deaths from methemoglobinemia (it cuts off oxygen to the brain). Because nitrates are difficult to control in processing, they are being used less often. However, they are still employed in long-curing processes, such as country hams, as well as dried, cured, and fermented sausages. In the early seventies, baby-food manufacturers voluntarily removed nitrates from their products. The U.S. Department of Agriculture, which has jurisdiction over meats, and the FDA, which has jurisdiction over processed poultry, have asked manufacturers to show that the use of nitrates is safe. Efforts to ban nitrates have failed because manufacturers claim there is no good substitute for them.

Nitrates change into nitrites on exposure to air. Our major intake of nitrates in foodstuffs comes primarily from vegetables or water supplies that are high in nitrate content, or from nitrates used as additives in the meat curing process. Nitrates are natural constituents of plants. They occur in very small amount in fruits but are high in certain vegetables— spinach, beets, radishes, eggplant, celery, lettuce, collards, and turnip greens—as high as more than 3,000 parts per million. The two most important factors responsible for large accumulations of nitrates in vegetables are the high levels of fertilization with nitrate fertilizers and the tendency of the species to accumulate nitrate.

**NITRITE. Potassium and Sodium.** Potassium nitrite is used as a color fixative in the more than $125 billion a year cured-meat business. Sodium nitrite has the peculiar ability to react chemically with the myoglobin molecule and impart red-bloodedness to processed meats, to convey tanginess to the palate, and to resist the growth of *Clostridium botulinum* spores. It is used as a color fixative in cured meats, bacon, bologna, frankfurters, deviled ham, meat spread, potted meats, spiced ham, Vienna sausages, smoke-cured tuna fish products, and in smoke-cured shad and salmon. Nitrite combines with natural stomach and food chemicals (secondary amines) to create nitrosamines, powerful cancer-causing agents. The U.S. Department of Agriculture, which has jurisdiction over processed meats, and the FDA, which has jurisdiction over processed poultry, asked manufacturers to show that the use of nitrites was safe and that nitrosamines were not formed in the products, as preliminary tests showed in bacon. Processors claimed there was no alternate chemical substitute for nitrite. They said alternate processing methods could be used but the products would not look or taste the same. Baby-food manufacturers voluntarily removed nitrites from baby foods in the early seventies. The FDA has found that adding Vitamin C to processed meats prevents or at least retards the formation of nitrosamines. In May 1978, the USDA announced plans to require bacon manufacturers to reduce their use of nitrite from 150 to 120 parts per million and to use preservatives that retard nitrosamine formation. Processors would have been required to keep nitrosamine levels to 10 ppm under the interim plan.

But in August 1978 a new concern about nitrite was raised. The USDA and the FDA issued a joint announcement that the substance has been directly linked to cancer by a Massachusetts Institute of Technology study. That work was later disputed. In 1982, amyl and butyl nitrites used by homosexual men were linked to Kaposi's Syndrome and other abnormalities of the immune system.

Researchers at Michael Reese Hospital linked infinitesimal amounts of nitrite to cancer in young laboratory mice, especially in the liver and lungs. Dr. Koshilya Rijhsinghani and her colleagues gave single doses of one three-thousandth (0.3 microgram) of a gram of nitrosamine for each gram of the animal's weight. This method differs from the way other researchers have induced cancer in mice with nitrosamines: repeated small doses or single large doses. Nitrosamines also produce cancer in hamsters similar to pancreatic cancers in humans.

In 1980, the FDA revoked its proposed phase-out because manufacturers said there was no adequate substitute for nitrites. In 1977 Germany banned nitrites and nitrates except in certain species of fish. However, a Committee on Nitrite and Alternative Curing Agents in Food, formed by the National Research Council in the United States, concluded that there was no single agent or process that could replace nitrite completely: "Several chemical and physical treatments appear to be comparable in inhibiting outgrowth of *Clostridium botulinum* spores in types of meat products but none confers the color and flavor that consumers have come to expect in nitrite-cured meats." Until the all-purpose agent comes along, or until consumer preference changes, the best compromise probably will be continued use of nitrite in conventional amounts with Vitamins C and E added to block formation of nitrosamines, or the use of smaller amounts of nitrite in combination with biological acidification, irradiation, or the chemicals potassium sorbate, sodium hypophosphite, or fumarate esters, the Committee said.

To reduce nitrosamines in bacon, the U.S. Department of Agriculture requires meat packers to add sodium ascorbate or sodium erythrobate (Vitamin Cs) to the curing brine. This offers only a partial barrier because ascorbate is soluble in water and its activity in fat is limited. Vitamin E, however, inhibits nitrosation in fatty tissues. The Committee suggested that both C and E be added to provide more complete protection.

If you must eat nitrite-laced meats, include a food or drink high in Vitamin C at the same time—for example, orange juice, grapefruit juice, cranberry juice, or lettuce.

**NITROGEN.** A gas which is 78 percent by volume of the atmosphere and essential to all living things. Odorless. Used for gas-packed foods and dressings for foods. In high concentrations it can asphyxiate. The final report to the FDA of the Select Committee on GRAS Substances stated in 1980 that it should continue its GRAS status with no limitations other than good manufacturing practices.

**NITROGEN OXIDES. Nitrous Oxide (see below), Nitric Oxide, Nitrogen Dioxide, Nitrogen Trioxide, Nitrogen Pentoxide.** Bleaching agent for cereal flour. Nitrogen dioxide is a deadly poison gas. Short exposure may cause little pain or discomfort but several days later, fluid retention and inflammation of the lungs can cause death. About 200 ppm can be fatal.

**NITROSYL CHLORIDE.** Nonexplosive, very corrosive reddish-yellow gas, intensely irritating to eyes, skin, and mucosa. Used as a bleaching agent for cereal flour. Inhalation may cause pulmonary edema and hemorrhage.

**NITROUS OXIDE. Laughing Gas.** A whipping agent for whipped cream and a propellant in pressurized containers for certain dairy and vegetable-fat toppings, slighly sweetish odor and taste. Colorless. An asphyxiant. Used in rocket fuel. Less irritating than other nitrogen oxides (*see*) but narcotic in high concentrations. The final report to the FDA of the Select Committee on GRAS Substances stated in 1980 that it should continue its GRAS status with no limitations other than good manufacturing practices.

*g*-NONALACTONE. Aldehyde C-18. Prunolide. Coconut Aldehyde. A synthetic berry, coconut, fruit, and nut flavoring agent for beverages, ice cream, ices, candy, baked goods, gelatin desserts, chewing gum, and icings. No known toxicity.

NONALOL. See Nonyl Alcohol.

NONANAL. Pelargonic Aldehyde. A synthetic flavoring that occurs naturally in lemon oil, rose, sweet orange oil, mandarin, lime, orris, and ginger. Used in lemon and fruit flavorings for beverages, ice cream, ices, candy, baked goods, gelatin desserts, and chewing gum. No known toxicity.

1, 3-NONANEDIOL ACETATE. A synthetic berry and fruit flavoring agent for beverages, ice cream, ices, candy, and baked goods. No known toxicity.

NONANOIC ACID. Pelargonic Acid. Nonoic Acid. Nonglic Acid. A synthetic flavoring agent that occurs naturally in cocoa and oil of lavender. Used in berry, fruit, nut, and spice flavorings for beverages, ice cream, ices, candy, baked goods, and shortenings. A strong irritant.

1-NONANOL. See Nonyl Alcohol.

NONANOL ISOVALERATE. See Nonyl Isovalerate.

3-NONANON-1-YL-ACETATE. A synthetic berry, rose, fruit, and cheese flavoring agent for beverages, ice cream, ices, candy, and baked goods. No known toxicity.

NONANOYL 4-HYDROXY-3-METHOXYBENZYLAMIDE. Perlargonyl Vanillylamide. A synthetic spice flavoring agent for candy, baked goods, and condiments. No known toxicity.

NONATE. See Isoamyl Nonanoate.

NONFAT DRY MILK. Milk from which the water and much of the fat have been removed. Comparisons between whole and dry milk: 100 grams fluid whole milk contains 68 calories; 87 grams of water; 3.5 grams of protein; 3.9 grams of fat; .7 gram of ash; 4.9 grams of carbohydrates; 118 milligrams of calcium; 93 milligrams of phosphorus; .1 milligram of iron; 50 milligrams of sodium; 140 milligrams of potassium; 160 international units of Vitamin A; .04 milligram of Vitamin $B_1$; .17 milligram of $B_2$; .1 milligram of nicotinic acid; and 1 milligram of Vitamin C. Total calories for one cup of milk is 166. Nonfat, dry milk has 362 calories per 100 grams; 3.5 grams of water; 35.6 grams of protein; 1 gram of fat; 7.9 grams of ash; total carbohydrates of 52 grams; 1,300 milligrams of calcium; 1,030 milligrams of phosphorus; .6 milligram of iron; 77 milligrams of sodium; 1,130 milligrams of potassium; 40 international units of Vitamin A; .35 milligram of Vitamin $B_1$; 196 milligrams of Vitamin $B_2$; 1.1 milligrams of nicotinic acid; and 7 milligrams of Vitamin C. The total calories for a tablespoon of dry nonfat milk is 28.

**NONNUTRITIVE SWEETENERS.** Sugar substitutes that contain no calories. Saccharin and cyclamates (*see both*) are examples.

**NONYLCARBINOL.** See 1-Decanol.

**NONYL ACETATE.** A synthetic, pungent, citrus and fruit flavoring agent, mushroomlike in odor. Used for beverages, ice cream, ices, candy, and baked goods. See Acetic Acid for toxicity.

**NONYL ALCOHOL. Nonalol.** A synthetic flavoring, colorless to yellow with a citronella oil odor. Occurs in oil of orange. Used in butter, citrus, peach, and pineapple flavorings for beverages, ice cream, ices, candy, baked goods, and chewing gum. Also used in the manufacture of artificial lemon oil. In experimental animals it has caused central nervous system and liver damage.

**NONYL ISOVALERATE.** A synthetic fruit and hazel nut flavoring agent for beverages, ice cream, ices, candy, and baked goods. No known toxicity.

**NOPINENE.** See β-Pinene.

**NORDIHYDROGUAIARETIC ACID (NDGA).** Occurs in resinous exudates of many plants. White or grayish white crystals, an antioxidant used in prepared piecrust mix, candy, lard, butter, ice cream, and pressure-dispensed whipped cream. In general food use, the percentage of fat or oil content including esential oil content should be no more than .02 percent NDGA. Lard containing 0.01 percent NDGA stored at room temperature for 19 months in diffused daylight showed no appreciable rancidity or color change. Canada banned the additive in 1967 after it was shown to cause cysts and kidney damage in a large percentage of tested rats. The FDA removed it from the GRAS list in 1968 and prohibited its use in products over which it has control. However, the U.S. Department of Agriculture, which controls antioxidants in lard and animal shortenings, still permits its use.

**NOVATONE.** See Acetanisole.

**NUTMEG. Nutmeg Oil.** A natural flavoring extracted from the dried ripe seed. Used in cola, vermouth, sausage, eggnog, and nutmeg flavorings for beverages, ice cream, ices, baked goods (2,000 ppm), condiments, meats, and pickles. Nutmeg *oil* is used in loganberry, chocolate, lemon, cola, apple, grape, muscatel, rum, sausage, eggnog, pistachio, root beer, cinnamon, dill, ginger, mace, nutmeg, and vanilla flavorings for beverages, ice cream, ices, candy, baked goods, chewing gum, condiments, meats, syrups, and icings. In common household use since the Middle

Ages, nutmeg is still a potentially toxic substance. Ingestion of as little as 3 whole seeds or 5 to 15 grams of grated spice can cause flushing of the skin, irregular heart rhythm, absence of salivation, and central nervous system excitation, including euphoria and hallucinations. On the FDA list for study of short-term mutagenic, subacute, teratogenic, and reproductive effects. The final report to the FDA of the Select Committee on Gras Substances stated in 1980 that while no evidence in the available information on it demonstrates a hazard to the public at current use levels, uncertainties exist requiring that additional studies be conducted. GRAS status continues while tests are being completed and evaluated.

**NUTRA-SWEET®.** See Aspartame.

# O

**OAK CHIP EXTRACT.** Extract from the white oak used in bitters and whiskey flavorings for beverages, ice cream, ices, candy, baked goods, and whiskey (1,000 ppm). No known toxicity.

**OAK MOSS, ABSOLUTE.** Extracted from the lichen that grows on a variety of oak trees. Used in fruit, honey, and spice flavorings for beverages, ice cream, ices, candy, baked goods, gelatin desserts, condiments, and soups. No known toxicity.

**OAT GUM.** A plant extract used as an antioxidant in butter, cream, and candy up to 1.5 percent. Also a thickener and stabilizer in pasteurized cheese spread and cream cheese (with other foods) up to .8 percent. Causes occasional allergic reactions, diarrhea, and intestinal gas. No known toxicity.

**OCIMUM BASILICUM.** See Basil.

**OCTADECANOIC ACID.** See Stearic Acid.

**9-OCTADECENOIC ACID.** See Oleic Acid.

**OCTAFLUOROCYCLOBUTANE.** A nonflammable gas. A refrigerant and propellant and aerating agent in foamed or sprayed food products. Used alone or in combination with carbon dioxide or nitrous oxide (*see both*). Nontoxic when used alone.

**2-OCTANONE.** A synthetic fruit and cheese flavoring agent for beverages, ice cream, ices, candy, and baked goods. No known toxicity.

**3-OCTANONE.** A synthetic flavoring that occurs naturally in oil of lavender. Used in citrus, coffee, peach, cheese, and spice flavorings for beverages, ice cream, ices, candy, and baked goods. No known toxicity.

**1-OCTEN-3-OL.** A synthetic fruit and spice flavoring agent for beverages, ice cream, ices, candy, baked goods, condiments, and soups. No known toxicity.

**1-OCTENYL SUCCINIC ANHYDRIDE.** A starch modifier incorporating up to 3 percent of the weight of the product. Limited to 2 percent in combination with aluminum sulfate (*see*). No known toxicity.

**OCTYL ALCOHOL. Caprylic Alcohol.** Colorless, viscous liquid soluble in water and insoluble in oil. Used in the manufacture of perfume and of food additives. Occurs naturally in the oils of lavender, lemon, lime, lovage, orange peel, and coconut. It has a penetrating, aromatic scent. No known toxicity.

**OCTYL BUTYRATE. Butyric Acid.** A synthetic strawberry, butter, citrus, fruit, cherry, melon, peach, pineapple, pumpkin, and liquor flavoring agent for beverages, ice cream, ices, candy, and baked goods. No known toxicity.

**OCTYL FORMATE. Formic Acid.** A synthetic flavoring, colorless, with a fruity odor. Used in citrus and fruit flavorings for beverages, ice cream, ices, candy, and baked goods. See Formic Acid for toxicity.

**OCTYL HEPTANOATE.** A synthetic citrus, coconut, and fruit flavoring agent for beverages, ice cream, ices, candy, and baked goods. No known toxicity.

**OCTYL ISOBUTYRATE. Isobutyric Acid.** A synthetic citrus, fruit, melon, peach, liquor, and wine flavoring agent for beverages, ice cream, ices, candy, and baked goods. No known toxicity.

**OCTYL ISOVALERATE. Isovaleric Acid.** A synthetic berry, butter, citrus, apple, cherry, grape, honey, and nut flavoring agent for beverages, ice cream, ices, candy, and baked goods. No known toxicity.

**OCTYL OCTANOATE. Octanoic Acid.** A synthetic citrus, grape, and pineapple flavoring agent for beverages, ice cream, ices, candy, and baked goods. No known toxicity.

**OCTYL PHENYLACETATE. Phenylacetic Acid.** A synthetic berry, apple, banana, grape, peach, pear, and honey flavoring agent for beverages, ice cream, ices, candy, and baked goods. No known toxicity.

**OCTYL PROPIONATE. Propionic Acid.** A synthetic berry, citrus, and melon flavoring agent for beverages, ice cream, ices, candy, and baked goods. No known toxicity.

**OIL OF NIOBE.** See Methyl Benzoate.

**OLEIC ACID.** Obtained from various animal and vegetable fats and oils. Colorless. On exposure to air it turns yellow to brown with a rancid odor. Used as a defoaming agent; as a synthetic butter, cheese, and spice flavoring agent for beverages, ice cream, ices, candy, baked goods, and condiments; as a lubricant and binder in various foods; and as a component in the manufacture of food additives. Low oral toxicity and mildly irritating to the skin. It caused tumors when injected under the skin of rabbits in 3,120-milligram doses per kilogram of body weight and when painted on the skin of mice in 62-milligram doses per kilogram of body weight. The final report to the FDA of the Select Committee on GRAS Substances stated in 1980 that it should continue its GRAS status with no limitations other than good manufacturing practices. The final report of the Select Committee also said that oleic acid should continue its GRAS status for packaging with no limitations other than good manufacturing practices.

**OLEINIC ACID.** See Oleic Acid.

**OLEORESIN.** A natural plant product consisting of essential oil and resin extracted from a substance, such as ginger, by means of alcohol, ether, or acetone. The solvent, alcohol, for example, is percolated through the ginger. Although the oleoresin is very similar to the spice from which it is derived, it is not identical because not all the substances in the spice are extracted. Oleoresins are usually more uniform and more potent than the original product. The normal use range of an oleoresin is from one-fifth to one-twentieth the corresponding amount for the crude spice. Certain spices are extracted as oleoresins for color rather than for flavor. Examples of color-intensifying oleoresins are those from paprika and tumeric (*see both*).

**OLIBANUM OIL. Frankincense.** The volatile distilled oil from the gum resin of a plant species found in Ethiopia, Egypt, Arabia, and Somaliland. One of the gifts of the Magi. Used in cola, fruit, and spice flavorings for beverages, ice cream, ices, candy, and baked goods. No known toxicity.

**ONION OIL.** From crushed onion seeds of the widely cultivated plant first discovered in Asia. Used in meat, onion, and spice flavorings for beverages, ice cream, ices, baked goods, condiments, meats, and pickles. No known toxicity. GRAS.

**ORANGE B.** Coal-tar dye. Coloring for casing of frankfurters and sausages. The color additive was limited to not more than 150 ppm by weight of finished food. In 1978, the FDA said use could result in exposure of consumers to beta-naphthylamine, a known cancer-causing agent. Although it was permanently listed by the FDA, the only manufacturer of it stopped making it.

**ORANGE BLOSSOMS.** *Orange blossoms, absolute,* is a natural flavoring derived from the fruit of the bitter plant species. Used in citrus and fruit flavorings for beverages, ice cream, ices, candy, baked goods, and chewing gum. The *flowers* provide a natural flavoring extract for citrus and cola flavorings for beverages (2,000 ppm). The orange *leaf extract* is used as a natural fruit flavoring for beverages, ice cream, ices, and baked goods. *Orange peel bitter oil* is expressed from the fresh fruit and is used in orange and fruit flavorings for beverages, ice cream, ices, candy, gelatin desserts, chewing gum, and liquors. No known toxicity. GRAS.

**ORANGE CRYSTALS.** See Methyl $\beta$-Naphthyl Ketone.

**ORANGE FLOWERS, BITTER OIL.** See Orange Blossoms.

**ORANGE LEAF.** See Orange Blossoms.

**ORANGE OIL (TERPENELESS).** The volatile oil expressed from the fresh peel of the ripe fruit of the sweet plant species. Intensely yellow or orange liquid. Used in grapefruit, orange, cola, pineapple, liquor, root beer, and ginger ale flavorings for beverages, ice cream, ices, baked goods, candy, gelatin desserts, puddings, chewing gum, and condiments. Used also in perfume and formerly as an expectorant. No known toxicity. GRAS.

**ORANGE OIL, DISTILLED.** The volatile oil distilled from the fresh fruit of the sweet plant species. Yellowish, very intense, pleasant odor. Used in orange and fruit flavorings for beverages, ice cream, ices, candy, baked goods, gelatin desserts, and chewing gum. No known toxicity.

**ORANGE PEEL, BITTER OIL.** See Orange Blossoms.

**ORANGE PEEL, SWEET EXTRACT.** From the fresh rind of the fruit. Sweetish, fragrant odor; slightly bitter taste. Used in orange and ginger ale flavorings for beverages, ice cream, ices, candy, and baked goods. No known toxicity.

**ORANGE PEEL, SWEET OIL.** From the fresh rind of the fruit. Sweetish, fragrant odor; slightly bitter taste. Used in blueberry, orange, cola, banana, pear, root beer, and ginger ale flavorings for beverages, ice cream, ices, candy, baked goods, condiments, meats, gelatin desserts, puddings (1,300 ppm), chewing gum (4,200 ppm), syrups, icings, liquors, and cereals. No known toxicity.

**ORANGE PEEL, SWEET OIL (TERPENELESS).** From the fresh rind of the fruit. Sweetish, fragrant odor; slightly bitter taste. Used in orange and fruit flavoring for beverages, ice cream, ices, candy, baked goods, gelatin desserts, and puddings. No known toxicity.

**ORCHIDEE.** See Isoamyl Salicylate.

**OREGANO. Mexican Oregano. Mexican Sage. Origanum.** The wild marjoram (*see*) plant, but spicier, originally found in Eurasia. Used in loganberry, cherry, sausage, root beer, and spice flavorings for beverages, baked goods, condiments (2,800 ppm), and meats. See Origanuum Oil for toxicity. GRAS.

**ORGANIC.** There are no federal standards for the term, but it usually means produce grown without pesticides, herbicides, or synthetic fertilizers on land that has been free of such chemicals for one to seven years.

**ORIGAN.** See Oregano.

**ORIGANOL.** See 4-Carvomenthenol.

**ORIGANUM OIL.** The volatile oil is obtained by steam distillation from a flowering herb. Yellowish red to dark brown, with a pungent odor. Used in vermouth, sausage, root beer, and spice flavorings for beverages, ice cream, ices, candy, baked goods, condiments, and meats. A teaspoonful can cause illness and less than an ounce has killed adults. GRAS.

**ORRIS. Concrete, Liquid, and Oil. White Flag.** The volatile oil obtained by steam distillation from the peeled, dried root of orris, a European plant. Used in raspberry, blackberry, strawberry, violet, cherry, nut, and spice flavorings for beverages, ice cream, ices, candy, baked goods, gelatin desserts, chewing gum, and icings. Also used in cosmetics, perfumes, and in toothpaste and powder. Causes frequent allergic reactions and is no longer used in American dusting powders for the bath. See Orris Root Extract.

**ORRIS ROOT EXTRACT.** Obtained from dried orris root. Has an intense odor. Used in chocolate, fruit, nut, vanilla, and cream soda flavorings for beverages, ice cream, ices, candy, baked goods, gelatin desserts, and chewing gum. Causes frequent allergic reactions.

**OX BILE. Oxgall.** Emulsifier from the fresh bile of male castrated bovines. Brownish green or dark green; viscous. Characteristic odor. Bitter, disagreeable taste. Used in dried egg whites up to .1 percent. No known toxicity. The final report to the FDA of the Select Committee on GRAS Substances stated in 1980 that it should continue its GRAS status with no limitations other than good manufacturing practices.

**OXIDES OF IRON.** Ochre, sienna, ferrous oxide, and other natural and synthetic oxides of iron varying in color from red, brown, or black to orange or yellow. Used for dyeing eggshells and in bottled soft drinks. See Iron for toxicity.

**OXIDIZED TALLOW.** A defoaming component used in yeast and beet sugar production in reasonable amounts required to inhibit foaming. See Tallow Flakes.

**2-OXOPROPANAL.** See Pyruvaldehyde.

**2-OXOPROPANOIC ACID.** See Pyruvic Acid.

**OXYSTEARIN.** A mixture of the glycerides (*see*) of partially oxidized stearic acids (*see*) and other fatty acids (*see*). Occurs in animal fat and used chiefly in manufacture of soaps, candles, cosmetics, suppositories, pill coatings. Tan, waxy. Used as a crystallization inhibitor in cottonseed and soybean cooking. In salad oils up to .125 percent. Also used as a defoamer in the production of beet sugar and yeast. The Select Committee of the Federation of American Societies for Experimental Biology advising on food additives recommended further study of this additive. The final report to the FDA of the Select Committee on Gras Substances stated in 1980 that while no evidence in the available information on it demonstrates a hazard to the public at current use levels, uncertainties exist, requiring that additional studies be conducted. GRAS status continues while tests are being completed and evaluated.

**OXYTETRACYCLINE.** An antibiotic substance used in feed to increase growth and found in edible tissue of chickens and turkeys. The carcasses are dipped in the solution to retard rancidity. Residues in the birds are permitted up to .0007 percent. Because it is an antimicrobial, it may cause sensitivity to light, nausea, inflammation of the mucous membranes of the mouth, and diarrhea.

# P

**PALATONE.** See Maltol.

**PALE CATECHU.** See Catechu, Extract.

**PALMA ROSA OIL. Geranium Oil.** The volatile oil obtained by steam distillation from a variety of partially dried grass grown in East India and Java. Used in rose, fruit, and spice flavorings for beverages, ice cream, ices, candy, and baked goods. Believed as toxic as other essential oils, causing illness after ingestion of a teaspoonful and death after ingestion of an ounce.

**PALMITIC ACID.** A mixture of solid organic acids obtained from fats, consisting chiefly of palmitic acid with varying amounts of stearic acid (*see*). It is white or faintly yellow and has a fatty odor and taste. Palmitic acid occurs naturally in allspice, anise, calamus oil, cascarilla bark, celery seed, butter acids, coffee, tea, and many animal fats and plant oils. Obtained from palm oil, Japan wax, or Chinese vegetable tallow. Used in butter and cheese flavorings for seasoning preparations. No known toxicity.

**PANTHENOL. Dexpanthenol. Vitamin B Complex Factor.** A viscous, slightly bitter liquid used as a supplement in foods medicinally to aid digestion and in liquid vitamins. It is formulated in hair products and cosmetic emollients; it allegedly combats graying hair. No known toxicity.

*d*-**PANTOTHENAMIDE. B Complex Vitamin. Vitamin B$_5$.** Made synthetically from royal jelly of the queen bee, yeast, and molasses. Cleared for use as a source of pantothenic acid activity in foods for special dietary use. Pantothenic acid (common sources are liver, rice bran, molasses) is essential for metabolism of carbohydrates, fats, and other important substances. Nerve damage has been observed in patients with low pantothenic acid. It is involved with the release of energy from carbohydrates in the breakdown of fats. Children and adults need from 5 to 10 milligrams per day. See Calcium Pantothenate.

*d*-PANTOTHENYL ALCOHOL. The final report to the FDA of the Select Committee on GRAS Substances stated in 1980 that it should continue its GRAS status with no limitations other than good manufacturing practices. See Calcium Pantothenate.

PAPAIN. A proteinase enzyme for meat tenderizing. Prepared from papaya, a fruit grown in tropical countries. Used for clearing beverages. Added to enriched farina to reduce cooking time. Used medically to prevent adhesions. It is deactivated by cooking, but because of its protein-digesting ability it can dissolve necrotic material with disastrous results. The usual grade used in food digests about 35 times its weight of lean meat. It may cause allergic manifestations. The final report to the FDA of the Select Committee on GRAS Substances stated in 1980 that it should continue its GRAS status with no limitations other than good manufacturing practices.

PAPRIKA. The finely ground pods of dried, ripe, sweet pepper. The strong, reddish orange powder is used in sausage and spice flavorings for baked goods (1,900 ppm), condiments, meats (7,400 ppm), and soups (7,-500 ppm). The *oleoresin* (*see*) is used in fruit, meat, and spice flavorings for beverages, ice cream, ices, candy, baked goods, condiments, and meats. Both paprika and paprika oleoresins are used as a red coloring. No known toxicity.

PARABENS. Butylparaben. Heptylparaben. Methylparaben. Propylparaben. The methyl and propylparabens and parahydroxybenzoate are the most commonly used preservatives in the United States, particularly in cosmetics. The parabens have a broad spectrum of antimicrobial activity, are safe to use—relatively nonirritating, nonsensitizing, and nonpoisonous—are stable over the pH (*see*) range, and are sufficiently soluble in water to be effective in liquids. Methyl and propylparaben are esters of parahydroxybenzoic acid. Neither occurs in nature. In foods, parabens function as preservatives that prevent the growth of molds and yeasts. They are used in baked goods, in sugar substitutes and in artificially sweetened jams, jellies, fats, and oils, and in frozen dairy desserts and many milk products. The only adverse effect of parabens found was that methylparaben caused birth defects in offspring of mice and rats fed 550 milligrams per kilogram of body weight daily during pregnancy, and in hamsters fed 300 milligrams under the same conditions.

PARAFFIN WAX. A colorless, somewhat translucent, odorless mass;

greasy feel. Used as a defoaming component in yeast and beet sugar production. Not digested or absorbed in the intestines. Used to cover food products. Cleared for use as a synthetic masticatory substance in chewing gum. Raises melting point in ointments, used in wax paper and candles, and in many industrial products. Used for wound dressing. When used in cosmetic surgery, paraffin has caused sloughing of the skin.

**PARSLEY.** The aromatic leaves of the annual herb cultivated everywhere. Used in spice flavorings for beverages, meats, soups, baked goods, and condiments. Parsley *oil* is obtained by steam distillation of the ripe seeds of the herb. Yellow to light brown, with a harsh odor, it is used in fruit and spice flavorings for beverages, ice cream, ices, candy, baked goods, and condiments. Parsley *oleoresin* (*see*) is used in spice flavorings for condiments. Parsley may cause sensitivity to light. GRAS.

**PARTIALLY DELACTOSED WHEY (PDW).** Used increasingly as a substitute for nonfat dry milk, which is more expensive. PDW is used in processed cheese foods and spreads. It is the result of the partial removal of lactose (*see*) from the milk ingredient whey (*see*).

**PARTIALLY DEMINERALIZED AND DELACTOSED WHEY.** Removal of some minerals as well as lactose (*see*). See Partially Delactosed Whey.

**PATCHOULY OIL.** The natural extract from the leaves of an East Indian herb mint. Yields a fragrant essential oil used in cola, fruit, nut, and spice flavorings for beverages, ice cream, ices, candy, baked goods, and chewing gum. No known toxicity.

**PEACH ALDEHYDE.** See γ-Undecalactone.

**PEACH KERNEL. Persic Oil.** Fixed oil from a seed. Smells like almonds. Used as a natural flavoring in conjunction with other natural flavorings. Also used as an emollient. No known toxicity.

**PEANUT OIL.** Expressed from seeds of a low-branch annual herb. A solvent, in salad oil, shortening, mayonnaise, and confections. Also used in conjunction with natural flavorings. Used in the manufacture of soaps and paints. Peanut butter is about 50 percent peanut oil suspended in peanut fibers. The oil acts as a mild cathartic and as a protective for the gastrointestinal tract when corrosive poisons have been swallowed. It is also an emollient for the skin and mucous membranes. The final report to the FDA of the Select Committee on GRAS Substances stated in 1980 that it should continue its GRAS status for packaging with no limitations other than good manufacturing practices.

**PEANUT STEARINE.** See Peanut Oil.

**PECTIN. Includes low methoxyl pectin and sodium pectinate.** Pectin is found in the roots, stems, and fruits of plants, and seems to function as a cementing agent. It is a coarse or fine powder, practically odorless, with a gluey taste. Richest source of pectin is lemon or orange rind, which contains about 30 percent of this polysaccharide. Used as a stabilizer, thickener, bodying agent for artificially sweetened beverages, syrups for frozen products, ice cream, ice milk, confections, fruit sherbets, water ices, French dressing, fruit jelly, preserves, and jams to compensate for a deficiency in natural pectin. Also used as an antidiarrheal agent. No known toxicity. The final report to the FDA of the Select Committee on GRAS Substances stated in 1980 that it should continue its GRAS status with no limitations other than good manufacturing practices.

**PEGU CATECHU EXTRACT.** See Catechu Extract.

**PELARGONALDEHYDE.** See Nonanal.

**PELARGONIC ACID.** See Nonanoic Acid.

**PELARGONIC ALDEHYDE.** See Nonanal.

**PELARGONYL VANILLYLAMIDE.** See Nonanoyl 4-Hydroxy-3-Methoxybenzylamide.

**PENNYROYAL OIL. Squaw Mint. Hedeoma.** From the dried leaves and flowering tops of plants raised from Canada to Florida and as far west as Nebraska. Used in mint flavorings for beverages, ice cream, ices, candy, and baked goods. Formerly used as an aromatic perspirant; to stimulate menstrual flow; for flatulence; an abortion inducer; and a counteractant for painful menstruation. Brain damage has been reported following doses of less than 1 teaspoon. Nausea, vomiting, bleeding, circulatory collapse, confusion, restlessness, and delirium have been reported.

**ω-PENTADECALACTONE. Thibetolide®. Angelica Lactone. Exaltolide.** A synthetic berry, fruit, liquor, wine, nut, and vanilla flavoring agent for beverages, ice cream, ices, candy, baked goods, gelatin desserts, and alcoholic beverages. No known toxicity.

**PENTADECANOLIDE.** See ω-Pentadecalactone.

**PENTANAL.** See Valeraldehyde.

**2, 3-PENTANEDIONE.** A synthetic flavoring agent that occurs naturally in coffee. Used in strawberry, butter, caramel, fruit, rum, and cheese flavorings for beverages, ice cream, ices, candy, baked goods, gelatin desserts, and puddings. No known toxicity.

**PENTANOIC ACID.** See Valeric Acid.

**1-PENTANOL. Pentyl Alcohol. N-Amyl Alcohol.** A liquid with a mild, pleasant odor, slightly soluble in water, used as a solvent. It is irritating to the eyes and respiratory passages and absorption may cause lack of oxygen in the blood.

**2-PENTANONE.** A synthetic flavoring that occurs naturally in pineapple. Used in fruit flavorings for beverages, ice cream, ices, candy, and baked goods. No known toxicity.

**4-PENTENOIC ACID.** A synthetic butter and fruit flavoring agent for beverages, ice cream, ices, candy, baked goods, and margarine. No known toxicity.

**PENTYL ALCOHOL.** See Amyl Alcohol.

**PENTYL BUTYRATE.** See Amyl Butyrate.

**PEPPER, BLACK.** A pungent product obtained from the dried, unripe berries of the East Indian pepper plant, *Piper nigrum.* Used in sausage and spice flavorings for beverages, baked goods, condiments, meats, soups, and pickles. Black pepper *oil* is used in meat and spice flavorings for beverages, ice cream, ices, candy, baked goods, condiments, and meats. Black pepper *oleoresin* (*see*) is used in sausage and pepper flavorings for beverages, ice cream, ices, candy, baked goods, condiments, and meats. Pepper was formerly used as a carminative to break up intestinal gas, to cause sweating, and as a gastric agent to promote gastric secretion. No known toxicity.

**PEPPER, RED.** See Cayenne Pepper.

**PEPPER, WHITE.** The pungent product obtained from the undecorticated (with the outer covering intact) ripe berries of the pepper plant. Used in sausage and spice flavorings for beverages, baked goods, condiments, meats, and soups. White pepper *oil* is used in spice flavorings for baked goods. White pepper *oleoresin* (*see*) is used in spice flavorings for meats. See Pepper, Black, for toxicity.

**PEPPER TREE OIL.** See Schinus Molle Oil.

**PEPPERMINT LEAVES.** See Peppermint Oil.

**PEPPERMINT OIL.** From the dried leaves and tops of a plant common to Asian, European, and American gardens. Used in chocolate, fruit, cordial, creme de menthe, peppermint, nut, and spice flavorings for beverages, ice cream, ices, candy (1,200 ppm), baked goods, gelatin desserts, chewing gum (8,300 ppm), meats, liquors, icings, and toppings. Peppermint has been used as a carminative to break up intestinal gas and as an antiseptic. Two patients who consumed large quantities of peppermint candy over a long period of time developed an irregular heart rhythm. GRAS.

**PEPSIN.** A digestive enzyme found in gastric juice that helps break down protein. The product used to aid digestion is obtained from the glandular layer of the fresh stomach of a hog. Slightly acid taste and a mild odor. No known toxicity.

**PEPTONES.** Secondary protein derivatives formed during the process of digestion—the result of the action of the gastric and pancreatic juices upon protein. Peptones are used as a foam stabilizer for beer and as a processing aid in baked goods, confections, and frostings. No known toxicity. Determined to be GRAS in 1982.

**PERACETIC ACID. Peroxyacitic Acid.** A starch modifier prepared from acetaldehyde (*see*). It is 40 percent acetic acid and highly corrosive. Acid odor; explodes violently on heating to 110°.

**PERLITE.** A filtering aid that the final report to the FDA of the Select Committee on GRAS Substances stated in 1980 should continue its GRAS status with no limitations other than good manufacturing practices.

**PEROXIDE. Benzoyl, Calcium, and Hydrogen.** *Benzoyl peroxide* is a compound used as a bleaching agent for flours, oils, and cheese. Has been used as a paste for treating poison ivy and for burns. May explode when heated. *Calcium peroxide* or *dioxide* is odorless, almost tasteless. Used as a dough conditioner and oxidizing agent for bread, rolls, and buns. Formerly an antiseptic. *Hydrogen peroxide* or *dioxide* is a compound used as a bleaching and oxidizing agent, a modifier for food starch, and a preservative and bactericide for milk and cheese. Bitter taste. May decompose violently if traces of impurities are present. A strong oxidant that can injure skin and eyes. Chemists are cautioned to wear rubber gloves and goggles when handling it. On the FDA list of additives to be studied for mutagenic, teratogenic, subacute, and reproductive effects.

**PERSIC OIL.** See Apricot Kernel; also Peach Kernel.

**PERUVIAN BALSAM.** See Balsam, Peru.

**PETITGRAIN OIL.** The volatile oil obtained by steam distillation from the leaves and small twigs of the bitter orange tree, a variety of citrus. Brownish to yellow, with a bittersweet odor. Used in loganberry, violet, apple, banana, cherry, grape, peach, pear, honey, muscatel, nut, ginger, and ginger ale flavorings for beverages, ice cream, ices, candy, baked goods, gelatin desserts, chewing gum, and condiments. No known toxicity.

**PETITGRAIN OIL (LEMON).** A fragrant, essential oil from a variety of citrus trees. Used in citrus and fruit flavorings for beverages, ice cream, ices, candy, and baked goods. No known toxicity. GRAS.

**PETITGRAIN OIL (MANDARIN).** The fragrant essential oil from a variety of citrus tree. Used in orange, tangerine, and grape flavorings for beverages, ice cream, ices, candy, baked goods, and gelatin desserts. No known toxicity. GRAS.

**PETROLATUM. Petroleum or Paraffin Jelly. Vaseline®.** Practically odorless and tasteless. A releasing agent and sealant for confections. A coating for fruits, vegetables, and cheese. A defoaming agent in yeast and beet sugar production. Used in baking products, a lubricant in meat-packing plants and used in dried-egg albumin. A protective dressing in medicine and used in cosmetics. When ingested, it produces a mild laxative effect. Not absorbed but may inhibit digestion.

**PETROLEUM. Crude or Mineral Oil.** A defoaming agent in food processing, a detergent agent in a fruit rinse, and for cleaning vegetables. See Mineral Oil for toxicity.

**PETROLEUM. Waxes.** A defoaming agent in processing beet sugar and yeast. Formerly used for bronchitis, tapeworms, and externally for arthritis and skin problems. No known toxicity.

**pH.** Chemical symbol representing a scale to measure acidity versus alkalinity. The pH of a solution is measured on a scale of 14. A truly neutral solution, neither acidic nor alkaline, such as water, would be 7. The desired pH for most crops is from 6 to 8. The pH of blood is 7.3; vinegar is 2.3; lemon juice is 8.2; and lye is 13. pH actually represents the hydrogen (H) ion concentration of a solution. "p" stands for the *power* of the hydrogen ion.

**α-PHELLANDRENE.** A synthetic flavoring agent that occurs naturally in allspice, star anise, angelica root, bay, dill, sweet fennel, black pepper, peppermint oil, and pimenta. Isolated from the essential oils of the eucalyptus plant. Used in citrus and spice flavorings for beverages, ice cream, ices, candy, and baked goods. Can be irritating to and absorbed through the skin. Ingestion can cause vomiting and diarrhea.

**PHENETHYL ALCOHOL.** A synthetic flavoring that occurs naturally in oranges, raspberries, and tea. Floral odor. Used in strawberry, butter, caramel, floral, fruit, and honey flavorings for beverages, ice cream, ices, candy, baked goods, gelatin desserts, and chewing gum. Practically all rose perfumes contain it. It is a strong local anesthetic and has caused central nervous system injury in mice.

**PHENETHYL ANTHRANILATE.** A synthetic butter, caramel, fruit, honey, and grape flavoring agent for beverages, ice cream, ices, candy, and baked goods. No known toxicity.

**PHENETHYL BENZOATE.** A synthetic fruit and honey flavoring agent for beverages, ice cream, ices, candy, baked goods, and chewing gum. No known toxicity.

**PHENETHYL BUTYRATE.** A synthetic strawberry, butter, caramel, floral, apple, peach, pineapple, and honey flavoring agent for beverages, ice cream, ices, candy, and baked goods. No known toxicity.

**PHENETHYL CINNAMATE.** A synthetic fruit flavoring for beverages, ice cream, ices, candy, baked goods, and puddings. No known toxicity.

**PHENETHYL FORMATE. Formic Acid.** A synthetic berry, apple, apricot, banana, cherry, peach, pear, plum, and honey flavoring agent for beverages, ice cream, ices, candy, and baked goods. See Formic Acid for toxicity.

**PHENETHYL ISOBUTYRATE.** A synthetic flavoring, slightly yellow, with a rose odor. Used in strawberry, floral, rose, apple, peach, pineapple, honey, and cheese flavorings for beverages, ice cream, ices, candy, and baked goods. No known toxicity.

**PHENETHYL ISOVALERATE.** A synthetic apple, apricot, peach, pear, and pineapple flavoring agent for beverages, ice cream, ices, candy, baked goods, and chewing gum. No known toxicity.

**PHENETHYL PHENYLACETATE.** A synthetic fruit and honey flavoring agent for beverages, ice cream, ices, candy, baked goods, and maraschino cherries. No known toxicity.

**PHENETHYL PROPIONATE.** A synthetic fruit and honey flavoring agent for beverages, ice cream, ices, candy, and baked goods. No known toxicity.

**PHENETHYL SALICYLATE.** A synthetic apricot and peach flavoring agent for beverages, ice cream, ices, candy, and baked goods. See Salicylic Acid for toxicity.

**PHENETHYL SENECIOATE.** A synthetic liquor and wine flavoring agent for ice cream, ices, candy, and alcoholic beverages.

**PHENETHYL TIGLATE.** A synthetic fruit and nut flavoring agent for beverages, ice cream, ices, candy, and baked goods. No known toxicity.

**PHENOXYACETIC ACID.** A synthetic fruit and honey flavoring agent for beverages, ice cream, ices, candy, and baked goods. Used as a fungicide to soften calluses and corns and other hard surfaces. A mild irritant.

**2-PHENOXYETHYL ISOBUTYRATE.** A synthetic fruit flavoring, colorless, with a roselike odor. Used in beverages, ice cream, ices, candy, and baked goods. No known toxicity.

**PHENYL ACETATE.** A synthetic flavoring agent prepared from phenol and acetic chloride. Used in berry, butter, caramel, floral, rose, fruit, honey, and vanilla flavorings for beverages, ice cream, ices, candy, and baked goods. Phenol is highly toxic. Death from 1.5 grams has been reported.

**4-PHENYL-2-BUTANOL.** A synthetic fruit flavoring for beverages, ice cream, ices, candy, and baked goods. No known toxicity.

**4-PHENYL-3-BUTEN-2-OL.** A synthetic fruit flavoring for beverages, ice cream, ices, candy, and baked goods. No known toxicity.

**4-PHENYL-3-BUTEN-2-ONE.** A synthetic chocolate, cocoa, fruit, cherry, nut, and vanilla flavoring agent for beverages, ice cream, ices, candy, baked goods, gelatin desserts, and shortening. No known toxicity.

**4-PHENYL-2-BUTYL ACETATE.** A synthetic fruit and peach flavoring agent for beverages, ice cream, ices, candy, and baked goods. See Acetic Acid for toxicity.

**PHENYL DIMETHYL CARBINYL ISOBUTYRATE.** See α-α-Dimethylbenzyl Isobutyrate.

**PHENYL 2-FUROATE.** A synthetic chocolate and mushroom flavoring agent for beverages, candy, and baked goods. No known toxicity.

**1-PHENYL-3-METHYL-3-PENTANOL.** A synthetic fruit flavoring agent for beverages, candy, and gelatin desserts. No known toxicity.

**1-PHENYL-1-PROPANOL.** A synthetic fruit and honey flavoring agent for beverages, ice cream, ices, candy, and baked goods. No known toxicity.

**3-PHENYL-1-PROPANOL.** A synthetic flavoring that occurs naturally in tea. Used in strawberry, apricot, peach, plum, hazelnut, pistachio, cinnamon, and walnut flavorings for beverages, ice cream, ices, candy, baked goods, liqueurs, and chewing gum. No known toxicity.

**3-PHENYL PROPYL ISOBUTYRATE.** A synthetic apple, apricot, peach, pear, pineapple, and plum flavoring agent for beverages, ice cream, ices, candy, and baked goods. No known toxicity.

**PHENYLACETIC ACID.** A synthetic flavoring agent that occurs naturally in Japanese mint, oil of neroli, and black pepper. A glistening, white solid with a persistent, unpleasant odor. Used in butter, chocolate, rose, honey, and vanilla flavorings for beverages, ice cream, ices, candy, baked goods, gelatin desserts, chewing gum, liquors, and syrups. No known toxicity.

**PHENYLACETALDEHYDE.** An oily, colorless flavoring agent with the odor of lilacs and hyacinths, derived from phenylethyl alcohol. Used in raspberry, strawberry, apricot, cherry, peach, honey, and spice flavorings for beverages, ice cream, ices, candy, baked goods, and chewing gum. The acetaldehyde of this compound is less irritating than formaldehyde (*see*) but is a stronger central nervous system depressant. In addition, it sometimes produces fluid in the lungs upon ingestion.

**PHENYLACETALDEHYDE 2,3-BUTYLENE GLYCOL ACETAL.** A synthetic floral and fruit flavoring agent for candy. See Phenylacetaldehyde for toxicity.

**PHENYLACETALDEHYDE DIMETHYL ACETAL.** A synthetic fruit, apricot, cherry, honey, and spice flavoring agent for beverages, ice cream, ices, candy, baked goods, and chewing gum. See Phenylacetaldehyde and Acetic Acid for toxicity.

**PHENYLACETALDEHYDE GLYCERYL ACETAL.** A synthetic floral and fruit flavoring agent for beverages, candy, ice cream, and ices. See Phenylacetaldehyde and Acetic Acid for toxicity.

**PHENYLALANINE.** An essential amino acid (*see*) considered essential for growth in normal human beings and not synthesized in the human body. Phenylalanine is involved in phenylketonuria (PHK), an affliction that, if not detected soon after birth, leads to mental deterioration in children. Restricting phenylalanine in diets results in improvement. Whole egg contains 5.4 percent and skim milk 5.1 percent. It can also be isolated commercially. For a dietary supplement, recommended intake for normal adults is 2.2 milligrams per day. The FDA has asked for further short-term study of this additive.

**2-PHENYLETHYL ISOVALERATE.** See Phenethyl Isovalerate.

**PHENYLETHYLACETATE.** A colorless liquid with a floral odor, insoluble in most oils. Used as a flavoring agent. No known toxicity.

**2-PHENYLPROPIONALDEHYDE.** A synthetic berry, rose, apricot, cherry, peach, plum, and almond flavoring agent for beverages, ice cream, ices, candy, and baked goods. No known toxicity.

**3-PHENYLPROPIONALDEHYDE.** A synthetic flavoring agent, slightly yellow, with a strong, floral odor. Used in berry, rose, apricot, cherry, peach, plum, and almond flavorings for beverages, ice cream, ices, candy, and baked goods. No known toxicity.

**2-PHENYLPROPIONALDEHYDE DIMETHYL ACETAL.** A synthetic berry, floral, rose, fruit, honey, mushroom, nut, and spice flavoring agent for beverages, ice cream, ices, candy, baked goods, chewing gum, and condiments. See Acetic Acid for toxicity.

**3-PHENYLPROPIONIC ACID.** A synthetic flavoring agent that occurs naturally in raspberries. Used in fruit and cheese flavorings for beverages, ice cream, ices, candy, baked goods, gelatin desserts, and dairy products. No known toxicity.

**3-PHENYLPROPYL ACETATE.** A synthetic flavoring, colorless, with a spicy floral odor. Used in berry, fruit, and spice flavorings for beverages, ice cream, ices, candy, baked goods, chewing gum, and condiments. Propyl acetate may be irritating to skin and mucous membranes and narcotic in high concentrations.

**2-PHENYLPROPYL BUTYRATE.** A synthetic flavoring used in beverages, ice cream, ices, candy and baked goods. No specific flavorings listed. No known toxicity.

**3-PHENYLPROPYL CINNAMATE.** A synthetic butter, caramel, chocolate, cocoa, coconut, grape, and spice flavoring agent for beverages, ice cream, ices, candy, and baked goods. No known toxicity.

**3-PHENYLPROPYL FORMATE. Formic Acid.** A synthetic currant, raspberry, butter, caramel, apricot, peach, and honey flavoring agent for beverages, ice cream, ices, candy, and baked goods. See Formic Acid for toxicity.

**3-PHENYLPROPYL HEXANOATE.** A synthetic fruit flavoring for beverages, ice cream, ices, candy, and baked goods. No known toxicity.

**2-PHENYLPROPYL ISOBUTYRATE.** A synthetic fruit flavoring for beverages, ice cream, ices, and candy. No known toxicity.

**3-PHENYLPROPYL ISOVALERATE.** A synthetic butter, caramel, apple, pear, and nut flavoring agent for beverages, ice cream, ices, candy, and baked goods. No known toxicity.

**3-PHENYLPROPYL PROPIONATE.** A synthetic apricot flavoring for beverages, ice cream, ices, and candy, and baked goods. No known toxicity.

**2-3 (3-PHENYLPROPYL) TETRAHYDROFURAN.** A synthetic fruit, honey and maple flavoring agent for beverages, ice cream, ices, candy, gelatin, puddings, and chewing gum. No known toxicity.

**PHOSPHATE.** A salt or ester of phosphoric acid (*see*). An emulsifier salt, texturizer, and sequestrant (*see*) in foods. Sodium phosphate is used in evaporated milk up to .1 percent of weight. A carbonated beverage contains phosphoric acid. Without sufficient phosphate there is abnormal parathyroid (gland) function, bone metabolism, intestinal absorption, malnutrition, and kidney malfunction. Chemicals that interfere with phosphate action include detergents, mannitol (an alcohol used as a dietary supplement, the basis of dietetic sweets), Vitamin D, and aluminum hydroxide (*see*), a leavening agent.

**PHOSPHATE, AMMONIUM. Dibasic and Monobasic.** See Ammonium Phosphate.

**PHOSPHATE, CALCIUM HEXAMETA-.** See Calcium Hexametaphosphate.

**PHOSPHATE, CALCIUM. Monobasic and Tribasic.** See Calcium Phosphate.

**PHOSPHATE, POTASSIUM. Monobasic and Dibasic.** See Potassium Phosphate.

**PHOSPHATED DISTARCH PHOSPHATE.** The final report to the FDA of the Select Committee on GRAS Substances stated in 1980 that there is no evidence in the available information that it is a hazard to the public when used as it is now and it should continue its GRAS status with limitations on amounts that can be added to food. See Modified Starches.

**PHOSPHORIC ACID.** A colorless, odorless solution obtained commercially from phosphate rock. Used as a sequestering (*see* Sequestrant) agent for rendered animal fat or a combination of such fat with vegetable fat. Also used as an acidulant and flavoring in soft drink beverages, jellies, frozen dairy products, bakery products, candy, cheese products, and in the brewing industry. In concentrated solutions, it is irritating to the skin and mucous membranes. The final report to the FDA of the Select Committee on GRAS Substances stated in 1980 that it should continue its GRAS status with no limitations other than good manufacturing practices.

**PHOSPHOROUS SOURCES: Calcium Phosphate, Magnesium Phosphate, Potassium Glycerophosphate, and Sodium Phosphate.** Mineral supplements for cereal products, particularly breakfast foods such as farina. They are also used in incendiary bombs and tracer bullets. Phosphorus was formerly used to treat rickets and degenerative disorders. See Phosphate.

**PHOSPHORUS CHLORIDE.** Phosphate derivative used as a starch modifier and a chlorinating agent. Intensely irritating to the skin, eyes, mucous membranes. Inhalation may cause fluid in the lungs.

**PIMENTA LEAF OIL. Jamaica Pepper. Allspice.** Derived from the dried ripe fruit of the evergreen shrub grown in the West Indies and Central and South America. Used in raspberry, fruit, nut, and spice flavorings for beverages, ice cream, ices, candy, baked goods, gelatin desserts, chewing gum, condiments, and meat products. No known toxicity. GRAS.

**PINE MOUNTAIN OIL.** See Pine Needle Oil and Pine Needle Dwarf Oil.

**PINE NEEDLE DWARF OIL. Pine Mountain Oil.** The volatile oil obtained by steam distillation from a variety of pine trees. Colorless, with a pleasant pine smell. Used in citrus, pineapple, and liquor flavorings for beverages, ice cream, ices, candy, and baked goods.

**PINE NEEDLE OIL. Pine Mountain Oil.** A natural flavoring extracted from a variety of pine trees. Used in pineapple, citrus, liquor, and spice flavorings for beverages, ice cream, ices, candy, and baked goods. Ingestion can cause intestinal hemorrhages.

**PINE SCOTCH OIL.** Volatile oil obtained by steam distillation from the needles of a pine tree. Colorless or yellowish, with an odor of turpentine. Used in various flavorings for beverages, candy, and baked goods. See Turpentine for toxicity.

**PINE TAR OIL.** A synthetic flavoring obtained from a species of pine wood. Used in licorice flavorings for ice cream, ices, and candy. Also used as a solvent, disinfectant, and deodorant. Irritating to the skin and mucous membranes. Large doses can cause central nervous system depression.

**α-PINENE.** A synthetic flavoring agent that occurs naturally in angelica root oil, anise, star anise, asafoetida oil, coriander, cumin, fennel, grapefruit, juniper berries, oils of lavender and lime, mandarin orange leaf, black pepper, peppermint, pimenta, and yarrow. It is the principal ingredient of turpentine (*see*). Used chiefly in the manufacture of camphor. Used in lemon and nutmeg flavorings for beverages, ice cream, candy, baked goods, and condiments. Also used in chewing gum base. Readily absorbed from the gastrointestinal tract, the skin, and respiratory tract. It is a local irritant, central nervous system depressant, and an irritant to the bladder and kidney. Has caused benign skin tumors from chronic contact. The fatal dose is estimated at 180 grams orally as turpentine.

**2-PINENE.** See α-Pinene.

**β-PINENE.** A synthetic flavoring that occurs naturally in black currant buds, coriander, cumin, black pepper, and yarrow herb. Used in citrus flavorings for beverages, ice cream, ices, candy (600 ppm), and baked goods (600 ppm). Also cleared for use in chewing gum base. See α-Pinene for toxicity.

**PINUS PUMILIO OIL.** See Pine Needle Dwarf Oil.

**PIPERIDINE.** A synthetic flavoring that occurs naturally in black pepper. Used in beverages, candy, baked goods, meats, soups, and condiments. Soapy texture. Has been proposed for use as a tranquilizer and muscle relaxant. No known toxicity.

**PIPERINE. Celery Soda.** A synthetic flavoring agent that occurs naturally in black pepper, it is used as a pungent brandy flavoring. It is also used as a nontoxic insecticide. Believed to be more toxic than the commercial pyrethrins.

**d-PIPERITONE.** A synthetic flavoring agent that occurs naturally in Japanese mint. Used in beverages, ice cream, ices, candy, and baked goods. Also used to give dentifrices a minty flavor. No known toxicity.

**PIPERONAL.** A synthetic flavoring agent that occurs naturally in vanilla and black pepper. White, crystalline powder, with a sweet floral odor. Used in strawberry, cola, cherry, rum, maple, nut, and vanilla flavorings in beverages, ice cream, ices, baked goods, gelatin puddings, and chewing gum. Used chiefly in perfumery. Ingestion of large amounts may cause central nervous system depression.

**PIPERONYL ACETATE.** A synthetic fruit flavoring agent for beverages, ice cream, ices, candy, and baked goods. See Piperonal for toxicity.

**PIPERONYL ALDEHYDE.** See Piperonal.

**PIPERONYL ISOBUTYRATE.** A synthetic fruit and cheese flavoring agent for beverages, ice cream, ices, candy, and baked goods. See Piperonal for toxicity.

**PIPERONYLPIPERIDENE.** See Piperine.

**PIPSISSEWA LEAVES EXTRACT. Love-in-Winter. Prince's Pine.** Extracted from the leaves of an evergreen shrub. Used in root beer, sarsaparilla, wintergreen, and birch beer flavorings for beverages and candy. Its leaves have been used as an astringent, diuretic, and tonic. The Cree name means "to break up"—bladder stones, that is.

**PLANTAIN.** The starchy fruit that is a staple item of diet throughout the tropics when cooked and that looks like a banana but is more angular and has a yellowish-green color.

**PLANTAROME.** See Yucca.

**POLYACRYLAMIDE.** A compound used as a film former in the imprinting of soft-shell gelatin capsules. Used in washing fruits and vegetables. No known toxicity.

**POLYACRYLIC ACID.** A polymer of acrylic acid used in clarification of sugar juice. Used as sizing in manufacture of nylon. A strong irritant.

**POLYDEXTROSE.** A reduced-calorie bulking agent developed by Pfizer, Inc., and approved for use in foods by the FDA in June 1981. The FDA says it is not a substitute for saccharin (*see*) nor a general sweetener but that it can replace sucrose (*see*) as a bulking agent in frozen desserts, cakes, and candies, and reduce calories in some products as much as 50 percent. According to Pfizer, it is a one-calorie-per-gram bulking agent capable of replacing higher calorie—four to nine calories-per-gram—ingredients such as sucrose, carbohydrates, and fats in many food products.

**POLYETHOXYLATED ALKYLPHENOL. Dodecyl, Nonyl, and Octyl.** Components of a commercial detergent for raw foods, followed by water rinsing. The only symptoms shown in animals poisoned with this substance is gastrointestinal irritation.

**POLYETHYLENE.** Chewing-gum base component. Used especially in form of films and sheets for packaging. No known toxicity.

**POLYETHYLENE GLYCOL. 400–2,000 molecular weight.** Defoaming agent in processed beet sugar and yeast. No known toxicity.

**POLYETHYLENE GLYCOL (600) DIOLEATE. Polyethylene glycol esters of mixed fatty acids from tall oil; Polyethylene glycol (400 through 6,000).** An agent in nonnutritive artificial sweeteners; a component of coatings and binders in tablet food; improves resistance to oxidation and moisture. See Polyols.

**POLYCLYCERATE 60.** See Glycerides.

**POLYGLYCEROL ESTERS.** Prepared from edible fats, oils, and fatty acids, hydrogenated or nonhydrogenated (*see* Hydrogenation). Derived from corn, cottonseed, palm, peanut, safflower, sesame, and soybean oils, lard, and tallow. Used as emulsifiers. No known toxicity.

**POLYISOBUTYLENE.** See Resin, Isobutylene.

**POLYLIMONENE.** A general fixative derived from citrus oils. It is used in candy (4,500 ppm), chewing gum, and baked goods (1,000 ppm). It can be a skin irritant and sensitizer. See *d*-Limonene.

**POLYMYXIN B₄.** A generic term for antibiotics obtained from fermentations of various media by strains of *Bacillus polymyxa.* Used as a bactericide in yeast culture for beer. May cause symptoms of renal irritation and damage.

**POLYOLS.** Alcohol compounds that absorb moisture. They have a low molecular weight: polyols with a weight above 1,000 are solids and less toxic than those weighing 600 or below. The latter are liquid and although higher in toxicity, very large doses are required to kill animals. Such deaths in animals have been found to be due to kidney damage. See Propylene Glycol and Polyethylene Glycol as examples.

**POLYOXYALKALENE GLYCOL.** Defoaming agent in beet sugar production. No known toxicity.

**POLYOXYETHYLENE GLYCOL.** Ester of edible cottonseed oil and fatty acids. Solubilizing agent in pickles. No known toxicity.

**POLYOXYETHYLENE GLYCOL (600) MONORICINOLEATE.** Defoaming component used in processing beet sugar and yeast. No known toxicity.

**POLYOXYETHYLENE (140) MONOSTEARATE.** Defoaming agent in processed food; emulsifier for frozen desserts. Application to the skin of mice has been shown to cause skin tumors. The compound has been fed to animals and does not appear to produce tumors on its own, but there is a suggestion that it allows cancer-causing agents to penetrate more quickly. On the FDA list for further study for long- and short-term effects.

**POLYOXYETHYLENE (20) SORBITAN MONOSTEARATE. Polysorbate 60.** An emulsifier and flavor-dispersing agent in shortening and edible oils. Used in whipped vegetable oil topping, cake, and cake mixes; cake icing or filling; sugar-type confection coatings; coconut spread; beverage mixes; confectionery; chicken bases; gelatin desserts; dressings made without egg yolks; solid-state, edible vegetable fat–water emulsions used as substitutes for milk or cream; dietary vitamin supplement; foaming agent in nonalcoholic beverage mix to be added to alcoholic beverages; and a wetting and dispersing agent for powdered processed foods. The FDA has asked for further study of this additive.

**POLYOXYETHYLENE (20) SORBITAN MONOOLEATE.** Emulsifier and defoamer in the production of beet sugar; a dietary vitamin and mineral supplement. Used in dill oil in spiced green beans, icing, frozen custard, iced milk, fruit, and sherbet. The FDA has asked for short-term mutagenic, teratogenic, subacute, and reproductive effects. No known toxicity.

**POLYOXYETHYLENE (20) SORBITAN MONOPALMITATE.** An emulsifier, flavor-dispersing agent, and defoaming agent. Used in whipped cream, beverages, confectionery, and soup. The FDA has asked for further study of the safety of this additive.

**POLYOXYETHYLENE (20) SORBITAN TRISTEARATE.** An emulsifier, defoaming agent, and flavor-dispersing agent. Used in cakes and cake mixes, including doughnuts, whipped mixes, whipped vegetable oil toppings, cake icings and fillings, ice cream, frozen custard, ice milk, fruit sherbet, and nonstandardized frozen desserts; solid-state edible vegetable fat–water emulsions used as substitutes for milk or cream in coffee; and as a wetting and dispersing agent in processed powdered food. No known toxicity.

**POLYOXYETHYLENE STEARATE.** A mixture of stearate (*see*) and ethylene oxide, it is a waxy solid added to bread to make it "feel fresh." It was fed to rats as one-fourth of their diets and resulted in the formulation of bladder stones, and subsequently a number of tumors. It is still on the market.

**POLYOXYPROPYLENE GLYCOL.** Defoaming agent for yeast and beet sugar. No known toxicity.

**POLYPROPYLENE GLYCOL.** Defoaming agent in processed beet sugar and yeast. No known toxicity.

**POLYSORBATE 80.** See Sorbitan Monooleate.

**POLYSORBATE 60.** See Polyoxyethylene (20) Sorbitan Monostearate.

**POLYVINYL ACETATE.** Used in a chewing-gum base. No known toxicity.

**POLYVINYL CHLORIDE (PVC). Chloroethylene Polymer.** Derived from vinyl chloride (*see*), it consists of white powder or colorless granules that are resistant to weather, moisture, acids, fats, petroleum products, and fungus. It has many uses in modern life, including plumbing, piping, conduits, siding, gutters, window and door frames, raincoats, toys, gaskets, film, sheeting, containers for toiletries, cosmetics, household chemicals, fibers for athletic supports, linings for reservoirs, adhesive and bonding agents, tennis court playing surfaces, flooring, and phonograph records. The use of PVC as a plastic wrap for food, including meats, and for human blood has alarmed some scientists. Human and animal blood can extract potentially harmful chemicals from the plastic. The chemicals are added to polyvinyl chloride to make it flexible, and they migrate from the plastic into the blood and into the meats in amounts directly proportional to the length of time of storage. The result can be contamination of the blood, causing lung shock, a condition in which the patient's blood circulation to the lungs is impeded. PVC has also caused tumors when injected under the skin of rats in doses of 100 milligrams per kilogram of body weight.

**POLYVINYLPOLYPYRROLIDONE.** Used in dietary products up to 40 milligrams per day. Also a clarifying agent in vinegar. See Polyvinylpyrrolidone for toxicity.

**POLYVINYLPYRROLIDONE.** Clarifying agent in vinegar and used as a plasma expander in medicine. In vinegar, up to .004 milligrams. It is not absorbed from the intestinal tract and may produce bulk evacuation, gas, and fecal impaction. It has damaged liver and kidneys when given intravenously. It is slowly excreted and may last in the system several months to a year. Found to cause cancer in experimental animals.

**POMEGRANATE BARK EXTRACT.** A flavoring from dried bark, stem, or root of trees in the Mediterranean region and elsewhere. Contains about 20 percent tannic acid (*see*); rind of fruit contains 30 percent. Formerly used as a teniafuge (to expel tapeworms). Overdose can cause nausea, vomiting, and diarrhea. GRAS.

**POPPY SEED.** The seed of the poppy. Used as a natural spice for flavoring for baked goods (8,600 ppm). Also used in the manufacture of paints, varnishes, and soaps. No known toxicity. GRAS.

**POT MARIGOLD.** See Marigold, Pot.

**POT MARJORAM.** See Marjoram, Pot.

**POTASSIUM ACETATE.** Colorless, water-absorbing crystals or powder, odorless or with a faint acetic aroma and a salty taste. Used as a buffer, antimicrobial preservative. Very soluble in water. Also used medicinally to treat irregular heartbeat and as a diuretic. No known toxicity.

**POTASSIUM ACID TARTRATE.** The salt of tartaric acid. Colorless, with a pleasant odor. An acid and buffer, it is the acid constituent of some baking powders. Used in effervescent beverages. It is also used in some confectionery products. Formerly a cathartic. No known toxicity.

**POTASSIUM ASPARTAME.** See Aspartame.

**POTASSIUM BICARBONATE.** Considered a miscellaneous and/or general-purpose food additive, it is present in fluids and tissues of the body as a product of normal metabolic processes. It is either colorless, odorless, transparent crystals or a white powder, slightly alkaline and salty to taste. Soluble in water. It is used in baking, low pH detergents, and as a laboratory reagent. The final report to the FDA of the Select Committee on GRAS Substances stated in 1980 that it should continue its GRAS status with no limitations other than good manufacturing practices.

**POTASSIUM BISULFITE.** Same uses as for sodium sulfite (*see*) in ale, beer, fruit-pie mix. The final report to the FDA of the Select Committee on GRAS Substances stated in 1980 that there is no evidence in the available information that it is a hazard to the public when used as it is now and it should continue its GRAS status with limitations on amounts that can be added to food.

**POTASSIUM BROMATE.** The compound is added as an improving agent in bread. The expected result is to obtain a fine spongelike quality with the action of oxygen. This method is used in Great Britain, the United States, and Japan. Legal allowance of potassium bromate is below 50 ppm. In 1980, potassium bromate was shown on the Ames Test (*see*) to be a mutagen.

**POTASSIUM BROMIDE.** A preservative used in washing fruits and vegetables. Used medically as a sedative and antiepileptic. In large doses it can cause central nervous system depression. Prolonged intake may cause bromism. Bromism's main symptoms are headache, mental inertia, slow heartbeat, gastric distress, skin rash, acne, muscular weakness, and occasionally violent delirium. Bromides can cross the placental barrier, and have caused skin rashes in the fetus.

**POTASSIUM CARBONATE. Salt of Tartar. Pearl Ash.** Odorless, with a strong alkaline taste. Used as an alkali in combination with potassium hydroxide (*see*) for extracting color from annatto seed (*see*). Also used in confections and cocoa products. Formerly employed as a diuretic to reduce body water and as an alkalizer. It is an irritant with caustic action. The final report to the FDA of the Select Committee on GRAS Substances stated in 1980 that it should continue its GRAS status with no limitations other than good manufacturing practices.

**POTASSIUM CASEINATE.** A texturizer used in ice cream, frozen custard, ice milk, and fruit sherbets. See Casein.

**POTASSIUM CHLORIDE.** A colorless, crystalline, odorless powder with a salty taste. A yeast food used in the brewing industry to improve brewing and fermentation and in the jelling industry. Small intestinal ulcers may occur with oral administration. Large doses ingested can cause gastrointestinal irritation, purging, weakness, and circulatory collapse. Used as a substitute for sodium chloride (*see*) in low-sodium dietary foods. The final report to the FDA of the Select Committee on GRAS Substances stated in 1980 that it should continue its GRAS status with no limitations other than good manufacturing practices.

**POTASSIUM CITRATE.** A transparent or white powder, odorless, with a cool, salty taste. Used as a buffer in confections and in artificially sweetened jellies and preserves. It is a urinary alkalizer and gastric antacid. No known toxicity. The final report to the FDA of the Select Committee on GRAS Substances stated in 1980 that it should continue its GRAS status with no limitations other than good manufacturing practices.

**POTASSIUM CORNATE.**  The potassium salt of corn oil (*see*).

**POTASSIUM GLUCONATE.**  The potassium salt of gluconic acid (*see*) used as a buffering agent that helps keep soda water bubbling. No known toxicity. The final report to the FDA of the Select Committee on GRAS Substances stated in 1980 that it should continue its GRAS status with no limitations other than good manufacturing practices.

**POTASSIUM GLYCEROPHOSPHATE.**  See Glycerides.

**POTASSIUM HYDROXIDE.**  An alkali used to extract color from annatto seed, a peeling agent for tubers and fruits, also in cacao products. Extremely corrosive. Ingestion may produce violent pain in the throat, bleeding, and collapse. Stricture of the esophagus may follow. Occasionally used to prevent the growth of horns in calves. The FDA banned household products containing more than 10 percent potassium hydroxide. The final report to the FDA of the Select Committee on GRAS Substances stated in 1980 that it should continue its GRAS status with no limitations other than good manufacturing practices.

**POTASSIUM HYPOPHOSPHATE.**  The final report to the FDA of the Select Committee on GRAS Substances stated in 1980 that it should continue its GRAS status with no limitations other than good manufacturing practices. See Phosphate Sources.

**POTASSIUM IODATE.**  See Iodine Sources.

**POTASSIUM IODIDE.**  In table salt as a source of dietary iodine restricted to .01 percent. It is also used in some drinking water. See Iodine Sources for use and toxicity. GRAS.

**POTASSIUM METABISULFITE.**  White or colorless, with an odor of sulfur dioxide (*see*), it is an antioxidant, preservative, and antifermentative in breweries and wineries. Also used for bleaching straw. The final report to the FDA of the Select Committee on GRAS Substances stated in 1980 that there is no evidence in the available information that it is a hazard to the public when used as it is now and it should continue its GRAS status with limitations on amounts that can be added to food.

**POTASSIUM-n-METHYLDITHIO-CARBAMATE.**  A bacteria-killing component in controlling microorganisms in cane sugar mills. Carbamates are used to prevent sprouting in potatoes and other products by stopping cell division, something we call mutations. Carbamate mutations may lead to defective children and to cancer.

**POTASSIUM NITRATE.**  See Nitrate, Potassium.

**POTASSIUM NITRITE.**  See Nitrite, Potassium.

**POTASSIUM PERMANGANATE.** Dark purple or bronzelike odorless crystals with a sweet, antiseptic taste, used as a starch modifier. Dilute solutions are mildly irritating; highly concentrated solutions are caustic.
**POTASSIUM PHOSPHATE. Monobasic, Dibasic, and Tribasic.** Colorless to white powder used as yeast food in the brewing industry and in the production of champagne and other sparkling wines. Has been used as a urinary acidifier. The final report to the FDA of the Select Committee on GRAS Substances stated in 1980 that it should continue its GRAS status with no limitations other than good manufacturing practices.
**POTASSIUM POLYMETAPHOSPHATE.** The final report to the FDA of the Select Committee on GRAS Substances stated in 1980 that it should continue its GRAS status with no limitations other than good manufacturing practices. See Potassium Phosphate for uses.
**POTASSIUM PYROPHOSPHATE.** Colorless, deliquescent crystals or granules, used as a sequestering agent, peptizing and dispersing agent, and in soaps and detergents. Low toxicity. The final report to the FDA of the Select Committee on GRAS Substances stated in 1980 that it should continue its GRAS status with no limitations other than good manufacturing practices.
**POTASSIUM SILICATE.** Colorless, waterless lump, it is used for inorganic protective coatings, for phosphorus on television tubes, in detergents, as a catalyst, and in adhesives. No known toxicity. The final report to the FDA of the Select Committee on GRAS Substances stated in 1980 that it should continue its GRAS status with no limitations other than good manufacturing practices.
**POTASSIUM SORBATE.** White crystalline powder used as a preservative; a mold and yeast inhibitor; and a fungistat in beverages, baked goods, chocolate, and soda fountain syrups, fresh fruit cocktail, tangerine puree (sherbet base), salads (potato, macaroni, cole slaw, gelatin), cheesecake, pie fillings, cake, cheeses in consumer-size packages, and artificially sweetened jellies and preserves. Low oral toxicity but may cause mild irritation of the skin. GRAS.
**POTASSIUM STEARATE.** A defoaming agent, with the slight odor of fat, in brewing. A strong alkali. No known toxicity.
**POTASSIUM SULFATE.** Colorless or white crystalline powder, with a bitter taste. A water corrective used in the brewing industry. Also used as a fertilizer and as a cathartic. Large doses can cause severe gastrointestinal bleeding.
**POTASSIUM SULFITE.** See Sulfites.
**POTATO STARCH.** A flour prepared from potatoes, ground to a pulp and washed free of fiber. A potential sensitizer. The final report to the

FDA of the Select Committee on GRAS Substances stated in 1980 that it should continue its GRAS status for packaging only with no limitations other than good manufacturing practices.

**POTASSIUM TRIPOLYPHOSPHATE.** White crystalline solid that is used in water-treating compounds, cleaners, and fertilizers; widely used as a sequestrant (*see*) in processed foods. The final report to the FDA of the Select Committee on GRAS Substances stated in 1980 that it should continue its GRAS status with no limitations other than good manufacturing practices.

**POTENTIATOR.** A flavor ingredient with little flavor of its own that augments or alters the flavor response, such as sodium glutamate and sodium inosinate.

**PREGELATINIZED STARCH.** When starch and water are heated, the starch molecules burst and form a gelatin. The final report to the FDA of the Select Committee on GRAS Substances stated in 1980 that it should continue its GRAS status with no limitations other than good manufacturing practices.

**PRESERVATIVES.** About 100 "antispoilants," which retard or prevent food from going "bad," are in common use. Preservatives for fatty products are called "antioxidants." Preservatives used in bread are labeled "mold" or "rope" inhibitors. They include sodium propionate and calcium propionate (*see both*). Preservatives to prevent mold and fungus growth on citrus fruits are called "fungicides." Among the most commonly used preservatives are sodium benzoate (*see*) to prevent the growth of microbes on cheese and syrups; sulfur dioxide (*see*) to inhibit discoloration in fruit juice concentrates, and nitrates and nitrites that are used to "cure" processed meats.

**PRICKLY ASH BARK.** A natural cola, maple, and root beer flavor extract from a prickly aromatic shrub or small tree bearing yellow flowers. Used in beverages, candy, and baked goods. No known toxicity. GRAS.

**PROLINE. L and DL forms.** An amino acid (*see*), used as a supplement but classified as nonessential. Usually isolated from wheat or gelatin. L-Proline is the naturally occurring form and DL-Proline is the synthetic. GRAS.

**PROPANE.** A gas, heavier than air, odorless when pure. It is used as fuel, and as a refrigerant. Cleared for use in combination with octafluorocyclobutane as a spray propellant and aerating agent for foamed and sprayed foods. May be narcotic in high concentrations. The final report to the FDA of the Select Committee on GRAS Substances stated in 1980 that it should continue its GRAS status with no limitations other than good manufacturing practices.

**PROPANOIC ACID.** See Propionic Acid.

**PROPENYLGLUAETHOL.** A synthetic chocolate, maple, nut, and vanilla flavoring agent for beverages, ice cream, ices, candy, baked goods, puddings, and chocolate. No known toxicity.

**PROPIONALDEHYDE. Propanal.** A synthetic flavoring agent that occurs naturally in apples and onions. Used in fruit flavorings for beverages, ice cream, ices, candy, and baked goods. Suffocating odor. May cause respiratory irritation.

**PROPIONIC ACID. Propanoic Acid.** A synthetic flavoring agent that occurs naturally in dairy products in small amounts and in apples, strawberries, tea, and violet leaves. Can be obtained from wood pulp waste liquor. Oily, with a slightly pungent, rancid odor. Used in butter and fruit flavorings for beverages, ice cream, ices, candy, baked goods, and cheese (600 ppm). Also an inhibitor and preservative. A perfume base. Salts have been used as antifungal agents to treat skin infections. The final report to the FDA of the Select Committee on GRAS Substances stated in 1980 that it should continue its GRAS status with no limitations other than good manufacturing practices.

**PROPYL ACETATE.** A synthetic currant, raspberry, strawberry, apple, cherry, peach, pineapple, and rum flavoring agent for beverages, ice cream, ices, candy, and baked goods. It may be irritating to skin and mucous membranes and narcotic in high concentrations.

**PROPYL ALCOHOL.** Obtained from crude fusel oil. Alcoholic and slightly overpowering odor. Occurs naturally in cognac green oil, cognac white oil, and onion oil. A synthetic fruit flavoring for beverages, ice cream, ices, candy, and baked goods. Mildly irritating to the eyes and mucous membranes. Ingestion causes symptoms similar to that of ethyl alcohol (*see*), also known as grain alcohol.

*p*-**PROPYL ANISOLE.** A synthetic flavoring agent, colorless to pale yellow, with an anise odor. Used in licorice, root beer, spice, vanilla, wintergreen, and birch beer flavoring for beverages, ice cream, candy, and baked goods. No known toxicity.

**PROPYL BENZOATE.** A synthetic fruit flavoring agent for beverages, ice cream, ices, candy, and baked goods. No known toxicity.

**PROPYL BUTYRATE.** Contains propyl alcohol (*see*) and butyric acid (*see*). A synthetic strawberry, banana, pineapple, plum, tutti-frutti, liquor, and rum flavoring agent for beverages, ice cream, ices, candy, and baked goods. See Propyl Alcohol and Butyric Acid for toxicity.

**PROPYL CINNAMATE. Cinnamic Acid.** A synthetic berry, floral, rose, apple, grape, and honey flavoring agent for beverages, ice cream, ices, candy, baked goods, and gelatins. No known toxicity.

**PROPYL FORMATE. Formic Acid.** A synthetic berry, apple, and rum flavoring agent for beverages, ice cream, ices, candy, and baked goods. See Formic Acid for toxicity.

**PROPYL 2-FURANACRYLATE.** A synthetic coffee and honey flavoring agent for beverages and candy. No known toxicity.

**PROPYL 2-FUROATE.** A synthetic chocolate and mushroom flavoring agent for candy, baked goods, and condiments. No known toxicity.

**PROPYL GALLATE.** A fine, white, odorless powder with a bitter taste used as an antioxidant for foods, fats, and oils. Also used in lemon, lime, fruit, and spice flavorings for beverages, ice cream, ices, candy, baked goods, and gelatin desserts. Reaffirmed as GRAS in the FDA's reevaluation in the following amounts: 0.02 percent maximum in fat or oil content of food; maximum of .015 percent in food prepared by the manufacturer.

**PROPYL HEPTANOATE.** A synthetic berry, coffee, fruit, cognac, and rum flavoring agent for beverages, ice cream, ices, candy, liqueurs, and baked goods. No known toxicity.

**PROPYL HEXANOATE.** A synthetic pineapple flavoring agent for beverages, ice cream, ices, and candy. No known toxicity.

**PROPYL-*p*-HYDROXYBENZOATE. Propylparaben.** A preservative used in beverages, candy, baked goods, artificially sweetened jellies and preserves. Also used in fruit flavorings for beverages, ice cream, ices, candy, and baked goods. Less toxic than benzoic (*see*) or salicylic (*see*) acid. Experimental animals showed no kidney or liver damage. On the FDA list for further study for short-term mutagenic, subacute, teratogenic, and reproductive effects. GRAS.

**PROPYL ISOVALERATE.** A synthetic strawberry, apple, banana, and peach flavoring agent for beverages, ice cream, ices, candy, and baked goods. No known toxicity.

**PROPYL MERCAPTAN.** A synthetic berry and onion flavoring agent for baked goods and pickles. No known toxicity.

**PROPYL METHOXYBENZENE.** See *p*-Propyl Anisole.

**PROPYL PHENYLACETATE.** A synthetic butter, caramel, rose, fruit, and honey flavoring agent for beverages, ice cream, ices, candy, and baked goods. See Acetic Acid for toxicity.

**PROPYL PROPIONATE.** Propyl alcohol and propionic acid. A synthetic banana, cherry, melon, peach, pineapple, plum, and rum flavoring agent for beverages, ice cream, ices, candy, and baked goods. See Propyl Alcohol and Propionic Acid for toxicity.

**PROPYLENE GLYCOL.** Viscous, slightly bitter-tasting solvent, wetting agent, and humectant. It is the most common moisture-carrying vehicle used in cosmetics other than water itself. It permeates better through the skin than glycerin and is less expensive, although it has been linked to more sensitivity reactions in cosmetics. It is being reduced and replaced in cosmetics by safer glycols such as butylene and polyethylene glycol. In food, it is used in confectionery, chocolate products, ice cream emulsifiers, shredded coconut, beverages, baked goods, toppings, icings, and meat products to prevent discoloration during storage. Used in antifreeze in breweries and dairy establishments. Practically nontoxic. Large oral doses in animals have been reported to cause central nervous system depression and slight kidney changes. The final report to the FDA of the Select Committee on GRAS Substances stated in 1980 that it should continue its GRAS status with no limitations other than good manufacturing practices.

**PROPYLENE GLYCOL ALGINATE. Kelcolid.®** The propylene glycol ester of alginic acid (*see*) derived from seaweed. Used as a stabilizer and defoaming agent. Cleared for use in French dressing and salad dressing under the food standard regulations. Use as a stabilizer in ice cream, frozen custard, ice milk, fruit sherbet, and water ices is permitted up to .5 percent of the weight of the finished product. The final report to the FDA of the Select Committee on GRAS Substances stated in 1980 that there is no evidence in the available information that it is a hazard to the public when used as it is now and it should continue its GRAS status with limitations on amounts that can be added to food.

**PROPYLENE GLYCOL MONOSTEARATE.** Cream-colored wax, which disperses in water and is soluble in hot alcohol. It is used as a lubricating agent and emulsifier; also as a dough conditioner in baked goods. Employed as a stabilizer of essential oils. Slightly more toxic than propylene glycol (*see*) in animals, and in large doses produces central nervous system depression and kidney injury. The final report to the FDA of the Select Committee on GRAS Substances stated in 1980 that it should continue its GRAS status with no limitations other than good manufacturing practices.

**PROPYLENE OXIDE. Propene Oxide.** Colorless, liquid starch modifier. No known toxicity.

**PROPYLIC ALCOHOL.** See Propyl Alcohol.

**3-PROPYLIDENEPHTHALIDE.** A synthetic fruit and spice flavoring agent for beverages, ice cream, ices, candy, and baked goods. No known toxicity.

**PROPYLPARABEN. Propyl *p*-Hydroxybenzoate.** Developed in Europe, the esters of *p*-hydroxybenzoic acid are widely used in the food, drug, and cosmetic industries as preservatives and bacteria and fungus killers. They are active against a variety of organisms. They are neutral, low in toxicity, slightly soluble, and active in all solutions—alkaline, neutral, or acid. Used medicinally to treat fungus infections. Can cause contact dermatitis and other allergic reactions. Less toxic than benzoic or salicylic acids (*see both*).

**PROPYLPARASEPT.** See Propyl *p*-Hydroxybenzoate.

**α-PROPYLPHENETHYL ALCOHOL.** A synthetic fruit flavoring agent for beverages, ice cream, ices, candy, and puddings. Toxicity similar to ethanol (*see*).

**PROTEIN.** Proteins are the chief nitrogen-containing constituents of plants and animals—essential constituents of every living cell. They contain (by weight) about 50 percent carbon, about 20 percent oxygen, about 15 percent nitrogen, about 7 percent hydrogen, and some sulfur; some proteins also contain iron and phosphorus. Proteins are colorless, odorless, and generally tasteless. They vary in solubility and readily undergo putrification, hydrolysis, and dilution with acids or alkalies. They are considered combinations of amino acids (*see*).

**PROTEIN HYDROZYLATES.** Used as flavor enhancers, particularly in meat products. See Protein and Hydrolysis.

**PROVITAMIN A.** See Carotene.

**PSYLLIUM SEED HUSK.** A stabilizer from the seed of the fleaseed plant used in frozen desserts up to .5 percent of the weight of the finished product. No known toxicity.

**PULEGONE.** Found in oils of plants, principally the pennyroyal. Pleasant odor, midway between camphor and peppermint. Used in peppermint flavorings for beverages, ice cream, ices, candy, and baked goods. See Pennyroyal Oil for toxicity.

**PULPS. From Wood, Straw, Bagasse, or Other Natural Sources.** A source of cellulose in food. The wood is treated with a mixture containing mainly sodium hydroxide (*see*). Treatment removes the fibrous lignin—the resinous substance that binds the fiber that lines the cells of wood. An indirect human food additive from packaging, the FDA's reevaluation in 1976 labeled pulps GRAS.

**PYRIDINE.** Occurs naturally in coffee and coal tar. Disagreeable odor. Sharp taste. Used in chocolate flavorings for beverages, ice cream, ices, candy, and baked goods. Also used as a solvent for organic liquids and compounds. Once used to treat asthma but may cause central nervous system depression and irritation of the skin and respiratory tract. Large doses can produce gastrointestinal disturbances and kidney and liver damage. Pyridine is absorbed from the respiratory and gastrointestinal tract. Small oral doses in man have produced loss of appetite, nausea, fatigue, and mental depression. After prolonged daily administration, kidney and liver damage resulted.

**PYRIDOXINE HYDROCHLORIDE. Vitamin B$_6$.** A colorless or white crystalline powder, added to evaporated milk base in infant foods. Present in many foodstuffs. Especially good sources are yeast, liver, and cereals. A coenzyme which helps in the metabolism of amino acids (*see*) and fat. Permits normal red blood cell formation. The final report to the FDA of the Select Committee on GRAS Substances stated in 1980 that it should continue its GRAS status with no limitations other than good manufacturing practices.

**PYROLIGNEOUS ACID AND EXTRACT.** A yellowish acid. Consists of 6 percent acetic acid (*see*), and small concentrations of creosote, methyl alcohol, and acetone (*see*). It is obtained by the destructive distillation of wood. Used as a synthetic flavoring in butter, butterscotch, caramel, rum, tobacco, smoke, and vanilla flavorings for beverages, ice cream, ices, candy, baked goods, puddings, and meats (300 ppm). The *extract* is used largely for smoking meats (300 ppm) and in smoke flavorings for baked goods (200 ppm) and alcoholic beverages. It is corrosive and may cause epigastric pain, vomiting, circulatory collapse, and death.

**PYROMUCIC ALDEHYDE.** See Furfural.

**PYROPHOSPHATE.** The salt of pyrophosphoric acid, it increases the effectiveness of antioxidants in lard and shortening and is also approved for a flavoring in the manufacture of caramel. In concentrated solutions it can be irritating to the skin and mucous membranes, and although it is approved as harmless to humans, its lethal oral dose in rats is quite low—40 milligrams per kilogram of body weight—compared to other chemicals that have a lethal oral dose of 3,890 milligrams or more.

**PYRORACEMIC ACID.** See Pyruvic Acid.

**PYRUVALDEHYDE.** A synthetic flavoring, yellowish, with a pungent odor. Formed as an intermediate in the metabolism or fermentation of carbohydrates and lactic acid (*see*). Used in coffee, honey, and maple flavorings for beverages, ice cream, ices, candy, and baked goods. No known toxicity.

**PYRUVIC ACID.** An important intermediate in fermentation and metabolism, it occurs naturally in coffee and when sugar is metabolized in muscle. It is reduced to lactic acid (*see*) during exertion. Pyruvic acid is isolated from cane sugar. It is a synthetic flavoring used in coffee and rum flavorings for beverages, ice cream, ices, candy, baked goods, and chewing gum. Has been used as a paste in the treatment of deep burns. No known toxicity.

# Q

**QUACK GRASS.** A couch grass, a pernicious weed in cultivated fields. See Dog Grass Extract.

**QUASSIA EXTRACT. Bitter Ash. Bitterwood.** From the wood and bark of a tree bearing bright scarlet flowers grown in Jamaica, the Caribbean Islands, and South America. So named for a black slave who discovered the medicinal value in the mid-eighteenth century. Slight odor, very bitter taste. Used in bitters, citrus, cherry, grape, liquor, root beer, sarsaparilla, and vanilla flavorings for beverages, baked goods, and liquors. Also used for fly poison on flypaper; to imitate hops; and as a bitter tonic and remedy for roundworms in children. No known toxicity.

**QUEBRACHO BARK EXTRACT.** Extract of a native Argentine tree, used in fruit, rum, and vanilla flavorings for beverages, ice cream, candy, ices, and baked goods. Closely related to the tranquilizer reserpine. Once promoted as an aphrodisiac, it can cause low blood pressure, nausea, abdominal distress, weakness, and fatigue.

**QUERCETIN-3-RUTINOSIDE.** See Rutin.

**QUERCUS ALBA.** See Oak Chip Extract.

**QUICK GRASS. Triticum.** See Dog Grass Extract.

**QUILLAIA. China Bark Extract.** See Quillaja.

**QUILLAJA. Soapbark. Quillay Bark. Panama Bark. China Bark.** The inner dried bark of a tree grown in South America. Used in fruit, root beer, and spice flavorings for beverages, ice cream, candy, and syrups. Formerly used internally to treat bronchitis, and externally as a detergent and local irritant. No known toxicity.

**QUINCE SEED EXTRACT.** From the seed of a plant known for its acid fruit, grown in Southeastern Asia and Europe. Used in fruit flavorings for beverages, ice cream, ices, and baked goods. No known toxicity.

**QUININE BISULFATE.** Most important alkaloid of cinchona bark (*see*), from trees that grow wild in South America and are cultivated in Java. Very bitter. Used in bitters flavoring for beverages and not to exceed 83 ppm in soda. Used to treat fever and as a local anesthetic and analgesic. No known toxicity.

**QUININE EXTRACT.** An extract of cinchona bark (*see*). A flavoring agent in numerous over-the-counter cold and headache remedies as well as in "bitter lemon" and tonic water, which may contain as much as 5 milligrams per 100 milliliters. Cinchonism, which may consist of nausea, vomiting, disturbances of vision, ringing in the ears, and nerve deafness, may occur from an overdose of quinine. If there is a sensitivity to quinine, such symptoms can result after ingesting tonic water. Quinine more commonly causes a rash.

**QUININE HYDROCHLORIDE.** A synthetic flavoring agent derived from cinchona bark (*see*) and used in bitters, citrus, and fruit flavorings for beverages. Some medical use as quinine sulfate (*see*). No known toxicity.

**QUININE SULFATE.** A synthetic flavoring agent derived from cinchona bark (*see*) and used in bitters flavoring for beverages. Also used medicinally to treat malaria; as an analgesic; and as a local anesthetic.

# R

**RACEMIC ACID.** See Tartaric Acid.

**RAPESEED OIL.** Canada has been seeking FDA clearance to sell rapeseed in the U.S. market. It would compete with soybeans and other oilseeds on the U.S. vegetable market. Rapeseed has become a major Canadian crop but has been barred from the United States because it contains erucic acid, which was cited in the early 1970s as a possible source of heart problems based on the result of tests on rats. New varieties of the seeds, *Canola*, have been developed that have low erucic acid levels. Small amounts of rapeseed oil are allowed in the United States for use in peanut butter and some cake mixes. The brownish-yellow oil is from a turniplike annual herb of European origin. Widely grown as a forage crop for sheep and hogs in the United States, it has a distinctly unpleasant odor. It is used chiefly in the United States as a lubricant and in rubber substitutes, but is also used in soft soaps and in some margarines. Can cause acnelike skin eruptions. When rats were fed a diet high in rapeseed oil over a lifetime, they showed significantly greater degenerative changes in the liver and a higher incidence of kidney damage than animals fed other vegetable oils.

**RDA.** Recommended Dietary Allowances of the Food and Nutrition Board, National Academy of Sciences–National Research Council.

**RED.** See FD and C Red (Nos. 3, 4, 40, and Citrus Red).

**REDUCING AGENT.** A substance that decreases, deoxidizes, or concentrates the volume of another substance. For instance, a reducing agent is used to convert a metal oxide into the metal itself. It is also a means of adding hydrogen agents to another substance (for example, when acetaldehyde is converted to alcohol in the final step of alcoholic fermentation). It is used in foods to keep metals from oxidizing and affecting the taste or color of fats, oils, salad dressings, and other foods containing minerals.

**RENNET. Rennin.** Enzyme from the lining membrane of the stomach of suckling calves. Used for curdling milk in cheese-making and in junket. Sometimes used as a digestant. No known toxicity. Reaffirmed GRAS in 1982.

**RESIN.** The brittle substance, usually translucent or transparent, formed from the hardened secretion of plants. See Gum.

**RESIN, ACRYLAMIDE—ACRYLIC ACID.** A clarifying agent in beet sugar and cane sugar juice. The acid is used in the synthesis of this acrylic resin. No known toxicity.

**RESIN, COUMARONE—INDENE.** A chewing-gum base and protective coating for citrus fruit. Coumarone is derived from coal tar and is used with a mixture of indene chiefly in the synthesis of coumarone resins. No known toxicity.

**RESIN, ISOBUTYLENE. Polyisobutylene.** A chewing-gum base made from the chemical used chiefly in manufacturing synthetic rubber. No known toxicity.

**RESIN, METHACRYLIC AND DIVINYL BENZENE.** A compound of fine particle size, weakly acidic. Used as an absorbent for Vitamin $B_{12}$ in nutritional supplement-type products. No known toxicity.

**RESIN, PETROLEUM HYDROCARBON.** A chewing-gum base synthesized from fuel oil. No known toxicity.

**RESIN, TERPENE. Alpha and Beta Pinene.** A chewing-gum base and coating for fresh fruits and vegetables. Pinene has the same toxicity as turpentine (*see*).

**RETINOIDS.** Derivatives of Vitamin A.

**RHATANY EXTRACT. Krameria.** A synthetic flavoring derived from the dried roots of either of two American shrubs. Used in raspberry, bitters, fruit, and rum flavorings for beverages, ice cream, ices, candy, chewing gum, and liquor. Also used as an astringent. Low oral toxicity. Large doses may produce gastric distress. Caused cancer when injected under the skin of rats, but no cancers have been reported as a result of ingestion.

**RHODENAL.** See Citronellal.

**RHODINOL. 3,7-Dimethyl-6-Octen-1-ol. Citronellol.** A synthetic flavoring agent isolated from geranium rose oil (*see*). Odor of roses. Used in strawberry, chocolate, rose, grape, honey, spice, and ginger ale flavorings for beverages, ice cream, ices, candy, baked goods, gelatin desserts, chewing gum, and jelly. No known toxicity.

**RHODINYL ACETATE. Acetic Acid.** An acidulant and synthetic flavoring, colorless to slightly yellow, with a light, fresh, roselike odor. Used in berry, coconut, apricot, floral, rose, and honey flavorings for beverages, ice cream, ices, candy, and baked goods. No known toxicity.

**RHODINYL BUTYRATE. Butyric Acid.** A synthetic raspberry, strawberry, and fruit flavoring agent for beverages, ice cream, ices, candy, baked goods, and chewing gum. No known toxicity.

**RHODINYL FORMATE. Formic Acid.** A synthetic flavoring, colorless to slight yellow, with a roselike odor. Used in raspberry, rose, apple, cherry, plum, pear, and pineapple flavorings for beverages, ice cream, ices, candy, baked goods, and gelatin desserts. See Formic Acid for toxicity.

**RHODINYL ISOBUTYRATE. Isobutyric Acid.** A synthetic raspberry, floral, rose, apple, pear, pineapple, and honey flavoring agent for beverages, ice cream, ices, candy, baked goods, and gelatin desserts. No known toxicity.

**RHODINYL ISOVALERATE. Isovaleric Acid.** A synthetic berry, rose, and fruit flavoring agent for beverages, ice cream, ices, candy, and baked goods. No known toxicity.

**RHODINYL PHENYLACETATE. Phenylacetic Acid.** A synthetic flavoring used in beverages, ice cream, ices, candy, and baked goods. No known toxicity.

**RHODINYL PROPIONATE. Propionic Acid.** A synthetic berry, rose, plum, and honey flavoring agent for beverages, ice cream, ices, candy, and baked goods. No known toxicity.

**RHODYMENIA PALMATA.** See Dulse.

**RIBOFLAVIN. Vitamin B$_2$. Lactoflavin. Vitamin G. B-Complex.** Formerly called B$_2$ or G. Riboflavin is a factor in the Vitamin B-complex. Every plant and animal cell contains a minute amount. Good sources are milk, eggs, malted barley, yeast, liver, kidney, heart. It is necessary for healthy skin and respiration, protects the eyes from sensitivity to light, and is used for building and maintaining many body tissues. Deficiency leads to lesions at the corner of the mouth and to changes in the cornea. Recommended daily requirements for infants is 4,000 micrograms per day and for adults 1,300 micrograms. Its yellow to orange-yellow color is used to dye egg-shells. Riboflavin and its more soluble form, riboflavin-5-phosphate, are added as enrichment to dry baby cereals, poultry stuffing, peanut butter, prepared breakfast cereals, enriched flour, enriched cornmeal, enriched corn grits, enriched macaroni, and enriched breads and rolls. GRAS.

**RIIBOFLAVIN-5-PHOSPHATE.** A more soluble form of riboflavin (*see*). The final report to the FDA of the Select Committee on GRAS Substances stated in 1980 that it should continue its GRAS status with no limitations other than good manufacturing practices.

**RICE STARCH.** A polysaccharide in rice that is used as an anticaking agent, thickener, and gelling agent. No known toxicity. The final report to the FDA of the Select Committee on GRAS Substances stated in 1980 that it should continue its GRAS status with no limitations other than good manufacturing practices.

**ROCHELLE SALT. Sodium Potassium Tartrate.** Used in manufacture of Seidlitz powders (a laxative), in baking powder, and in the silvering of mirrors. No known toxicity.

**ROSA ALBA.** See Rose, Absolute.

**ROSA CANINA.** See Rose Hips Extract.

**ROSA CENTIFOLIA.** See Rose, Absolute.

**ROSE, ABSOLUTE.** Same origin as for Rose Bulgarian (*see*). Used as a berry, rose, fruit, and nut flavoring agent for beverages, ice cream, ices, candy, and baked goods. No known toxicity except for allergic reactions. GRAS.

**ROSE BULGARIAN. True Otto Oil. Attar of Roses.** Derived from dried petals of a variety of roses collected just before expanding. Grown in Western Asia, Europe, and the United States. Rose extracts are used for a variety of flavors including loganberry, raspberry, strawberry, orange, rose, violet, cherry, grape, peach, honey, muscatel, maple, almond, pecan, and ginger ale flavorings for beverages, ice cream, ices, candy, baked goods, gelatin desserts, chewing gum, and jellies. Also used in mucilage, coloring matter, and as a flavoring in pills. No known toxicity except for allergic reactions. GRAS.

**ROSE GERANIUM OIL.** See Geranium Rose Oil.

**ROSE HIPS EXTRACT. Hipberries.** The fruits or berries from wild rose bushes. Rich in ascorbic acid (*see*). Widely used by organic food enthusiasts. Used as a natural flavoring in a number of foods. No known toxicity.

**ROSE LEAVES EXTRACT.** Derived from the leaves of the genus *Rosa*. Used in raspberry and cola beverages. No known toxicity except for allergic reactions. GRAS.

**ROSELLE.** *Hibiscus sabdariffa.* An herb cultivated in the East Indies, it is used for making tarts and jellies, and gives a tart taste to acid drinks. It is also used as a natural red food coloring for soft drinks, tea-type products, punches, apple jelly, and pectin jelly but it is not stable in carbonated beverages. No known toxicity.

**ROSEMARY. Garden Rosemary.** A meat and spice flavoring from the fresh aromatic flowering tops of the evergreen shrub grown in the Mediterranean. Light blue flowers and gray green leaves. Used for beverages, condiments, and meats. The oil is obtained by steam distillation. Colorless or pale yellow with the odor of rosemary. Used in citrus, peach, meat, and ginger flavorings for beverages, ice cream, ices, candy, baked goods, condiments, and meats. Also used in perfumery. A teaspoonful may cause illness in an adult, and an ounce may cause death. GRAS.

**ROSMARINUS OFFICINALIS.** See Rosemary.

**RUBBER, BUTADIENE STYRENE. Latex.** A chewing gum base. No known toxicity.

**RUBBER, SMOKED SHEET.** A chewing gum base. No known toxicity.

**RUE.** A spice agent obtained from fresh aromatic blossoming plants grown in Southern Europe and the Orient. Fatty odor. Used in baked goods. The *oil*, obtained by steam distillation, is used in blueberry, raspberry, coconut, grape, peach, rum, cheese, nut, and spice flavorings for beverages, ice cream, ices, candy, baked goods, and condiments. Formerly used medically to treat menstrual disorders and hysteria. In 1976 the FDA confirmed rue as GRAS in all categories of food at a maximum use level of 2 parts per million. The final report to the FDA of the Select Committee on GRAS Substances stated in 1980 that there is no evidence in the available information that it is a hazard to the public when used as it is now and it should continue its GRAS status with limitations on amounts that can be added to food.

**RUM ETHER.** A synthetic flavoring, consisting of water, ethanol, ethyl acetate, methanol, ethyl formate, acetone, acetaldehyde, and formaldehyde (*see all*). Used in butter, liquor, and rum flavorings for beverages, ice cream, ices, candy, baked goods, gelatin, chewing gum, and alcoholic beverages (1,600 ppm). No known toxicity.

**RUTIN.** Pale yellow crystals found in many plants, particularly buckwheat. Used as a dietary supplement for capillary fragility. No known toxicity.

# S

**SACCHARIN.** An artificial sweetener in use since 1879, it is 300 times as sweet as natural sugar but leaves a bitter aftertaste. It was used along with cyclamates (*see*) in the experiments that led to the banning of the latter in 1969. The FDA proposed restricting saccharin to 15 milligrams per day for each kilogram of body weight or about 1 gram a day for a 150-pound person. Then, on March 9, 1977, the FDA announced the use of saccharin in foods and beverages would be banned because the artificial sweetener had been found to cause malignant bladder tumors in laboratory animals. The ban was based on the findings of a study sponsored by the Canadian government that found that 7 out of 38 animals developed tumors, 3 of them malignant. In addition, 100 offspring were fed saccharin, and 14 of them developed bladder tumors. In contrast, 100 control rats were not fed saccharin and only 2 developed tumors. At the time of the FDA's announcement, 5 million pounds of saccharin were being consumed per year, 74 percent of it in diet soda, 14 percent in dietetic food, and 12 percent as a "tabletop" replacement for sugar. There was an immediate outcry, led vociferously by the Calorie Control Council, an organization made up of commercial producers and users of saccharin. The FDA, urged by Congress, then delayed the ban. The moratorium on prohibiting the use of saccharin has been extended indefinitely. Since 1977, however, saccharin containers carry labels warning that saccharin may be hazardous to your health.

Saccharin has exhibited mutagenic activity (genetic changes) in the early-warning Ames Test (*see*) for carcinogens. When administered orally to mice, mutagenic activity was demonstrated in the urine of these animals as well as in tissue tests. Highly purified saccharin was not mutagenic in tissue tests, but the urine of mice to which this material had been administered exhibited mutagenic effects on another strain. Two other sweeteners, neohesperidin dihydrochalcone and xylitol, had no detectable mutagenic activity. Congress's Office of Technology Assessment, in view of evidence to date, strongly endorsed the scientific basis of the FDA's proposed ban. "This review of animal studies leads to the conclusion that saccharin is a carcinogen for animals," the OTA panel said. Clouding the risk of assessment, however, is that up to 20 parts per million of unknown chemical impurities contaminated those doses fed rats in the Canadian study that led to the FDA's original move. The impurities themselves proved mutagenic in the Ames Test.

On November 6, 1978, the Committee of the Institute of Medicine and National Research Council reported that it had reached the conclusion that saccharin is a potential carcinogen in humans. The extremely low potency of saccharin as a carcinogen was emphasized by the committee. However, they expressed special concern that children under 10 years of age were consuming diet sodas and other saccharin-containing products in increasing amounts. Exposure in children, the committee noted, may have special significance because of the long time required for some cancers to develop. There were some "worrisome data" regarding consumption by women of child-bearing age, children, and teenagers. The concern about fetal exposure grew out of earlier findings of increased bladder cancers in male rats fed high-saccharin diets or born to mothers who were on high-saccharin diets during pregnancy. The committee concluded that it is most likely that saccharin, acting by itself, is the carcinogenic agent, rather than any impurities that may be associated with its manufacture. The fight to keep saccharin on the market spotlighted the Delaney Amendment, which prohibits known carcinogens from being added to food, and a move to weaken that amendment persists. In 1969, Britain banned saccharin except as an artificial sweetener. In 1950, France banned it except as a nonprescription drug. Germany restricts its use to certain foods and beverages which must state on the label that it is in the product.

**SAFFLOWER OIL.** The edible oil expressed or extracted from safflower seeds. Safflower is an Old World yellow herb with large, orange-red flower heads. The oil thickens and becomes rancid on prolonged exposure to air. It is used in salad oils and shortenings, and as a vehicle for medicines. As a dietary supplement it is alleged to be a preventive in the development of atherosclerosis—fat-clogged arteries. A drug consisting of the dried flowers of safflower is used in medicines in place of saffron (*see*). No known toxicity.

**SAFFRON. Crocus. Vegetable Gold. Spanish or French Saffron.** The dried stigmas of the crocus grown in Western Asia and Southern Europe. Orange-brown; strong, peculiar aromatic odor; bitterish, aromatic taste. Almost entirely employed for coloring and flavoring. Used in bitters, liquor, and spice flavorings for beverages, baked goods, meats, and liquors. Cleared by the USDA Meat Inspection Department for coloring sausage casings, oleomargarine, shortening, and for marking ink. The *extract* is used in honey and rum flavorings for beverages, ice cream, ices, candy, baked goods, and condiments, and it goes into yellow coloring. Saffron was formerly used to treat skin diseases. No known toxicity. GRAS.

**SAFROL.** See Sassafras Bark Extract.

**SAGE.** The flowering tops and leaves of the shrubby mints. Spices include Greek sage and Spanish sage. The genus is *Salvia,* so named for the plant's supposed healing powers. Greek sage is used in fruit and spice flavorings for beverages, baked goods, and meats (1,500 ppm). Greek sage *oil,* obtained by steam distillation, is used in berry, grape, liquor, meat, creme de menthe, nutmeg, and sage flavorings for beverages, ice cream, ices, candy, baked goods, chewing gum, condiments, meats, and pickles. Greek sage *oleoresin* (*see*) is used in sausage and spice flavorings for condiments and meats. Spanish sage oil is used in fruit and spice flavorings for beverages, ice cream, ices, candy, baked goods, condiments, and meats. Greek sage is used in medicine. No known toxicity. GRAS.

**SAIGON CINNAMON.** See Cinnamon.

**SAIGON CINNAMON LEAF OIL.** See Cinnamon.

**SAINT-JOHN'S-BREAD.** See Carob Bean.

**SALICYLALDEHYDE. Salicylic Aldehyde.** A synthetic flavoring made by heating phenol (very toxic) and chloroform. Occurs naturally in cassia bark. Clear, bitter almondlike odor, burning taste. Used in butter, caramel, violet, fruit, muscatel, nut, spice, cinnamon, cassia, and vanilla flavorings for beverages, ice cream, ices, candy, baked goods, chewing gum, condiments, and liqueurs. Used chiefly in perfumery. Lethal dose in rats is 1 gram per kilogram of body weight.

**SALICYLATES. Amyl, Phenyl, Benzyl, Menthyl.** Salts of salicylic acid (*see*). Those who are sensitive to aspirin may also be hypersensitive to FD and C Yellow No. 5, a salicylate, and to a number of foods that naturally contain salicylate, such as almonds, apples, apple cider, apricots, blackberries, boysenberries, cloves, cucumbers, currants, gooseberries, oil of wintergreen, oranges, peaches, pickles, plums, prunes, raisins, raspberries, strawberries, and tomatoes.

**SALICYLIC ACID.** A synthetically prepared powder obtained by heating phenol (very toxic) with carbon dioxide, which is used as a preservative in food products. It occurs naturally in the form of esters in several plants, notably wintergreen leaves and the bark of sweet birch. Also used in manufacture of aspirin; in medicine it is used as a remedy for rheumatic and gout conditions. The dose for external antimicrobial use is topically 2–20 percent concentration in lotions, ointments, powders, and plasters. Absorption of large amounts may cause vomiting, abdominal pain, increased respiration, acidosis, mental disturbances, and skin rash in sensitive individuals.

**SALICYLIC ETHER.** See Ethyl Salicylate.

**SALTPETER. Potassium Nitrate. Niter.** See Nitrate, Potassium. Acute intoxication is unlikely because large doses cause vomiting and because it is rapidly excreted. Potassium poisoning disturbs the rhythm of the heart and orally poisoned animals die from respiratory failure. Prolonged exposure to even small amounts may produce anemia, methemoglobinemia (lack of oxygen in the blood), and kidney damage.

**SALVIA.** See Sage.

**SAMBUCUS.** See Elder Flowers.

**SANDALWOOD OIL, EAST INDIAN.** The volatile oil obtained by steam distillation from the dried, ground roots and heartwood of trees grown in the East Indies. Yellow, somewhat viscous, with a strong odor. Used in floral, fruit, honey, and ginger ale flavorings for beverages, ice cream, ices, candy, baked goods, and chewing gum. Also used for incense and as a fumigant. No known toxicity.

**SANDALWOOD OIL, WEST INDIAN.** Less soluble than the East Indian variety above. See Amyris Oil.

**SANDALWOOD OIL, YELLOW. Arheol.** Same origin as East Indian sandalwood oil (*see*). A floral, fruit, honey, and ginger ale flavoring agent for beverages, ice cream, ices, candy, baked goods, and chewing gum. No known toxicity.

**SANTALOL.** See Arheol.

**SANTALUM ALBUM.** See Sandalwood Oil.

**SANTALYL ACETATE. Acetic Acid.** A synthetic flavoring agent obtained from sandalwood oils (*see*). Used in floral, pear, and pineapple flavorings for beverages, ice cream, ices, candy, baked goods, and chewing gum. No known toxicity.

**SANTALYL PHENYLACETATE. Phenylacetic Acid.** A synthetic flavoring obtained from sandalwood oils (*see*). Used in butter, caramel, fruit, and honey flavorings for beverages, ice cream, ices, candy, and baked goods. No known toxicity.

**SANTOQUIN. Ethoxyquin.** A yellow liquid antioxidant and herbicide. It has been found to cause liver tumors in newborn mice.

**SAP.** See Sodium Acid Pyrophosphate.

**SARSAPARILLA EXTRACT.** The dried root from tropical American plants. Used in cola, mint, root beer, sarsaparilla, wintergreen, and birch beer flavorings for beverages, ice cream, ices, candy, and baked goods. Still used for psoriasis; formerly used for the treatment of syphilis. No known toxicity.

**SASSAFRAS BARK EXTRACT. Safrol. Safrol-free.** Extracted with dilute alcohol from the bark of the tree. Used in rum and root beer flavorings for beverages, ice cream, ices, candy, and baked goods. Safrol is a constituent of several essential oils, notably of sassafras, of which it constitutes 80 percent. The lethal dose of safrol in rabbits is 1 gram per kilogram of body weight. Sassafras by itself has no known toxicity. It is used as a topical antiseptic, to mask the odor of medicines, and to break up intestinal gas.

**SASSAFRAS LEAVES. Safrol-free.** Same origin as the bark extract. Used in soups (30,000 ppm). See Sassafras Bark Extract for toxicity.

**SAUNDERS WHITE OIL.** See Sandalwood Oil.

**SAVORY.** A flavoring from the aromatic mints, known as summer savory and winter savory. The dried leaves of summer savory is a spice used in baked goods, condiments, and meats. Summery savory oil is obtained from the dried whole plant. It is used as a spice in condiments, candy, and baked goods. Summer savory oil oleoresin (*see*) is a spice used in candy, baked goods, and condiments. Winter savory oil and oleoresin spices are used in candy, baked goods, and condiments. No known toxicity. GRAS.

**SCHINUS MOLLE OIL.** A natural flavoring extract from the tropical pepper tree, *Schinus molle*. Used in candy, baked goods, and condiments. No known toxicity. GRAS.

**SEBACIC ACID.** See Dibutyl Sebacate.

**SEQUESTRANTS.** Substances that render ions (usually from metal) inactive by absorbing them. This is how water is softened. Sequestrants are added to food to attract the trace metals to remove them. They prevent physical and chemical changes that affect color, flavor, texture, or appearance. Ethylenediamine tetraacetic acid (EDTA) (*see*) is an example. It is used in carbonated beverages.

**SERINE. L and DL forms.** An amino acid (*see*), nonessential, taken as a supplement. On the FDA list requiring further information.

**SESAME. Seeds and Oils.** The edible seeds of an East Indian herb, which has a rosy or white flower. The seeds, which flavor bread, crackers, cakes, confectionery, etc., yield a pale yellow, bland-tasting, almost odorless oil used in the manufacture of margarine. The oil has been used as a laxative and skin softener, and contains elements active against lice. Bland taste flavoring. No known toxicity except for allergies. GRAS.

**SHADDOCK EXTRACT.** An extract of *Citrus grandis* and named for a seventeenth-century sea captain who brought the seeds back from the East Indies to Barbados. Shaddock is a very large, thick-rinded, pear-shaped citrus fruit related to and largely replaced by the grapefruit. No known toxicity.

**SHEA BUTTER.** The natural fat obtained from the fruit of the karite tree. Also called karite butter, it is chiefly used as a food. No known toxicity.

**SHELLAC.** A resinous excretion of certain insects feeding on appropriate host trees, usually in India. As processed for marketing, the lacca, which is formed by the insects, may be mixed with small amounts of arsenic trisulfide (for color) and with rosin. White shellac is free of arsenic. Shellac is used as a candy glaze and polish up to .4 percent. May cause skin irritation.

**SHORTENING.** A fat such as a butter, lard, or vegetable oil used to make cake, pastry, bread, etc., light and flaky.

**SIBERIAN FIR OIL.** See Pine Needle Oil.

**SILICA AEROGEL. Silicon Dioxide.** A finely powdered, microcellular silica foam having a minimum silica content of 89.5 percent. Chemically and biologically inert, it is used as an antifoaming agent in beverages and as a surface active agent. Used chiefly in manufacture of glass. See Silicon Dioxide for toxicity. The final report to the FDA of the Select Committee on GRAS Substances stated in 1980 that it should continue its GRAS status with no limitations other than good manufacturing practices.

**SILICATES.** The simplest silicate is sand, a molecule formed by joining one silicon atom with two oxygen atoms.

**SILICON DIOXIDE. Silica.** Transparent, tasteless crystals or powder, practically insoluble in water. Occurs in nature as agate, amethyst, chalcedony, cristobalite, flint, quartz, sand, and tridymite. Used as a defoaming agent in beer production, Cleared for use as a food additive and as an anticaking agent at a level not to exceed 2 percent in salt and salt substitutes, in BHT (see butylated hydroxytoluene), in vitamins up to 3 percent, in urea up to 1 percent, in sodium propionate (*see all*) up to 1 percent. Also used in ceramics and in scouring and grinding compounds. Prolonged inhalation of the dust can injure lungs. The final report to the FDA of the Select Committee on GRAS Substances stated in 1980 that it should continue its GRAS status for packaging with no limitations other than good manufacturing practices.

**SILICONES.** Any of a large group of fluid oils, rubbers, resins, and compounds derived from silica, which occurs in 12 percent of all rocks. Sand is a silica. Water repellent, they are stable over a wide range of temperatures. Used as an anticaking agent in foods and in waterproofing and lubrication. No known toxicity, except if inhaled.

**SLOE BERRIES. Blackthorn Berries.** The fruit of the common juniper. The extract is a natural flavoring used in berry, plum, and liquor flavorings for beverages, ice cream, ices, candy, baked goods, and cordials (up to 43,000 ppm). Sloe gin is flavored with sloe berries. No known toxicity. GRAS.

**SMALLAGE.** See Lovage.

**SMELLAGE.** See Lovage.

**SMOKE FLAVORING SOLUTIONS.** Condensates from burning hardwood in a limited amount of air. The solutions are used to flavor various foods, primarily meats, and as an antioxidant to retard bacterial growth. It is also permitted in cheeses and smoke-flavored fish. The Select Committee of the Federation of American Societies for Experimental Biology (FASEB), under contract to the FDA, concluded that smoke flavorings in general pose no hazard to the public when used at current levels and under present procedures but uncertainties exist which require further study. The committee also said there are insufficient data upon which to base an evaluation of smoked yeast flavoring, produced by exposing food grade yeast to wood smoke. It is used to flavor soups, cheese, crackers, dip, pizza, and seasoning mixes.

**SMOKED SHEET RUBBER.** See Rubber, Smoked Sheet.

**SNAKEROOT OIL. Canadian Oil.** Derived from the roots of the plant, which had a reputation for curing snakebites. Grown from Canada to North Carolina and Kansas. Used in ginger, ginger ale, wintergreen, and birch beer flavorings for beverages, ice cream, ices, candy, baked goods, and condiments. No known toxicity.

**SOAP. Sodium Oleate and Sodium Palmitate.** Any salt of a fatty acid, usually made by saponification of a vegetable oil with caustic soda. Hard soap consists largely of sodium oleate or sodium palmitate. Used medically as an antiseptic, detergent, or suppository; as a laxative and antacid. GRAS for food packaging.

**SOAPBARK.** See Quillaja.

**SODIUM ACETATE.** Transparent crystals highly soluble in water. Used as a preservative in licorice candy. In industrial forms it is used in photography and dyeing processes, and in foot and bottle warmers because of its heat retention. Medically it is used as an alkalizer. It was also used as a diuretic to reduce retention of fluids and as an expectorant. No known toxicity. The final report to the FDA of the Select Committee on GRAS Substances stated in 1980 that it should continue its GRAS status for packaging with no limitations other than good manufacturing practices.

**SODIUM ACID PYROPHOSPHATE (SAP).** A white mass or freeflowing powder used as a buffer. It is a slow-acting acid constituent of a leavening mixture for self-rising and prepared cakes, doughnuts, waffles, muffins, cupcakes, and other types of flours and mixes. Also used in canned tuna fish. The U.S. Department of Agriculture has proposed that SAP be added to hot dogs and other sausages to accelerate the development of a rose-red color, thus cutting production time by some 25 to 40 percent. It is related to phosphoric acid, which is sometimes used as a gastric acidifier. No known toxicity. The final report to the FDA of the Select Committee on GRAS Substances stated in 1980 that it should continue its GRAS status with no limitations other than good manufacturing practices.

**SODIUM ACID SULFITE.** See Sodium Bisulfite.

**SODIUM ALGINATE.** See Alginates.

**SODIUM ALUMINATE.** A strong alkaline employed in the manufacture of lake colors used in foods (*see* FD and C Lakes). Also used in water-softening and printing. The final report to the FDA of the Select Committee on GRAS Substances stated in 1980 that it should continue its GRAS status for packaging with no limitations other than good manufacturing practices.

**SODIUM ALUMINOSILICATE.** A chemical substance used in dental compounds, colored lakes (*see* FD and C Lakes) for foods, and in washing compounds. The final report to the FDA of the Select Committee on GRAS Substances stated in 1980 that it should continue its GRAS status with no limitations other than good manufacturing practices.

**SODIUM ALUMINUM PHOSPHATE.** A white, odorless powder, insoluble in water, used as a buffer in self-rising flour. Used with sodium bicarbonate (*see*). Used also in various cheeses. No known toxicity. The final report to the FDA of the Select Committee on GRAS Substances stated in 1980 that it should continue its GRAS status with no limitations other than good manufacturing practices.

**SODIUM ALUMINUM SULFATE.** A bleaching agent for flour at no more than 6 parts by weight, alone, or in combination with potassium aluminum, calcium sulfate, and other compounds. No known toxicity.

**SODIUM ASCORBATE. Vitamin C Sodium.** Aside from its use in Vitamin C preparations, it can serve as an antioxidant in chopped meat and other foods to retard spoiling; also used in curing meat. No known toxicity. The final report to the FDA of the Select Committee on GRAS Substances stated in 1980 that it should continue its GRAS status with no limitations other than good manufacturing practices.

**SODIUM BENZOATE. Benzoate of Soda.** White, odorless powder or crystals; sweet, antiseptic taste. Works best in slightly acid media. Used as a flavoring and in liver function tests and as a preservative in margarine, codfish, bottled soft drinks, maraschino cherries, mincemeat, fruit juices, pickles, confections, fruit jelly, preserves, and jams. Also used in the ice for cooling fish. Once used medicinally for rheumatism and tonsillitis. The lethal dose in dogs and cats is 2 grams but an adult human male has taken as much as 50 grams without ill effect. It can cause intestinal upset. In an FDA reevaluation, it was confirmed as GRAS for 0.1 percent use in food. It has been reported to cause allergic reactions.

**SODIUM BICARBONATE. Bicarbonate of Soda. Baking Soda. Sodium Acid Carbonate.** An alkali prepared by the reaction of soda ash with carbon dioxide and used in prepared pancakes, biscuit, and muffin mixes; a leavening agent in baking powders; in various crackers and cookies; to adjust acidity in tomato soup, ices, and sherbets, in pastes and beverages; in syrups for frozen products; confections; and self-rising flours. Also used in cornmeals and canned peas. Also as a fire extinguisher. Used medicinally as an antacid and to take the sting out of insect bites. It may alter the urinary excretion of other drugs thus making those drugs either more toxic or less effective. GRAS.

**SODIUM BISULFITE. Sodium Acid Sulfite. Sodium Hydrogen Sulfite.** A white powder with a disagreeble taste used as a bleaching agent in ale, wine, beer, and other food products. Commercial bisulfite consists chiefly of sodium metabisulfite (*see*). Used externally for parasitic skin diseases. Concentrated solutions are highly irritating to the skin and mucous membranes. Sodium bisulfite can change the genetic material of bacteria which can change cytosine—a compound of nucleic acid (the heart of the cell)—into uracil, also a nucleic acid compound. Nucleic acids are the fundamental substances of heredity, and changes in them are considered mutations. The final report to the FDA of the Select Committee on GRAS substances stated in 1980 that there is no evidence in the available information that it is a hazard to the public when used as it is now and it should continue its GRAS status with limitations on amounts that can be added to food.

**SODIUM BORATE.** See Boron Sources.

**SODIUM CALCIUM ALUMINOSILICATE.** Used to prevent salt and dry mixes from caking. No known toxicity. The final report to the FDA of the Select Committee on GRAS Substances stated in 1980 that it should continue its GRAS status with no limitations other than good manufacturing practices.

**SODIUM CARBONATE. Soda Ash.** Colorless or white odorless crystals occurring naturally as thermonatrite, natron, or natrite. Usually obtained commercially. Used as a neutralizer for butter, cream, fluid milk, and ice cream; in the processing of olives before canning; and in cocoa products. A strong alkali used as lye. Used to treat skin rashes, and as a water softener. Has been used as mouthwash and vaginal douche. Ingestion of large quantities may produce corrosion of the gastrointestinal tract, vomiting, diarrhea, circulatory collapse, and death. The final report to the FDA of the Select Committee on GRAS Substances stated in 1980 that it should continue its GRAS status with no limitations other than good manufacturing practices.

**SODIUM CARBOXYMETHYL CELLULOSE.** Made from a cotton byproduct, it occurs as a white powder or granules. Used as a stabilizer in ice cream, beverages, confections, baked goods, icings, toppings, chocolate milk, chocolate-flavored beverages, gassed cream (pressure-dispensed whipped cream), syrup for frozen products, variegated mixtures, cheese spreads, and in certain cheeses. Also used in French dressing, artificially sweetened jellies and preserves, gelling ingredients, mix-it-yourself powdered drinks, and baby foods. Used to extend and stabilize baked pies. Medicinally used as a laxative (1.5 grams orally), antacid (15–30 milligrams of 5 percent solution), and in pharmacy for preparing suspensions. It has been shown to cause cancer in animals. The final report to the FDA of the Select Committee on GRAS Substances stated in 1980 that it should continue its GRAS status with no limitations other than good manufacturing practices.

**SODIUM CASEINATE. Casein.** A white odorless powder from cow's milk. Used as a texturizer in ice cream, frozen custard, ice milk, and sherbet. Cleared by the USDA Meat Inspection Department for use in imitation sausage, nonspecific loaves, soups, and stews. No known toxicity. The final report to the FDA of the Select Committee on GRAS Substances stated in 1980 that it should continue its GRAS status with no limitations other than good manufacturing practices.

**SODIUM CHLORIDE.** Common table salt. In addition to seasoning it is used as a pickling agent, a preservative for meats, vegetables, butter. Prevents browning in cut fruit. Not generally considered toxic, but can adversely affect persons with high blood pressure and kidney disease. Accidental substitution of salt for lactose in baby formulas has caused poisonings. The final report to the FDA in 1980 of the Select Committee on GRAS Substances stated that there are insufficient data to determine that it is not deleterious to health when used at current levels. Therefore, safer usage conditions must be established or it must be removed from food.

**SODIUM CHLORITE.** A powerful oxidizer prepared commercially and used to modify food starch (*see* Modified Starch) up to .5 percent. Used as a bleaching agent for textiles and paper pulp and in water purification. Toxicity depends upon concentration.

**SODIUM CITRATE.** White odorless granules, crystals, or powder, with a salty taste. Prevents "cream plug" in cream and "feathering" when cream is used in coffee, an emulsifier in ice cream, processed cheese, evaporated milk; a buffer to control acidity and retain carbonation in beverages, in frozen fruit drinks, confections, fruit jellies, preserves, and jams. It attaches itself to trace metals present in water and inhibits their entering the living cell. Proposed as a replacement for phosphates in detergents but also causes algal growth and removes the necessary trace metals from water as well as the toxic ones. Can alter urinary excretion of other drugs, thus making those drugs either less effective or more toxic. The final report to the FDA of the Select Committee on GRAS Substances stated in 1980 that it should continue its GRAS status with no limitations other than good manufacturing practices.

**SODIUM DEHYDROACETATE. Dehydroacetic Acid.** A preservative, white, odorless, powdered, with an acrid taste. Used in cut or peeled squash and as a plasticizer, fungicide, and bactericide in antienzyme toothpaste. It is a kidney-tube blocking agent, and can cause impaired kidney function. Large doses can cause vomiting, ataxia, and convulsions. There are no apparent allergic skin reactions.

**SODIUM DIACETATE.** A compound of sodium acetate and acetic acid (*see*); a white crystalline solid. Smells like vinegar. Used as a preservative. Inhibits molds and rope-forming bacteria in baked goods. No known toxicity. The final report to the FDA of the Select Committee on GRAS Substances stated in 1980 that it should continue its GRAS status with no limitations other than good manufacturing practices.

**SODIUM DIALKYLPHENOXYBENZENEDISULFONATE.** Used in lye mixtures for peeling fruits and vegetables. No known toxicity.

**SODIUM DODECYL BENZENESULFONATE.** Used in commercial detergents to treat raw food products, which is followed by a water rinsing. It may cause skin irritations, and if swallowed, will cause vomiting.

**SODIUM ERYTHORBATE. Sodium Isoascorbate.** A white odorless powder, it is an antioxidant used in pickling brine up to 7.5 ounces per 100 gallons and in meat products up to ¾ of an ounce per 100 pounds. Also used in beverages and baked goods; in cured cuts and cured, pulverized products to accelerate color fixing in curing. No known toxicity. The final report to the FDA of the Select Committee on GRAS Substances stated in 1980 that it should continue its GRAS status with no limitations other than good manufacturing practices.

**SODIUM 2-ETHYL 1-HEXYLSULFATE.** A component of a commercial detergent for washing raw foods, followed by water rinsing. No known toxicity.

**SODIUM FERRIC EDTA.** Prepared from disodium ethylenediaminetetraacetic acid and ferric nitrate. Used as an iron source. The final report to the FDA of the Select Committee on GRAS Substances stated in 1980 that there were insufficient relevant biological and other studies upon which to base an evaluation of it when it is used as a food ingredient.

**SODIUM FERRICITROPYROPHOSPHATE.** A white powder used in food enrichment. It is less prone to induce rancidity than other orthophosphates. The final report to the FDA of the Select Committee on GRAS Substances stated in 1980 that there were insufficient relevant biological and other studies upon which to base an evaluation of it when it is used as a food ingredient. See Iron Sources.

**SODIUM FORMATE.** White, deliquescent granules or crystalline powder, with the slight odor of formic acid (*see*). It is used in dyeing and printing fabrics and as a buffering agent. The final report to the FDA of the Select Committee on GRAS Substances stated in 1980 that it should continue its GRAS status for packaging with no limitations other than good manufacturing practices.

**SODIUM GLUCONATE. Gluconic Acid. Sodium Salt.** A pleasant-smelling compound, it is used as a sequestering agent. The final report to the FDA of the Select Committee on GRAS Substances stated in 1980 that it should continue its GRAS status with no limitations other than good manufacturing practices.

**SODIUM HEXAMETAPHOSPHATE.** An emulsifier, sequestering agent, and texturizer. Used in breakfast cereals, angel food cake, flaked fish, ice cream, ice milk, bottled beverages, reconstituted lemon juice, puddings, processed cheeses, artificially sweetened jellies, potable water supplies to prevent scale formation and corrosion, and in pumping pickle for curing hams and shoulders, etc. Because it keeps calcium, magnesium, and iron salts in solution, it is an excellent water softener and detergent; used in Calgon®, Giltex®, and other such products. Lethal dose in dogs is 140 milligrams per kilogram of body weight. The final report to the FDA of the Select Committee on GRAS Substances stated in 1980 that it should continue its GRAS status for packaging with no limitations other than good manufacturing practices.

**SODIUM HYDROSULFITE.** A bacterial inhibitor and antifermentative in the sugar and syrup industries. Slight odor. No known toxicity. The final report to the FDA of the Select Committee on GRAS Substances stated in 1980 that it should continue its GRAS status for packaging with no limitations other than good manufacturing practices.

**SODIUM HYDROXIDE. Caustic Soda. Soda Lye.** An alkali used as a modifier for food starch; as a glazing agent for pretzels; as a peeling agent for tubers and fruits; in the refining process for vegetable oils and animal fats to neutralize free fatty acids; in sour cream and butter; cocoa products; and canned peas as a neutralizer. The FDA banned use of more than 10 percent in household liquid drain cleaners. Its ingestion causes vomiting, prostration, and collapse. Inhalation causes lung damage. The final report to the FDA of the Select Committee on GRAS Substances stated in 1980 that it should continue its GRAS status for packaging with no limitations other than good manufacturing practices.

**SODIUM HYDROXIDE GELATINIZED STARCH.** Starch (*see*) that has been gelatinized with sodium hydroxide. The final report to the FDA of the Select Committee on GRAS Substances stated in 1980 that there were insufficient relevant biological and other studies upon which to base an evaluation of it when it is used as a food ingredient.

**SODIUM HYPOCHLORITE.** A preservative used in the washing of cottage cheese curd. Also used medically as an antiseptic for wounds. Ingestion may cause corrosion of mucous membranes, esophageal or gastric perforation. The aqueous solutions are Eau de Javelle, Clorox, Dazzle.

**SODIUM HYPOPHOSPHATE.** White crystals, soluble in water, used as a sequestrant (*see*). The final report to the FDA of the Select Committee on GRAS Substances stated in 1980 that it should continue its GRAS status with no limitations other than good manufacturing practices.

**SODIUM INOSINATE.** See Inosinate.

**SODIUM IRON PYROPHOSPHATE.** See Sodium Pyrophosphate.

**SODIUM ISOASCORBATE.** See Erythorbic Acid.

**SODIUM LACTATE.** A colorless, transparent salt of lactic acid, nearly odorless. It is used as an antioxidant, bodying agent, and humectant. Used medicinally as a systemic and urinary alkalizer. No known toxicity.

**SODIUM LAURYL SULFATE (SLS).** Used in commercial detergents to treat raw foods, followed by a water rinsing. Also an ingredient of toothpaste and a whipping aid in cake mixes and dried egg products. On the FDA list of further studies on the safety of this widely used additive.

**SODIUM METABISULFITE.** A bacterial inhibitor in wine, ale, and beer; an antifermentative in sugar and syrups; preservative for fruit and vegetable juices; antibrowning agent in cut fruits, frozen apples, dried fruits, prepared fruit pie mix, peeled potatoes, and maraschino cherries. The Select Committee on GRAS Substances found the additive did not present a hazard when used at present levels but that increased use would require additional safety data.

**SODIUM METAPHOSPHATE.** A dough conditioner. The final report to the FDA of the Select Committee on GRAS Substances stated in 1980 that it should continue its GRAS status with no limitations other than good manufacturing practices. See Sodium Hexametaphosphate.

**SODIUM METASILICATE.** An alkali usually prepared from sand and soda ash. Used as a peeling solution for peaches and as a denuder for tripe "in amounts sufficient for the purpose." The FDA has charged that sodium metasilicate in nonphosphate detergents "is a caustic substance, corrosive to skin, harmful if swallowed, and the cause of severe eye irritations."

**SODIUM METHYL NAPHTHALENE SULFONATE.** In solutions for peeling fruits and vegetables; water rinse. No known toxicity.

**SODIUM METHYL SULFATE.** Used in processing of pectin (*see*). No known toxicity.

**SODIUM MONOALKYLPHENOXYBENZENEDISULFONATE.** Used in lye for peeling fruits and vegetables. No known toxicity.

**SODIUM NITRATE.** See Nitrate, Sodium.

**SODIUM NITRITE.** See Nitrite, Sodium.

**SODIUM OLEATE. Sodium Salt of Oleic Acid.** White powder, fatty odor, alkaline. Used in soaps. The final report to the FDA of the Select Committee on GRAS Substances stated in 1980 that it should continue its GRAS status for packaging with no limitations other than good manufacturing practices.

**SODIUM PALMITATE. Sodium Salt of Palmitic Acid** (*see*). The final report to the FDA of the Select Committee on GRAS Substances stated in 1980 that it should continue its GRAS status for packaging with no limitations other than good manufacturing practices.

**SODIUM PANTOTHENATE. Vitamins $D_1$ and $D_2$.** Used as a dietary supplement. The final report to the FDA of the Select Committee on GRAS Substances stated in 1980 that it should continue its GRAS status with no limitations other than good manufacturing practices.

**SODIUM PECTINATE.** A stabilizer and thickener for syrups for frozen products, ice cream, ice milk, confections, fruit sherbets, French dressing and other salad dressings, fruit jelly, preserves, jams. Used in "quantities which reasonably compensate for the deficiency, if any, of natural pectin content of the fruit ingredients." No known toxicity. GRAS.

**SODIUM PHOSPHATE.** The final report to the FDA of the Select Committee on GRAS Substances stated in 1980 that it should continue its GRAS status with no limitations other than good manufacturing practices. See Phosphorous Sources.

**SODIUM PHOSPHOALUMINATE.** The acid salt of phosphoric acid. An ingredient of baking powders and other leavening mixtures. GRAS for packaging. See Phosphoric Acid for toxicity.

**SODIUM POTASSIUM TARTRATE. Rochelle Salt.** A buffer for confections, fruit jelly, preserves, and jams. For each 100 pounds of saccharin in the above products 3 ounces of sodium potassium tartrate is used. Also used in cheese. Used medically as a cathartic. No known toxicity. GRAS.

**SODIUM PROPIONATE.** Colorless or transparent odorless crystals which gather water in moist air. Used as a preservative, and to prevent mold and fungus in foodstuffs. It has been used to treat fungal infections of the skin but can cause allergic reactions. The final report to the FDA of the Select Committee on GRAS Substances stated in 1980 that it should continue its GRAS status with no limitations other than good manufacturing practices.

**SODIUM PYROPHOSPHATE.** Used to decrease the amount of cooked-out juices in canned hams, pork shoulders, and bacon at 5 percent phosphate in pickle; 0.5 percent phosphate in product (only clear solution may be injected into hams). It is also used in cold water puddings and processed cheese. It is an emulsifier salt and a texturizer as well as a sequestrant. The FDA labeled it GRAS for use as a sequestrant.

**SODIUM SACCHARIN.** See Saccharin.

**SODIUM SALT.** See Sodium Benzoate.

**SODIUM SESQUICARBONATE. Lye.** Produced on a large scale from sodium carbonate and a slight excess of sodium bicarbonate (*see both*). Used as a neutralizer for butter, cream, fluid milk, ice cream, in the processing of olives before canning, cacao products, and canned peas. Chiefly used in laundering in conjunction with soap. Irritating to skin and mucous membranes. The final report to the FDA of the Select Committee on GRAS Substances stated in 1980 that it should continue its GRAS status with no limitations other than good manufacturing practices.

**SODIUM SILICATE. Water Glass. Soluble Glass.** In the forms of crystallike pieces or lumps. Used in packaging. Strongly alkaline. Irritating to skin. If swallowed, causes vomiting and diarrhea. The final report to the FDA of the Select Committee on GRAS Substances stated in 1980 that it should continue its GRAS status for packaging with no limitations other than good manufacturing practices.

**SODIUM SILICO ALUMINATE.** Anticaking agent used in table salt up to 2 percent; dried egg yolks up to 2 percent; in sugar up to 1 percent; and in baking powder up to 5 percent. Slightly alkaline. No known toxicity.

**SODIUM SORBATE.** The final report to the FDA of the Select Committee on GRAS Substances stated in 1980 that it should continue its GRAS status with no limitations other than good manufacturing practices. See Calcium Sorbate.

**SODIUM STEARATE.** Alkaline; white, powdery, soapy texture; slight tallowlike odor. Used as an emulsifier in foods. Also used in suppositories and toothpaste, and as a waterproofing agent. Has been used to treat skin diseases. No known toxicity.

**SODIUM STEARYL FUMARATE.** A fine white powder used as a dough conditioner in yeast and leavened bakery products in amounts not exceeding .5 percent by weight of flour used. Also used as a conditioning agent in dehydrated potatoes in an amount not exceeding 1 percent by weight. No known toxicity.

**SODIUM STEAROYL-2-LACTYLATE.** The sodium salt of a lactylic ester of fatty acid. Prepared from lactic acid and fatty acids. It is used as an emulsifier, plasticizer, or surface active agent in an amount not greater than required to produce the intended physical or technical effect, and where standards of identity do not preclude use, in the following: bakery mixes, baked products, cake icings, fillings and toppings, dehydrated fruits and vegetables, dehydrated fruit and vegetable juices; frozen desserts, liquid shortenings for household use; pancake mixes, precooked instant rice, pudding mixes, solid-state edible vegetable fat–water emulsions used as substitutes for milk or cream in coffee; and with shortening and edible fats and oils when such are required in the foods listed above. See Lactic Acid for toxicity.

**SODIUM SULFATE.** Occurs in nature as the minerals mirabilite and thenardite. Used in chewing-gum base; medicinally to reduce body water. Used chiefly in manufacture of dyes, soaps, and detergents. Taken by mouth it stimulates gastric mucous production and sometimes inactivates a natural digestive juice—pepsin. Fatally poisoned animals show only diarrhea and intestinal bloating with no gross lesions outside the intestinal tract.

**SODIUM SULFITE.** Slightly pink, odorless powder, with a salty taste, used as a bacterial inhibitor in wine, brewing, and distilled-beverage industries. Also an antifermentative in the sugar and syrup industries and a preservative in fruit and vegetable juices, meats, and egg yolks. Prevents browning in cut fruits, and is used in frozen apples, dried fruit, prepared fruit pie mix, peeled potatoes, maraschino cherries, dried fruits, and glacéed fruits. Used to bleach straw, silk, and wool; a developer in photography; treats upset stomachs and combats fungus infections. The Select Committee on GRAS Substances found that sodium sulfite did not present a hazard when used at present levels but that additional data would be necessary if significant increase in consumption occurred.

**SODIUM TAUROCHOLATE. Taurocholic Acid.** The chief ingredient of the bile of carnivorous animals. Used as an emulsifier in dried egg white up to .1 percent. It is a lipase accelerator. Lipase is a fat-splitting enzyme in the blood, pancreatic secretion, and tissues. No known toxicity.

**SODIUM TETRAPHOSPHATE. Sodium Polyphosphate.** Used as a sequestering agent. The final report to the FDA of the Select Committee on GRAS Substances stated in 1980 that it should continue its GRAS status with no limitations other than good manufacturing practices. Also see Phosphates.

**SODIUM THIOSULFATE.** An antioxidant used to protect sliced potatoes and uncooked French fries from browning and as a stabilizer for potassium iodide in iodized salt. Also used to neutralize chlorine and to bleach bone. It is an antidote for cyanide poisoning and has been used in the past to combat blood clots; used to treat ringworms and mange in animals. Poorly absorbed by the bowel. The final report to the FDA of the Select Committee on GRAS Substances stated in 1980 that it should continue its GRAS status with no limitations other than good manufacturing practices.

**SODIUM *p*-TOLUENE SULFOCHLORAMINE. Chloramine T.** A water-purifying agent and a deodorant used to remove weed odor in cheese. Suspected of causing rapid allergic reaction in the hypersensitive. Poisoning by Chloramine T is characterized by pain, vomiting, sudden loss of consciousness, circulatory and respiratory collapse, and death.

**SODIUM TRIMETAPHOSPHATE.** A starch modifier. No known toxicity.

**SODIUM TRIPOLYPHOSPHATE (STPP).** A texturizer and sequestrant cleared for use in food starch modifiers. A water softener. Also cleared by the USDA Meat Inspection Department to preserve meat by decreasing cooked-out juices in canned hams, pork shoulders, chopped ham, and bacon. Also used as a dilutant for Citrus Red No. 2 (*see*). Moderately irritating to the skin and mucous membranes. Ingestion of large amounts can cause violent purging. It may deplete the body of calcium if taken in sufficient amounts and such a case of low calcium was reported in a patient poisoned with water softener. The final report to the FDA of the Select Committee on GRAS Substances stated in 1980 that it should continue its GRAS status for packaging with no limitations other than good manufacturing practices.

**SORBATE, CALCIUM.** See Calcium Sorbate.

**SORBIC ACID. Acetic Acid. Hexadienic Acid. Hexadienoic Acid. Sorbistat.** A white, free-flowing powder that is obtained from the berries of the mountain ash. Also made from chemicals in the factory. It is used in cosmetics as a preservative and humectant. A mold and yeast inhibitor, it is used in foods, especially cheeses and beverages. It is also used in baked goods, chocolate syrup, fresh fruit cocktail, soda-fountain-type syrups, tangerine purée (sherbet base), salads (potato, macaroni, cole slaw, gelatin), cheesecake, pie fillings, cake, cheese in consumer-size packages, and artificially sweetened jellies and preserves. Percentages range from .003 in beverages to .2 percent in cheeses. Practically nontoxic but may cause a slight skin irritation. When injected under the skin of laboratory animals in 2,600-milligram doses per kilogram of body weight, it caused cancer. The final report to the FDA of the Select Committee on GRAS Substances stated in 1980 that it should continue its GRAS status with no limitations other than good manufacturing practices.

**SORBITAN MONOOLEATE. Polysorbate 80.** An emulsifying agent for special dietary products and pharmaceuticals, a defoamer in yeast production, and a chewing gum plasticizer. An unintentionally administered daily dose of 19.2 grams per kilogram of body weight for 2 days to a 4-month-old baby caused no harm except loose stools.

**SORBITAN MONOPALMITATE.** An emulsifier and flavor-dispersing agent used as an alternate for sorbitan monostearate (*see*) in cake mixes. No known toxicity.

**SORBITAN MONOSTEARATE.** An emulsifier, defoaming, and flavoring dispersing agent. Used in cakes and cake mixes, whipped vegetable oil toppings, cookie coatings, cake icings and fillings, solid-state edible vegetable fat–water emulsions used as substitutes for milk or cream in coffee, coconut spread, beverages, confectionery, baked goods. Percentages range from 1 to .0006 percent. No single dose is known to be lethal in animals, and man has been fed a daily single dose of 20 grams without harm.

**SORBITAN TRISTEARATE.** An emulsifier and alternate for sorbitan monostearate (*see*) in candy coatings. No known toxicity.

**SORBITOL.** A white, crystalline, sweet, water-soluble powder, first found in ripe berries of the mountain ash. Also occurs in other berries (except grapes) and in cherries, plums, pears, apples, seaweed, and algae by the breakdown of dextrose. A sugar substitute for diabetics. Used in candy as a thickener, in vegetable oils as a sequestrant, as a stabilizer and sweetener in frozen desserts for special dietary purposes, as a humectant and texturizing agent in shredded coconut and dietetic fruits and soft drinks. Medically used to reduce body water, as a cathartic, for intravenous feeding, and to increase absorption of vitamins in pharmaceuticals. Industrially used in plasticizers and resins to control moisture on printing rolls, in leather and tobacco; used in writing inks to ensure a smooth flow from the point of the pen; and as an antifreeze. The FDA has asked for further study of sorbitol. Although it has a sweetening effect similar to sugar, its safety for diabetics has yet to be proved. It may alter the absorption of other drugs, making them less effective or more toxic. It can cause diarrhea and gastrointestinal disturbances when taken in excess.

**SORBOSE.** Derived from sorbitol (*see*) by fermentation. Used in the manufacture of Vitamin C (accounts for nearly 1,000 tons of ascorbic acid (*see*) produced yearly). No known toxicity. The final report to the FDA of the Select Committee on GRAS Substances stated in 1980 that it should continue its GRAS status for packaging with no limitations other than good manufacturing practices.

**SORGHUM.** The second most widely grown feed grain in the United States. Only 2 to 3 percent of the crop is used for human food in America, but it is the reverse in Africa and Asia. However, a new high-lysine sorghum plant has been developed that is twice as nutritious in protein as the common variety and is 50 percent richer in lysine, the essential amino acid. The syrup, produced by evaporation from the stems and the juice, resembles cane sugar but contains a high proportion of invert sugars (*see*) as well as starch and dextrin (*see both*). Very sweet, it is used as a texturizer and sweetener in foods. No known toxicity.

**SORGHUM GRAIN SYRUP.** Produced from the dried sorghum juice. See Sorghum.

**SOYBEAN. Bean, Oil, and Flour.** Soybeans came originally from Eastern Asia but are now cultivated in the midwestern United States. The oil is made up of 40 percent protein, 17 percent carbohydrates, 18 percent oil, and 4.6 percent ash. It contains ascorbic acid, Vitamin A, and thiamine. Debittered soybean flour contains practically no starch and is widely used in dietetic foods. Soybean oil is used in defoamers in the production of beet sugar and yeast, in the manufacture of margarine, shortenings, candy, and soap. Soybean is used in many products including MSG, dough mixes, Lea and Perrins Worcestershire Sauce, Heinz's Worcestershire Sauce, La Choy Oriental Soy Sauce, soy sauce, salad dressings, pork link sausages, luncheon meats, hard candies, nut candies, milk and coffee substitutes. It is made into soybean milk, soybean curd, and soybean cheese. About 300 million bushels of soybeans are grown yearly in the U.S.A., one third more than in China. No known toxicity but it may cause allergic reactions. The final report to the FDA of the Select Committee on GRAS Substances stated in 1980 that it should continue its GRAS status with no limitations other than good manufacturing practices.

**SOY SAUCE. Fermented or Hydrolyzed.** A hydrolysis product of soybeans. A combination of mold fermentation and acid hydrolysis is used. The molds employed are *Aspergillus flavus, A. niger,* and *A. oryzae.* Soy sauce consists of a mixture of amino acids, peptides, polypeptides, peptones, simple proteins, purines, carbohydrates, and other organic compounds suspended in an 18 percent sodium chloride solution. In 1983, some manufacturers produced soy sauce with a lower salt content. Used directly on food as a flavoring. The final report to the FDA of the Select Committee on GRAS Substances stated in 1980 that there is no evidence in the available information that it is a hazard to the public when used as it is now and it should continue its GRAS status with limitations on amounts that can be added to food.

**SPANISH HOPS.** See Ditanny of Crete.

**SPANISH ORIGANUM.** See Origanum Oil.

**SPEARMINT FLAVORING. Garden Mint. Green Mint.** Fresh ground parts of an aromatic herb used in spearmint flavoring for beverages, meats, and condiments (1,000 ppm). Widely cultivated in the United States. The volatile, colorless *oil* (principal active constituent contains at least 50 percent carvone; *see*), obtained by steam distillation of the flowering plant, is used in butter, caramel, citrus fruit, garlic, soy, and spice flavorings for beverages, ice cream, ices, candy, baked goods, condiments (100,000 ppm), fats, oils, and icings (50,000 ppm). Has been used to break up intestinal gas, but has no known toxicity. GRAS.

**SPERM OIL (HYDROGENATED)** (*see* Hydrogenation). Obtained from the sperm whale. Yellow, thin liquid; slightly fishy odor if not of good quality. Used as a release agent or lubricant in baking pans and as an industrial lubricant. No known toxicity.

**SPIKE LAVENDER.** A pale yellow liquid obtained from flowers in the

Mediterranean region and used chiefly in perfume and for fumigating against moths. Used in fruit, floral, mint, and spice flavorings for beverages, ice cream, ices, candy, and baked goods. No known toxicity. GRAS.

**SPIRAL FLAG OIL.** See Costus Root Oil.

**SPIRIT OF NITROUS ETHER.** See Ethyl Nitrite.

**SPRUCE OIL.** See Hemlock Oil.

**STABILIZERS.** Used in foods to get a uniform consistency or texture and to maintain the stability of mixtures. Chocolate milk needs a stabilizer to keep the particles of chocolate from settling to the bottom of the container. Calcium salt (*see*) is used as a stabilizer in canned tomatoes to keep them from falling apart. Among the most widely used stabilizers are the gums such as gum arabic and agar-agar (*see both*).

**STANNOUS CHLORIDE. Tin Dichloride.** An antioxidant used for canned asparagus, canned soda (11 ppm), and other foods. Soluble in water and a powerful reducing agent, particularly in manufacture of dyes, and tinning agent. Used to revive yeast. Low systemic toxicity but may be highly irritating to the skin and mucous membranes. On the FDA list for further study for mutagenic, teratogenic, subacute, and reproductive effects. GRAS.

**STAR ANISE. Chinese Anis.** Fruit of *Illicium verum* from China, called star because of the fruit's shape. The *extract* is used in fruit, licorice, anise, liquor, sausage, root beer, sarsaparilla, vanilla, wintergreen, and birch beer flavorings for beverages, ice cream, ices, candy, meats (1,000 ppm), and liqueurs. The *oil* is used in blackberry, peach, licorice, anise, liquor, meat, root beer, spice, wintergreen, and birch beer flavorings for beverages, ice cream, ices, candy, baked goods, meats, syrups, and liqueurs. The fruit is a source of anise oil (*see* Anise). Star anise has been used as an expectorant and carminative. Japanese star anise is *Illicium anisatum* and contains a toxic lactone called anisatin, unknown in the Chinese variety. No known toxicity. GRAS.

**STARCH. Acid-Modified, Pregelatinized, and Unmodified.** Starch is stored by plants and is taken from grains of wheat, potatoes, rice, corn, beans, and many other vegetable foods. Insoluble in cold water or alcohol but soluble in boiling water. Comparatively resistant to naturally occurring enzymes and this is the reason processors "modify" starch (*see* Modified Starch) to make it more digestible. Starch is modified with propylene oxide, succinic anhydride, 1-octenyl succinic anhydride, aluminum sulfate, or sodium hydroxide (*see all*). Starch is a major component of cereals and many vegetables. The average United States diet has about 180 grams per person daily. Modified starch contributes about a gram per person per day. The source of starch and the type of modification are not usually identified on the label, since the FDA does not require it. The modified starches used in foods are most often bleached starch, acetylated distarch adipate, distarch phosphate, acetylated distarchphosphate, and hydroxypropyl distarchphosphate. The latter three are commonly used in baby foods. The final report to the FDA of the Select Committee on GRAS Substances said that there was no information that starch acetate was hazardous to the public when used as it is now and it should continue its GRAS status with limitations on amounts that can be added to food. On the other hand, starch sodium succinate, starch sodium octenyl succinate, and starch sodium hypochlorite oxidized were said not to demonstrate a hazard to the public at current use levels, but uncertainties do exist, requiring additional studies to be conducted. However, GRAS status continues while tests are being completed and evaluated. Acid-modified and pregelatinized starches were said, in the final report, to be GRAS, requiring no limitations other than good manufacturing practices.

**STEARIC ACID. Octadecanoic Acid.**   Occurs naturally in some vegetable oils, cascarilla bark extract, and as a glyceride (*see*) in tallow and other animal fats and oils. Prepared synthetically by hydrogenation (*see*) of cottonseed and other vegetable oils. Slight tallowlike odor. Used in butter and vanilla flavorings for beverages, baked goods, and candy (4,000 ppm). Also a softener in chewing-gum base, used in suppositories, ointments, vanishing creams, and other cosmetics. A possible sensitizer for allergic types. The final report to the FDA of the Select Committee on GRAS Substances stated in 1980 that it should continue its GRAS status for packaging with no limitations other than good manufacturing practices.

**STEARYL CITRATE.**   A metal scavenger to prevent adverse effects of trace metals in foods and an antioxidant to prevent rancidity in oleomargarine. See Citrate Salts for toxicity. The final report to the FDA of the Select Committee on GRAS Substances stated in 1980 that it should continue its GRAS status with no limitations other than good manufacturing practices.

**STEARYL-2-LACTYLIC ACID.**   Occurs in tallow and other animal fats, as well as in animal and vegetable oils. Used to emulsify shortening in non-yeast-leavened bakery products and pancake mixes. Also used to emulsify cakes, icings, and fillings. No known toxicity.

**STEARYL MONOGLYCERIDYL CITRATE.**   The soft, practically tasteless, off-white, waxy solid used as an emulsion stabilizer in shortening with emulsifiers. It is prepared by the chemical reaction of citric acid on monoglycerides of fatty acids (*see*). No known toxicity.

**STERCULEN. Sterculia.** See Karaya Gum.

**STPP.** See Sodium Tripolyphosphate.

**STORAX. Styrax. Sweet Oriental Gum.** A liquid balsam obtained from the trunk of a small tree. American storax is produced chiefly in Honduras. Used in strawberry, fruit, and spice flavorings for beverages, ice cream, ices, candy, baked goods, chewing gum, and toppings. Used in medicine as a weak antiseptic and in perfumery. Has been used as an expectorant. Moderately toxic.

**STRAWBERRY ALDEHYDE.** See Ethyl 3-Methyl-3-Phenylglycidate.

**STYRACIN.** See Cinnamyl Cinnamate.

**STYRAX EXTRACT. Storax.** Extract of large shrubs that yield commercially important resins such as storax and benzoin. Used in chocolate, fruit, and liquor flavorings for beverages, ice cream, ices, candy, baked goods, and gelatin desserts. See Storax and Benzoin for toxicity.

**STYROLENE ACETATE.** See α-Methylbenzyl Acetate.

**STYRYL CARBINOL.** See Cinnamyl Alcohol.

**SUBACUTE.** A zone between acute and chronic or the process of a disease that is not overt. Subacute endocarditis, for example, is an infection of the heart. It is usually due to a "strep" germ and may follow a temporary infection after a tooth extraction.

**SUCCINIC ACID.** Occurs in fossils, fungi, lichens, etc. Prepared from acetic acid (*see*). Odorless, very acid taste. The acid is used as a plant-growth retardant. Also a buffer and neutralizing agent. Used in perfumes. Has been used as a laxative. Lethal dose in rats is 8.40 milligram per kilogram. The final report to the FDA of the Select Committee on GRAS Substances stated in 1980 that it should continue its GRAS status with no limitations other than good manufacturing practices.

**SUCCINIC ANHYDRIDE.** A starch modifier up to 4 percent. See Modified Starch.

**SUCCINYLATED MONOGLYCERIDES.** Surfactants (*see*) used as a dough conditioner to add loaf volume and firmness. See Glycerides and Succinic Acid.

**SUCROSE. Sugar. Saccharose. Cane Sugar (15–20 percent). Beet Sugar (10–17 percent).** A sweetening agent for food. Table sugar can stimulate the production of fat in the body, apart from its calorie content in the diet, and may be particularly fat-producing in women on the "pill." Sugar is used also as a starting agent in fermentation production, in pharmacy as a preservative, as an antioxidant (in the form of invert sugar), as a demulcent, as a substitute for glycerol (*see*), as coating for tablets. No known toxicity. The final report to the FDA of the Select Committee on GRAS Substances stated in 1980 that there is no evidence in the available information that it is a hazard to the public when used as it is now and it should continue its GRAS status with limitations on amounts that can be added to food.

**SUCROSE FATTY ACID ESTERS.** Derived from sucrose (*see*) and edible tallow, the FDA gave permission in 1982 for their use as components of protective coatings for fruits.

**SUCROSE OCTAACETATE.** Prepared from sucrose (*see*). A synthetic flavoring used in bitters, spice, and ginger ale flavorings for beverages. Used in adhesives; a denaturant for alcohol. No known toxicity.

**SULFAMIC ACID.** White crystalline solid, moderately soluble in water, it is odorless. Used as a plasticizer and fire retardant for paper and other cellulosics; as a stabilizing agent for chlorine and hypochlorite, bleaching paper pulp, and as a catalyst for urea-formaldehyde resin. Low toxicity. The final report to the FDA of the Select Committee on GRAS Substances stated in 1980 that it should continue its GRAS status for packaging with no limitations other than good manufacturing practices.

**SULFATED TALLOW.** Fat from fatty tissues of sheep and cattle which becomes solid at 40 to 46 degrees F. It is a defoaming agent in yeast and beet sugar production in "amounts reasonably required to inhibit foaming." See Tallow Flakes for toxicity.

**SULFITE DIOXIDE.** See Sulfites.

**SULFITES. Sodium, Potassium, and Ammonium.** Preservatives, antioxidants, and antibrowning agents used in foods. There are six sulfiting agents that are currently listed as GRAS chemical preservatives. They are sulfur dioxide, sodium sulfite, sodium and potassium bisulfite, and sodium and potassium metabisulfite (*see all*). Under the current listing, sulfiting agents may be used as preservatives in any food, except meat or food that is a recognized source of Vitamin $B_1$. These agents have been used in many processed foods and in cafeterias and restaurants to prevent fruits, green vegetables, potatoes, and salads from turning brown, as well as to enhance their crispness.

The FDA had sulfiting agents under review in 1983. As part of this review, a proposal to affirm the GRAS status of sulfur dioxide, sodium bisulfite, and sodium and potassium metabisulfite (*see all*), with specific use limitations, was published in the *Federal Register* of July 9, 1982. The agency did not propose to affirm the GRAS status of sodium sulfite and potassium bisulfite because it had no evidence to indicate their current use in food.

Reactions to sulfites can include acute asthma attacks, loss of consciousness, anaphylactic shock, diarrhea, and nausea occurring soon after ingesting sulfiting agents. The FDA asked medical doctors for reports of untoward effects of sulfites among their patients. In the meantime, the FDA is reviewing the information on sulfites. Sulfiting agents are listed on the ingredient labeling of packaged foods—except alcoholic beverages—but unless they ask and are told, allergic individuals may not know sulfiting agents are used in restaurant food preparation.

A citizens' petition was submitted by the Center for Science in the Public Interest, Washington, D.C., on October 28, 1982, that asked the agency to restrict the use of sulfiting agents to a safe residue level in food or require labels on those food products in which sulfiting agents must be used at higher levels to perform essential public health functions.

In the meantime, the California Grape and Tree Fruit League recommended that the Food and Drug Administration affirm as GRAS sulfiting agents used in sulfur dioxide fumigation within specific limitations and include its use as an ingredient to treat fresh grapes. Stating that the compound is essential to the marketing, transport, storage, and export of table grapes, the group claimed lack of any known substitute for the gaseous compound effective in preventing mold-rot and other storage fungi and in prolonging storage life. A spokesperson for the Wine Institute, which represents 460 domestic winemakers, said that many of the sulfur compounds in wine are natural parts of fermentation, but they also are added to many wines. As of this writing, the FDA still had the subject of sulfiting agents under review.

**SULFOACETATE DERIVATIVES OF MONOGLYCERIDES AND DIGLYCERIDES.** Used as emulsifiers. The final report to the FDA of the Select Committee on GRAS Substances stated in 1980 that there were insufficient relevant biological and other studies upon which to base an evaluation of them when they are used as food ingredients.

**SULFO-*p*-TOLUENE. Sodium Chloramine.** A water-purifying agent and a deodorant used to remove onion and weed odors in cheese. Toluene may cause mild anemia and is narcotic in high concentrations.

**SULFUR DIOXIDE.** A gas formed when sulfur burns. Used to bleach vegetable colors and to preserve fruits and vegetables; a disinfectant in breweries and food factories; a bleaching agent in gelatin, glue, and beet sugars; an antioxidant, preservative, and antibrowning agent in wine, corn syrup, table syrup, jelly, dried fruits, brined fruit, maraschino cherries, beverages, dehydrated potatoes, soups, and condiments. Should not be used on meats or on foods recognized as a source of Vitamin A because it destroys the vitamin. Very poisonous, highly irritating. Often cited as an air pollutant. Inhalation produces respiratory irritation and death when sufficiently concentrated. The final report to the FDA of the Select Committee on GRAS Substances stated in 1980 that there is no evidence in the available information that it is a hazard to the public when used as it is now and it should continue its GRAS status with limitations on amounts that can be added to food.

**SULFURIC ACID. Oil of Vitriol.** A clear, colorless, odorless, oily acid used to modify starch (*see*) and to regulate acidity-alkalinity in the brewing industry. It is very corrosive and produces severe burns on contact with the skin and other body tissues. Inhalation of the vapors can cause serious lung damage. Dilute sulfuric acid has been used to stimulate appetite and to combat overalkaline stomach juices. Ingestion of undiluted sulfuric acid can be fatal. The final report to the FDA of the Select Committee on GRAS Substances stated in 1980 that it should continue its GRAS status with no limitations other than good manufacturing practices.

**SUNFLOWER SEED OIL.** Oil obtained by milling the seeds of the large flower produced in the United States, USSR, India, Egypt, and Argentina. A pale yellow oil, and bland, it contains a large amount of Vitamin E (*see* Tocopherols) and forms a "skin" after drying. Used in food and salad oils and as a resin in soap manufacturing. No known toxicity.

**SUNSET YELLOW.** See FD and C Yellow No. 6.

**SUPERGLYCERINATED FULLY HYDROGENATED RAPESEED OIL.** Used in some margarines and emulsions. See Rapeseed Oil, Glycerin, and Hydrogenation.

**SURFACE ACTIVE AGENTS.** See Surfactants.

**SURFACTANTS.** The more than 194 million pounds of compounds that are produced annually to make it easier to effect contact between surfaces. By 1985 production is expected to reach nearly 800 million pounds. Surfactants separate individual particles or clumps of particles called "flocs" so as to impart "favorable" properties to a wide variety of foods, drugs, and cosmetics. Surfactants may be classified as emulsifiers, dispersants, wetting and foaming agents, detergents, viscosity modifiers, and stabilizers. For example, in peanut butter, a surfactant keeps oil and water mixtures from separating; in cosmetics, it makes lotions more spreadable; salad dressings and cheeses are thickened by surfactants, which make them pour better.

**SWEET FLAG.** See Calamus.

**SYNTHETIC.** Made in the laboratory and not by nature. Vanillin, for example, made in the laboratory may be identical to vanilla extracted from the vanilla bean but vanillin cannot be called "natural."

**TAGETES. Meal, Extract, and Oil.** The *meal* is the dried, ground flower petals of the Aztec marigold, a strong-scented, tropical American herb, mixed with no more than .3 percent ethoxyquin, a herbicide and antioxidant. The *extract* is taken from tagetes petals. Both the meal and the extract are used to enhance the yellow color of chicken skin and eggs. They are incorporated in chicken feed, supplemented sufficiently with the yellow coloring xanthophyll. The coloring is exempt from certification. The oil is extracted from the Aztec flower and used in fruit flavorings for beverages, ice cream, ices, candy, baked goods, gelatin, desserts, and condiments. No known toxicity.

**TALC. Talcum. French Chalk.** The lumps are known as soapstone or steatite. An anticaking agent added to vitamin supplements to render a free flow; also a chewing gum base. Talc is finely powdered native magnesium silicate, the same that is used in dusting powder and paints. There is no acute toxicity, but there is a question about its being a cancer-causing agent. It is suspected that the high incidence of stomach cancer among the Japanese is due to the fact that the Japanese prefer that their rice be treated with talc, a mineral whose chemical composition is similar to the known cancer-causing agent asbestos. Furthermore, talc-based powders have been linked to ovarian cancer. In Boston's Brigham and Women's Hospital, of 215 women with ovarian cancer, 32 had used talcum powder on their genitals and sanitary napkins. GRAS for packaging food.

**TALL OIL. Liquid Rosin.** A byproduct of the wood pulp industry. *Tall* is Swedish for "pine." It may be a mild irritant and sensitizer. The final report to the FDA of the Select Committee on GRAS Substances stated in 1980 that it should continue its GRAS status for packaging with no limitations other than good manufacturing practices.

**TALLOW FLAKES. Suet. Dripping.** Animal fat obtained in North America mainly from sheep and cattle. Used as a defoaming agent in yeast and beet sugar production. In miniature pigs in one year, feeding tallow caused moderate-to-severe atherosclerosis (clogging of the arteries) similar to that in humans in type and location of lesions. The final report to the FDA of the Select Committee on GRAS Substances stated in 1980 that it should continue its GRAS status for packaging with no limitations other than good manufacturing practices.

**TAMARIND.** Partially dried ripe fruit of large tropical tree grown in the East Indies and Africa. Preserved in sugar or syrup. Used as a natural food flavoring. Pulp contains about 10 percent tartaric acid (*see*). Has been used as a cooling laxative drink. No known toxicity.

**TANGERINE OIL.** The oil obtained by expression from the peels of the ripe fruit from several related tangerine species. Reddish orange, with a pleasant orange aroma. Used in blueberry, mandarin orange, tangerine, and other fruit flavorings for beverages, ice cream, ices, candy, baked goods, gelatin desserts, and chewing gum. No known toxicity. GRAS.

**TANNIC ACID.** Occurs in the bark and fruit of many plants, notably in the bark of the oak species, in sumac, cherry, wild bark, and in coffee and tea. It is used to clarify beer and wine, and as a refining agent for rendered fats. As a flavoring it is used in butter, caramel, fruit, brandy, maple, and nut flavorings for beverages, ice cream, ices, candy, baked goods, and liquor (1,000 ppm). Used medicinally as a mild astringent. When applied, it may turn the skin brown. Low toxicity orally, but large doses may cause gastric distress. Can cause tumors and death by injection, but not, evidently, by ingestion. However, scientists have asked for further study. The final report to the FDA of the Select Committee on GRAS Subtances stated in 1980 that there is no evidence in the available information that it is a hazard to the public when used as it is now and it should continue its GRAS status with limitations on amounts that can be added to food.

**TANNIN.** See Tannic Acid.

**TAPIOCA STARCH.** A preparation of cassava, the tapioca plant. Used for thickening liquid foods such as puddings, juicy pies, and soups. No known toxicity. The final report to the FDA of the Select Committee on GRAS Substances stated in 1980 that it should continue its GRAS status for packaging with no limitations other than good manufacturing practices.

**TAR OIL.** Distilled from wood tar, a black residue insoluble in water. The principal toxic ingredients are phenols (very toxic) and other aromatic hydrocarbons such as naphthalenes. Toxicity estimates are hard to make because even the United States Pharmacopoeia does not specify the phenol content of official preparations. However, if ingested, it is estimated that one ounce would kill. See Pine Tar Oil, which is a rectified tar oil used as a licorice food flavoring.

**TARA GUM. Peruvian Carob.** Obtained by grinding the endosperms of the seeds of an evergreen tree common to Peru. The whitish-yellow, nearly odorless powder that is produced is used as a thickening agent and stabilizer. No known toxicity. See also Locust Bean Gum.

**TARAXACUM ERYTHROSPERMUM.** See Dandelion Root Extract.

**TARTARIC ACID.** Described in ancient times as being a residual of grape fermentation, it occurs naturally in grapes and a few other fruits and is sold today as a byproduct of wine making. It is the acidic constituent of some baking powders and is used to adjust acidity in frozen dairy products, jellies, bakery products, beverages, confections, dried egg whites, candies, artificially sweetened preserves up to 4 percent. It has been used medicinally as a laxative and is used in refrigerant drinks. Essentially nontoxic but in concentrated solutions it may be irritating. GRAS.

**TARTRATE, SODIUM POTASSIUM.** The final report to the FDA of the Select Committee on GRAS Substances stated in 1980 that it should continue its GRAS status with no limitations other than good manufacturing practices. See Sodium Potassium Tartrate.

**TARTRAZINE. FD and C Yellow No. 5.** Bright orange-yellow powder used in foods, drugs, and cosmetics and as dye for wool and silk. Those allergic to aspirin are also allergic to tartrazine. Allergies have been reported in persons eating sweet corn, soft drinks, and cheese crackers—all colored with Yellow No. 5. It is derived from coal tar.

**TAUROCHOLIC ACID. Cholic Acid. Cholyltaurine.** Occurs as a sodium salt in bile. It is formed by the combination of the sulfur-containing amino acid, taurine, and cholic acid. It aids digestion and absorption of fats. It is used as an emulsifying agent in foods. The final report to the FDA of the Select Committee on GRAS Substances stated in 1980 that it should continue its GRAS status with no limitations other than good manufacturing practices.

**TBHQ.** See Tertiary Butylhydroquinone.

**TEA.** The leaves, leaf buds, and internodes of plants having leaves and fragrant white flowers, prepared and cured to make an aromatic beverage. Cultivated principally in China, Japan, Sri Lanka, and other Asian countries. Tea is a mild stimulant and its tonic properties are due to the alkaloid caffeine; the tannin makes it astringent. See Caffeine and Tannic Acid for toxicity. GRAS.

**TERATOGENIC.** From the Greek *terat* (monster) and Latin *genesis* (origin): the origin or cause for the introduction of a monster—or a defective fetus.

**TERPENE.** A class of unsaturated hydrocarbons. Its removal from products improves their flavor.

**β-TERPINEOL.** A colorless, viscous liquid with a lilaclike odor, insoluble in mineral oil and slightly soluble in water. It is primarily used as a flavoring agent but is also employed as a denaturant (*see*). It has been used as an antiseptic. In concentrations of 2 percent, it may cause burns, but in cosmetics less than 1 percent has been found to be harmless. Can be a sensitizer.

**TERPINOLENE.** A synthetic citrus and fruit flavoring agent for food, beverages, ice cream, ices, candy, and baked goods. See Turpentine for toxicity.

**TERPINYL ACETATE. Acetic Acid.** A synthetic flavoring agent that occurs naturally in cardamom. Clear, colorless, with a lavender odor. Used in berry, lime, orange, cherry, peach, plum, and meat flavorings for beverages, ice cream, ices, candy, baked goods, chewing gum, condiments, and meats. See Turpentine for toxicity.

**TERPINYL ANTHRANILATE.** A synthetic fruit flavoring agent for beverages, ice cream, ices, candy, and baked goods. See Turpentine for toxicity.

**TERPINYL BUTYRATE.** A synthetic fruit flavoring agent for beverages, ice cream, ices, candy, baked goods, and chewing gum. See Turpentine for toxicity.

**TERPINYL CINNAMATE.** A synthetic fruit flavoring agent for beverages, ice cream, ices, candy, and baked goods. See Turpentine for toxicity.

**TERPINYL FORMATE. Formic Acid.** A synthetic fruit flavoring agent for beverages, ice cream, ices, candy, baked goods, and liqueurs. See Turpentine for toxicity.

**TERPINYL ISOBUTYRATE.** A synthetic fruit flavoring agent for beverages, ice cream, ices, candy, and baked goods. See Turpentine for toxicity.

**TERPINYL ISOVALERATE.** A synthetic fruit flavoring for beverages, ice cream, ices, candy, and baked goods. See Turpentine for toxicity.

**TERPINYL PROPIONATE.** A synthetic fruit flavoring agent, colorless, with a lavender odor. Used in beverages, ice cream, ices, candy, and baked goods. See Turpentine for toxicity.

**TERRA JAPONICA.** See Catechu Extract.

**TERTIARY BUTYLHYDROQUINONE (TBHQ).** This antioxidant is finally on the market after years of pushing by food manufacturers to get it approved. It contains the petroleum-derived butane (*see*) and is used either alone or in combination with the preservative-antioxidant butylated hydroxyanisole (BHA) and/or butylated hydroxytoluene (BHT) (*see both*). (Hydroquinone combines with oxygen very rapidly and becomes brown when exposed to air.) The FDA said that TBHQ must not exceed 0.02 percent of its oil and fat content. Death has occurred from the ingestion of as little as 5 grams. Ingestion of a single gram (a thirtieth of an ounce) has caused nausea, vomiting, ringing in the ears, delirium, a sense of suffocation, and collapse. Industrial workers exposed to the vapors—without obvious systematic effects—suffered clouding of the eye lens. Application to the skin may cause allergic reactions.

**TETRADECANAL.** See Myristaldehyde.

**TETRADECANOIC ACID.** See Ethyl Myristate.

**TETRADECYL ALDEHYDE.** See Myristaldehyde.

**TETRAHYDROFURFURYL BUTYRATE. Butyric Acid.** A synthetic fruit flavoring agent for beverages, ice cream, ices, candy, and baked goods. May be irritating to the skin and mucous membranes.

**TETRAHYDROFURFURYL PROPIONATE. Propionic Acid.** A synthetic chocolate, honey, and maple flavoring agent for beverages, ice cream, ices, candy, and baked goods. Also used as a solvent for intravenous drugs. Moderately irritating to skin and mucous membranes.

**TETRAPOTASSIUM PYROPHOSPHATE.** An emulsifier. See Tetrasodium Pyrophosphate.

**TETRASODIUM PYROPHOSPHATE (TSPP).** Used in cheese emulsification, in cleansing compounds, oil well drilling, water treatment, and as a general sequestering agent to remove rust stains. It is alkaline and irritating and ingestion can cause nausea, diarrhea, and vomiting. GRAS for use in packaging.

**TEXTURIZER.** In food terminology, the chemicals used to improve the texture of various foods. For instance, canned tomatoes, canned potatoes, and canned apple slices tend to become soft and fall apart, unless the texturizer calcium chloride (*see*), for example, or its salts are added, which keep the product firm.

**THALOSE®.** A blend of food-grade acidulants (*see*) that contains propylene glycol, and the acids citric, lactic, phosphoric, and tartaric (*see all*), and water and salt. Adding this compound to sugar permits a reduction in the amount of sugar required to achieve a desired sweetness (1 ounce of liquid Thalose added to 32 pounds of sugar causes the perceived sweetness to be increased by 90 percent). One pint added to sugar will result in a saving of 500 pounds of sugar without reducing sweetness. Thalose itself is not sweet and does not alter the flavor or aroma of the foods to which it is added. It does not contribute calories but will reduce the caloric level of the end product by lowering the amount of carbohydrates in the compound. Thalose can be used in beverages, bakery and confectionery products, and in ice cream, as long as the physical properties of sugar are not needed (sugar is often used as a thickening agent and texturizer). All of the substances contained in this extender are GRAS and comply with the FDA provisions for food-grade ingredients.

**THAMNIDIUM ELEGANS.** A grayish white mold used for aging meat. It is related to the typical bread mold. No known toxicity.

**THEINE.** See Caffeine.

**THIAMINE HYDROCHLORIDE. Vitamin B₁.** A white crystalline powder used as a dietary supplement in prepared breakfast cereals, peanut butter, poultry, stuffing, baby cereals, skimmed milk, bottled soft drinks, enriched flours, enriched farina, cornmeal, enriched macaroni and noodle products, and enriched bread and rolls. Acts as a helper in important energy-yielding reactions in the body. Practically all $B_1$ sold is synthetic. The vitamin is destroyed by alkalies and alkaline drugs such as phenobarbital. No known toxicity. The final report to the FDA of the Select Committee on GRAS Substances stated in 1980 that it should continue its GRAS status with no limitations other than good manufacturing practices.

**THIAMINE MONONITRATE. Vitamin $B_1$.** A white crystalline powder, used as a diet supplement in multivitamin capsules and enriched flour. It is a more stable form of thiamine in dry mixes. A potential allergen. No known toxicity. The final report to the FDA of the Select Committee on GRAS Substances stated in 1980 that it should continue its GRAS status with no limitations other than good manufacturing practices.

**THIBETOLIDE®.** See ω-Pentadecalactone.

**THICKENERS.** Many natural gums and starches are used to add body to mixtures. Pectin (*see*), for instance, which is used in fruits naturally low in this gelling agent, enables manufacturers to produce jams and jellies of a marketable thickness. Algin (*see* Alginates) is used to make salad dressings that will not be runny.

**2-THIENYL MERCAPTAN.** A synthetic flavoring agent that occurs naturally in coffee. Used in coffee flavoring for candy and baked goods. No known toxicity.

**THIETHYL CITRATE.** An antioxidant used primarily in dried egg whites. See Citric Acid. GRAS.

**THIODIPROPIONIC ACID.** An antioxidant employed in the manufacture of food packaging material. Based on a sulfur and propionic acid (*see*). No known toxicity.

**THIODIPROPTONIC ACID.** An antioxidant in general food use. Percent of fat or oil, including essential oil, content of food is up to .02. The final report to the FDA of the Select Committee on GRAS Substances stated in 1980 that there is no evidence in the available information that it is a hazard to the public when used as it is now and it should continue its GRAS status with limitations on amounts that can be added to food.

**THIOLLYL ETHER.** See Allyl Sulfide.

**THISTLE, BLESSED. Holy Thistle.** Extract of the prickly plant. Cleared for use as a natural flavoring in alcoholic beverages. No known toxicity.

**THREONINE. L and DL forms.** An essential amino acid (*see*), the last to be discovered (1935). Prevents the buildup of fat in the liver. Occurs in whole eggs, skim milk, casein, and gelatin. On the FDA list for further study. GRAS.

**THYME.** A seasoning from the dried leaves and flowering tops of the wild or creeping thyme grown in Eurasia and throughout the United States. Used in meat, tuna, and spice flavorings for beverages, candy, baked goods, meats, and soups (1,000 ppm). Has been used in cough medicines, and it is a muscle relaxant. No known toxicity. GRAS.

**THYME OIL.** The volatile oil obtained by distillation from the flowering thyme (*see*). Colorless, yellow, or red, with a pleasant odor. Used in sausage, spice, and thyme flavorings for beverages, ice cream, ices, candy, baked goods, chewing gum, condiments, meats, and soups. A muscle relaxant. No known toxicity. GRAS.

**THYME WHITE OIL.** Obtained from the plant and used in fruit, liquor, and thyme flavorings for beverages, ice cream, ices, candy, baked goods, condiments, meats, and wine. A muscle relaxant. No known toxicity.

**THYMOL.** Occurs naturally in Dittany of Crete, oil of lavender, origanum oil, and thyme (*see all*). Used in fruit, peppermint, and spice flavorings for beverages, ice cream, ices, candy, baked goods, and chewing gum. Oral dose as medicine is .067 grams. It can cause vomiting, diarrhea, dizziness, and cardiac depression when taken in sufficient amounts.

**TIGLIC ACID.** See Allyl Tiglate.

**TITANIUM DIOXIDE.** A white pigment that occurs naturally in minerals and is used for coloring candy, gums, and a marking ink for confectionery. As a natural color, it is not subject to FDA certification. High concentrates of the dust may cause lung damage. The amount of dioxide may not exceed 1 percent by weight of food. A pound has been ingested without apparent ill effects.

**TOCOPHEROLS. Vitamin E.** Obtained by the vacuum distillation of edible vegetable oils. Used as a dietary supplement and as an antioxidant for essential oils, rendered animal fats, or a combination of such fats with vegetable oils. Helps form normal red blood cells, muscle, and other tissues. Protects fat in the body's tissues from abnormal breakdown. Experimental evidence shows Vitamin E may protect the heart and blood vessels and retard aging. The final report to the FDA of the Select Committee on GRAS Substances stated in 1980 that it should continue its GRAS status with no limitations other than good manufacturing practices.

**TOLU BALSAM. Extract and Gum.** Extract from the Peruvian or Indian plant. Contains cinnamic acid and benzoic acid (*see both*). Used in butter, butterscotch, cherry, and spice flavorings for beverages, ice cream, ices, candy, baked goods, and chewing gum. The gum is used in fruit, maple, and vanilla flavorings for beverages, ice cream, ices, candy, baked goods, and syrups. Mildly antiseptic and may be mildly irritating to the skin.

**α-TOLUALDEHYDE.** See Phenylacetaldehyde.

**TOLUALDEHYDE GLYCERYL ACETAL.** A synthetic chocolate, fruit, cherry, coconut, and vanilla flavoring agent for beverages, ice cream, ices, candy, and baked goods. No known toxicity.

**TOLUALDEHYDES (MIXED o, m, p).** Synthetic berry, loganberry, fruit, cherry, muscatal, peach, apricot, nut, almond, and vanilla flavoring agents for beverages, ice cream, ices, candy, baked goods, gelatin desserts, chewing gum, and maraschino cherries. No known toxicity.

**TOLYL ACETATE. Acetic Acid.** A synthetic butter, caramel, fruit, honey, nut, and spice flavoring agent for beverages, ice cream, ices, candy, baked goods, chewing gum, and condiments. No known toxicity.

**o-TOLYL ACETATE. Acetic Acid.** A synthetic butter, caramel, fruit, cherry, and honey flavoring agent for beverages, ice cream, ices, candy, baked goods, gelatin desserts, and chewing gum. No known toxicity.

**p-TOLYL ACETATE. Acetic Acid.** A synthetic butter, caramel, fruit, honey, nut, and spice flavoring agent for beverages, ice cream, ices, candy, baked goods, chewing gum, and condiments. No known toxicity.

**4-(p-TOLYL)-2-BUTANONE.** A synthetic fruit flavoring agent for beverages, ice cream, ices, candy, and baked goods. No known toxicity.

**p-TOLYL ISOBUTYRATE.** A synthetic fruit flavoring agent for beverages, ice cream, ices, candy, and baked goods. No known toxicity.

**p-TOLYL LAURATE. Dodecanoic Acid.** A synthetic miscellaneous flavoring agent for beverages, ice cream, ices, candy, and baked goods. No known toxicity.

**p-TOLYL PHENYLACETATE.** A synthetic butter, caramel, fruit, honey, and nut flavoring agent for beverages, ice cream, ices, candy, and baked goods. No known toxicity.

**2-(p-TOLYL) PROPIONALDEHYDE.** A synthetic caraway flavoring agent for beverages, ice cream, ices, candy, baked goods, and liqueurs. No known toxicity.

**TOLYLACETALDEHYDE.** A synthetic berry, loganberry, fruit, cherry, muscatel, peach, apricot, nut, almond, and vanilla flavoring agent for beverages, ice cream, ices, candy, baked goods, gelatin desserts, chewing gum, and maraschino cherries. No known toxicity.

**p-TOLYLACETALDEHYDE.** A synthetic honey and nut flavoring agent for ice cream, ices, candy, and baked goods. No known toxicity.

**TONKALIDE.** See δ-Hexalactone.

**TRAGACANTH.** See Gum Tragacanth.

**TRIACETIN. Glyceryl Triacetate.** See (tri-) Acetin.

**TRIBUTYL ACETYLCITRATE.** A synthetic fruit flavoring agent for beverages. No known toxicity.

**TRIBUTYRIN. Glyceryl Tributyrate.** A colorless, somewhat oily liquid that occurs naturally in butter. It has a characteristic odor and bitter taste. It is soluble in alcohol. Used as a flavoring agent in beverages, ice cream, candy, baked goods, margarine, and puddings. No known toxicity.

**TRICALCIUM PHOSPHATE.** An anticaking agent in table salt; used also in vanilla powder and vanilla-vanillin powder; as a bleaching agent in flour at not more than six parts by weight alone or in combination with potassium alum, calcium sulfate (*see*), and other compounds. Also a dietary supplement. No known toxicity.

**TRICALCIUM SILICATE.** Used in table salt and baking powder as an anticaking agent up to 2 percent. On the FDA list to be studied for subacute, mutagenic, teratogenic, and reproductive effects. No known toxicity. GRAS.

**TRICHLOROETHYLENE (TCE).** Residue in decaffeinated coffee powder. Used in spice oleoresins as a solvent. Moderate exposure can cause symptoms similar to alcohol inebriation, and its analgesic and anesthetic properties make it useful for short operations. High concentrations have a narcotic effect. Deaths have been attributed to irregular heart rhythm. Tests conducted by the National Cancer Institute showed that this chlorinated hydrocarbon caused cancer of the liver in mice. Rats failed to show significant response, a fact which may be attributed to the cancer-resistance of the strain used. Despite the species difference in cancer response, the NCI concluded that the TCE test clearly showed the compound caused liver cancer in mice. The findings are considered definitive for animal studies and serve as a warning of possible carcinogenicity in humans. However, the extent of the possible human risk cannot be predicted reliably on the basis of these studies alone. A related compound, vinyl chloride (*see*), does cause liver cancer in humans.

**2-TRIDECENAL.** A synthetic citrus and fruit flavoring agent for beverages, ice cream, ices, candy, baked goods, and chewing gum. No known toxicity.

**TRIETHANOLAMINE.** A coating agent for fresh fruit and vegetables. Its principal toxic effect in animals has been attributed to overalkalinity. Gross pathology has been found in the gastrointestinal tract in fatally poisoned guinea pigs.

**TRIETHYL CITRATE. Citric Acid.** An odorless, practically colorless, bitter liquid. Used in dried eggs as a sequestrant and to prevent rancidity. See Citrate Salts for toxicity. The final report to the FDA of the Select Committee on GRAS Substances stated in 1980 that it should continue its GRAS status with no limitations other than good manufacturing practices.

**2-4-5 TRIHYDROXYBUTYROPHENONE (THBP).** An antioxidant used alone or in combination with other antioxidants. Total antioxidant not to exceed .02 percent of the oil or fat content of any product. Also used in the manufacture of food packaging materials, with a limit of .005 percent in food. On the FDA list for further study of this widely used additive.

**TRIISOPROPANOLAMINE.** A component of a coating used for fresh fruits and vegetables. No known toxicity.

**2-6-6-TRIMETHYL BICYCLO-(3.1.1)-2 HEPTENE.** See α-Pinene.

**1, 3, 7-TRIMETHYL-2-6-DIOXOPURINE.** See Caffeine.

**TRITICALE.** A man-made cross between wheat (*see* Dog Grass, Triticum) and rye (secale), but more nutritious than wheat. The protein content of bread made with it is 10 percent higher and its essential amino acid, lysine (*see*), exceeds wheat bread by 50 percent. The crop is the result of seven years' development and is being offered both as an ingredient and as a basic food substance. A number of novel products are being made from it, including ethnic breads. Two slices of Tritibread (made with triticale) supply 12 percent of the U.S. Recommended Daily Allowance for protein, 30 percent for thiamine, and 10 percent for riboflavin, niacin, and iron. Tritibread is intended for baked goods, ready-to-eat cereals, and malt products; also as a thickener, emulsifier, fortifier, and supplement. Once accepted, triticale can be an important nutritious addition to the food supply.

**TRITICUM.** See Dog Grass.

**TRYPTOPHAN.** An essential amino acid (*see*) which is a precursor of niacin and, like niacin, is capable of preventing and curing pellagra. It is a partial precursor of the brain hormone serotonin and is indispensable for the manufacture of certain cell proteins. The FDA has called for further study of this additive. GRAS.

**TUBEROSE EXTRACT.** From a Mexican bulbous herb commonly cultivated for its white, spike flowers. Used in peach flavorings for beverages, ice cream, ices, candy, and baked goods. No known toxicity. GRAS.

**TUMERIC. Turmeric.** Derived from an East Indian herb. An aromatic pepperlike but somewhat bitter taste. The cleaned, boiled, sun-dried, pulverized root is used in coconut, ginger ale, and curry flavorings for puddings, condiments, meats, soups, and pickles; also for yellow coloring used to color sausage casings, oleomargarine, shortening, and marking ink. The *extract* is used in fruit, meat, and cheese flavorings for beverages, condiments, meats, soup bases, and pickles. The *oleoresin* (*see*) is obtained by extraction with one or more of the solvents acetone, ethyl alcohol, ethylene dichloride (*see all*), and others. It is used in spice flavorings for condiments, meats, pickles, and brine. No known toxicity. GRAS.

**TUNU EXTRACT. Tuno.** From a Central American tree closely related to the rubber tree. Cleared for use as a natural masticatory substance of vegetable origin in chewing gum base. No known toxicity.

**TURMERIC.** See Tumeric.

**TURPENTINE. Gum and Steam Distilled.** Any of the various resins obtained from coniferous trees. A yellowish, viscous exudate with a characteristic smell, both forms are used in spice flavorings for baked goods. Steam-distilled turpentine is used also in candy. Turpentine is irritating to skin and mucous membranes, and can cause severe kidney irritation. It is readily absorbed from the gastrointestinal tract, the lungs, and skin. In addition to being a local irritant, it is a central nervous system depressant. Death is usually due to respiratory failure. As little as 15 milliliters has killed children.

**TYROSINE. L and DL forms.** A widely distributed amino acid (*see*) termed nonessential because it does not seem to be necessary for growth. Used as a dietary supplement. The FDA has asked for further study of this additive. GRAS.

# U

**2,3-UNDECADIONE.** A synthetic butter flavoring agent for beverages, ice cream, ices, candy, and baked goods. No known toxicity.

**γ-UNDECALACTONE. 4-Hydroxyundecanoic Acid. γ-Lactone. γ-Undecyl Lactone. γ-Heptyl Butyrolactone. Aldehyde C-14 Pure (so-called). Peach Aldehyde.** A synthetic fruit flavoring, colorless or yellow, with a strong peach odor. Used for beverages, ice cream, ices, candy, baked goods, gelatin desserts, and chewing gum. No known toxicity.

**UNDECANAL.** A synthetic flavoring agent. Colorless to slightly yellow, with a sweet, fatty odor. Used in lemon, orange, rose, fruit, and honey flavorings for beverages, ice cream, ices, candy, baked goods, and chewing gum. No known toxicity.

**9-UNDECANAL.** A synthetic citrus and nut flavoring agent for beverages, ice cream, ices, candy, and baked goods. No known toxicity.

**10-UNDECANAL.** A synthetic citrus, floral, and fruit flavoring agent for beverages, ice cream, ices, and candy. No known toxicity.

**2-UNDECANONE.** A synthetic flavoring agent that occurs naturally in rue and hops oil. Used in citrus, coconut, peach, and cheese flavorings for beverages, ice cream, ices, candy, baked goods, and puddings. No known toxicity.

**10-UNDECEN-1-YL ACETATE.** A synthetic citrus and fruit flavoring agent for beverages, ice cream, ices, candy, and baked goods. No known toxicity.

**UNDECYL ALCOHOL.** A synthetic lemon, lime, orange, and rose flavoring agent for beverages, ice cream, ices, candy, and baked goods. No known toxicity.

**UREA.** Occurs in urine and other body fluids as a product of protein metabolism. Used in yeast food and wine production up to 2 pounds per gallon. Also in fertilizer, animal feeds, in the making of plastics, in ammoniated dentifrices, and in baked goods such as pretzels. Used medicinally to reduce body water and intracranial and eye pressures. No known toxicity. The final report to the FDA of the Select Committee on GRAS Substances stated in 1980 that it should continue its GRAS status for packaging with no limitations other than good manufacturing practices.

# V

**VALERAL.** See Valeraldehyde.

**VALERALDEHYDE. Pentanal.** A synthetic flavoring agent which occurs naturally in coffee extract. Used in fruit and nut flavorings for beverages, ice cream, ices, candy, and baked goods. Has narcotic properties and is a mild irritant.

**VALERIAN ROOT. Extract and Oil.** A flavoring extracted from the dried roots of a widely cultivated herb in the United States and Europe. Used in cheese, fruit, maple, black walnut, walnut, and vanilla flavorings for beverages, ice cream, ices, candy, baked goods, and condiments. The yellowish green to brown oil is used in raspberry, cheese, grape, peach, honey, maple, and black walnut flavorings for beverages, ice cream, ices, candy, baked goods, and gelatin desserts. Has been used as a sedative. No known toxicity.

**VALERIC ACID.** A synthetic flavoring agent that occurs naturally in apples, cocoa, coffee, oil of lavender, peaches, and strawberries. Colorless, with an unpleasant odor. Used in butter, butterscotch, fruit, rum, and cheese flavorings for beverages, ice cream, ices, candy, and baked goods. Also used in perfumery. No known toxicity.

**VALERIC ALDEHYDE.** See Valeraldehyde.

**γ-VALEROLACTONE.** A synthetic vanilla flavoring agent for beverages, ice cream, ices, candy, and baked goods. No known toxicity.

**VALINE. L and DL forms.** An essential amino acid (*see*) classified as essential. Occurs in the largest quantities in fibrous protein. It is indispensable for growth and nitrogen balance. The FDA has asked for further study of this nutrient. GRAS.

**VANAY®.** See (*tri*) Acetin.

**VANILLA.** A natural flavoring from the cured, full-grown but unripe fruit of the genus *Vanilla* grown in Mexico and the West Indies. Used in butter, butterscotch, caramel, chocolate, fruit, and vanilla flavorings for beverages, ice cream, ices, candy, baked goods, puddings, syrups, icings, and toppings. No known toxicity. GRAS.

**VANILLA EXTRACT.** Derived from the vanilla bean. Contains not less than 35 percent aqueous ethyl alcohol (*see*) and one or more of the following ingredients: glycerin, propylene glycol, sugar (including invert sugar) and corn syrup. Used in many foods and beverages as flavorings. No known toxicity.

**VANILLAL.** See Ethyl Vanillin.

**VANILLIN.** Occurs naturally in vanilla (*see*) and potato parings but is an artificial flavoring. Odor and taste of vanilla. Made synthetically from eugenol (*see*); also from waste of wood pulp industry. One part vanillin equals 400 parts vanilla pods. Used in butter, chocolate, fruit, root beer, and vanilla flavorings for beverages, ice cream, ices, candy, baked goods, gelatin desserts, puddings, syrups (30,000 ppm), toppings, margarine, chocolate products, and liqueurs. The lethal dose in mice is 3 grams per kilogram of body weight. GRAS.

**VANILLIN ACETATE. Vanillin.** A synthetic spice and vanilla flavoring agent for beverages, ice cream, ices, candy, and baked goods.

**VERATRALDEHYDE.** A synthetic fruit, nut, and vanilla flavoring agent for beverages, ice cream, ices, candy, baked goods, and puddings. Derived from vanillin. May have narcotic and irritant effects but no specific data.

**VERATRIC ALDEHYDE.** See Veratraldehyde.

**VIBURNUM PRUNIFOLIUM.** See Haw Bark.

**VINEGAR.** See Acetic Acid.

**VINEGAR NAPHTHA.** See Ethyl Acetate.

**VINYL ACETATE.** A starch modifier not to exceed 2.5 percent in modified starch (*see*). Vapors in high concentration may be narcotic; animal experiments show low toxicity.

**VIOLA ODORATA.** See Violet Extract, leaves.

**VIOLAXANTHIN.** Natural orange-red coloring isolated from yellow pansies and Valencia orange peel. Soluble in alcohol. See Xanthophyll. No known toxicity.

**VIOLET EXTRACT. Flowers and Leaves.** From the plant widely grown in the United States. Used in berry, violet, and fruit flavorings for beverages, ice cream, ices, candy, and baked goods. No known toxicity. GRAS.

**VIRIDINE.** See Phenylacetaldehyde Dimethyl Acetal.

**VITAMIN A. Acetate and Palmitate.** An anti-infective, antixerophthalmic vitamin, essential to growth and development. Deficiency leads to retarded growth in the young, diminished visual acuity, night blindness, and skin problems. Insoluble in water. Toxic when children or adults receive more than 100,000 units daily over several months. Recommended daily dietary allowance is 1,500 units for infants and 4,500 units for adults and 2,000–3,500 units for children. It is used to fortify Mellorine (vegetable-fat imitation ice cream), skim milk, dietary infant formula, blue cheese, Gorgonzola cheese, milk, and oleomargarine (1 pound of margarine contains 15,000 USP units of Vitamin A). The final report to the FDA of the Select Committee on GRAS Substances stated in 1980 that there is no evidence in the available information that it is a hazard to the public when used as it is now and it should continue in GRAS status with limitations on amounts that can be added to food.

**VITAMIN B₁ HYDROCHLORIDE.** See Thiamine Hydrochloride.

**VITAMIN B₂.** See Riboflavin.

**VITAMIN B₆.** See Pyridoxine Hydrochloride.

**VITAMIN B₁₂. Cyanocobalamin.** An antipernicious anemia factor used as a growth factor in feed for hogs, chickens, and turkeys when they are given antibiotics. It is a coenzyme in the synthesis of materials for the nucleus of all cells. It contributes to the health of the nervous system and normal red blood cell formation. Recommended daily allowance is 5 milligrams per day. It occurs predominantly in foods of animal origin. The final report to the FDA of the Select Committee on GRAS Substances stated in 1980 that it should continue its GRAS status with no limitations other than good manufacturing practices.

**VITAMIN C.** See Ascorbic Acid.

**VITAMIN D₂. Calciferol.** Nutritional factor added to prepared breakfast cereals, Mellorine (vegetable-fat imitation ice cream), Vitamin D milk, evaporated and skim milks, margarine, infant dietary formulas, enriched flour, self-rising flour, enriched cornmeal and grits, enriched macaroni and noodle products (250–1,000 USP), enriched farina, and enriched bread, rolls, etc. Vitamin D speeds the body's production of calcium and has been found to cause calcium deposits and facial deformities and subnormal IQs in children of mothers given too much Vitamin D. Nutritionists recommend 400 units per day for pregnant women. Some pregnant women taking vitamin pills and vitamin enriched milk and foods consume as much as 2,000 to 3,000 units daily. The final report to the FDA of the Select Committee on GRAS Substances stated in 1980 that there is no evidence in the available information that it is a hazard to the public when used as it is now and it should continue its GRAS status with limitations on amounts that can be added to food.

**VITAMIN D₃. Activated 7-Dehydrocholesterol.** Approximately as effective as Vitamin D₂ (*see*). The final report to the FDA of the Select Committee on GRAS Substances stated in 1980 that there is no evidence in the available information that it is a hazard to the public when used as it is now and it should continue its GRAS status with limitations on amounts that can be added to food.

**VITAMIN E.** See Tocopherols.

**VITAMIN G.** See Riboflavin.

**VITAMIN H.** See Biotin.

**VIVERRA CIVETTA SCHREBER.** See Civet, Absolute.

**VIVERRA ZIBETHA SCHREBER.** See Civet, Absolute.

# W

**WALNUT HULL EXTRACT.** The extract of the edible nut of the English walnut tree. Used in walnut flavorings for beverages, ice cream, ices, candy, and baked goods. No known toxicity.

**WAXY MAIZE. Corn Starch.** The soft, sticky material from the inside of the corn kernel. The final report to the FDA of the Select Committee on GRAS Substances stated in 1980 that it should continue its GRAS status with no limitations other than good manufacturing practices. See Starch.

**WETTING AGENTS.** Any of numerous water-soluble agents that promote spreading of a liquid on a surface or its penetration into a material such as the skin. They lower surface tension for better contact and absorption. See Surfactants.

**WHEAT.** A cereal grain that yields a fine white powder. Wheat is avoided by some allergic people. Breads, cakes, crackers, cookies, pretzels, pastries, and noodles are made of wheat; also, breakfast foods such as Cream of Wheat, Pablum, Grapenuts, Wheaties, Puffed Wheat, Shredded Wheat, and bran; sauces, soups, gravies; Postum, Ovaltine, malted milk; sausages, hamburger, and meat loaf. Nontoxic.

**WHEAT GLUTEN.** A mixture of proteins present in wheat flour and obtained as an extremely sticky yellowish-gray mass by making a dough and then washing out the starch. It consists almost entirely of two proteins, gliadin and glutelin. It contributes to the porous and spongy structure of breads. Also used in cosmetic powders and creams as a base. No known toxicity.

**WHEAT STARCH.** A minor part of starch production in the U.S. The final report to the FDA of the Select Committee on GRAS Substances stated in 1980 that it should continue its GRAS status for packaging with no limitations other than good manufacturing practices. See Wheat.

**WHEY. Milk Serum. Serum Lactis.** The water part of milk remaining after the separation of the casein (*see*). Cleared by the U.S. Department of Agriculture's Meat Inspection Department to bind and extend imitation sausage, and for use in soups and stews. Nontoxic.

**WHITE FLAG EXTRACT.** See Orris.

**WILD CHERRY. Wild Black Cherry Bark.** Dried stem bark collected in autumn in North America. Used in cherry flavorings for foods and medications and as a cough medicine. No known toxicity. GRAS.

**WILD GINGER. Canadian Oil.** See Snakeroot Oil.

**WILD THYME EXTRACT.** The flowering tops of a plant grown in Eurasia and throughout the United States. The dried leaves are used as a seasoning in food and in emollients and fragrances. It has also been used as a muscle relaxant. No known toxicity. GRAS.

**WINTERGREEN. Extract and Oil. Methyl Salicylate. Checkerberry Extract.** Obtained naturally from betula, sweet birch, or teaberry oil. Present in certain leaves and bark but usually prepared by treating salicylic acid (*see*) with methanol. Wintergreen *extract* is used in root beer and wintergreen flavorings for beverages and candy (5,000 ppm). The *oil* is used for checkerberry, raspberry, teaberry, fruit, nut, root beer, sassafras, spice, and wintergreen flavorings for beverages, ice cream, ices, candy, baked goods (1,500 ppm), and chewing gum (3,900 ppm). Wintergreen is a strong irritant. Ingestion of relatively small amounts may cause severe poisoning and death (average lethal dose in children is 10 milliliters and in adults 30 milliliters). Symptoms of poisoning are nausea, vomiting, acidosis, pulmonary edema, pneumonia, and convulsions. Can be fatal. Very irritating to the mucous membranes and skin and can be absorbed rapidly through the skin. Like other salicylates, it has a wide range of interaction with other drugs, including alcohol, antidiabetic medications, Vitamin C, and tranquilizers.

**WORMWOOD. Absinthium.** A European woody herb with a bitter taste, used in bitters and liquor flavoring for beverages and liquors. The *extract* is used in bitters, liquor, and vermouth flavorings for beverages, ice cream, candy, and liquors, and in making absinthe. The *oil* is a dark green to brown and a narcotic substance. Used in bitters, apple, vermouth, and wine flavorings for beverages, ice cream, ices, candy, baked goods, and liquors. In large doses or frequently repeated doses, it is a narcotic poison, causing headache, trembling and convulsions. Ingestion of the volatile oil or of the liquor, absinthe, may cause gastrointestinal symptoms, nervousness, stupor, coma, and death.

# X

**XANTHAN GUM.** A polysaccharide gum produced on a commercial basis from the fermentation of corn sugar by the bacterium *Xanthomonas campestris.* The United States Agriculture Department has asked for the use of xanthan gum as a necessary ingredient in packaging meat and poultry products. It is now used to thicken, suspend, emulsify, and stabilize water-based foods, such as dairy products and salad dressings. It is also used as a "pseudoplasticizer" in salad dressings to help them pour well. No known toxicity.

**XANTHOPHYLL. Vegetable Lutein.** A yellow coloring originally isolated from egg yolk, now isolated from petals of flowers. Occurs also in colored feathers of birds. One of the most widespread carotenoid alcohols (a group of red and yellow pigments) in nature. Provisionally listed for use in food. Although carotenoids can usually be turned into Vitamin A, xanthophyll has no Vitamin A activity.

**XANTHOXYLUM AMERICANUM. Ash Bark. Toothache Tree. Angelica Tree.** The dried bark or berries of this tree, which grows in Canada, south of Virginia, and Missouri, is used to ease the pain of toothaches, to soothe stomachaches, and as an antidiarrheal medicine. No known toxicity.

**XYLITOL.** Formerly made from birchwood but now made from waste products from the pulp industry. Xylitol has been reported to have a diuretic effect but, according to Kauko K. Makinen, Ph.D., professor in biochemistry of the Institute of Dentistry, Turku, Finland, the diuretic effect of xylitol has not been unequivocally substantiated. He said the test group in Finland, which has had the longest experience with xylitol, reported no diuretic effect and he said none has been reported among consumers in European countries and the United States. Dr. Makinen said that the preliminary reports on the possible carcinogenicity of xylitol were based on studies in England in which large doses of xylitol were given to rats and mice during their entire life. He said the animals were from a cancer-prone strain and that any carbohydrate was bound to have an effect. He said sorbitol at the same dosage level caused a similar effect as xylitol, yet the former is widely accepted as a food additive. Xylitol is now used in eleven European countries and the United States and Canada. It is also used in large amounts in the Soviet Union as a diabetic sweetener. Xylitol has been evaluated by the Joint FAO/WHO Expert Committee on Food Additives in Geneva, April 11–20, 1983. On the basis of submitted data, the committee accepted that the adverse effects observed in the British studies were species-specific and cannot be extrapolated to humans. Therefore, no limit on daily intake was set and no additional toxicological studies were recommended. Xylitol has been reported to sharply reduce cavities in teeth.

# Y

**YARA YARA.** See $\beta$-Naphthyl Methyl Ether.

**YARROW. Milfoil.** A strong-scented Eurasian herb now widely grown in North America. Used in liquor, root beer, and spice flavorings for beverages and liquor. Can cause sensitivity to light.

**YEAST.** A dietary source of folic acid, it is used in enriched farina, enriched cornmeals and corn grits, and in bakery products. It is also used in hot dogs, hamburger and frankfurter buns and rolls, pretzels, milk fortified with vitamins, meat fried in cracker crumbs, mushrooms, truffles, cheeses of all kinds, vinegars, catsup, barbeque sauce, fermented brews, and all dried fruits. Any yeast is a type of one-celled fungus. Ordinary yeast produces the enzymes invertase and zymase, which eventually convert cane sugar to alcohol and carbon dioxide in the fermentation process. Some of the living organisms pressed into a damp, starchy, or other absorbent material give a product know as "baker's yeast," which is not as potent as brewer's yeast. No known toxicity.

**YEAST AUTOLYZATES.** Concentrated soluble components of hydrolyzed brewers' or bakers' yeasts, a byproduct of brewing. They provide a good source of B vitamins. The final report to the FDA of the Select Committee on GRAS Substances stated in 1980 that while no evidence in the available information on it demonstrates a hazard to the public at current use levels, uncertainties exist, requiring that additional studies be conducted. GRAS status continues while tests are being completed and evaluated.

**YEAST-MALT SPROUT EXTRACT.** A flavor enhancer.

**YELLOW NO. 5.** All foods containing Yellow No. 5, the most widely used color additive, will have to identify the color by name on the label. The action is to enable people allergic to the color to avoid it.

**YELLOW PRUSSIATE OF SODA. Sodium Ferrocyanide.** An anticaking agent, it is used in table salt to prevent the formation of clumps and keep it free flowing. The additive is produced by heating sodium carbonate and iron with organic materials. The average daily diet in the

United States contains 0.6 milligrams of sodium ferrocyanide per person. The UN Joint FAO/WHO Expert Committee on Food Additives considers 1.5 milligrams daily an acceptable and safe intake for a 132-pound human.

**YELLOW WAX.** See Beeswax.

**YERBA SANTA FLUID EXTRACT. Holy Herb.** Fruit flavoring derived from evergreen shrubs grown in California. Used in beverages, ice cream, ices, candy, and baked goods, and to mask the bitter taste of drugs. Also used as an expectorant. No known toxicity.

**YLANG-YLANG OIL. Cananga Oil.** A yellow essential oil with a fine floral odor from the flowers of a tree grown in the Philippines and Java. Light yellow, very fragrant. Used in raspberry, cola, violet, cherry, rum, and ginger ale flavorings for beverages, ice cream, ices, candy, baked goods, chewing gum, and icings. Used in perfumes, cosmetics, and soap. No known toxicity. GRAS.

**YUCCA. Joshua Tree. Mohave Extract.** A root beer flavoring from a southwestern U.S. plant. Used for beverages, ice cream, and ices. No known toxicity.

# Z

**ZEAXANTHIN.** Natural yellow coloring from corn and marigolds. One of the most widespread carotenoids (*see*) in nature, it has a bluish luster. No known toxicity.

**ZEODARY.** A bark extract from the East Indies used as a bitters and ginger ale flavoring for beverages. No known toxicity. GRAS.

**ZINC SOURCES: Zinc Acetate, Zinc Carbonate, Zinc Chloride, Zinc Gluconate, Zinc Hydrosulfate, Zinc Oxide, Zinc Sulfate.** Zinc is a blue-white lustrous metal known since very early times. It is a mineral source and added as a nutrient to food. Ingestion of the salts may cause nausea, vomiting, and purging. The final report to the FDA of the Select Committee on GRAS Substances said that zinc chloride was not known to be hazardous to the public when used as it is now and it should continue its GRAS status with limitations on amounts that can be added. Zinc gluconate and zinc hydrosulfate were given GRAS status with no limitations other than good manufacturing practices.

**ZINGERONE.** A synthetic flavoring occurring naturally in ginger. Used in fruit, root beer, sarsaparilla, spice, ginger ale, wintergreen, and birch beer flavorings for beverages, ice cream, ices, candy, baked goods, and chewing gum. No known toxicity.

**ZINGIBER OFFICINALE ROSC.** See Ginger.

**ZINGIBERONE.** See Zingerone.

# BIBLIOGRAPHY

Adams, Catherine F., *Nutritive Value of American Foods in Common Units.* Washington, D.C.: Agriculture Handbook No. 456, U.S. Department of Agriculture, 1975.

Bowes, Helen N., and Charles F. Church, *Food Values of Portions Commonly Used.* 11th ed., rev. Philadelphia: J. B. Lippincott Co., 1970.

*Chemicals Used in Food Processing.* Washington, D.C.: National Academy of Sciences, Publication 1274, 1965.

*The Condensed Chemical Dictionary.* 9th ed. Revised by Gessner G. Hawley. New York: Van Nostrand Reinhold, 1976.

Done, Alan, *Toxic Reactions to Common Household Products.* Paper read at the Symposium on Adverse Reactions Sponsored by the Drug Service Center for Disease Control, December 1976, San Francisco.

*Food Chemicals Codex.* 1st ed. Washington, D.C.: National Academy of Sciences Publication 1406, 1966.

Gleason, Marion N., et al., *Clinical Toxicology of Commercial Products.* Baltimore: The Williams & Wilkins Co., 1969.

Gordon, Lesley, *A Country Herbal.* New York: Mayflower Books, 1980.

*Handbook of Food Additives.* Edited by Thomas E. Furia. Cleveland: The Chemical Rubber Co., 1968.

Martin, Eric W., et al., *Hazards of Medications.* Philadelphia: J. B. Lippincott Co., 1971.

*The Merck Index.* 8th, 9th, and 10th eds. Rahway, N.J.: Merck, Sharp and Dohme Research Laboratories, 1968, 1976, 1983.

*The Merck Manual.* 11th ed. Edited by Charles E. Lyght. Rahway, N.J.: Merck, Sharp and Dohme Research Laboratories, 1966.

Miall, L. Mackenzie, and D. W. A. Sharp. *A New Dictionary of Chemistry.* 4th ed. New York: John Wiley & Sons, Inc., 1968.

*Physicians' Desk Reference.* Oradell, N.J.: Medical Economics, 1973.

*Recommended Dietary Allowances.* Rev. ed. Washington, D.C.: National Academy of Sciences, 1980.

*Sourcebook on Food and Nutrition.* 3rd ed. Edited by Joannis Scarpa, Ph.D., Helen Kiefer, Ph.D., and Rita Tatum. Chicago: Marquis Academic Media, 1982.

*Stedman's Medical Dictionary.* 24th ed. Baltimore: The Williams & Wilkins Co., 1982.

*Suspected Carcinogens: A Subfile of the NIOSH Toxic Substance List.* Rockville, Md.: Tracor Jitco, Inc., U.S. Department of Health, Education and Welfare, 1975.

*Suspected Carcinogens: A Subfile of the Registry of Toxic Effects of Chemical Substances.* Cincinnati: U.S. Department of Health, Education and Welfare, Public Health Services, Center for Disease Control, 1976.

*Toxicants Occurring Naturally in Foods.* 2nd ed. Washington, D.C.: National Academy of Sciences, 1973.

Watt, Bernice, and Annabel Merrill, et al., *Composition of Foods: Raw, Processed, Prepared.* Washington, D.C.: Agriculture Handbook No. 8, U.S. Department of Agriculture, 1963.

White, John Henry, *A Reference Book of Chemistry,* 3rd ed. New York: Philosophical Library, 1965.

Winter, Ruth, *Cancer-Causing Agents: A Preventive Guide.* New York: Crown Publishers, Inc., 1979.